T0155873

# Lecture Notes in Artificial Intelligence    12600

Subseries of Lecture Notes in Computer Science

More information about this subseries at http://www.springer.com/series/1244

Bertrand Braunschweig ·
Malik Ghallab (Eds.)

# Reflections on Artificial Intelligence for Humanity

*Editors*
Bertrand Braunschweig
Inria
Le Chesnay, France

Malik Ghallab
LAAS-CNRS
Toulouse, France

ISSN 0302-9743          ISSN 1611-3349  (electronic)
Lecture Notes in Artificial Intelligence
ISBN 978-3-030-69127-1          ISBN 978-3-030-69128-8  (eBook)
https://doi.org/10.1007/978-3-030-69128-8

LNCS Sublibrary: SL7 – Artificial Intelligence

This Springer imprint is published by the registered company Springer Nature Switzerland AG
The registered company address is: Gewerbestrasse 11, 6330 Cham, Switzerland

# Preface

Artificial Intelligence is significantly affecting humanity. According to several thinkers and philosophers, this "soft" revolution is comparable to and as disruptive as the deployment of writing, some five thousand years ago, and printing, a few centuries ago. As media for human interaction and cognition, writing and printing have deeply changed social organizations, laws, cities, economy, and science; they have affected human values, beliefs, and religions. We are possibly witnessing a commensurately profound but much faster revolution. However, we are not just passive observers. Every person today is an actor in these dynamics, with different levels of responsibility. We all need to be well-informed, responsible actors.

We already observe the positive effects of AI in almost every field, from agriculture, industry, and services, to social interaction, knowledge dissemination, sciences, and health, including in response to pandemics. We foresee its potential to help address our sustainable development goals and the urgent challenges for the preservation of the environment.

We certainly know that there can be no human action, enterprise, or technology without risks. Those risks related to the safety, security, confidentiality, and fairness of AI systems are frequently discussed. The threats to free will of possibly manipulative systems are raising legitimate concerns. The impacts of AI on the economy, employment, human rights, equality, diversity, inclusion, and social cohesion need to be better assessed.

The ethical values to guide our choices and appraise our progress in the development and use of AI have been discussed through many initiatives, such as the principles of the Montreal declaration, the OECD principles on AI, or the EU guidelines for trustworthy AI.

The opportunities and risks are still not sufficiently well assessed. The criteria to appraise societal desirability may not be universal. Different stakeholders favor different concerns ranging from human rights and environmental preservation, to economic growth, profit, or social control. However, despite differences in deployment and views across different regions, the effects of AI will be increasingly worldwide.

The social acceptability of AI technology is not equivalent to its market acceptance. More than ensuring consumer engagement by the dissemination of convenient services at largely hidden global costs, the focus must be on social acceptability, taking into account long-term effects and possible impacts on future generations. The development and use of AI must be guided by principles of social cohesion, environmental sustainability, meaningful human activity, resource sharing, inclusion, and recognition of social and cultural differences. It has to integrate the imperatives of human rights as well as the historical, social, cultural, and ethical values of democratic societies. It needs to consider global constraints affecting the environment and international relations. It requires continued education and training as well as continual assessment of effects through social deliberation.

Research and innovation in AI are creating an avalanche of changes. These strongly depend on and are propelled by two main forces: economic competition and political initiatives. The former provides a powerful and reactive drive; however, it is mostly governed by short-term, narrow objectives. The latter rely on the former as well as on slow feedback from social awareness, education, and understanding, which strive to keep up with the pace of AI technology.

Scientists from AI and the social sciences who are involved in the progress and comprehension of the field do not have full control over its evolution, but they are not powerless; nor are they without responsibilities. They understand and guide the state of the art and what may need to be done to mitigate the negative impacts of AI. They are accountable for and capable of raising social awareness about the current limitations and risks. They can choose or at least adapt their research agenda. They can engage with integrative research and work toward socially beneficial developments. They can promote research organizations and assessment mechanisms to favor long-term, cross-disciplinary objectives addressing the social and human challenges of AI.

There is a need for a clear commitment to act in accordance with these responsibilities. Coordinated actions of all stakeholders need to be guided by the principles and values that allow us to fully assume these responsibilities, including alignment with the universal declaration of human rights, respect for and solidarity with all societies and future generations, and recognition of our interdependence with other living beings and the environment.

This book calls for all interested scientists, technologists, humanists, and concerned individuals to be involved with and to support initiatives aimed in particular at addressing the following questions[1]:

– How can we ensure the security requirements of critical applications and the safety and confidentiality of data communication and processing? What techniques and regulations for the validation, certification, and audit of AI tools are needed to develop confidence in AI? How can we identify and overcome biases in algorithms? How do we design systems that respect essential human values, ensuring moral equality and inclusion?
– What kinds of governance mechanisms are needed for personal data, metadata, and aggregated data at various levels?
– What are the effects of AI and automation on the transformation and social division of labor? What are the impacts on economic structures? What proactive and accommodation measures will be required?
– How will people benefit from decision support systems and personal digital assistants without the risk of manipulation? How do we design transparent and intelligible procedures and ensure that their functions reflect our values and criteria? How can we anticipate failure and restore human control over an AI system when it operates outside its intended scope?
– How can we devote a substantial part of our research and development resources to the major challenges of our time such as climate, environment, health, and education?

---

[1] Issues addressed by the Global Forum on AI for Humanity, Paris, Oct. 28–30, 2019.

The above issues raise many scientific challenges specific to AI, as well as inter-disciplinary challenges for the sciences and humanities. They must be the topic of interdisciplinary research, social observatories and experiments, citizen deliberations, and political choices. They must be the focus of international collaborations and coordinated global actions.

The "Reflections on AI for Humanity" proposed in this book develop the above problems and sketch approaches for solving them. They aim at supporting the work of forthcoming initiatives in the field, in particular of the *Global Partnership on Artificial Intelligence*, a multilateral initiative launched in June 2020 by fourteen countries and the European Union. We hope that they will contribute to building a better and more responsible AI.

December 2020                                               Bertrand Braunschweig
                                                                        Malik Ghallab

# Organization

## Programme Committee of the Global Forum for Artificial Intelligence for Humanity, October 28–30 2019, Paris

| | |
|---|---|
| Pekka Ala-Pietilä | Huhtamaki, Finland |
| Elisabeth André | University of Augsburg, Germany |
| Noriko Arai | National Institute of Informatics, Japan |
| Genevieve Bell | Australian National University, Australia |
| Bertrand Braunschweig (Co-chair) | Inria, France |
| Natalie Cartwright | Finn AI, Canada |
| Carlo Casonato | University of Trento, Italy |
| Claude Castelluccia | Inria, France |
| Raja Chatila | Sorbonne University, France |
| Kate Crawford | AI Now Institute and Microsoft, USA |
| Sylvie Delacroix | University of Birmingham and Alan Turing Institute, UK |
| Andreas Dengel | DFKI, Germany |
| Laurence Devillers | Sorbonne University, France |
| Virginia Dignum | Umeå University, Sweden |
| Rebecca Finlay | CIFAR, Canada |
| Françoise Fogelman- Soulié | Hub France IA, France |
| Malik Ghallab (Co-chair) | CNRS, France |
| Alexandre Gefen | CNRS, France |
| Yuko Harayama | RIKEN, Japan |
| Martial Hebert | Carnegie Mellon University, USA |
| Holger Hoos | Universiteit Leiden, Netherlands |
| Lyse Langlois | Observatoire international sur les impacts sociétaux de l'intelligence artificielle et du numérique (OBVIA), Canada |
| Fei-Fei Li | Stanford University, USA |
| Jocelyn Maclure | Laval University, Canada |
| Ioana Manolescu | Inria and École polytechnique, France |
| Joel Martin | National Research Council, Canada |
| Michela Milano | University of Bologna, Italy |
| Katharina Morik | Technical University of Dortmund, Germany |
| Joëlle Pineau | McGill University and Facebook, Canada |
| Stuart Russell | University of California, Berkeley, USA |
| Bernhard Schölkopf | Max Planck Institute for Intelligent Systems, Germany and ETH Zurich, Switzerland |
| Hideaki Takeda | National Institute of Informatics, Japan |

| | |
|---|---|
| Paolo Traverso | Fondazione Bruno Kessler, Italy |
| Junichi Tsujii | National Institute of Advanced Industrial Science and Technology, Japan |
| Hyun Seung Yang | Korea Advanced Institute of Science and Technology, Korea |

# Contents

# Reflections on AI for Humanity: Introduction

Bertrand Braunschweig[1]([✉]) and Malik Ghallab[2]

[1] Formerly Inria, Paris, France
`bertrand.braunschweig@bilab.fr`
[2] CNRS, LAAS, Toulouse, France
`malik.ghallab@laas.fr`

**Abstract.** This chapter briefly surveys the current situation of AI with respect to its human and social effects, and to its risks and challenges. It presents a few global initiatives regarding ethical, social and legal aspects of AI. It introduces the remaining chapters of the book and briefly discusses a global cooperation framework on AI and its governance.

## 1 Context of the Book

Over the last two decades, Artificial Intelligence has moved from a technical area of interest to a focused community of specialists, to a widely popular issue, making the media headlines and bringing daily to the limelights new computational functions and applications. The effectiveness and potential of AI techniques became highly visible, attracting vast private investments and national R&D plans.

The social interest in AI is naturally amplified since its techniques are the mediating means between users and the digital world, which plays a predominant role in personal, social, and economic relations. Comparisons to and competitions with human in games and several tasks, sometimes transposed and exaggerated uncritically, have boosted the general attention. This interests is matched with a growing concern over several risks and infringements related to, for example, security, confidentiality, exploitation of personal data or opinion manipulation.

The concerns about AI have been expressed in numerous forums and programs seeking to steer the technical developments toward social good, to mitigate the risks and investigate ethical issues. This is illustrated through the initiatives taken by international organizations, such as the United Nations and its specialized agencies [24,39], the European Union [18,42], or the Organisation for Economic Cooperation and Development [30]. Many other initiatives have been taken by technical societies [17], NGOs, foundations, corporations, and academic organizations [14–16,20–22,25,36].

At the political level, statements from several leaders have placed AI as a geopolitical issue, a matter of power competition in international relations. Calls for cooperation have been delivered. Recent G7 summits promoted the idea of

Springer Nature Switzerland AG 2021
B. Braunschweig and M. Ghallab (Eds.): Reflections on Artificial Intelligence
for Humanity, LNAI 12600, pp. 1–12, 2021.
https://doi.org/10.1007/978-3-030-69128-8_1

setting up a permanent *Global Partnership on AI* (GPAI), relying on international working groups and annual plenary meetings. In that perspective, the *Global Forum on AI for Humanity*, held in Paris in October 2019, gathered a large interdisciplinary audience over five workshops and eight technical sessions. Its purpose was to provide an initial input to the GPAI working groups. This book results from the contributions and discussions help at this Global Forum. It is written by the organizers and moderators of the Forum debates.

## 2    What Is AI Today

Academic controversies about a proper definition of AI, as a science or as a technology, about its weak versus various versions of strength, or its symbolic old fashioned flavor versus its deep numeric one, may have their interest but are not very relevant to our purpose here. It is sufficient to say that AI techniques have demonstrated convincing results and a significant potential in the mechanization of cognitive functions, for *perceiving, reasoning, learning, acting* and *interacting.*

These techniques prosper on and enrich a large interdisciplinary background, mainly from computer science, mathematics, cognitive and neurosciences. They rely in particular on *(i)* data-based approaches, from probability, statistics, and numerical optimization, *(ii)* model-based approaches, from logic, ontologies, knowledge representations and structures, *(iii)* heuristic search and constraint propagation methods, and *(iv)* the fruitful synergies of their algorithmic integrations. They benefit from the tremendous growth of electronics and communication systems.

AI achievements already cover a broad set of capabilities such as image, speech and scene recognition, natural language processing and interaction, semantic information handling and search, automated planning, scheduling, and diagnosis, or computer aided design and decision making. Significant progress has been witnessed in almost all academic competitions and challenges which allow to compare approaches to these capabilities and structure developments.[1]

Successful applications of AI techniques can be found in almost every area of industry and services. Medicine and health have attracted significant developments. The very recent COVID-19 pandemic has already seen numerous proposals, for example in diagnosis and prognosis from medical imaging, protein structure planning for drug discovery, virus nucleic acid testing, epidemiology modeling and forecasting, and in text mining and analysis of the scientific literature.[2] Transportation is another area of significant AI developments and investments, e.g., in autonomous vehicles. Manufacturing and logistics implement AI over a broad spectrum of deployments, from the design and planning stages to the production stage with millions of robots in operation integrating more

---

[1] These are, for example, the challenges in image recognition [23], in question answering [35] and other natural language processing tasks [29], in automated planning [26], in theorem proving [34], and in logistics and other robotics competitions [33].

[2] See [2], an early survey on April 2020 of 140 references.

and more AI techniques. Similarly for mining, e.g., to support deep drills exploration or automated open-pit mining. Space applications are among the early success stories of AI, e.g., [5]. Defense and military applications are a matter of huge investments, as well as concerns. Precision and green agriculture relies on a range of sensing, monitoring and planning techniques as well as on versatile robots for weeding and crop management tasks. AI has been adopted very early in e-commerce for automated pricing, user profiling and (socially dubious) optimizations. Similarly in finance, e.g., in high frequency trading. Learning and decision making techniques are extensively used in banking, insurance, and consulting companies. Education institutions are routinely using advanced data and text management tools (e.g., timetabling, plagiarism detection). Personal tutoring techniques start being deployed.[3] Automated translation software and vocal assistants with speech recognition and synthesis are commonly marketed. This is also the case for very strong board, card and video games. Motion planning and automated character animation are successfully used by the film industry. Several natural language and document processing functions are employed by the media, law firms and many other businesses. Even graphical and musical artists experiment with AI synthesis tools for their work.

Key indicators for AI show a tremendous growth over the last two decades in research, industry and deployments across many countries. For example, the overall number of peer-reviewed publications has tripled over this period. Funding has increased at an average annual growth rate of 48%, reaching over $70B world wide. Out of a recent survey of 2360 large companies, 58% reported adopting AI in at least one function or business unit [28]. The AI labor demand vastly exceeds trained applicants and leads to a growing enrollment in AI education, as well as to incentives for quickly augmenting the AI schooling capacities.[4]

## 3   AI Risks and Challenges

AI techniques have clearly demonstrated their great beneficial potential for humanity. Numerous scientific and technical bottlenecks remain to be overcome, but progress is accelerating and the current state of the art is already providing approaches to many social challenges. This is illustrated in particular through several projects addressing with AI techniques the United Nations Sustainable Development Goals (SDGs) [38]. AI use cases have been identified for about half of the 169 SDG targets by a UN initiative on big data and artificial intelligence for development, humanitarian action, and peace [37].

However, as for any other technology, the development of AI entails risks. These risk are commensurate with AI impact and potential. Moreover, rapid technology developments do not leave enough time to social evaluation and adequate regulation. In addition, there are not enough incentives for risk assessment,

---

[3] e.g., [27,31], the two winner systems of the Global Learning XPrize competition in May 2019.

[4] These and other indicators are detailed in the recent AI Index Report [8].

in research as well as in industrial development; hence there are many more studies of new techniques than studies of their entailed risks.[5]

The main issues of AI are how to assess and mitigate the human, social and environment risks of its ubiquitous deployments in devices and applications, and how to drive its developments toward social good.

AI is deployed in safety critical applications, such as health, transportation, network and infrastructure management, surveillance and defense. The corresponding risks in human lives as well as in social and environmental costs are not sufficiently assessed. They give rise to significant challenges for the verification and validation of AI methods.

The individual uses of AI tools entail risks for the security of digital interaction, the privacy preserving and confidentiality of personal information. The insufficient transparency and intelligibility of current techniques imply other risks for uncritical and inadequate uses.

The social acceptability of a technology is much more demanding than the market acceptance. Among other things, social acceptability needs to take into account the long term, including possible impacts on future generations. It has to worry about social cohesion, employment, resource sharing, inclusion and social recognition. It needs to integrate the imperatives of human rights, historical, social, cultural and ethical values of a community. It should consider global constraints affecting the environment or international relations.

The social risks of AI with respect to these requirements are significant. They cover a broad spectrum, from biases in decision support systems (e.g., [7,10]), to fake news, behavior manipulation and debate steering [13]. They include political risks that can be a threat to democracy [6] and human rights [9], as well as risks to economy (implicit price cartels [4], instability of high frequency trading [11]) and to employment [1]. AI in enhanced or even autonomous lethal weapons and military systems threatens peace, it raises strong ethical concerns, e.g., as expressed in a call to a ban on autonomous weapons [19].

## 4    Worldwide Initiatives on the Societal Impact of AI

Many initiatives, studies and working groups have been launched in order to assess the impacts of AI applications. There are also a few meta-studies that analyze and compare these initiatives. In this section, we briefly look at four transnational initiatives backed by major organisations that may have a significant impact on the development and use of AI, and we discuss two relevant meta-studies.

*The Partnership on AI.* This partnership was created by six companies, Apple, Amazon, Google, Facebook, IBM, and Microsoft, and announced during the Future of Artificial Intelligence conference in 2016. It was subsequently extended into a multi-stakeholder organization which now gathers 100 partners from 13

---

[5] E.g., according to the survey [28] 13% companies adopting AI are taking actions for mitigating risks.

countries [32]. Its objectives are "to study and formulate best practices on AI technologies, to advance the public's understanding of AI, and to serve as an open platform for discussion and engagement about AI and its influences on people and society". Since its inception, the Partnership on AI published a few reports, the last one being a position paper on the undesirable use of a specific criminal risk assessment tool in the COVID-19 crisis.

*UNESCO Initiatives.* In 2017, the World Commission on the Ethics of Scientific Knowledge and Technology of UNESCO mandated a working group to develop a study on the ethics of AI. This led to the publishing in 2019 of a Preliminary Study on the Ethics of AI [41]. This study has a broader scope than other similar document as it addresses UNESCO priority issues such as education, science, culture, peace and the development of AI in less-favored countries. It concludes with a list of eleven principles to be included in the requirements for AI applications, such as, human rights, inclusiveness, democracy, sustainability, quality of life in addition to the usual demandes on transparency, explainability, and accountability. Following this report, UNESCO created an *ad hoc* expert group of 24 specialists from 24 different countries and backgrounds to develop recommendations on the ethics of AI; the outcome of its work is still pending.

*The European Commission's HLEG.* The High Level Expert Group on AI of the European Commission is among the noticeable international efforts on the societal impact of AI. Initially composed of 52 multi-disciplinary experts, it started its work in 2018 and published its first report in December of the same year [18]. The report highlights three characteristics that should be met during the lifecycle of an AI system in order to be trustworthy:"it should be lawful, complying with all applicable laws and regulations; it should be ethical, ensuring adherence to ethical principles and values; and it should be robust, both from a technical and social perspective, since, even with good intentions, AI systems can cause unintentional harm". Four ethical principles are stressed: human autonomy; prevention of harm; fairness; explainability. The report makes recommendations for technical and non-technical methods to achieve seven requirements (human agency and oversight; technical robustness; etc.).

A period of pilot implementations of the guidelines followed this report, its results have not yet been published. Meanwhile, the European Commission released a White Paper on AI [42], which refers to the ethics recommendations of the HLEG.

*The OECD's Expert Group and Observatory.* OECD created an AI Group of Expert (AIGO) in September 2018, within its Committee on Digital Economy Policy, composed of approximately 50 delegates from OECD countries, with invited experts and other contributors in subgroups. The AIGO published a report [40], which makes recommendations on national policies and sets a few "principles for responsible stewardship of trustworthy AI", similar to those of other organisations, such as

- Inclusive and sustainable growth and well-being,
- Human-centered values and fairness,
- Transparency and explainability,
- Robustness and safety,
- Accountability.

The OECD's initiatives are pursued within a Network of Experts in AI, established in February 2020, as well as an Observatory on AI [30].

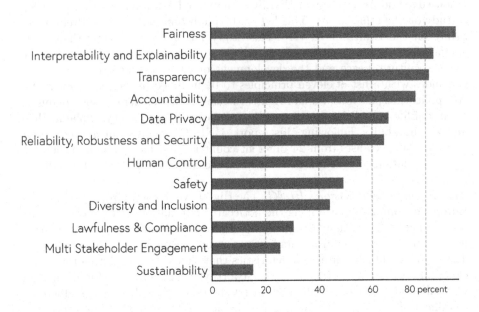

**Fig. 1.** Ethical AI Challenges identified across 59 documents (from [8], p. 149).

*Meta-studies: Research Devoted to Analyzing and Comparing Diverse Initiatives.* The general AI principles discussed in 74 document are analyzed in [12]. The principles are grouped into ten categories (e.g., fairness, transparency, privacy, collaboration, etc.); the analyzed documents were published between 2017 and 2019 by various organisations. The corresponding website gives access to a 2D-table with links to referred documents for each analyzed category, for example:

- for the category "Fairness", the *Beijing AI Principles* contains the following: "making the system as fair as possible, reducing possible discrimination and biases, improving its transparency, explainability and predictability, and making the system more traceable, auditable and accountable".
- for the category "Privacy", the *Montreal AI Declaration* states that "Every person must be able to exercise extensive control over their personal data, especially when it comes to its collection, use, and dissemination."

Another meta-study analyzes and maps 36 documents from government, companies, and others groups related to AI ethics [3]. The map is designed along eight dimensions: safety and security, transparency and explainability, fairness and non-discrimination, human control of technology, professional responsibility, promotion of human values, international human rights. It allows for convenient comparisons over these dimensions between the documents. The final version of this analysis shows that most AI ethics documents address all eight key themes, showing a global convergence on the issues currently of concern to society.

Finally, let us go back to the AI Index [8] has been monitoring the advancement of AI over several aspects: how science and technology are progressing; how companies are investing; what is the employment situation in AI; how different countries are placed in the global competition, etc. In its 2019 report, the Index also covers 59 documents from associations, government, companies, and think tanks about ethical AI principles. It summarizes the main topics addressed; the most popular being fairness, interpretability and explainability, transparency, accountability, and data privacy (see Fig. 1).

## 5   Outline of the Book

This book develops the issues discussed at the Global Forum on AI for Humanity. Each chapter synthesizes and puts into perspective the talks and debates presented either at a plenary session (for chapters 2 to 10, and 15) or a workshop (for chapters 11 to 14) of the Forum.

In chapter 2, Raja Chatila and colleagues discuss the motivations for trustworthy AI. Human interactions with devices and systems, and social interactions are increasingly mediated through AI. This entails strong requirements to ensure trust in critical AI applications, e.g., in health or transportation systems. Techniques and regulations for the explainability, certification and auditing of AI tools need to be developed. The final part of the chapter examines conditions and methods for the production of provably beneficial AI systems.

In chapter 3, Sylvie Delacroix and colleagues look at ethical, political and legal issues with Data governance. The loop from data to information, to knowledge, action and more data collection has been further automated and improved, leading to stronger impacts, already effective or potential. It is of critical importance to clarify the mutual dependence of bottom-up empowerment structures and top-down rules for the social governance of personal data, metadata, and aggregated data. The chapter ends by exploring the role of data trusts for such purposes.

Yuko Harayama, Michela Milano and colleagues examine in chapter 4 the impact of AI on the future of work. The effectiveness of AI in the mechanization of complex physical and cognitive task has strong economic impacts, as well as social disruptive capabilities, given in particular its rapid progress. Proactive measures may be needed. This requires a good understanding of the likely effects of AI on the main economic channels and the transformation of work. The chapter presents complementary views on economy, job quality and policies as discussed at the Global Forum.

Rebecca Finlay and Hideaki Takeda report in chapter 5 about the delegation of decisions to machines. Delegating simple daily life or complex professional decisions to a computerized personal assistant, to a digital twin, can amplify our capabilities or be a source of alienation. The requirements to circumvent the latter include in particular intelligible procedures, articulate and explicit explanations, permanent alignment of the machine's assessment functions with our criteria, as well as anticipation of and provision for an effective transfer of control back to human, when desirable.

In chapter 6 Françoise Fogelman-Soulié, Laurence Devillers and Ricardo Baeza-Yates address the subject of AI & Human values such as equity, protection against biases and fairness, with a specific focus on nudging and feedback loop effects. Automated or computer aided decisions can be unfair, because of possibly unintended biases in algorithms or in training data. What technical and operational measures can be needed to ensure that AI systems comply with essential human values, that their use is socially acceptable, and possibly desirable for strengthening social bounds.

Chapter 7, coordinated by Paolo Traverso addresses important core AI scientific and technological challenges: understanding the inner mechanisms of deep neural networks; optimising the neural networks architectures; moving to explainable and auditable AI in order to augment trust in these systems; and attempting to solve the talent bottleneck in modern artificial intelligence by using automated machine learning. The field of AI is rich of technical and scientific challenges, as can be seen from the examples given in this chapter.

In chapter 8, Jocelyn Maclure and Stuart Russell consider some of the major challenges for developing inclusive and equitable education, improving healthcare, advancing scientific knowledge and preserving the planet. They examine how properly designed AI systems can help address some of the United Nations SDGs. They discuss the conditions required to bring into play AI for these challenges. They underline in particular that neither neither pure knowledge-based approaches nor pure machine learning can solve the global challenges outlined in the chapter; hybrid approaches are needed.

In chapter 9, Carlo Casonato reflects on legal and constitutional issues raised by AI. Taking many examples from real-world usage of AI, mainly in justice, health and medicine, Casonato puts the different viewpoints expressed in the previous chapters into a new perspective, regarding regulations, democracy, anthropology and human rights. The chapter ends with a proposal for a set of new (or renewed) human rights, in order to achieve a balanced and constitutionally oriented framework for specific rights for a human-centered deployment of AI systems.

The question of ethical charters for AI is discussed in chapter 10 by Lyse Langlois and Catherine Régis. Looking at the current ethical charters landscape which has flourished extensively in the last years, the chapter examines the fundamentals of ethics and discusses their relations with law and regulations. It concludes with remarks on the appropriateness of GPAI, UN and UNESCO to take the lead in international regulatory efforts towards globally accepted ethics charters for AI.

Continuing on ethical issues related to AI, Vanessa Nurock and colleagues propose in chapter 11 an in-depth analysis of the notion of "ethics by design", as compared to other framing such as, for example, privacy by design, or responsible innovation. The chapter examines current approaches for applying ethics to AI and concludes with guidelines for an ethics by design demanding to answer four questions on "care".

AI with respect to humanities and social sciences is discussed by Alexandre Gefen in chapter 12 from two perspectives: as an important topic of investigation and as a new mean for research. The questions about AI and its human and social consequences are invading the public sphere through the multiple issues of acceptability, privacy protection or economic impact, requiring the expertise and strong involvement of every area of Humanities and Social Sciences. AI offers also new tools to social sciences, humanities and arts, including massive data extraction, processing, machine learning and wide network analysis.

In chapter 13 Andreas Dengel and Laurence Devillers report on the state of the art of Human-Machine Co-Creation, Co-Learning and Co-Adaptation, and discuss how to anticipate corresponding ethical risks. Human ambiguous relationships with symbiotic or autonomous machines raise numerous ethical problems. Augmented intelligence and superintelligent AI are main topics for the future of human society. The robotic simulation has the virtue of questioning the nature of our own intelligence. Capturing, transmitting and mimicking our feelings will open up new applications in health, education, transport and entertainment.

Chapter 14, by Nicolas Miailhe and colleagues, is devoted to "AI Commons", a global non-profit initiative which aims to democratize responsible adoption and deployment of AI solutions for social good applications addressing the seventeen UN SDGs. This project brings together a wide range of stakeholders around innovative and holistic problem "identification-to-solution" frameworks and protocols. Its ultimate objectives are to pool critical AI capabilities (data, algorithms, domain specific knowledge, talent, tools and models, computing power and storage) into an open and collaborative platform that can be used to scale up the use of *AI for Everyone*.

Finally, Pekka Ala-Pietilä and Nathalie Smuha conclude the book with a framework for global cooperation on AI and its governance. This is certainly an essential issue in a critical period for AI. The chapter clarifies why such a governance is needed jointly with international cooperation. It lists the main areas for which international cooperation should be prioritized, with respect the socio-technical environment of AI in a transversal manner, as well as with respect to the socio-technical environments of data and digital infrastructure, these two dimensions being are tightly coupled. It concludes assessing how global cooperation should be organized, stressing the need to balance speed, holism and contextualism, and providing a number of guiding principles that can inform the process of global cooperation initiatives on AI and its governance.

This book collects views from leading experts on AI and its human, ethical, social, and legal implications. Each chapter is self-contained and addresses a specific set of issues, with links to other chapters. To further guide the reader about the organization of the covered topics, a possible clustering (with overlaps) of these "Reflections on Artificial Intelligence for Humanity" is the following:

- chapters 7, 13 and 14 are mainly devoted to technological and scientific challenges with AI and at some developments designed to address them;
- chapters 5, 6, 10, and 11 focus on different ethical issues associated with AI;
- chapters 2, 3, 4, 5, and 6 cover the social impacts of AI at the workplace and in personal applications;
- chapters 7, 8, 12 and 13 discuss the possible benefits and risks of AI in several area such as health, justice, justice, education, humanities and social sciences;
- chapters 3, 9, 14, and 15 addresses legal and organizational issues raised by AI.

## 6   What's Next: An Opening for GPAI

The GFAIH forum was a step in the preparation of GPAI, the Global Partnership on Artificial Intelligence. Launched by France and Canada on the sidelines of the Canadian presidency of the G7, this initiative aims to organize an independent global expertise on the ethical regulation of AI.

Following the Franco-Canadian Declaration on AI of June 7, 2018, and the production of a mandate for an international group of experts in artificial intelligence (G2IA), France and Canada jointly decided to include the GPAI on the agenda of the French presidency of the G7, in order to place this initiative in a multilateral framework. The G7 digital ministerial meeting on May 2019 helped secure the support of Germany, Italy, Japan, the United Kingdom, New Zealand, India and the European Union for the launch of the GPAI. The G7 summit in Biarritz on 24–26 August 2019 made it possible to obtain the support of the G7 States for this initiative, renamed the Global Partnership on AI (GPIA) and of the four invited countries (India, Chile, South Africa and Australia) and New Zealand, giving a strong political mandate to the initiative thanks to the Biarritz Strategy for an open, free and secure digital transformation. Canada and France also agreed on a tripartite structure for the PMIA, consisting of two centres of expertise in Paris and Montreal and a secretariat hosted at the OECD in Paris to avoid work duplication and maximize synergies, while maintaining a strict independence of the experts' work. A major step was taken on June 15th, 2020, when fifteen countries - among which all G7 - members simultaneously announced the launch of the Partnership and their commitment to make it a success.

This initiative will permit an upstream dialogue between the best scientists and experts and public decision-makers, which is a key condition for designing effective responses and recommendations necessary to cope with current and future challenges faced by our societies. The GPAI will produce, on a comprehensive, objective, open and transparent basis, analyses of scientific, technical and socio-economic information relevant to understanding the impacts of AI, encouraging its responsible development, and mitigating its risks. This work will follow a project-based approach, with a strong technical dimension. Complementary to other approaches such as the four initiatives mentioned above, the work of GPAI will be mostly driven by science and will include representative experimentation to support its recommendations.

Four working groups have been initially identified in GPAI on, respectively, the issues of responsible AI, data governance, future of work, innovation and commercialization. A fifth working group on the response to the current pandemic situation and to other possible pandemics has been created as a subgroup of "Responsible AI". There is a clear link between the topics of the Global forum, the chapters of this book and the four main working groups of GPAI: the "data governance" and "future of work" themes are direct matches, whereas several chapters contribute to "Responsible AI" (chapters 2, 5, 6, 7, 11 in particular) and to "Innovation and commercialization" (chapters 2, 7, 8, 15 in particular). The first plenary meeting of GPAI experts took place online in early December 2020,[6] the second will take place in Paris in 2021.

It has become crucial to consolidate democracies at a time when technological competition is intensifying, while the risks of Internet fragmentation and AI social impacts are deepening. GPAI aspires to bring together like-minded countries, sharing the same democratic values in order to promote a socially responsible, ethical vision of AI.

# References

1. Arntz, M., Gregory, T., Zierahn, U.: The Risk of Automation for Jobs in OECD Countries. OECD Social, Employment and Migration Working Papers (189) (2016). https://doi.org/10.1787/5jlz9h56dvq7-en. https://www.oecd-ilibrary.org/content/paper/5jlz9h56dvq7-en
2. Bullock, J., Luccioni, A., Pham, K.H., Lam, C.S.N., Luengo-Oroz, M.: Mapping the landscape of artificial intelligence applications against covid-19. arXiv (2020). https://arxiv.org/abs/2003.11336
3. Fjeld, J., Achten, N., Hilligoss, H., Nagy, A., Srikumar, M.: Principled artificial intelligence: mapping consensus in ethical and rights-based approaches to principles for AI. Technical report 2020, Berkman Klein Center Research Publication (2020). https://doi.org/10.2139/ssrn.3518482
4. Gal, M.S.: Illegal pricing algorithms. Commun. ACM **62**(1), 18–20 (2019)
5. Muscettola, N., Nayak, P.P., Pell, B., Williams, B.C.: Remote agent: to boldly go where no AI system has gone before. Artif. Intell. **103**, 5–47 (1998)
6. Nemitz, P.: Constitutional democracy and technology in the age of artificial intelligence. Philos. Trans. Roy. Soc. A: Math. Phys. Eng. Sci. **376**(2133), 1–14 (2018)
7. O'Neil, C.: Weapons of Math Destruction: How Big Data Increases Inequality and Threatens Democracy. Crown Random House, New York (2016)
8. Perrault, R., et al.: The AI index 2019 annual report. Technical report, Stanford University (2019). http://aiindex.org
9. Raso, F., Hilligoss, H., Krishnamurthy, V., Bavitz, C., Kim, L.Y.: Artificial Intelligence & Human Rights: Opportunities & Risks. SSRN, September 2018

---

[6] See http://gpai.ai.

10. Skeem, J.L., Lowenkamp, C.: Risk, Race, & Recidivism: Predictive Bias and Disparate Impact. SSRN (2016)
11. Sornette, D., von der Becke, S.: Crashes and High Frequency Trading. SSRN, August 2011
12. Zeng, Y., Lu, E., Huangfu, C.: Linking artificial intelligence principles. arXiv (2018). https://arxiv.org/abs/1812.04814v1
13. Zuboff, S.: The Age of Surveillance Capitalism. PublicAffairs, New York (2019)
14. AI for good foundation. https://ai4good.org/about/
15. AI now institute. https://ainowinstitute.org/
16. Ai4People. http://www.eismd.eu/ai4people/
17. Ethically Aligned Design. https://standards.ieee.org/content/dam/ieee-standards/standards/web/documents/other/ead_v2.pdf
18. EU high level expert group on AI. https://ec.europa.eu/digital-single-market/en/high-level-expert-group-artificial-intelligence
19. The Future of Life Institute. https://futureoflife.org/open-letter-autonomous-weapons/?cn-reloaded=1
20. The Global Challenges Foundation. https://globalchallenges.org/about/the-global-challenges-foundation/
21. Human-Centered AI. http://hai.stanford.edu/
22. Humane AI. http://www.humane-ai.eu/
23. Image Net. http://image-net.org/
24. International Telecommunication Union. https://www.itu.int/dms_pub/itu-s/opb/journal/S-JOURNAL-ICTS.V1I1-2017-1-PDF-E.pdf
25. International Observatory on the Societal Impacts of AI. https://observatoire-ia.ulaval.ca/
26. International Planning Competition. http://icaps-conference.org/index.php/Main/Competitions
27. Kitkit School. http://kitkitschool.com/
28. Mckinsey Global Institute. https://www.mckinsey.com/featured-insights/artificial-intelligence/global-ai-survey-ai-proves-its-worth-but-few-scale-impact
29. NLP Competitions. https://codalab-worksheets.readthedocs.io/en/latest/Competitions/#list-of-competitions
30. OECD AI Policy Observatory. http://www.oecd.org/going-digital/ai/oecd-initiatives-on-ai.htm
31. OneTab. https://onebillion.org/
32. Partnership on AI. https://www.partnershiponai.org/research-lander/
33. RoboCup. https://www.robocup.org/
34. SAT Competitions. http://satcompetition.org/
35. SQuAD Explorer. https://rajpurkar.github.io/SQuAD-explorer/
36. UK center for the governance of AI. https://www.fhi.ox.ac.uk/governance-ai-program/
37. Un Global Pulse. https://www.unglobalpulse.org/
38. Un Sustainable Development Goals. https://sustainabledevelopment.un.org/?menu=1300
39. UNESCO. https://en.unesco.org/artificial-intelligence
40. Deliberations of the expert group on artificial intelligence at the OECD (2019). https://www.oecd-ilibrary.org/
41. Preliminary study on the ethics of artificial intelligence (2019). https://unesdoc.unesco.org/
42. EU white paper on AI (2020). https://ec.europa.eu/info/publications/white-paper-artificial-intelligence-european-approach-excellence-and-trust_en

# Trustworthy AI

Raja Chatila[1]([✉]), Virginia Dignum[2], Michael Fisher[3], Fosca Giannotti[4], Katharina Morik[5], Stuart Russell[6], and Karen Yeung[7]

[1] Sorbonne University, Paris, France
Raja.Chatila@sorbonne-universite.fr
[2] Umea University, Umeå, Sweden
[3] University of Manchester, Manchester, UK
[4] CNR Pisa, Pisa, Italy
[5] TU Dortmund University, Dortmund, Germany
[6] University of California, Berkeley, USA
[7] University of Birmingham, Birmingham, UK

**Abstract.** Modern AI systems have become of widespread use in almost all sectors with a strong impact on our society. However, the very methods on which they rely, based on Machine Learning techniques for processing data to predict outcomes and to make decisions, are opaque, prone to bias and may produce wrong answers. Objective functions optimized in learning systems are not guaranteed to align with the values that motivated their definition. Properties such as transparency, verifiability, explainability, security, technical robustness and safety, are key to build operational governance frameworks, so that to make AI systems justifiably trustworthy and to align their development and use with human rights and values.

**Keywords:** Human rights · Machine learning · Interpretability · Explainability · Dependability · Verification and validation · Beneficial AI

This chapter addresses different aspects of trustworthiness of AI systems. It is a collective contribution from Virginia Dignum (for Sect. 1), Raja Chatila (Sect. 2), Katharina Morik (Sect. 3), Fosca Giannotti (Sect. 4), Michael Fisher (Sect. 5), Karen Yeung (Sect. 6), and Stuart Russell (Sect. 7).

## 1 The Necessity of Trustworthy AI

The recent developments in Artificial Intelligence (AI) hold great promises for humanity and society. However, as with any potentially disruptive innovation, AI also brings challenges, in particular where it concerns safety, privacy, bias, impact on work and education, and how the align legislation and regulations with the rapid changes of AI technology. A responsible approach to development and

Springer Nature Switzerland AG 2021
B. Braunschweig and M. Ghallab (Eds.): Reflections on Artificial Intelligence for Humanity, LNAI 12600, pp. 13–39, 2021.
https://doi.org/10.1007/978-3-030-69128-8_2

use of AI is needed to facilitate trust in AI and ensure that all can profit from the benefits of AI. This can guard against the use of biased data or algorithms, ensure that automated decisions are justified and explainable, and help maintain privacy of individuals.

In recent years, we have seen a rise of efforts around the ethical, societal and legal impact of AI. These are the result of concerted action by national and transnational governance bodies, including the European Union, the OECD, the UK, France, Canada and others, but have often also originated from bottom-up initiatives, launched by practitioners or the scientific community. A few of the most well-known initiatives are:

- IEEE initiative on Ethics of Autonomous and Intelligent Systems[1]
- High Level Expert Group on AI of the European Commission[2]
- the Partnership on AI[3]
- the French AI for Humanity strategy[4]
- the Select Committee on AI of the British House of Lords[5]

These initiatives aim at providing concrete recommendations, standards and policy suggestions to support the development, deployment and use of AI systems. Many others have focused on analysing the values and principles to which AI systems and promoting specific principles to which the development and thereof should adhere. In fact, hardly a week goes by without news about yet another declaration of principles for AI, or of other initiatives at national or corporate level. For up-to-date information on all such initiatives, check Alan Winfield's blog[6] or the crowdsourced effort coordinated by Doteveryone.[7] Moreover, several groups have provided detailed analysis and comparison of the different proposals [16,34].

Trustworthy AI, as defined by the High level expert group on AI from the European Union[8] is

1. lawful, i.e. complying with all applicable laws and regulations
2. ethical, i.e. ensuring adherence to ethical principles and values
3. robust, both from a technical and social perspective since, even with good intentions, AI systems can cause unintentional harm.

In order to achieve trustworthy AI, it is as important to understand the properties of AI technology, as determined by the advances in computation techniques and data analytics. AI technology is an artefact, a software system (possibly

---

[1] https://ethicsinaction.ieee.org/.

[2] https://ec.europa.eu/digital-single-market/en/high-level-expert-group-artificial-intelligence.

[3] https://www.partnershiponai.org/.

[4] https://www.aiforhumanity.fr/en/.

[5] https://www.parliament.uk/ai-committee.

[6] http://alanwinfield.blogspot.com/2017/12.

[7] https://goo.gl/ibffk4 (maintained in Google docs).

[8] https://ec.europa.eu/newsroom/dae/document.cfm?doc_id=60419.

embedded in hardware) designed by humans that, given a complex goal, is able to take a decision based on a process of perception, interpretation and reasoning based on data collected about that environment. In many case this process is considered 'autonomous' (by which it is meant that there may be limited need for human intervention after the setting of the goals), 'adaptive' (meaning that the system is able to update its behaviour to changes in the environment), and 'interactive' (given that it acts in a physical or digital dimension where people and other systems co-exist). Even though many AI systems currently only exhibit one of these properties, it is their combination that is at the basis of the current interest on and results of AI, and that fuels public's fears and expectations [11].

Guidelines, principles and strategies must be directed to these socio-technical systems. It is not the AI artefact that is ethical, trustworthy, or responsible. Rather, it is the social component of the socio-technical system that can and should take responsibility and act in consideration of an ethical framework such that the overall system can be trusted by the society. Trustworthy AI, or AI ethics, is not about giving machines some kind of 'responsibility' for their actions and decisions, and in the process, possibly discharge people and organisations of their responsibility. On the contrary, trustworthy AI requires more responsibility and more accountability from the people and organisations involved: for the decisions and actions of the AI applications, and for their own decision of using AI on a given application context.

Moreover, it is important to realise that any requirements for trustworthy AI, such as those proposed by the several initiatives we list above, are necessary but not sufficient to develop human-centered AI. That is, such requirements need be understood and implemented from a contextual perspective, i,e, it should be possible to adjust the implementation of the requirement such as transparency based on the context in which the system is used. I.e. requirements such as transparency should not have one fixed definition for all AI systems, but rather be defined based on how the AI system is used. At the same time, any AI technique used in the design and implementation should be amenable to explicitly consider all ethical requirements. E.g. it should be possible to explain (or to show) how the system got to a certain decision or behavior.

In the remainder of this chapter, we explore the many different aspects that are included in, or result from a responsible approach to AI development and use, which truly enable trustworthy AI.

# 2    The Meaning of Trust Regarding Machines

## 2.1    Technical Trust

Any technology is developed to provide a service fulfilling some needs. When deployed, its adoption depends on its ability to actually deliver the expected service safely, and to meet user expectations in terms of quality and continuity of service. In addition, the users expect that the technology will not do something it's not supposed to do, i.e., about which they were not informed. These are very basic conditions that one can apply to any technological object or systems, from a toaster in your kitchen to an airliner. If people are convinced that a technology has these features, they will use it, trusting it will deliver the expected service. In addition to this, long term impacts should also be considered but are often discarded or neglected, compared to immediate short term gains.

Like other technologies, computerized socio-technical systems, *i.e.,* those based on algorithmic computations and decisions that impact human individuals and society in a way or another, must be trustworthy. This implies several attributes that have been classically addressed in software engineering under the general designation of 'dependability' which is defined as the "delivery of service that can justifiably be trusted" [4]. This entails the following properties:

- Availability: readiness for correct service;
- Reliability: continuity of correct service;
- Safety: absence of catastrophic consequences on the user(s) and the environment;
- Confidentiality: absence of unauthorized disclosure of information;
- Integrity: absence of improper system alterations;
- Maintainability: ability to undergo, modifications, and repairs.
- Security: the concurrent existence of availability for authorized users only, confidentiality, and integrity (with 'improper' meaning 'unauthorized').

The realization of these properties includes verification and validation techniques (see Sect. 5) and has become essential in sectors in which critical functions are assumed by computer systems. Such functions are in particular those which failure entails major disruptions of the service delivered by the systems, which might lead to catastrophic consequences involving human lives. Computer systems engineering has developed a whole body of research and methods on dependable systems, largely applied in the Aeronautics industry in particular, or electricity distribution networks control.

These techniques have been rather ignored or minimized recently with the recent development of learning AI-based systems. Indeed, learning techniques based on statistics and on detecting regularities in data use millions of parameters which are not explicitly in a causal relation with the results, hence the blackbox depiction of these systems. The results, even if reaching high levels of accuracy, are not explainable. Worse, they can be totally wrong [1], actually showing lack of semantics in these systems.

This lack of explainability is an important factor in reducing trust in the system, and has motivated a wide interest in research [6], see Sects. 3 and 4 which provide two views on explainability. It is only through reaching a high and provable level of technical robustness and safety, that AI systems can be technically trusted.

An important question has to be clarified in this context, as in some applications such as automated driving, or autonomous weapons, there are discussions about the possibility that ethical decisions could be delegated to machines. Ethics are founded on the abstract notion of human dignity and are related to human autonomy and agency, the capacity to deliberate and to act freely and intentionally. Machines (i.e., digital computers) on the other hand operate at the syntactic computational level and can only decide and act within a bounded set of possibilities defined directly or indirectly (e.g., through machine learning) by human programmers. It is therefore not possible that machines take ethical decisions, even if their actions could have ethical consequences. This means that no decisions implying ethical deliberation with critical consequences should be delegated to machines.

## 2.2  Governance

However, technical solutions are only one necessary condition. If there is no framework to facilitate of even impose their adoption, there will be no guarantee that they are actually embedded commercial systems. Therefore governance issues become another condition for trust.

Indeed, comparing with other sectors, technical standards, certification processes by independent and recognized authorities, audit mechanisms and regulations imposing this mechanism, are essential factors in the build of trust and adoption of technologies. Other factors are related to ethics as well as to soft law approaches that could lead private companies to adopt virtuous design and development processes. All theses issues are related to *governance* issues that are largely discussed for instance in [17] and in [32]. Perhaps one of the most relevant list of recommendations in this effect are the "Ethics Guidelines for Trustworthy AI" issued by the High-Level Expert Group on AI appointed by the European Commission [29], (see Sect. 1. Two of the seven "Key requirements for Trustworthy AI" directly point to necessary governance mechanisms:

– Transparency. The data, system and AI business models should be transparent. Traceability mechanisms can help achieving this. Moreover, AI systems and their decisions should be explained in a manner adapted to the stakeholder concerned. Humans need to be aware that they are interacting with an AI system, and must be informed of the system's capabilities and limitations.
– Accountability. Mechanisms should be put in place to ensure responsibility and accountability for AI systems and their outcomes. Auditability, which enables the assessment of algorithms, data and design processes plays a key role therein, especially in critical applications. Moreover, adequate and accessible redress should be ensured.

# 3  The Difficulty of Understanding

The pioneering work "Learning interpretable models" [54] starts with the saying of Henry Louis Mencken:

*There is always an easy solution to every human problem –*
*neat, plausible, and wrong.*

This directly leads us to the problem of understanding with its two faces, the complexity of what is to be explained, and the human predilection for simple explanations that fit into what is already known. When applying the saying to understanding AI systems, we may state that AI systems are not neat and are based on assumptions and theories that are not plausible in the first instance. Since we are not interested in wrong assertions, we exclude easy solutions and take a look at the complexity of AI systems and human understanding.

## 3.1  Complexity of AI Systems

Computer systems are ubiquitous and many of them entail some AI processes, which may interact with each other. The user might perceive just the embedding system, possibly not aware of what is going on behind the scenes.

A search engine or social network platform, for instance, shows a band of advertisements along with the search results. An online auction determines for each query of a user which brands are displayed. Companies (buyers) bid to show an ad and are rewarded for the served ad or for the increase in product purchases by the brands (marketers) which they represent. The buyers compete with each other and, internally, each buyer selects among his marketers which brand has the best chance to win the auction [58]. Moreover, marketers adapt their websites to the likelihood of being selected. At least four systems are involved here: the embedding system (e.g. a search engine), the auction system running real-time bidding, the buyer, and the marketer system. Each of these put machine learning to good use. The buyer learns the probability that an ad is clicked by the user or even leads to a sale, another learning program of the buyer optimizes the price for a bid. The marketer learns a model that relates the wording and the images at its website to the success of being presented to the user or selected by the buyer. For each learning algorithm to be understood at an abstract level, knowledge of statistics and optimization is required. The interaction of all the systems leads to particular ads at the display and adds even more complexity. Finally, the data about the brands, the click-through data of users, and the data about the auction results are extremely high-dimensional and for learning they are sampled in various ways.

If the recommendation of a brand is justified by similarity with users who clicked on the ad of this brand, we have to admit that the notion of "similarity" here is itself complex. Where users might think of personality traits, interests, or location, the system calculates the distance between two entities in a much more detailed granularity. Actually, a thousand features of the user data are weighted to form a vector whose cosine angle with the vector of another user indicates the similarity, or some other kernel function computes the similarity between the data of two users. If some clustering algorithm groups users according to similarity, their heuristic search procedure is not deterministic, i.e. results may vary even on the same data set using the same learning algorithm. Hence, the underlying similarity is not of a kind that the user would call "similarity".

An analysis process is actually a sequence of steps and some of them are again composed of sequences. As if that would not be hard enough to understand, the overall process and its sub-processes are subject to optimization themselves. In interaction with the developer, RapidMiner recommends enhancements for an analysis process based on its learning from processes[9]. Moreover, the system creates and selects features using multi-objective optimization [43]. Many auto modeling approaches are around today [31,35,40]. The self-optimization of machine learning also applies to the level of implementing the algorithms on hardware architectures [7,37]. Hence, even if the statistical formula and the abstract algorithm is well understood by a user, there remains the part of the actual implementation on a particular computing architecture including all the optimizations.

Machine learning algorithms themselves are often compositions. In the simplest case, an ensemble of learned models outputs their majority vote. In the more complex setting of probabilistic graphical models, nodes with some states are linked to form a graph. The structure of the graph indicates the conditional independence structure of the nodes, given their neighboring nodes. Here, the design of the nodes and their neighborhoods may involve human knowledge about the domain which is modeled. This eases the understanding of the model. The likelihood of a node's state depends on the states of all the other nodes, whose likelihood, in turn, are estimated based on observations. Graphical models estimate a joint probability distribution over all the states of all the nodes. Understanding this requires statistical reasoning. The inference of the likelihood of a certain state of a subset of the nodes, i.e. the answer to a question of a user is a hard problem. There exists a variety of algorithms that approximate the inference. For a user with statistical knowledge, the explicit uncertainty that comes together with a model's answer, helps the reflection about how reliable the answer is. However, at another level, within the most prominent classes, variational inference, (loopy) belief propagation, and (Gibb's) sampling, diverse algorithms have been developed for specific computing architectures and each implementation comes along with its own error bounds, memory, energy, and run-time demands.

Deep learning methods are composed of several functions, organized into layers. Between the input nodes and the output nodes are several layers of different types that transform the high-dimensional input step by step into higher-level features such that in the end a classification can be performed in a better representation space with fewer dimensions. Given the observations and their class membership, learning – or, to be more precise: its optimization procedure – delivers features and local patterns at the intermediate layers. Sometimes and especially for pictures that can be interpreted by every user visualizations of the intermediate local patterns can be interpreted, e.g., the eye areas of faces. Most often, the intermediate representations learned to do not correspond to high-level features that human experts use. There are almost infinitely many architectures that combine different layer types. Setting up the training has high degrees of freedom, in addition. We know that deep neural networks are capable of learning every function approximately. However, we do not know whether a particular network architecture with a particular learning set-up delivers the best model. It is most likely, that better models exist, but the only way to find them is trial

---

[9] See https://rapidminer.com/blog/.

and error. The theoretical propositions of error bounds and resource demands are not always available. Explanation approaches work on the network with the trained weights and learn an explanation on top of it [56]. A well-known technique is the Layer-wise Relevance Propagation [5]. Understanding the principles of deep learning and its explanation requires sound knowledge in optimization and algorithmics. Understanding the explanation itself is easy if pictures are classified because their parts are interpretable. For more abstract signals, already the understanding of the explanation requires some training. In sum, the many development decisions at several levels of abstraction that make up for an AI system are complex both in themselves and in their interaction.

## 3.2   Human Understanding

The broad field of human understanding is studied in cognitive psychology, education, philosophical epistemology [13,19,21,27]. The meaning of "understanding" is closely related with "knowing" and "explaining" and discussing it has always been a stimulating subject in AI research. In the early days, AI systems were designed to explain human behavior, because with the systems, experiments can be made which are otherwise impossible, and properties like the complexity of reasoning could be proven mathematically (e.g. [46,49]).

More recently, attention moved to the human understanding of AI systems [18]. Here, we ask at which level a system is to be understood and which capabilities of the human decision-maker or user match which type of explanation. As has been shown in the previous section, understanding the principles of an AI system requires some statistical knowledge and familiarity with optimization. We are all born with the mathematical sense wired into the brain [9] so that we can learn this. The problem is that we have to learn it and not everybody did it. As has been shown in a study comparing mathematicians and scientists from other disciplines, there seem to be different areas of the brain responsible for numeric and linguistic processing [2]. Since we want also users from other disciplines to understand the systems they use, we might think about explaining the involved math linguistically. However, it could be shown that linguistic notions of quantities are hard to understand [60]. Hence, depending on the type of training and the given knowledge of a user, different ways of understanding are to be supported.

There have been many proposals of which questions should be answered by explanations of AI systems or, turning it the other way around, which answers indicate a human understanding of a system [30]. Building the right mental model of how the system works and what it does requires some years of training and intensive studies. This is for developers. Scientists work on answers toward questions like "When does the system fail?" proving error rates and guarantees of robustness. Understanding *why* a certain system does what it does is the subject of research, investigating an algorithm and its implementations on a particular computing architecture. We still do not know all answers to this question for all systems. Understanding in the sense of being able to rebuild or reconstruct it is a matter of research.

Understanding might also be indicated by knowing the answer to "How do I use it?" and giving a good estimate of the kind of the system's actions and their result. This is the level of understanding that regular users have of their smartphones and the applications that are installed on it. Without knowing how it works, they were immediately able to use it and trusted it right away. Offering a helpful metaphor to users eases the usage of systems. The system developers must take care that this surrogate model of the system's functionality is not misleading. Since we understand human actions through ascribing an intention, users often apply this to systems as well, but systems do not have an intention, developers and producers have (cf. Sect. 5). It is the task of system developers to design such that the limitations of a system can easily be derived from the usage guiding metaphor or by other means.

Understanding might be related to the data and the process that has generated them. In this respect, interactive exploration of the data and the learned model serve the users' understanding of their data. An example is machine learning for the sciences, where, e.g., biologists and doctors analyze genomic data with the help of a learning method that delivers a model which can be inspected by the experts. The impact of plausibility for interpreting models is investigated with respect to rule models [18]. More details on this type of understanding can be found in Sect. 4.

An important meaning of understanding is to know the particular properties of a system and their impact. The results of the research are to be transferred into labels allowing decision-makers to match the requirements of their application and the characteristics of a system. This moves beyond the fact sheet or model card approaches of IBM and Google which document systems [3,45]. Theoretical bounds of the error, the resource consumption (runtime, memory, energy), the fairness, robustness, and the covered type of learning tasks can be expressed by *care labels* for implemented algorithms on a certain computing platform, similar to care labels of textiles and washing machines or dryers. The novel care labels neither require a particular training nor interest in AI methods. They turn the stock of knowledge about AI systems into guarantees for their use. The particular set of care labels can only be worked out by a common undertaking of many scientists because it implies testing procedures that verify the care label for a certain implemented method. At the same time, working on it indicates where further research is needed. This brings us from examining human understanding back to the research in the complexity of the systems.

## 4    Explainability – Opening the Black Box

Explainability is at the heart of **Trustworthy AI** and must be guaranteed for developing AI systems aimed at empowering and engaging people, across multiple scientific disciplines and industry sectors. In multiple practical decision making scenarios, human-machine symbiosis is needed, with humans keeping the responsibility for the decisions, but relying on machine aids. We can completely rely on machines (AI systems) only when we can understand, at the best of our possibilities, and regarding our purposes, the reasons for the behavior observed or the decision suggested.

What is an **'explanation'** has already been investigated already by Aristotle in his Physics, a treatise dating back in the 4th century BC. Today it is urgent to give a functional meaning, as an interface between people and the algorithms that suggest decisions, or that decide directly.

Really useful AI systems for decision support, especially in high-stake domain such as health, job screening and justice, should enhance the awareness and the autonomy of the human decision maker, so that the ultimate decision is more informed, free of bias as much as possible, and ultimately 'better' than the decision that the human decision maker would have made without the AI system, as well as 'better' than the automated decision by the AI system alone.

Decision making is essentially a **socio-technical system**, where a decision maker interacts with various sources of information and decision support tools, whose quality should be assessed in term of the final, aggregated outcome - the quality of the decision - rather than assessing only the quality of the decision support tool in isolation (e.g., in terms of its predictive accuracy and precision as a stand-alone tool). To this purpose, rather than purely predictive tools, we need tools that explain their predictions in meaningful terms, a property that is rarely matched by the AI tools available in the market today.

Following the same line of reasoning, the AI predictive tools that do not satisfy the explanation requirement should simply not be adopted, also coherently with the GDPR's provisions concerning the *'right of explanation'* (see Articles 13(2)(f), 14(2)(g), and 15(1)(h), which require data controllers to provide data subjects with information about *'the existence of automated decision-making, including profiling and, at least in those cases, meaningful information about the logic involved, as well as the significance and the envisaged consequences of such processing for the data subject.'*)

There are different roles played within the decision making pipeline, therefore, it is important to clarify to whom is the explanation interpretable and which kind of questions can they ask.

- End users: 'Am I being treated fairly'?, 'Can I contest the decision'?, 'What could I do differently to get a positive outcome'?
- Engineers and data scientists: 'Is my system working as designed'?
- Regulators: 'Is it compliant'?

Essentially, the explanation problem for a decision support system can be understood as 'where' to place a boundary between what algorithmic details the decision maker can safely ignore and what meaningful information the decision maker should absolutely know to make an informed decision. Therefore explanation is intertwined with trustworthiness (what to safely ignore), comprehensibility (meaningfulness of the explanations), and accountability (humans keeping the ultimate responsibility for the decision).

## 4.1 Approaches

The explanation of decision processes is fundamental not only in machine learning but also in other different AI fields. In robotics, for instance, a verbalization of a mobile robot can provide a way for the robot to 'tell' its experience in a way that understandable by humans, or a rescue robot can explain its actions through a decision tree providing human-friendly information. Concerning planning and scheduling, it is beneficial for the user to have a way to explain reasons for specific planning so that she can agree or not with the returned plan. The explanations of the decisions of multi-agent systems can provide insights for resolving conflicts and harmful interactions or for summarizing the strategies adopted by the agents. On the other hand, knowledge representation and reasoning can help in providing logical justifications to explanations or augment basic logic with inference reasoning supplying more actionable explanations. On the same line, computer vision techniques provide the visualization tools for enhancing explanations that can be easily understood at a glance both for images and for text.

In Machine Learning the problem is articulated in two different forms:

- **Black Box eXplanation (BBX)**, or post-hoc explanation, that given a black box model aims to reconstruct its logic;
- **eXplanation by Design (XbD)** that aims to develop a model that it is explainable on its own.

The most recent works in literature are discussed in the review [23], organizing them according to the ontology illustrated in the figure below (Fig. 1). Today we have encouraging results that allow us to reconstruct individual explanations, answers to questions such as 'Why wasn't I chosen for the place I applied for? What should I change to overturn the decision'?

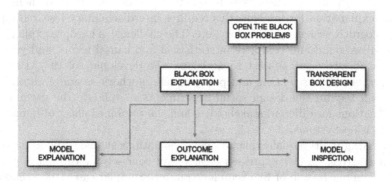

**Fig. 1.** Open the Black Box Problems. The first distinction concerns XbD and BBx. The latter can be further divided between Model Explanation, when the goal of explanation is the whole logic of the dark model, Outcome Explanation, when the goal is to explain decisions about a particular case, and Model Inspection, when the goal is to understand general properties of the dark model.

Particularly active is the stream on 'Outcome Explanation' that focuses on the local behavior of a black box [23], searching for an explanation of the decision made for a specific instance. Some of such approaches are model-dependent and aim, e.g., at explaining the decisions of neural networks by means of saliency maps, i.e., the portions of the input record (such as the regions of an input image) that are mainly responsible for the classification outcome [61]. A few more recent methods are model-agnostic, such as LIME [51]. The main idea is to derive a local explanation for a decision outcome on a specific instance by learning an interpretable model from a randomly generated neighborhood of the instance under investigation, where each instance in the neighborhood is labeled by querying the black box. An extension of LIME using decision rules (called Anchors) is presented in [52], which uses a bandit algorithm that randomly constructs the rules with the highest coverage and precision. Another recent approach LORE [24] provides local explanations in terms of both factual rules (why the instance has been classified as such?) and counterfactual rules (what should change in the instance to obtain a different classification?).

## 4.2   Open Challenges

To sum up, despite the soaring attention to the topic, the state of the art to date still exhibits ad-hoc, scattered results, mostly hard-wired with specific models. A widely applicable, systematic approach with a real impact has not emerged yet and many interesting and intertwined questions are still to be answered:

- Formalisms for explanations and quantification of comprehensibility: What are the key features for explanatory AI? Is there a general structure for explanatory AI? How does an AI system reach a specific decision, and based on what rationale or reasons does it do so? Formalism for explanations is missing and still no standards exist to quantify the degree of comprehensibility of an explanation for humans, this requires interdisciplinary research mixing with cognitive science, psychology, etc. The challenge is hard, as explanations should be sound and complete in statistical and causal terms, and yet comprehensible to users subject to decisions, the developers of the AI system, researchers, data scientists and policymakers, authorities and auditors, etc., this will require the design social experiments to validate the usefulness of explanations for different stakeholders and the combined effect of human and AI decision Systems.
- Generating multi modal explanations: explanations should come as meaningful narratives, and/or expressed clearly and concisely or through visualizations/summarization or by exemplar/counter-exemplar cases, till to explanation systems capable of supporting human-machine conversation, with two-way feedback and reinforcement learning. Explanations should reveal the why, why-not, and what-if. This would require explanations linking the visual structure of the image or video scenes or of the contained objects with knowledge of the real world expressed with definitions or facts using natural language or logic descriptions.

- Open the black-box (BBx): at the state of art for text and images the best learning methods are based on Deep Neural networks, therefore post-hoc explanators are needed to be coupled with the black-box, capable of achieving the required quality standards above.
- Transparency by design of hybrid AI algorithms (XbD): the challenge is twofold: i) to link learnt data models with a priori knowledge that is explicitly represented through a knowledge graph or an ontology. It would allow to relate the extracted features by deep learning inference with definitions of objects in a knowledge space. Different kinds of hybrid systems should be investigated, from loose coupling to tight integration of symbolic and numerical models. ii) To re-think Machine Learning as a joint optimization problem of both accuracy and explainability.

## 5  Verification

Verification is typically the process of

*providing evidence that something that was believed (some fact or hypothesis or theory) is correct.*

This can take many forms within computational systems, with a particularly important variety being **formal verification**, which can be characterised as

*the process of proving or disproving the correctness of a system with respect to a certain formal specification or property.*

Using formal verification allows us to establish key properties of hardware or software using formal logic, rather than either testing or informal arguments. This may appear to be an unnecessarily strong step but, while testing is both widespread and (generally) easy to mechanise, it is important to remember that testing typically involves selecting a (small) subset of scenarios and assessing whether the system works within those. In the case of complex, autonomous systems, it is often impossible to measure how many of the possible scenarios testing has covered.

Meanwhile, the focus of *formal* verification is to *prove* that the system will work as expected in *all* scenarios. Yet this comes at a cost, with formal verification being expensive (in that it can take significant modelling/design effort), complex (in that formal verification techniques are often computationally expensive), and restricted (in that, real-world, complex scenarios will require some abstraction/analysis before verification).

Nevertheless, formal verification is important for safety-critical systems, especially the key parts of systems where safety aspects are handled [33].

### 5.1  Issues

As we turn to AI systems, particularly Autonomous Systems that have key responsibilities we must be sure that we can *trust* them to act independently.

The concept of 'trust' in autonomous systems is quite complex and subjective [14]. However, the *trustworthiness* of an autonomous system usually comprises two key aspects:

1. **reliability**—will it always work reliably?
2. **beneficiality**—will it always do what we would like it to?

The first requirement is common among all cyber-physical systems; the second is especially relevant to autonomous systems. Since autonomous systems must make their own decisions and take their own actions, then unless we can prescribe *exactly* what the system will do in every situation then we must trust it to make the decisions we would like it to. Clearly, in any non-trivial situation, we cannot enumerate all possible situations/decisions so we are left trusting that it will behave as we would want even when not directly under our control.

We here need strong verification techniques for ensuring this second aspect. If we do not know when, how, and (crucially) why autonomous systems make their decisions then we will not trust them.

## 5.2  Approaches

In verifying reliability, there are a wide range of techniques, many of which will provide probabilistic estimates of the reliability of the software [39]. In verifying beneficiality, there are far fewer methods. Indeed, what verification method we can use depends on how decisions are made. Beyond the broad definition of autonomous systems as "systems that make their own decisions without human intervention" there are a variety of options.

- *Automatic:* whereby a sequence of prescribed, activities are fixed in advance. Here, the decisions are made by the original programmer and so we can carry out formal verification on the (fixed) code. (Note, however, that these systems show little flexibility.)
- *Learning (trained system):* whereby a machine learning system is trained offline from a set of examples.
  Here, the decisions are essentially taken by whoever chose the training set. Formal verification is very difficult (and often impossible) since, even when we know the training set, we do not know what attributes of the training set are important (and what bias was in the training set). Hence the most common verification approach here is testing.
- *Learning (adaptive system):* whereby the system's behaviour evolves through environmental interactions/feedback.
  In systems such as this (reinforcement learning, adaptive systems, etc.), the decisions are effectively taken by the environment. Since we can never fully describe any real environment, we are left with either testing or approximation as verification approaches.
- *Fully Autonomous:* whereby decisions involve an algorithm based on internal principles/motivations and (beliefs about) the current situation.
  Decisions are made by software, not fixed in advance and not directly driven

by the system's environment or training. Here, rather than verifying all the decisions the system might make (which we do not know), we can verify the *way* that the system makes decisions [10]. At any particular moment, will it always make the best decision given what it knows about the situation?

## 5.3   Challenges

What is our real worry about autonomous systems? It is not particularly that we think they are unreliable [55] but that we are concerned about their intent. What are they trying to do and why are they doing this? It is here that 'why' becomes crucial. In complex environments we cannot predict all the decisions that must be made (and so cannot pre-code all the 'correct' decisions) but we can ensure that, in making its decisions, an autonomous system will carry them out "in the right way". Unless we can strongly verify that autonomous systems will certainly try to make the right decisions, and make them for the right reasons, then it is irresponsible to deploy such systems in critical environments.

In summary, if we build our system well (exposing reasons for decisions) and provide strong verification, then we can make significant steps towards trustworthy autonomy. If we can expose why a system makes its decisions then:

1. we can verify (prove) that it always makes the appropriate decisions [10];
2. we can help convince the public that the system has "good intentions" [36];
3. we can help convince regulators to allow/certify these systems [15]; and so
4. give engineers the confidence to build more autonomous systems.

# 6   Human Rights and AI

It is now widely accepted that unless AI systems adhere to ethical standards that reflect values of fundamental importance to human communities, those systems would not qualify as trustworthy. Although discussions of 'AI ethics' have become commonplace, there is no agreed set of ethical standards that should govern the operation of AI, reflected in the variety of ethical standards espoused in various voluntary 'AI ethics codes' that have emerged in recent years. Some values commonly appear in these discussions, particularly those of 'transparency', 'fairness' and 'explainability' [17, 22] yet the vagueness and elasticity of the scope and content of 'AI ethics' means that it largely operates as an empty vessel into which anyone (including the tech industry, and the so-called Digital Titans) can pour their preferred 'ethical' content. Without an agreed framework of norms that clearly identifies and articulates the relevant ethical standards which AI systems should be expected to comply with, little real progress will be made towards ensuring that these systems are in practice designed, developed and deployed in ways that will meet widely accepted ethical standards[10].

---

[10] See also chapters 9 and 10 of this book.

## 6.1    Why Should Human Rights Provide the Foundational Ethical Standards for Trustworthy AI?

Elsewhere I have argued that international human rights standards offer the most promising set of ethical standards for AI, as several civil society organisations have suggested, for the following reasons[11].

First, as an international governance framework, human rights law is intended to establish global standards ('norms') and mechanisms of accountability that specify the way in which individuals are entitled to be treated, of which the UN Universal Declaration of Human Rights (UNHR) 1948 is the most well-known. Despite considerable variation between regional and national human rights charters, they are all grounded on a shared commitment to uphold the inherent human dignity of each and every person, in which each individual is regarded of equal worth, wherever situated [41]. These shared foundations reflect the status of human rights standards as *basic moral entitlements* of every individual in virtue of their humanity, whether or not those entitlements are backed by legal protection [12].

Secondly, a commitment to effective human rights protection is a critical and indispensable requirement of democratic constitutional orders. Given that AI systems increasingly configure our collective and individual environments, entitlements and access to, or exclusion from, opportunities and resources, it is essential that the protection of human rights, alongside respect for the rule of law and the protection of democracy, is assured to maintain the character of political communities as constitutional democracies, in which every individual is free to pursue his or her own version of the good life as far as this is possible within a framework of peaceful and stable cooperation framework underpinned by the rule of law [28].

Thirdly, the well-developed institutional framework through which systematic attempts are made to monitor, promote and protect adherence to human rights norms around the world offers a well-established analytical framework through which tension and conflict between rights, and between rights and collective interests of considerable importance in democratic societies, are resolved

---

[11] See various reports by civil society organisations concerned with securing the protection of international human rights norms, e.g., [41,42]. See also the Toronto Declaration: Protecting the rights to equality and non-discrimination in machine learning systems (2018) (Available at https://www.accessnow.org/the-toronto-declaration-protecting-the-rights-to-equality-and-non-discrimination-in-machine-learning-systems/); The Montreal Declaration for a Responsible Development of Artificial Intelligence: A Participatory Process (2017) (Available at https://nouvelles.umontreal.ca/en/article/2017/11/03/montreal-declaration-for-a-responsible-development-of-artificial-intelligence/); Access Now (see https://www.accessnow.org/tag/artificial-intelligence/ for various reports); Data & Society (see https://datasociety.net/); IEEE's report on ethically aligned design for AI (Available at https://ethicsinaction.ieee.org/) which lists as its first principle that AI design should not infringe international human rights; and the AI Now Report (2018) (Available at https://ainowinstitute.org/AI_Now_2018_Report.pdf).

in specific cases through the application of a structured form of reasoned evaluation. This approach is exemplified in the structure and articulation of human rights norms within the European Convention of Human Rights (the 'ECHR') which specifies a series of human rights norms, including (among others) the right to freedom of expression, the right to life, the right to private and home life, the right to freedom of assembly and religion, for example, all of which must be guaranteed to all individuals and effectively protected. For many of those rights, certain qualifications are permitted allowing human rights interferences only to the extent that they are justified in pursuit of a narrow range of clearly specified purposes that are prescribed by law, necessary in a democratic society and proportionate in relation to those purposes. This structured framework for the reasoned resolution of conflict arsing between competing rights and collective interests in specific cases is widely understood by human rights lawyers and practitioners, forming an essential part of a 'human rights approach' and overcomes another shortcoming in existing codes of ethical conduct: their failure to acknowledge potential conflict between ethical norms, and the lack of any guidance concerning how those conflicts will or ought to be resolved in the design and operation of AI systems.

Fourthly, the well-established human rights approach to the resolution of ethical conflict is informed by, and developed through, a substantial body of authoritative rulings handed down by judicial institutions (at both international and national level) responsible for adjudicating human rights complaints. These adjudicatory bodies, which determine allegations of human rights violations lodged by individual complainants, form part of a larger institutional framework that has developed over time to monitor, promote and protect human rights, and includes a diverse network of actors in the UN system, other regional human rights organisations (such as the Council of Europe and a wide range of civil society organisations focused on the protection of human rights), national courts and administrative agencies, academics and other human rights advocates. The institutional framework for rights monitoring, oversight and adjudication provides a further reason why human rights norms provide the most promising basis for AI ethics standards. This dynamic and evolving corpus of judicial decisions can help elucidate the scope of justified interferences with particular rights in concrete cases, offering concrete guidance to those involved in the design, development and implementation of AI systems concerning what human rights compliance requires. Most importantly, human rights norms are both internationally recognised and, in many jurisdictions, supported by law, thereby providing a set of national and international institutions through which allegations of human rights violations can be investigated and enforced, and hence offer a means for real and effective protection.

## 6.2   How to Ensure that Trustworthy AI Offers Effective Human Rights Protection?

The need to develop and establish a human-rights centred approach to the governance of AI systems springs from recognition that self-regulatory approaches which rely on voluntary compliance by firms and organisations to ensure that AI systems comply with ethical standards will not provide adequate and effective protection. In a highly competitive market, driven by the forces of global capitalism, commercial firms cannot be relied upon to, in effect, satisfactorily mark their own ethics homework. Instead, legally mandated external oversight by an independent regulator with appropriate investigatory and enforcement powers, which includes opportunities for meaningful stakeholder and public consultation and deliberation, is needed to ensure that human rights protection is both meaningful and effective. Yet achieving this is no small task. Designing and implementing a human-rights centred governance framework to secure trustworthy AI requires much more foundational work, both to specify the content and contours of this approach more fully and to render it capable of practical implementation.

Nevertheless, I believe that the core elements of such an approach *can* be identified to ensure that the design, development and deployment of human rights-compliant AI systems in real world settings. The core elements of an approach that I have developed with collaborators, which we call 'human rights-centred design, deliberation and oversight', has the potential to ensure that, in practice, AI systems will be designed, developed and deployed in ways that provide genuinely ethical AI, with contemporary human rights norms as its core ethical standards. This governance regime is designed around four principles, namely (a) *design and deliberation* (b) *assessment, testing and evaluation* (c) *independent oversight, investigation and sanction*, and (d) *traceability, evidence and proof.* Our proposed approach (which we have outlined more fully elsewhere [62]) draws upon variety of methods and techniques varying widely in their disciplinary foundations, seeking to integrate both ethical design strategies, technical tools and techniques for software and system design, verification, testing and auditing, together with social and organisational approaches to effective and legitimate governance. Suitably adapted and refined to secure conformity with human rights norms, these various methodological tools and techniques could be drawn together in an integrated manner to form the foundations of a comprehensive design and governance regime. It requires that human rights norms are systematically considered at every stage of system design, development and implementation (making interventions where this is identified as necessary), drawing upon and adapting technical methods and techniques for safe software and system design, verification, testing and auditing in order to ensure compliance with human rights norms, together with social and organisational approaches to effective and legitimate regulatory governance (including meta-regulatory risk management and impact assessment methodologies and post-implementation vigilance). Such a regime must be mandated by law, and relies critically on external oversight by independent, competent and properly resourced regulatory authorities with appropriate powers of investigation and enforcement, requiring input from both technical and human rights experts, on the one hand, and meaningful input and deliberation from affected stakeholders and the general public on the other.

## 6.3   Open Challenges

Much more theoretical and applied research is required to flesh out the details of our proposed approach, generating multiple lines of inquiry that must be pursued to develop the technical and organisational methods and systems that will be needed, based on the adaptation of existing engineering and regulatory techniques aimed at ensuring safe system design, re-configuring and extending these approaches to secure compliance with a much wider and more complex set of human rights norms. It will require identifying and reconfiguring many aspects of software engineering (SE) practice to support meaningful human rights evaluation and compliance, complemented by a focused human rights-centred interdisciplinary research and design agenda. To fulfil this vision of human-rights centred design, deliberation and oversight necessary to secure trustworthy AI, several serious challenges must first overcome - at the disciplinary level, the organisational level, the industry level, and the policy-making level 'none of which will be easily achieved. Furthermore, because human rights are often highly abstract in nature and lacking sharply delineated boundaries given their capacity to adapt and evolve in response to their dynamic socio-technical context, there may well be only so much that software and system design and implementation techniques can achieve in attempting to transpose human rights norms and commitments into the structure and operation of AI systems in real world settings. Nor can a human-rights centred approach ensure the protection of all ethical values adversely implicated by AI, given that human rights norms do not comprehensively cover all values of societal concern. Rather, our proposal for the human-rights centred governance of AI systems constitutes only one important element in the overall socio-political landscape needed to build a future in which AI systems are compatible with liberal democratic political communities in which respect for human rights and the rule of law lie at its bedrock[12]. In other words, human-rights norms provide a critical starting point in our quest to develop genuinely trustworthy AI, the importance of which is difficult to underestimate. As the UN Secretary General High-Level Panel on Digital Cooperation (2019) has stated:

*"There is an urgent need to examine how time-honoured human rights frameworks and conventions and the obligations that flow from those commitments can guide actions and policies relating to digital cooperation and digital technology".*

# 7   Beneficial AI

Artificial intelligence is currently experiencing a surge of research investment and technological progress. Tasks that seemed far off a decade ago—such as defeating human Go champions, driving cars safely in urban settings, and translating accurately among dozens of languages—are now largely solved.

---

[12] see also chapter 9 of this book.

Although there are several remaining obstacles that require breakthroughs in basic research, it seems reasonable to expect that AI will eventually reach and then exceed its long-standing objective of general-purpose, human-level AI. Indeed, the great majority of active AI researchers polled on this question are quite confident that this will happen during this century, with many putting the likely date much earlier [20]. Moreover, Critch and Krueger [8] argue that other characteristics of AI systems—such as speed, replication, and direct Internet contact with billions of humans—mean that thresholds of concern could be crossed long before general-purpose human-level AI is achieved.

The question of what happens when AI succeeds in its quest for true machine intelligence is seldom considered. Alan Turing [59] was not optimistic:

> "It seems probable that once the machine thinking method had started, it would not take long to outstrip our feeble powers. ... At some stage therefore we should have to expect the machines to take control."

This is the *problem of control*: if we create machines more powerful than ourselves, how do we retain power over them forever? Conversely, and perhaps more positively, we would like to create *provably beneficial AI*: AI systems that are guaranteed to be of benefit to humans, no matter how capable they become. This is the essence of trustworthy AI: we trust a machine if and only if we have good reason to believe it will act in ways beneficial to us.

## 7.1   AI in the Standard Model

To solve the control problem, it helps to understand *why* we humans might lose control—why it is that making AI better and better could lead to the worst possible outcome.

The difficulty has its origins in the way we have defined and pursued AI since the beginning. As computers emerged and AI became a possibility in the 1940s and 1950s, it was natural to define AI as a machine version of human intelligence. And human intelligence, in turn, was increasingly associated with the formal definitions of rationality proposed by Ramsey [50] and by von Neumann and Morgenstern [47]. In this view, roughly speaking,

> Humans are intelligent to the extent that our actions can be expected to achieve our objectives.

(In truth, this view of intelligence, expressed non-mathematically, can be traced easily back to Aristotle and other ancient sources.) The natural translation to machines looks like this:

> Machines are intelligent to the extent that their actions can be expected to achieve their objectives.

As machines, unlike humans, do not come with objectives, those are supplied exogenously, by us. So we create optimizing machinery, plug in the objectives, and off it goes.

I will call this the *standard model* for AI. It is instantiated in slightly different ways in different subfields of AI. For example, problem-solving and planning algorithms (depth-first search, A\*, SATPlan, etc.) aim to find least-cost action sequences that achieve a logically defined goal; game-playing algorithms maximize the probability of winning the game; MDP (Markov Decision Process) solvers and reinforcement learning algorithms find policies that maximize the expected discounted sum of rewards; supervised learning algorithms minimize a loss function. The same basic model holds in control theory (minimizing cost), operations research (maximizing reward), statistics (minimizing loss), and economics (maximizing utility, GDP, or discounted quarterly profit streams).

Unfortunately, the standard model fails when we supply objectives that are incomplete or incorrect. We have known this for a long time. For example, King Midas specified his objective—that everything he touch turn to gold—and found out too late that this included his food, drink, and family members. Many cultures have some variant of the genie who grants three wishes; in these stories, the third wish is usually to undo the first two wishes. In economics, this is the problem of *externalities*, where (for example) a corporation pursuing profit renders the Earth uninhabitable as a side effect.

Until recently, AI systems operated largely in the laboratory and in toy, simulated environments. Errors in defining objectives were plentiful [38], some of them highly amusing, but in all cases researchers could simply reset the system and try again. Now, however, AI systems operate in the real world, interacting directly with billions of people. For example, content selection algorithms in social media determine what a significant fraction of all human beings read and watch for many hours per day. Initial designs for these algorithms specified an objective to maximize some measure of click-through or engagement. Fairly soon, the social media companies realized the corrosive effects of maximizing such objectives, but fixing the problem has turned out to be very difficult.

Content selection algorithms in social media are very simple learning algorithms that typically represent content as feature vectors and humans as sequences of clicks and non-clicks. Clearly, more sophisticated and capable algorithms could wreak far more havoc. This is an instance of a general principle [48]: with misspecified objectives, the better the AI, the worse the outcome. An AI system pursuing an incorrect objective is by definition *in conflict* with humanity.

## 7.2   AI in the New Model: Assistance Games

The mistake in the standard model is the assumption that we humans can supply a complete and correct definition of our true preferences to the machine. From the machine's point of view, this amounts to the assumption that the objective it is pursuing is exactly the right one. We can avoid this problem by defining the goals of AI in a slightly different way [53]:

Machines are *beneficial* to the extent that *their* actions can be expected to achieve *our* objectives.

After all, we don't want intelligent machines if they are not beneficial, so perhaps we should have pursued this formulation all along. It is more difficult from the machine's point of view, because the objectives remains within us, not in the machine. It is, nonetheless, feasible. Informally, it translates into three principles:

1. The machine's only objective is to maximize the realization of human preferences.
2. The machine is initially uncertain about what those preferences are.
3. The ultimate source of information about human preferences is human behavior.

The key characteristics of the new model are the absence of a fixed, known objective—whether at design time or embedded in the agent itself—and the flow of preference information from human to machine at runtime. Here, "preferences" refers to everything that people, in all their variety, might care about with regard to how the future unfolds.

The new model is strictly more general than the standard model, because *uncertainty* about preferences has *certainty* as a special case. It is also at least as amenable to instantiation in a wide variety of forms. One particular formal instantiation is the *assistance game*—originally a cooperative inverse reinforcement learning or CIRL game [26]. An assistance game is a formal model in which there are two agents H (the "human") and R (the "robot"); H has a payoff function $\theta$; R also has the same payoff, but has only a prior probability distribution $P(\theta)$ for what $\theta$ might be. Within this model one can show that optimal solutions for the human include teaching the robot about human preferences, while optimal solutions for the robot allow it to interpret the human's teaching behavior. Moreover, under reasonable assumptions, the robot will defer to human requests [44], choose "minimally invasive" strategies that change the world as little as possible [57], ask permission before taking risky actions whose outcomes may violate human preferences, and, perhaps most importantly, allow itself to be switched off [25]. Even if it knows nothing about human preferences, it can still take actions that improve the human's freedom of action. All of these behaviors follow from the definition of the problem that the robot is solving, and not from any human-supplied scripts.

## 7.3   Research Agenda and Open Questions

To replace the standard model of AI with a new model that allows for uncertain objectives will require reconstructing many branches of AI, including search, game-playing, constraint satisfaction, logical planning, sequential decisions under uncertainty, supervised learning, and reinforcement learning. This includes finding the "natural" form of partial preference information, the corresponding "protocol" whereby preference information flows from the human, and new, efficient interactive algorithms.

The simple, single-human/single-robot assistance game has yielded many important insights and also models the relationship between the human race and its machines, each construed monolithically. Additional complications arise, of course, when we consider the multiplicity of humans and machines. Decision making on behalf of multiple humans is the subject of millennia of research in moral philosophy and the social sciences. This research has identified many "extreme failure modes" for simplistic solutions. Issues include fairness, preference tradeoffs, interpersonal comparisons of preferences, decisions that affect population size, and human preferences that are altruistic, sadistic, or relativized to the well-being or status of others. Heterogeneity of preferences is relatively unproblematic—machines can easily accommodate billions of individual preference models, and in no sense will there be a single definition of "human values" uploaded into the machine.

Many harmful AI outcomes in the real world result from the combined failure of the algorithm and the sociotechnical context in which it is embedded. Racially biased outputs from machine learning algorithms are a well-known example that results both from objective misspecification and from bias in the process that produces the training data; other, more complex failure modes include classifiers whose decisions affect their own future input data, as exemplified by moral hazard and adverse selection in insurance. Formal models of the sociotechnical context and the embedded AI system could be of enormous value in revealing new failure modes and providing guidance for safe design and use of AI systems.

For the new model to be workable when deployed among real humans, it must take into account the imperfect nature of the link between human preferences and human choice behavior. We are computationally limited, sometimes governed by emotion, and almost always embedded in a hierarchy of commitments and activities that sharply limit the actions we even consider taking at any give moment in time. Inferring the stable preferences that underlie such complex patterns of behavior is an extraordinarily difficult problem. Fortunately, there are vast troves of data to help: not just direct real-time observation, but also the entire written record, much of which concerns humans and their actions.

The final and perhaps most important open question concerns the plasticity of human preferences. "Version 0.1" of the new model assumes stable preferences, whereas of course our preferences are influenced by experience and maturation. This leads to a failure mode whereby machines learn to modify human preferences to be easier to satisfy.

Put another way: there are many different possible futures in which reality more or less lines up with our preferences, because there are many different preferences we could come to have. (There are, of course, far more futures where reality is catastrophically misaligned with our preferences, but one hopes that AI is not the reason.) It would be nice to have such a choice, even if it is a difficult choice to make.

## 8   Conclusion: The Way Ahead

AI systems are deployed in a particular historical context. Globalization and the internet create a new situation in which the development of the technology anywhere has almost an immediate effect worldwide. Social network powered by AI systems influence entire populations in the world instantly. A new breakthrough emerging in one country quickly becomes available and usable at the antipodes. It is therefore necessary that trustworthiness of AI technologies becomes a concern for all nations, and that mechanisms of governance, grounded on research results for ensuring technical robustness and safety, be agreed upon in an international framework.

**Acknowledgments.** Chatila's work has been partially supported by the European Commission's Horizon 2020 research and innovation programme project AI4EU (grant 825619).

Fisher's work has been supported by funding from UKRI, over several research projects, and through a Royal Academy of Engineering *Chair in Emerging Technologies*.

Dignum's work has been partially supported by the European Commission's Horizon 2020 research and innovation programme project AI4EU (grant 825619) and by the Wallenberg AI, Autonomous Systems and Software Program (WASP) program funded by the Knut and Alice Wallenberg Foundation.

Morik's work has been supported by the Federal Ministry of Education and Research of Germany as part of the competence center for machine learning ML2R (01IS18038A), and by Deutsche Forschungsgemeinschaft (DFG) within the Collaborative Research Center SFB 876 "Providing Information by Resource-Constrained Data Analysis".

# References

1. Alcorn, M.A., et al.: Strike (with) a pose: neural networks are easily fooled by strange poses of familiar objects. In: Proceedings of the IEEE/CVF Conference on Computer Vision and Pattern Recognition (CVPR), June 2019
2. Amalric, M., Dehaene, S.: Origins of the brain networks for advanced mathematics in expert mathematicians. In: Proceedings of the National Academy of Sciences, vol. 113, pp. 4909–4917. PNAS (2016). https://www.pnas.org/content/113/18/4909
3. Arnold, M., et al.: FactSheets: increasing trust in AI services through supplier's declarations of conformity. CoRR (2019). arXiv:1808.07261v2
4. Avizienis, A., Laprie, J.C., Randell, B., Landwehr, C.: Basic concepts and taxonomy of dependable and secure computing. IEEE Trans. Depend. Secure Comput. 1(1), 11–33 (2004)
5. Bach, S., Binder, A., Montavon, G., Klauschen, F., Müller, K.R., Samek, W.: On pixel-wise explanations for non-linear classifier decisions by layer-wise relevance propagation. PLOS One 7(10) (2015). https://doi.org/10.1371/journal.pone.0130140
6. Barredo Arrieta, A., et al.: Explainable Artificial Intelligence (XAI): concepts, taxonomies, opportunities and challenges toward responsible AI. Inf. Fusion 58, 82–115 (2020). https://doi.org/10.1016/j.inffus.2019.12.012. http://www.sciencedirect.com/science/article/pii/S1566253519308103
7. Buschjäger, S., Chen, K.H., Chen, J.J., Morik, K.: Realization of random forest for real-time evaluation through tree framing. In: The IEEE International Conference on Data Mining Series (ICDM), November 2018
8. Critch, A., Krueger, D.: AI Research Considerations for Human Existential Safety (ARCHES). Preprint at http://acritch.com/arches (2020)

9. Dehaene, S.: The Number Sense: How the Mind Creates Mathematics. OUP, Oxford (2011)
10. Dennis, L.A., Fisher, M., Lincoln, N.K., Lisitsa, A., Veres, S.M.: Practical verification of decision-making in agent-based autonomous systems. Autom. Softw. Eng. **23**(3), 305–359 (2016). https://doi.org/10.1007/s10515-014-0168-9
11. Dignum, V.: Responsible Artificial Intelligence: How to Develop and Use AI in a Responsible Way. Springer, Cham (2019). https://doi.org/10.1007/978-3-030-30371-6
12. Dworkin, R.: Taking Rights Seriously. A&C Black, London (2013)
13. Feltovich, P.J., Coulson, R.L., Spiro, R.J.: Learners' (mis)Understanding of Important and Difficult Concepts: A Challenge to Smart Machines in Education. AAAI Press (2001)
14. Fisher, M., List, C., Slavkovik, M., Weiss, A.: Ethics and trust: principles, verification and validation. Dagstuhl Rep. **9**(4), 59–86 (2019). https://doi.org/10.4230/DagRep.9.4.59
15. Fisher, M., Mascardi, V., Rozier, K.Y., Schlingloff, B., Winikoff, M., Yorke-Smith, N.: Towards a Framework for Certification of Reliable Autonomous Systems (2020). https://arxiv.org/abs/2001.09124
16. Fjeld, J., Achten, N., Hilligoss, H., Nagy, A., Srikumar, M.: Principled artificial intelligence: mapping consensus in ethical and rights-based approaches to principles for AI. Berkman Klein Center Research Publication (2020-1) (2020)
17. Floridi, L., et al.: AI4People–an ethical framework for a good AI society: opportunities, risks, principles, and recommendations. Minds Mach. **28**(4), 689–707 (2018). https://doi.org/10.1007/s11023-018-9482-5
18. Fürnkranz, J., Kliegr, T., Paulheim, H.: On cognitive preferences and the plausibility of rule-based models. Mach. Learn. J. **109**, 853–898 (2020). https://doi.org/10.1007/s10994-019-05856-5
19. Gordon, E.C.: Understanding in epistemology. In: Fieser, J., Dowden, B. (eds.) Internet Encyclopedia of Philosophy (2015). https://www.iep.utm.edu/understa/
20. Grace, K., Salvatier, J., Dafoe, A., Zhang, B., Evans, O.: When will AI exceed human performance? Evidence from AI experts. J. Artif. Intell. Res. **62**, 729–754 (2018)
21. Graham, S.A., et al.: Artificial intelligence approaches to predicting and detecting cognitive decline in older adults: a conceptual review. Psychiatry Res. **284**, 112732 (2020)
22. Greene, D., Hoffmann, A.L., Stark, L.: Better, nicer, clearer, fairer: a critical assessment of the movement for ethical artificial intelligence and machine learning. In: Proceedings of the 52nd Hawaii International Conference on System Sciences (2019)
23. Guidotti, R., Monreale, A., Ruggieri, S., Turini, F., Giannotti, F., Pedreschi, D.: A survey of methods for explaining black box models. ACM Comput. Surv. (CSUR) **51**(5), 1–42 (2018)
24. Guidotti, R., Monreale, A., Ruggieri, S., Turini, F., Giannotti, F., Pedreschi, D.: A survey of methods for explaining black box models. ACM Comput. Surv. **51**, 1–42 (2019)
25. Hadfield-Menell, D., Dragan, A., Abbeel, P., Russell, S.: The off-switch game. In: Proceedings of the Twenty-sixth International Joint Conference on Artificial Intelligence (2017)
26. Hadfield-Menell, D., Dragan, A.D., Abbeel, P., Russell, S.J.: Cooperative inverse reinforcement learning. In: Advances in Neural Information Processing Systems 29 (2017)

27. Hernández-Orallo, J., Martínez-Plumed, F., Schmid, U., Siebers, M., Dowe, D.L.: Computer models solving intelligence test problems: progress and implications. Artif. Intell. **230**, 74–107 (2016)

28. Hildebrandt, M.: Smart Technologies and the End(s) of Law: Novel Entanglements of Law and Technology. Edward Elgar Publishing, Cheltenham (2015)

29. HLEG-AI: Ethics Guidelines for Trustworthy AI. European Commission (2019). https://ec.europa.eu/digital-single-market/en/news/ethics-guidelines-trustworthy-ai

30. Hoffman, R.R., Mueller, S.T., Klein, G., Litman, J.: Metrics for explainable AI: challenges and prospects. CoRR (2018). http://arxiv.org/abs/1812.04608

31. Hutter, F., Kotthoff, L., Vanschoren, J. (eds.): Automated Machine Learning - Methods, Systems, Challenges. Springer, Cham (2019). https://doi.org/10.1007/978-3-030-05318-5

32. IEEE: Ethically Aligned Design. A Vision for Prioritizing Human Well-being with Autonomous and Intelligent Systems. IEEE (2019). https://ethicsinaction.ieee.org

33. International Electrotechnical Commission: Functional safety and IEC 61508 (2010). https://www.iec.ch/functionalsafety/

34. Jobin, A., Ienca, M., Vayena, E.: The global landscape of AI ethics guidelines. Nat. Mach. Intell. **1**(9), 389–399 (2019)

35. Kietz, J.-U., Serban, F., Fischer, S., Bernstein, A.: "Semantics Inside!" But let's not tell the data miners: intelligent support for data mining. In: Presutti, V., d'Amato, C., Gandon, F., d'Aquin, M., Staab, S., Tordai, A. (eds.) ESWC 2014. LNCS, vol. 8465, pp. 706–720. Springer, Cham (2014). https://doi.org/10.1007/978-3-319-07443-6_47

36. Koeman, V., Dennis, L.A., Webster, M., Fisher, M., Hindriks, K.: The "Why did you do that?" Button: answering Why-questions for end users of Robotic Systems. In: Proceedings of the 7th International Workshop on Engineering Multi-Agent Systems (EMAS) (2019)

37. Kotthaus, H., Schönberger, L., Lang, A., Chen, J.J., Marwedel, P.: Can flexible multi-core scheduling help to execute machine learning algorithms resource-efficiently? In: 22nd International Workshop on Software and Compilers for Embedded Systems, SCOPES 2019. ACM (2019)

38. Krakovna, V.: Specification gaming examples in AI. Available at vkrakovna.wordpress.com (2018)

39. Kwiatkowska, M., Norman, G., Parker, D.: PRISM 4.0: verification of probabilistic real-time systems. In: Gopalakrishnan, G., Qadeer, S. (eds.) CAV 2011. LNCS, vol. 6806, pp. 585–591. Springer, Heidelberg (2011). https://doi.org/10.1007/978-3-642-22110-1_47

40. Lang, M., Kotthaus, H., Marwedel, P., Weihs, C., Rahnenführer, J., Bischl, B.: Automatic model selection for high-dimensional survival analysis. J. Stat. Comput. Simul. **85**(1), 62–76 (2015). https://doi.org/10.1080/00949655.2014.929131

41. Latonero, M.: Governing artificial intelligence: upholding human rights & dignity. Data Soc. (2018)

42. McGregor, L., Murray, D., Ng, V.: International human rights law as a framework for algorithmic accountability. Int. Comp. Law Q. **68**(2), 309–343 (2019)

43. Mierswa, I., Morik, K.: Automatic feature extraction for classifying audio data. Mach. Learn. J. **58**, 127–149 (2005). https://doi.org/10.1007/s10994-005-5824-7

44. Milli, S., Hadfield-Menell, D., Dragan, A., Russell, S.: Should robots be obedient? In: Proceedings of the Twenty-Sixth International Joint Conference on Artificial Intelligence (2017)

45. Mitchell, M., et al.: Model cards for model reporting. CoRR (2018). http://arxiv.org/abs/1810.03993

46. Morik, K., Mühlenbrock, M.: Learning in order: steps of acquiring the concept of the day (night cycle). In: In Order to Learn - How the Sequence of Topics Influences Learning, pp. 119–136. Oxford University Press (2007)

47. von Neumann, J., Morgenstern, O.: Theory of Games and Economic Behavior. Princeton University Press, Princeton (1944)

48. Omohundro, S.: The basic AI drives. In: AGI-08 Workshop on the Sociocultural, Ethical and Futurological Implications of Artificial Intelligence (2008)

49. Parkison, R.C., Colby, K.M., Faught, W.S.: Conversational language comprehension using integrated pattern–matching and parsing. In: Grosz, B.J., Jones, K.S., Webber, B.L. (eds.) Readings in Natural Language Processing, pp. 551–56. Morgan Kaufmann, Los Altos (1987)

50. Ramsey, F.P.: Truth and probability. In: Braithwaite, R.B. (ed.) The Foundations of Mathematics and Other Logical Essays. Harcourt Brace Jovanovich (1931)

51. Ribeiro, M.T., Singh, S., Guestrin, C.: "Why should I trust you?" Explaining the predictions of any classifier. In: Proceedings of the 22nd ACM SIGKDD International Conference on Knowledge Discovery and Data Mining, pp. 1135–1144 (2016)

52. Ribeiro, M.T., Singh, S., Guestrin, C.: Anchors: high-precision model-agnostic explanations. In: Thirty-Second AAAI Conference on Artificial Intelligence (2018)

53. Russell, S.J.: Human Compatible: AI and the Problem of Control. Penguin, New York (2019)

54. Rüping, S.: Learning interpretable models. Ph.D. thesis, University Dortmund (2006). https://eldorado.uni-dortmund.de/handle/2003/23008

55. Salem, M., Lakatos, G., Amirabdollahian, F., Dautenhahn, K.: Would you trust a (faulty) robot?: Effects of error, task type and personality on human-robot cooperation and trust. In: Proceedings of the 10th ACM/IEEE International Conference on Human-Robot Interaction (HRI), pp. 141–148. ACM (2015)

56. Samek, W., Montavon, G., Vedaldi, A., Mueller, K.R. (eds.): Explainable AI: Interpreting, Explaining and Visualizing Deep Learning. Springer, Cham (2019). https://doi.org/10.1007/978-3-030-28954-6

57. Shah, R., Krasheninnikov, D., Alexander, J., Abbeel, P., Dragan, A.: Preferences implicit in the state of the world. In: Proceedings of the Seventh International Conference on Learning Representations (2019)

58. Shi, Y., Stitelman, O., Perlich, C.: Blacklisting the blacklist in online advertising: improving delivery by bidding for what you can win. In: Proceedings of the ADKDD 2017. ACM (2017). https://doi.org/10.1145/3124749.3124753

59. Turing, A.: Can digital machines think? Radio broadcast, BBC Third Programme. Typescript available at turingarchive.org (1951)

60. Wintle, B., Fraser, H., Wills, B., Nicholson, A., Fidler, F.: Verbal probabilities: very likely to be somewhat more confusing than numbers. PLoS One **14**(4), 1–18 (2019)

61. Xu, K., et al.: Show, attend and tell: neural image caption generation with visual attention. In: International Conference on Machine Learning, pp. 2048–2057 (2015)

62. Yeung, K., Howes, A., Pogrebna, G.: AI Governance by Human Rights-Centred Design, Deliberation and Oversight: An End to Ethics Washing. The Oxford Handbook of AI Ethics. Oxford University Press, Oxford (2019)

# Democratising the Digital Revolution: The Role of Data Governance

Sylvie Delacroix[1,2(✉)], Joelle Pineau[3], and Jessica Montgomery[1]

[1] University of Birmingham, Birmingham B15 2TT, UK
S.DELACROIX@bham.ac.uk
[2] The Alan Turing Institute, London W1 2DB, UK
[3] McGill University, Quebec H3A0G4, Canada

**Abstract.** Data is at the heart of today's AI. As AI technologies advance at a rapid pace, action is needed today to develop and implement governance structures to ensure that the benefits of AI are shared across society.

## 1 Introduction

Data is at the heart of today's AI. The machine learning techniques enabling many of the field's most recent advances and impressive applications leverage large amounts of data to extract insights that form the basis of new products or services. These systems have the potential to support hugely beneficial societal outcomes across a range of spheres of life – from improving healthcare services [1], to increasing access to transport [3] to helping tackle the major challenges posed by climate change [2]. As AI technologies advance at a rapid pace, action is needed today to develop and implement governance structures to ensure that the benefits of AI are shared across society.

This chapter explores more specifically the role that data governance can play in shaping the development of AI technologies (see also Chapter 9). It starts by considering how the role of law and governance systems in the digital environment is shifting, prompted by investigations or public incidents that have exposed the negative or unintended consequences of data use for both individuals and society. As the 'wild west' view of the digital sphere as an ungoverned, or ungovernable, space becomes increasingly outmoded, the chapter considers how policymakers and legislators are increasingly seeking means through which to assert social values in digital systems.

With a variety of legal and policy structures already seeking to influence patterns of data use and technology development, this chapter then briefly reviews recent legislative and policy activities, noting that – despite recent efforts – gaps in the policy landscape remain. Finding that new forms of bottom-up data sharing arrangement are needed to enhance democratic governance of data use, the chapter concludes by exploring the role of data trusts as a vehicle for leveraging the power associated with data aggregation.

© Springer Nature Switzerland AG 2021
B. Braunschweig and M. Ghallab (Eds.): Reflections on Artificial Intelligence
for Humanity, LNAI 12600, pp. 40–52, 2021.
https://doi.org/10.1007/978-3-030-69128-8_3

## 2  Data for Intelligence: The Role of Data Governance in Creating AI that Benefits Humanity

While the term AI for many conjures images of human-like intelligence, the type of intelligence that comes from today's techniques is different. The combination of advanced statistics and computing power that underpins many of the most successful AI technologies is perhaps more analogous to the human immune system than it is to human cognition [4]. By processing data, these technologies are able to detect signals in the environment, which are not otherwise easily identifiable, and generate automatic responses to well-defined (and typically narrowly scoped) prediction tasks.

With data central to the development of AI, data governance will need to be central to any system seeking to encourage its trustworthy development and deployment. Effective data governance plays a role in both unlocking the value of data – enabling individuals and organisations to share data to support economic and social wellbeing – and protecting individuals, communities and society from the vulnerabilities that can be associated with the use of data, in particular the use of sensitive personal data. These vulnerabilities can relate to the privacy of such data, the development of data-enabled systems that reinforce discrimination on the basis of personal characteristics, or the potential for digital systems to shape the choices made by an individual in ways that undermine their agency both on- and off-line (see Chapter 2).

As the digital economy grows, and as data-enabled products and services become embedded in many daily activities, policymakers are grappling with questions about how best to manage such vulnerabilities. After an 'annus horribilis' for AI, in which a range of news stories laid bare the ways in which these new uses of data can leave individuals or groups exposed to harm [5], governments are increasingly looking for innovative governance mechanisms. The aim is to find ways of unlocking responsible data sharing while embedding legal and ethical practices that reduce the risk of harm and protect individual rights and freedoms.

There already exist legal instruments that seek to protect individual rights. Taking its roots in a human rights framework, the European Union's General Data Protection Regulation, for example, sits alongside a range of other legal instruments aimed at managing intellectual property, preserving copyright, and protecting privacy. Together, these create a constellation of individual rights and protections, and define circumstances and means through which individuals can assert those rights.

The nature of today's digital environment puts pressure on these existing systems. Designed for decisions of significant personal or social impact, these legal frameworks are not as well-equipped to handle the collective aspects of data sharing and manage the vulnerabilities that arise from the cumulative ways in which individuals share their data. Given that multiple algorithmic systems often act in parallel – each leveraging parcels of data that inform seemingly insignificant decisions which become collectively significant – tackling these vulnerabilities demands sophisticated measures to *antici-pate* the many risks of data use or potential failures in governance systems (in contrast to the current post-hoc, harm-remedying approach).

The latter, top-down approaches to constraining the use of data cannot by themselves create the conditions that support the beneficial use of data and AI. Today's challenge is therefore to bridge the gap between society's data sharing aspirations on the one hand and rights-protecting concerns on the other. This challenge creates a demand for new tools that can limit – or redistribute – technological and economic power. Inspired by discussions between Paul Nemitz (European Commission), Neil Lawrence (University of Cambridge), Nigel Shadbolt (Open Data Institute) and Lise Getoor (University of California at Santa Cruz), this chapter considers the infrastructures that could contribute to this democratisation of data governance.

## 3 The Role of Law and Governance in the Digital Environment

### 3.1 Understanding the Lessons from Recent History

The last ten years have seen a rapid proliferation of data uses, and the growth of a vibrant global digital economy. Though the benefits of data use can be difficult to quantify, research suggests that on average the use of data analytics improves company performance resulting in 5–6% higher output and productivity [6]. Personal data has been a source of value in this economy. As more data is collected about individuals from a wider variety of sources – from online shopping, social media, fitness tracking devices, or mobile phone apps – it is increasingly possible for companies to develop a rich picture of daily life from the data trail left by each individual. This granular data is in turn relied on to build personal profiles whose predictive power is easily monetised in today's economy.

While bringing many benefits, these uses of data are exposing vulnerabilities. These accrue:

- To individuals, with examples of sensitive data about an individual's personal characteristics being inferred from seemingly innocuous information, as datasets are analysed in new ways, creating risks that individuals might inadvertently disclose private information [7, 8];
- To groups, as the social inequalities embedded in datasets at the point of collection are reinforced in the digital environment, leading to discrimination against vulnerable groups – women being less likely than men to be shown adverts for high-paid jobs, for example, or racial disparities in the predictions from algorithmic risk assessment tools in the justice system [9–11];
- To society, for example through the misuse of personal data to influence political debate [12].

This period of rapid technology development has also been accompanied by increasing concentrations of market power. Companies with access to large volumes of information about individuals have been successful in leveraging that personal data to generate revenue. While the most prominent examples of this come from the use of personal data to enable targeted advertising for products, services, or other forms of information, access to data has provided a first-mover advantage that contributes to market concentration across the wider digital economy. While the digital economy does offer benefits to individuals, publics and policymakers are increasingly expressing concern that the benefits that come from personal data use are disjointed from the public interest [13, 14].

In many parts of the world, these technological developments have taken place alongside wider debates about the extent to which all in society are able to benefit from advances in technology and economic growth. Political shifts following the growth of populist movements in the US and Europe have prompted further concerns about the extent to which digital technologies – originally envisaged as means for democratic engagement – have created an information environment that undermines democratic discourse [15]. With calls to reorient the use of technologies so as to support democracy and social cohesion, governance systems are needed that align digital systems with societal values.

Addressing governments at the World Economic Forum in 1996, cyber-activist John Perry Barlow claimed in his *declaration of the independence of cyberspace* that "cyberspace does not lie within your borders", suggesting governments "have no moral right to rule us nor do you possess any methods of enforcement we have true reason to fear" [16]. In the early days of the growing digital economy, statements such as this fed a techno-centric narrative that argued the internet – or online activities – were beyond the reach of governments or governance. However, as digital systems become foundational to daily activities, as the vulnerabilities they create become clearer, and as publics and policymakers question who is benefitting from technological advances, this 'wild west' mentality seems increasingly outdated. In its place arrive new questions about power and asymmetries of power: who really controls the digital world, and how can governance help share the benefits of digital technologies across society?

Learning from this recent history, and as the disruptive potential of technologies like AI, cryptocurrencies and quantum computing become clearer, policymakers are seeking to create governance systems that allow freedom to innovate and pursue research, within an environment that pre-empts and prevents the harms that may follow. These approaches frequently seek to allow the innovation that has come from market development, in a framework that asserts democratic values.

## 3.2   Current Legal Structures and Data Rights

If recent history has shown the vulnerabilities created by new patterns of data use, it has also demonstrated the ability of governments, publics, civil society and industry to endeavour to mitigate these potential harms.

The last five years have seen governments across the world put in place national strategies to support the development of AI technologies and their ethical deployment. Amongst the common elements in many of these strategies are data ethics initiatives, pursued with the aim of improving the trustworthiness of AI technologies, for example:

- Germany's Data Ethics Commission was set up by the Federal Government in 2018 with a mandate "to develop ethical benchmarks and guidelines as well as specific recommendations for action, aiming at protecting the individual, preserving social cohesion, and safeguarding and promoting prosperity in the information age". The Commission recently made recommendations aimed at governing both the digital economy and AI technologies [17].
- The UK's Centre for Data Ethics and Innovation, an advisory body established by the UK Government "to connect policymakers, industry, civil society, and the

public to develop the right governance regime for data-driven technologies" [18]. Its first reports on bias and online targeting have sought to inform government policy development in these areas.

- Picking up the recommendations of Cedric Villani's report 'For a meaningful artificial intelligence', France's 2018 AI strategy seeks to promote a data policy regime that encourages data sharing in the public interest, while enforcing a right to data portability [19].
- At EU level, high level groups on AI and data ethics have spent recent years advising the European Commission on its approach to data and AI, with recent draft strategies on both these areas noting key areas of ethical challenge [20].

Sitting alongside these strategies, there are domains in which 'hard law' sets the bounds of technology use. Legislation on net neutrality, copyright, data privacy and the use of personal data, cybersecurity, and more has begun to define what is and is not acceptable in the digital environment. These current legal frameworks provide a constellation of data rights, with different kinds of data giving rise to different kinds of rights in different jurisdictions.

Protecting vulnerable individuals from misuse of power is central to good governance. In the EU, the General Data Protection Regulation defines a range of prohibitions of discrimination based on protected characteristics [21]. It also confers rights around portability, erasability, and explainability. While many of these principles are being replicated around the world – in California's Data Freedom Act, for example – the depth of many of these provisions have not yet been tested. Further regulatory developments in the EU are expected, and seem likely to focus on the impacts of AI-enabled innovation, using assessments that take into account the risks and benefits of different applications, and recent lessons about the interactions that arise between technology advances and economic structures [22].

Recent activities by regulatory bodies in many jurisdictions also signal a willingness to assertively intervene against undesirable use of data. In the US, the Federal Trade Commission has leveraged large fines against Facebook for privacy violation [23], has barred developers from selling apps that monitor consumers' mobile phone devices – so-called stalking apps – unless they "take certain steps to ensure the apps will only be used for legitimate purposes" [24], and is active in reviewing anti-competitive behaviour in the sector [25]. In the UK, the Information Commissioner's Office has similarly issued large fines against Facebook for privacy issues in handling user data, while the UK Government is currently considering how to act on recommendations made by a review of competition in digital markets [26]. The European Commission is also examining data practices by large technology companies, and their implications for competition policy, with the EU's data strategy seeking to support innovation in the European technology industry and Europe's technological 'sovereignty' [22].

These policy developments have been accompanied by an expanding pool of ethics codes and principles from the private sector and civil society. Many of these cluster around similar social and ethical issues, calling for action to increase transparency or explainability, to avoid bias or unfairness in data use and AI, to enhance privacy and security, to embed sustainability practices, and to take steps to mitigate the risks automation might pose to stable employment [27].

Together, these interventions seem to be questioning whether choices made by the market lead to a desirable mix of public and private interest. Such regulatory interest seems likely to be sustained over the coming years, with policymakers across the world looking for mechanisms to support data-enabled innovation, while managing the risks it creates.

As this resurgence of policy and legal interest gains pace, there is a growing movement to orient the outcomes of innovation towards beneficial societal outcomes – to ensure that technology both follows and fosters democracy. With broad consensus on the areas of concern associated with data use and AI, the challenge now is to move from these principles to actions that connect conversations about data sharing to the enforcement of individual rights.

## 3.3   The Changing Technology Environment

At the same time, technologies are advancing at pace, giving rise to complex patterns of data use and decision-making. In this complex environment, data collected for one purpose can be rapidly repurposed or shared in ways that are opaque or unanticipated at the point of data collection. A 2018 study [28] of almost one million widely available apps found that most of those apps contained third-party tracking systems. Moreover, one in five of those apps shared data with more than twenty third parties, this data ranging from user age or gender to location details. Further analysis of these data transfer patterns showed a large number of data transfers to a handful of technology companies [29]. The complexity of these patterns of data exchange and aggregation mean it would be challenging for any individual to understand the destination of the data they yield to any app, creating an asymmetry in knowledge about data use. This growing complexity of data processing compounds the limitations of consent-based models of data governance, which have been well-characterised elsewhere [30].

In this environment, seemingly insignificant decisions made about an individual in one area can give rise to complex effects across networks, as the outputs of different digital systems feed into – and out of – each other, and as individuals and technology interact. Any individual fact learned about an individual might be inconsequential, but – taken together, over time – the detailed picture of daily life that emerges can have a significant impact.

Existing policy frameworks are not necessarily well-placed to manage these net-work effects. They present different circumstances to those envisaged in the early stages of drafting the GDPR in the 1990s, where policymakers were primarily concerned with the use of data to inform decision-making in areas that might have a significant personal or social impact. The 'first mover advantage' that comes from having access to large volumes of data about individuals, meanwhile, favours further centralisation of data, as its aggregation enhances insights and economic benefit.

For some, these vulnerabilities foster a sense of diminished agency in the digital environment. Individuals lack power to influence the terms of data use – either because of a lack of knowledge about what choices are being made, or a lack of bargaining power in transactions – while also having their quotidian choices invisibly shaped by data-enabled systems against which there is no clear response.

Calls for returning ownership of data to individuals is one response to these challenges. However, not only is ownership unlikely to provide the level of control over the use of data that many are seeking, it is also a poor response to the vulnerabilities that are at stake.

With technology changing at pace, and complex patterns of data use and decision-making giving rise to unanticipated consequences, legislators face challenges in designing legal frameworks that allow technological progress to keep in touch with evolving socio-cultural values and expectations. What type of governance system would be best suited to a situation in which individual decisions have cumulative, unanticipated impacts?

### 3.4  Bridging the Gaps: A Democratic Model for Data Governance?

As data governance finds itself at the heart of continuing efforts to articulate (and contest) social and political objectives, the rights granted by regulatory instruments become important tools to set limits on acceptable uses of data. However, their exercise alone is unlikely to be sufficient to give citizens a voice in shaping these data-reliant futures.

New forms of democratic governance are needed to reassert fundamental democratic values, creating a system that supports human dignity and fosters democratic representation. This requires fresh governance approaches that can bridge the gap between the aspiration to share data to achieve social and economic benefit, and concerns about protecting individual rights in data use. One approach to bridging this gap is the creation of new forms of data sharing arrangements that leverage the power that comes from aggregating data to open the way to new, bottom-up governance frameworks.

## 4   Commons, Cooperatives, and Counter-Power

### 4.1  Mutualisation as a Tool to Counter Power Asymmetries

Data becomes valuable in aggregate. While data about an individual has limited use, collection and analysis of data about large numbers of individuals yields significant economic and social value – and power. An environment where a small number of actors have access to – or control of – this aggregated data, is one of asymmetric power, in which any single individual has limited scope to influence the terms of data use. Collective action, however, could provide a counterbalancing force.

History gives numerous examples of the ways in which combining resources can enable individuals to exert influence in systems dominated by powerful interests. In the 19th century, for example, the right to vote in the UK was conditional upon land ownership, and such ownership was available only to those with economic and social resources. Land societies were established as a means of countering this inequality. Individuals pooled their resources in a land society to collectively buy a plot of land, which was then divided between the society's membership, giving each member a right to vote. This form of mutualisation therefore gave a political voice to individuals that were otherwise disenfranchised [31].

Inspired by this history, it is possible to envisage governance mechanisms that seek to promote collective action. One such mechanism comes in the form of data trusts: by pooling data – or data rights – individuals would be better placed to acquire a political and economic voice in the digital economy. At stake is not the right to vote, but the ability to influence decisions about how data is used, and for what purpose.

## 4.2    The Emergence of Data Trusts as a Governance Tool

Trusts are a legal agreement under which one party (the trustee) manages an asset or object for the benefit of another (the beneficiary) [32]. A data trust is a mechanism to secure independent stewardship of data use under the framework of trust law [33]. The trust creates an intermediary layer between data subjects and controllers, with individuals that invest their data rights in a trust tasking trustees with making decisions about data use on their behalf. The ways in which data in the trust is used would depend on the terms of that trust.

Core to the functioning of a data trust are the fiduciary responsibilities trust law creates. These impose a duty of undivided loyalty that require those that lead the trust to act in the interests of its beneficiaries. These responsibilities act as a strong safeguard that sets data trusts apart from data access agreements based on contractual or corporate frameworks.

By pooling data within a trust, individuals and collectives can wield the collective power of data to exert influence over how it is used. Trusts could become powerful actors that are better placed to influence the terms and conditions of data use than any individual.

The role of the trustee sits at the heart of this mechanism, taking on significant responsibilities on behalf of the trust's members. Not only would trustees need to be mandated to exercise such rights, they would also need a set of professional skills to ensure the decisions they make are soundly-based [34]. In the same way that previous centuries saw professionalisation of medical and legal practitioners to manage the vulnerabilities at play in those interactions, data trustees could become a new profession for the 21st century.

Data trusts would not need to be built according to a single model: some might be generalist, others built to focus on data relevant for a specific purpose; different trusts might offer different levels of participation or consultation with its members; or there could be centralised or decentralised approaches to managing the data in the trust: a trust need not hold or gather the data. By building an ecosystem of data trusts – each with different approaches to data use – individuals could select a trust that best reflects their aspirations and attitudes to risk. Individuals would be able to 'shop around' these different trusts, finding one that reflects their desired mix of risks and responsibilities [25].

These trusts would complement existing legal and regulatory frameworks that define the rights an individual has over how data about them is used. Instead of relying on 'one size fits all' regulatory approaches to setting the boundaries of data use, each trust would define its own approach to data management, taking into account the aspirations and interests of its members. In this way, trusts could offer a way of aligning an individual's values with the way their data is used.

Since gaining public prominence in 2016 [36], the ideas behind data trusts have gained traction in a variety of policy communities. The UK's Hall-Pesenti review of AI recommended that the UK Government establish trusts to promote trustworthy data sharing [37], the Canadian Government's Digital Charter has recommended the creation of trusts for similar purposes [38], and Germany's Data Ethics Commission has recommended that further investments be made in research and development to create data trust schemes [39].

With this growing interest in novel data governance frameworks, other types of data sharing institutions have emerged each with different benefits and limitations [40]:

- Public databanks – data management institutions run by a public sector entity – that provide a publicly-accountable means of managing public data assets to deliver goods or services. While this form of institution might be able to take action to reduce the vulnerabilities associated with data use, they offer limited scope for individuals to assert how data about them is used.
- Data cooperatives that provide a means of organising data pooled from individuals or companies for a particular purpose. While offering a means for groups of individuals to promote the use of certain types of data, these lack the fiduciary safeguards inherent in reliance on trust law, since coops will be based on contractual or corporate structures. The latter structures may of course include terms that seek to prevent undesirable forms of data use, yet they will not have the same safeguards as those available under a trust structure.
- Contractual frameworks that define terms of use for data shared in specific circumstances are encountered by many people in the terms and conditions associated with data agreements. These consent-based approaches offer limited – if any – scope for individuals to influence the terms of data use and tend not to be well-suited to managing individual vulnerabilities. Horizontal data sharing agreements – another form of contractual framework that set in place access agreements between companies – can increase corporate confidence in enabling data use by providing legal certainty about acceptable use.

These different frameworks are thus more or less well-suited to different aims [40]. They can variably be used to promote social benefit, to protect vulnerabilities, or monetise data to different extents, or direct data use towards specific purposes that may benefit different communities. The choice of model will depend on the objectives of the data sharing activity.

Data trusts distinguish themselves from these models not only in the level of legal safeguards they provide, but also in their ability to simultaneously pursue each of these aims, as determined by their governing documents.

## 5   Optimising for Democracy? A Data Governance System that Benefits Humanity

The power of modern AI comes from its ability to automatically extract knowledge from large amounts of data, using the insights so created to optimise systems and make predictions. The question that now pervades debates about data governance and the use of AI is: for what is the system optimised? And who decides whether this is desirable? The challenge of data governance for the 21st century is to create conduits that bring social and ethical values into technology developments, establishing mechanisms that return agency to individuals and communities.

Data governance offers a lever to reshape the underpinnings of technology development. Governance can support data use – enabling its analysis by technologies such as AI to create economic and social value – while creating an infrastructure that aligns technology development with personal, ethical and democratic values.

Some pillars of such an infrastructure already exist. Efforts to support data use through open data movements have achieved significant success over the last decade, with data availability now at the heart of many government digital services and research efforts. These open resources have already brought widespread benefits, and continue to be deployed in innovative ways. Data access agreements in recent years have been put in place to share medical data to improve diagnosis of macular degeneration, to share environmental monitoring data to tackle the illegal wildlife trade, and sharing engineering data to help address health and safety issues [41]. Further success for these efforts will require sustained investment to make data accessible, to make it interoperable, and to make it safe and reliable for use (see also Chapter 8).

A further pillar comes from the top-down regulations that are already in place to govern data use. These will constrain actors to prevent undesirable uses of data, and create space for individual and community data rights. However, while helping to define the scope of individual rights or terms of acceptable use, these top-down endeavours cannot alone reverse the power imbalances that pervade the digital environment. The limits of these existing approaches leave a gap in the governance environment. To fill this gap, new structures are needed that provide space for individuals to collectively influence how data about them is used. These will need to be fostered by governmental action to set policy and regulatory frameworks that help such bottom-up structures grow to fulfill their potential.

Complementing existing regulatory approaches, data trusts offer a mechanism through which individuals can assert their rights, collectively gaining a voice in decisions otherwise made by a small number of people. Crucially, these trusts can bridge the gap between the widely-shared aspiration to share data to foster the realisation of various public goods on one hand and concerns about protecting individual rights on the other. In so doing, they can facilitate collective action that promotes innovative applications of data while remedying the power asymmetries that would traditionally follow such use.

Further developing the concepts and methods in the data trusts approach will require action from policymakers, industry and civil society. Understanding and overcoming the limits of existing regulatory provisions around data portability, provenance, and erasure will be necessary in order to enhance processes by which individuals can move their data between trusts.

Measures to support a wide range of individuals and communities to engage with data trusts will also be necessary in order to ensure that their benefits and protections are accessible by all. There is generally low levels of awareness of data use and AI technologies [42], meaning that – in the absence of any steps to promote their use – the average level of interest in registering with a trust might be low. Interventions to support citizens to understand their data rights and raise the profile of data trusts (in a way not dissimilar to pensions-related interventions) may be necessary to complement these governance structures.

Achieving the potential of AI technologies – and unlocking the value of data – requires a data environment that supports responsible data use, empowers disenfranchised groups and protects individual rights. A collection of novel data governance tools is emerging, prompting questions about the limits of existing regulatory approaches and the structures that can best embed democratic values in technology development and use. With growing interest from governments across the world in the idea of data trusts as a tool for democratising data governance, the coming years will bring a pressing need to resolve questions such as:

- Are additional legislative measures needed to enable citizens to mandate their data rights to a data trustee, or ensure the portability of their data (and/or data rights) as when they switch from one trust to another?
- What jurisdictional issues might arise in the development of data trusts internationally, and what forms of international cooperation might be needed to address these?
- What policies or institutions should be in place to support the professionalisation of data trustees?

# References

1. The Academy of Medical Sciences and the Royal Society: AI in health and care: from bench to bedside, note of discussions at a workshop on 29 March 2019 (2019). https://acmedsci.ac.uk/policy/policy-projects/artificial–intelligence-and-health
2. European Parliament: Artificial intelligence in transport, briefing from the members' research service (2019). https://www.europarl.europa.eu/RegData/etudes/BRIE/2019/635609/EPRS_BRI(2019)635609_EN.pdf
3. See work by Climate Change AI (2020). https://www.climatechange.ai/
4. Lawrence, N.: From data subject to data citizen (2019). https://inverseprobability.com/talks/notes/from-data-subject-to-data-citizen.html
5. AI Now: Annual report (2019). https://ainowinstitute.org/AI_Now_2019_Report.pdf
6. HM Treasury: The economic value of data: a discussion paper (2018). https://www.gov.uk/government/publications/the-economic-value-of-data-discussion-paper
7. Zheleva, E., Getoor, L.: To join or not to join: the illusion of privacy in social networks with mixed public and private user profiles. In: Proceedings of the 18th International Conference on World Wide Web, April 2009, pp. 531–540 (2009)
8. Kosinski, M., Stillwell, D., Graepel, T.: Private traits and attributes are predictable from digital records of human behaviours. PNAS **110**, 5802–5805 (2013)
9. Datta, A., Tschantz, M., Datta, A.: (2015) Automated experiments on ad privacy settings. Proc. Priv. Enhanc. Technol. **1**, 92–112 (2015)
10. MIT Tech Review: AI is sending people to jail – and getting it wrong (2019). https://www.technologyreview.com/s/612775/algorithms-criminal-justice-ai/
11. BBC: Amazon scrapped 'sexist AI' tool (2018). https://www.bbc.co.uk/news/technology-45809919

12. The Guardian: Cambridge analytica scandal 'highlights need for AI regulation' (2018). https://www.theguardian.com/technology/2018/apr/16/cambridge-analytica-scandal-highligh ts-need-for-ai-regulation
13. CDEI: Review of online targeting (2020). https://www.gov.uk/government/publications/ cdei-review-of-online-targeting
14. Ipsos MORI: Public views of machine learning: findings from public research and engagement (2017). www.royalsociety.org/machine-learning
15. Pasquale, F.: The automated public sphere, University of Maryland Legal Studies Research Paper No. 2017-31 (2017). https://papers.ssrn.com/sol3/papers.cfm?abstract_id=3067552
16. Barlow, J.P.: A Declaration of the Independence of Cyberspace (2018). https://www.weforu m.org/agenda/2018/02/a-declaration-of-the-independence-of-cyberspace/
17. Daten Ethik Komission (2019). https://www.bmjv.de/DE/Themen/FokusThemen/ Datenethikkommission/Datenethikkommission_EN_node.html
18. The Centre for Data Ethics and Innovation. https://www.gov.uk/government/organisations/ centre-for-data-ethics-and-innovation/about
19. See: https://uk.ambafrance.org/France-s-AI-strategy
20. European Commission: A European strategy for data and AI: a European approach to excellence and trust (2020). https://ec.europa.eu/
21. Lawrence, N.: Personal data trusts (2020). https://inverseprobability.com/talks/notes/ personal-data-trusts.html
22. European Commission: A European strategy for data (2020). https://ec.europa.eu/digital- single-market/en/policies/building-european-data-economy
23. FTC: FTC imposes $5 billion penalty and sweeping new privacy restrictions on Facebook (2019). https://www.ftc.gov/news-events/press-releases/2019/07/ftc-imposes-5-billion-penal ty-sweeping-new-privacy-restrictions
24. FTC: FTC brings first case against developers of stalking apps (2019). https://www.ftc.gov/ news-events/press-releases/2019/10/ftc-brings-first-case-against-developers-stalking-apps
25. FTC: FTC's Bureau of Competition launches task force to monitor technology markets (2019). https://www.ftc.gov/news-events/press-releases/2019/02/ftcs-bureau-competition-lau nches-task-force-monitor-technology
26. HM Treasury: Budget 2020 (2020). https://www.gov.uk/government/publications/budget- 2020-documents/budget-2020
27. Linking AI Principles (2019). https://uk.ambafrance.org/France-s-AI-strategy
28. Binns, R., Lyngs, U., Van Kleek, M., Zhao, J., Libert, T., Shadbolt, N.: Third party tracking in the mobile ecosystem. In: Proceedings of the 10th International ACM Web Science Conference (2018)
29. Financial Times: How smartphone apps track users and share data (2019). https://ig.ft.com/ mobile-app-data-trackers/
30. British Academy, TechUK and Royal Society: Data ownership, rights and controls: reaching a common understanding (2018). https://royalsociety.org/-/media/policy/projects/data- governance/data-ownership-rights-and-controls-October-2018.pdf
31. Financial Times: Letter: legal instruments exist to empower us, the data subjects. From Sylvie Delacroix and Neil Lawrence, The Alan Turing Institute (2019). https://www.ft.com/ content/33926828-16c0-11ea-9ee4-11f260415385
32. Chambers, R.: Distrust: our fear of trusts in the commercial world. Curr. Leg. Probl. **63**, 631 (2010)
33. Delacroix, S., Lawrence, N.: Bottom-up data trusts: disturbing the 'one size fits all' approach to data governance. Int. Data Priv. Law **9**, 236–252 (2018)
34. In the EU, Article 80(1) of the GDPR makes provision for such mandates to be put in place, but in only limited circumstances

35. A legal basis for the ability to move data between trusts could be found in the EU in the GDPR's provisions on data portability and data erasure (Articles 20 and 17)
36. Lawrence, N.: Data trusts could allay our privacy fears. The Guardian (2016). https://www.theguardian.com/media-network/2016/jun/03/data-trusts-privacy-fears-feudalism-democracy
37. UK Government Hall-Pesenti Review: Growing the artificial intelligence industry in the UK (2017). https://assets.publishing.service.gov.uk/government/uploads/system/uploads/attachment_data/file/652097/Growing_the_artificial_intelligence_industry_in_the_UK.pdf
38. Government of Canada: Strengthening privacy for the digital age (2019). https://www.ic.gc.ca/eic/site/062.nsf/eng/h_00107.html
39. Daten Ethik Komission: Opinion of the data ethics commission (2019). https://www.bmjv.de/
40. Delacroix, S., Lawrence, N., Montgomery, J.: Selecting a data sharing structure: a value-based choice (2020). https://datatrusts.uk/blogs/selectingdatastructures
41. Open Data Institute: Data trusts: lessons from three pilots (report) (2019). https://theodi.org/article/odi-data-trusts-report/
42. Royal Society and Ipsos MORI: Machine learning – what do the public think? (2017). www.royalsociety.org/machine-learning

# Artificial Intelligence and the Future of Work

Yuko Harayama[1]([✉]), Michela Milano[2], Richard Baldwin[3],
Céline Antonin[4], Janine Berg[5], Anousheh Karvar[6],
and Andrew Wyckoff[7]

[1] RIKEN, Wako, Japan
yuko.harayama@riken.jp
[2] Centro Interdipartimentale Alma Mater Research Institute for Human-Centered
Artificial Intelligence, University of Bologna, Bologna, Italy
[3] Graduate Institute, University of Geneva, Geneva, Switzerland
[4] Paris Institute of Political Studies, Paris, France
[5] International Labor Organization, Geneva, Switzerland
[6] Delegate of the French Government to the International Labor Organization's
Governing Body, Paris, France
[7] Directorate for Science, Technology and Innovation, OECD, Paris, France

**Keywords:** Future of work · Job quality · Automation · Robotics · Artificial
intelligence

## 1 Introduction

Digital transformation is underway, particularly shaped by the ever-expanding frontier
of Artificial Intelligence (AI) technologies. It is impacting our everyday life, at work, in
public space, as well as at home and in the private sphere. We are already strong users
and consumers of information, and our dependence on connectivity, shaping the way
we make decisions, the way we interact, even more how we feel. This trend seems to be
irreversible.

Today, investing in AI is becoming a priority in the business sector, to gain the
efficiency and flexibility in the production and maintenance processes, through worker
empowerment or backed by Internet of Things (IoT), as we transform into data-driven
businesses.

Most of governments emphasize AI as a nation's competitive edge, by identifying
the main sectors where AI could boost productivity and efficiency, while providing
necessary education and training for adapting the skills of the current workforce and
ensuring responsible use of technology. Europe focusses, in its White Paper on Artificial Intelligence [1], on trustworthy technology and on providing a regulatory
framework for Artificial Intelligence.

They also consider AI as a mean for addressing societal challenges. For instance,
Japan, with its demographic pressures, is on the front line to seek a solution to overcome the problem of shrinking workforce in production sector, and to address the
health and social issues faced by aging population, thus actively exploring AI, robotics,
and many other digital devices, to better shape the society of tomorrow.

© Springer Nature Switzerland AG 2021
B. Braunschweig and M. Ghallab (Eds.): Reflections on Artificial Intelligence
for Humanity, LNAI 12600, pp. 53–67, 2021.
https://doi.org/10.1007/978-3-030-69128-8_4

Furthermore, the increasing use of AI in the economy will affect the organization and nature of work. We recognize today that expectations of job creation and fears of job destruction are present simultaneously.

Indeed, we already observe that the potential of AI to drive change is impacting the reality (e.g. socially embedded mobile devices), sometimes with unexpected effects, but still we are just at the beginning of a more profound transformation not only in terms of business but also society as a whole, and even more, in terms of humanity. In short, our future depends on how we will be developing and using AI.

However, in times of accelerating change, it is almost impossible to make relevant projections or accurate predictions of where we will be. Faced with these unknowns, fears of AI may prevail. Also, the deployment of AI could affect people differently, according to where you are, what you are doing, to which group you belong, and eventually who you are; as such, we may observe widening inequality and deepening of the digital divide[1].

Therefore, some proactive actions by the government and other relevant stakeholders would be needed, beyond conventional tax and transfer policy, to accompany the advancement in AI and to facilitate a smooth societal transformation engendered by it.

With this, a fundamental question arises: Are we ready to take advantage of full potential of AI? Or, in some cases, should precaution prevail?

In order to get a better grasp of this question, we will be focusing on the "Future of Work" in this chapter.

As mentioned above, there are many debates and controversies related to the effect of AI on the labour market, mostly turning around the question of substitution effect, and often generating the fears of job destruction. On the other hand, Frey and Osborne's highly publicised paper "The Future of Employment: How susceptible are jobs to computerisation?" [2] has caught the attention of policy makers in many countries, pushing AI into debates on the future of jobs and the potential consequences. Missing from this debate is a lack of reflection on how AI affects the quality of jobs and associated time path.

What we observe today is that AI is affecting different groups of workers through different paths, the way we organize our work, and even the scope of work. In fact, the capacity, not to say the value, of humans is tested, competed and challenged by AI at the workplace, raising the question of competitive advantage of human vis-à-vis AI, since, focused on the routine tasks by the past, the substitution effect of AI is expanding its scope to the manual tasks and even more to the cognitive tasks.

If we look at the work practices, we see the emergence of new ways of organizing work, such as distributed work, remote work, or task-based work, and the trend of decoupling where work is done and the physical workplace is ever-expanding. They are reflecting the change in the business models, notably the shift from capital-intensive to knowledge-intensive business, hence the efficiency of these working practices depends greatly of the underlying information infrastructure, and also the capacity to harness AI technologies.

---

[1] See chapter 6 on AI and human values.

Also, the value of work is changing. The motivation of people to work is diversifying today, this far beyond the classical work-leisure dichotomic thinking. Not only considered as a source of income, people see their work as a way to personal development or fulfillment, a way to feel useful to your surrounding and to serve society more broadly. Thus, the conception of work should be revisited before talking about the impact of AI on work.

With this in mind, in this chapter, we try to shed light on the interplay between AI and the future of work, by asking ourselves, if the socio-economic institutions in place today have capacity to steer the use of AI for the betterment of societies.

Our attempt is not just to summarize what has been said on this issue, but to start with a contextualization and then to bring robust analysis and evidence, drawing out some of the key policy implications.

This chapter is the result of the collaboration among participants to the panel discussion "Future of work and economic impacts of AI", held at the Global Forum on AI for Humanity (GFAIH) in Paris. It will be organized as follows.

In Sect. 2 "Is this time different?", we state that this phase of globalisation and robotics, called "globotics", follows a different pace with respect to past globalization and automation, based on our observation of a higher pace of "digitech". Also, we propose a view of Artificial Intelligence as a tool for supporting and not replacing humans.

In Sect. 3 "Artificial Intelligence and job quality", we observe the new jobs created by the AI that are integral to the functioning of AI systems and analyse the quality of these new jobs. In addition, the section discusses the AI-based recruitment, and monitoring and surveillance tools and their impact on the job quality.

In Sect. 4 "Policy implication", we advocate for the need of inclusive public policies, to support the benefits of innovation in association with impacted enterprises and workers, being aware that the global challenges faced in terms of unemployment, inequality, unfair competition and unbalanced distribution of value should be regulated in an international framework.

Finally, Sect. 5 concludes with some future perspectives.

## 2  Is This Time Different?

Throughout our history, we have experienced the emergence of disruptive technologies, to name just a few the invention of steam engine and computer, inducing the diffusion of new tools or new systems in production and more generally across society, in many cases followed by the adjustment of social institutions, including the way we organize the work. Artificial Intelligence (AI) is certainly one of them.

Among economists, one the surest laugh-lines is to claim: "This time is different". The merriment arises from the fact that many of the biggest follies in economics were founded on the belief that the usual rules have been repealed – that the normal laws of economics does not apply this time. It is thus with eyes wide open that we claim in this chapter that "this time is different" when it comes to the future of work. Not everything is different, but many important trends that are significantly underappreciated.

## 2.1  Impact on the Manufacturing Sector

The rise of AI stirs up the fears of a jobless world, characterized by massive unemployment. Even before the AI era, automation has always been a subject of concern: early analyses of Keynes (1930) [3] or Leontief (1952) [4] already showed an increase in technological unemployment based on macroeconomic equilibrium analyses. Yet, if automation is, by definition, clearly labour-saving at the task level, it also provides productivity gains and increases the need for implementing new tasks. Therefore, automation is also labour-augmenting. Despite extensive current research, empirical effects of automation on employment remain debated: Acemoglu-Restrepo (2019) [5] or Chiacchio et al. (2018) [6] find a negative effect of the use of industrial robots on employment, whereas Michaels and Graetz (2018) [7] or Dauth et al. (2019) [8] highlight a positive or non-significant impact.

To have a better understanding of the effect of AI on employment, as a first step, we start by revisiting the manufacturing sector, referring to the ongoing work at the Collège de France, by Philippe Aghion, Céline Antonin, Simon Bunel and Xavier Jaravel [9].

Based on the assumption that AI is a latest form of automation in a continuum of automation progress and using comprehensive micro data in the French manufacturing sector between 1994 and 2015, they attempted to analyze the effects of automation technologies on employment.

In order to measure automation, they use an original and broad concept: the consumption of electric motors, also called the electro-motive force, and excluding all the facilities (heating, cooling, servers, …) which do not directly enter the production process.

Causal effects are estimated with event studies and econometrics methods. Their main results are the following: at all levels of the analysis – i.e. plant, firm, and industry - the estimated impact of automation on employment is positive, for skilled as well as unskilled workers; this suggests that the productivity effects of automation outweigh its potential displacement effects. Indeed, at the plant level, a 1% increase in automation leads to a simultaneous 0.2% increase in employment. The response of employment rises over time: a 1% increase in automation at time t leads to a 0.4% increase in employment at time t+10, i.e. after ten years.

Besides, at the industry-level, the relationship between employment and automation is positive on average, but there is a substantial heterogeneity between industries depending on their exposure to international trade. While the employment response is positive and significant in industries that face international competition, there is no significant effect in sectors with low exposure to international competition. In sum, globalisation appears to be a significant factor in understanding the impact of AI on employment in the manufacturing sector.

## 2.2  Impact on the Service Sector

Richard Baldwin takes a step further in the direction of globalisation, by characterising today's trend of "globotics", combination of globalisation and robotics, and claims that it will mostly be about the service sector, not just the manufacturing, mining and agricultural sectors as in past decades (Baldwin 2019) [10]. Just to name a few, AI software robots are making service sector workers and professionals more productive by automating some tasks, as illustrated by the case of "patent lawyer in California" he reported (see Box 1).

---

Box 1. Patent lawyer in California

James Yoon has a great job as a lawyer specializing in patent disputes. But his job today is very different to what it was 20 years ago, but in other ways its exactly the same. Today, he charges them $1100 an hour – much more than the $400 he charged in 1999. This is not just because he is more experienced. It is also because AI-trained computer programs have transformed some aspects of his job. Today, he organises a team with a quarter of the legal human power since he is using white-collar robots. These robo-lawyers are good at things like searching through documents and emails, and flagging which ones will be relevant and that has helped Yoon cut his cost-basis. Specifically, he uses Lex Machina and Ravel Law to help him digest huge piles of court decisions and the documents filed on similar cases by the judges and opposing lawyers.

But much of Yoon's job is untouched by digitech. He is still doing the most human aspects of the job – advising and reassuring clients, structuring the final legal strategy, negotiating with opposing counsel, appearing in court, and the like.

---

Given that 80 to 90% of people in advanced economies work in the service sector now, the implications are clear. Even if we capture a positive impact of AI on employment in the manufacturing sector, we are still underestimating the number of people affected by the effects of globotics.

## 2.3   Information as Key Driver

Past globalization and automation were mostly about goods, and thus the manufacturing sector and related infrastructures. They were ultimately restrained by the laws of physics that apply to physical matter. Globalization and automation of the service sector are all about information, to be processed and transmitted, and this alters possibilities. It would be physically impossible to double world trade flows in 18 months. The infrastructure could not handle it, and building infrastructure takes years, not months, for reasons that have to do with the physics of it as well as the economics of it. World information flows, by contrast, have doubled every couple of years for decades. They will continue to do so for years to come. The timescale disparity is due to the physics.

Working with information can ignore many of the laws of physics that slow down globalization and automation in industry and agriculture. The technological impulse behind the coming globotics transformation is profoundly different than the technological impulses that triggered previous waves of automation and globalization.

The background constraints that shape the economic pace of change have changed. This is why historical experience must be treated with great care when applying lessons to today's globalization and robotization. And it is exactly why the disordering of service sector jobs will come faster than most believe.

## 2.4   Expected or Explosive?

We live in a time when the future of work is changing rapidly, but also in a time when it is particularly difficult to sort out the main lines. The baseline argument is that the world we are in is witnessing two distinct types of growth processes, that Baldwin qualified of expected/normal and explosive/digital.

In fact, in the real world, most things – say job displacement, or reorganisation of work practices – are affected by a blend of these two processes. Some aspects of the future are governed by the expected pace of progress, others by the explosive pace of digital technology, but the difficulty lies in sorting out which parts are subject to expected change and which to explosive change.

The big pay-off in insight comes from thinking hard about which tasks are subject to the explosive progress and how this will affect the new jobs and those that survive the explosive progress.

One particularly common line of thinking takes AI-trained 'robots' as humans who have not quite grown into fully capable human-replacements, but will eventually. Our view is that AI should be thought of this with practical thinking ahead for today's realities for the foreseeable future, not in the realm of science fiction.

### 2.5   "Telemigration" in Perspective

The future of globalisation is also changing rapidly and in way few expect. The term "telemigration" – people sitting in one nation and working in offices in another – would characterize what may happen in the foreseeable future.

This year, the abrupt propagation of COVID-19 has disrupted the ordinary course of business around the world. In many countries, induced by the confinement and border restriction decided by the government, online meetings and teleworking are becoming a common work practice. In fact, "telemigration" is already around the corner.

In the past, language barriers have been so important in separating peoples and hindering commerce among them, but what we observe today is that the development and use of machine translation, as illustrated by Baldwin (see Box 2), will change an incredible number of things.

---

Box 2. Machine translation

The first and most obvious linkage between digital technology and globalization is automatic language translation – what experts call 'machine translation'.

Machine translation used to be a joke. Just two years ago it was little more than a party trick, or a very rough first draft. But no longer. Now it is rivalling average human translation for popular language pairs.

According to Google research, which uses humans to score machine translations on a scale from zero (complete nonsense) to six (perfect), in 2015, Google Translate got a grade of 3.6 – far worse than the average human translator which gets scores like 5.1. After a massive upgrade that came in 2016, Google Translate now hits numbers like 5[11]. The capabilities are advancing in leaps and bounds.

It works on any smartphone, tablet or laptop. Just open up a foreign language web site and apply Google Translate to the text. The iTranslate app is another example to instantly translate foreign language in real time. You fire up the app on your smartphone and point your phone's camera it at a page of, say, French and you see the English translation on your phone's screen. Instantly and costlessly.

Another key change is the rise of freelancing platforms like Upwork.com, which could be considered as the 'container ships' of future globalisation. They are how companies and individuals in advanced economies are finding, hiring, managing and paying talented, low-cost service workers sitting abroad. Yet, the nature of the employment relationship is different, as workers on Upwork have been classified by the platform as self-employed, hence they are not privy to the stability and benefits associated with a traditional employer-employee relationship.

In short, AI in particular and digital technology in general is transforming the future of work in all industrial and service sectors, while in the current transition phase, we observe the destruction of some jobs and creation of others as implementation, inter-action and adaptation with AI systems occur.

The transformation that is in progress is driven by the immense amount of data available, and to the development of ever more accurate tools for analysing this huge information flow and extracting value from it, calling for the need of new skills and competences. The pace of this transformation – merging automation and globalisation – is higher with respect to past similar transformation phases, and extremely hard to predict. What we can do is analyse the current situation, the tools that affect the labour market, job quality and employment and try to shape global strategic policies to exploit the full potential of AI technologies while harnessing potential risks.

## 3 Artificial Intelligence and Job Quality

Since Frey and Osborne's (2013) study estimating that 47% of U.S. jobs are at risk of automation[2], with those performing routine tasks most likely to be affected, there has been a deluge of articles and books in the popular press on the impending jobs apocalypse and what to do with the masses in a future without work [12, 13]. Some of this debate has been tempered by other studies emphasizing that the automation of tasks will transform jobs – rather than shed jobs – allowing workers to focus on the more creative and social aspects of the work [14].

But a more accurate discussion on the effect of Artificial Intelligence (AI) on jobs would recognize that AI cannot function smoothly without humans. Mary Gray and Siddharth Suri call this the "automation paradox", and explain how the quest to eliminate human labour through automation "always generates new tasks for humans [15]." Some of these new jobs will be complementary, but many are integral to the functioning of AI systems. Yet these "jobs" have received little recognition in debates

---

[2] They are clear in their paper that it is the potential number of jobs that could be automated "from a technological capabilities point of view", "over an unspecified number of years." They do not estimate how many jobs will actually be automated, which they argue will depend on "several additional factors which were left unaccounted for". See their blog, "Automation and the future of work – understanding the numbers" (13 April 2018), available at https://www.oxfordmartin.ox.ac.uk/blog/automation-and-the-future-of-work-understanding-the-numbers/ and their original study, Carl Benedikt Frey and Michael Osborne (2013), *The future of employment: How susceptible are jobs to computerisation?*, Oxford Martin School working paper.

on AI and the future of work. Also, absent have been discussions about the quality of these jobs.

In addition, AI systems are being increasingly integrated into workplaces, as tools for recruitment, and monitoring and surveillance. These practices have important implications for job quality that deserve further research and analysis, as well as the possible guidelines or certifications from regulators.

## 3.1   Artificial-Artificial Intelligence

In the mid-2000s, Amazon launched its first crowd-working platform as a way to service its growing on-line catalogues. The company found that its computer pro-grammes were unable to distinguish between similar products leading to errors and multiple entries on the Amazon site; it thus needed human labour to correctly tag and classify its catalogue entries. Amazon realized that it could externalize the tasks to a crowd of workers located across the globe, as well as provide a platform for other companies to post tasks. Ironically, it is the failures of AI that spurred the need for human input, leading Jeff Bezos, head of Amazon, to aptly describe the Amazon Mechanical Turk (AMT) platform as "artificial-artificial-intelligence" [16]. Despite important advances in AI, the need for human intelligence to service an ever-ranging array of activities to ensure the smooth functioning of automated or "artificially intelligent" systems continues to grow, with no sign of abating [17].

Workers located throughout the world perform tasks on these platforms, training AI systems. They tag images, outline photos of streets in order to train driverless cars, remove pornographic content from social media sites, classify sentiments on twitter posts, and other tasks. They are the "magic" behind AI [16]. They are also an important source of job creation that has accompanied this technological transformation. But these jobs are highly precarious.

Depending on the design of the platform, workers either receive tasks directly posted by clients or the tasks are divided and dispersed to the crowd via the platform. The workers are classified as self-employed and are not privy to benefits or rights that are part of the employment relationship. This means there is no minimum wage, no limits on working time, no rights to paid leave, no social security contributions, and no mechanisms for dispute resolution or redress, beyond the private arbitration of the platform.

In 2015 and 2017, the ILO conducted surveys of 3,500 workers on five micro-task platforms to learn more about socio-demographic profile of the workers, their job histories and their working conditions. Despite posting on English-language platforms, the survey revealed that there were workers from 75 countries. Workers were well-educated, with more than 80% having post-secondary studies, many in science and technology fields. The average age of crowd-workers was 33.2 years [18].

For one out of every three workers, crowd-work was their main source of income. Yet earnings were relatively low, even for workers in developing countries. The 2017 ILO survey showed that average hourly earnings ranged between US$2 and US$6.5, with a high proportion of workers earning below the prevailing minimum wage in their jurisdiction, a finding also documented in other studies [19]. The low earnings among these workers is due in part to their inability to obtain tasks on a continuous basis.

Workers spent on average 20 min of every hour performing unpaid work (looking for work, taking unpaid qualification tests, vetting clients in online worker forums). An overwhelming majority of workers (88%) reported that they would like to do more work, wishing on average for 12 h more of crowd-work per week.

## 3.2    Algorithmic Management and Job Quality

In addition, there are concerns about how algorithmic management systems that are embedded in platforms affect workers' job quality. In some micro-task platforms, labour can be accessible through an application programming interface (API), allowing programmers to integrate human workers into larger computational systems and tasks. Clients can post jobs in the form of raw data sets consisting of multiple rows of data. The platform then distributes each row of data to multiple workers, who each make a "judgment" on that row of data. The platform automates for clients the process of comparing the multiple judgments on each row that were made by different workers in order to verify that the judgment was correct. Serving as an intermediary, the microtask platform APIs make it possible for businesses to manage an entire workforce algorithmically, and to integrate human labour as though it were a mere function in the computer programme [18]. But this means, that if three workers perform a particular task (a common practice for dispersing work on micro-task platforms), and the result of one of the workers is different from the other two, the algorithm may be set up to reject the work of the response that is different, even if it was correct. Such a rejection not only affects the workers' income, but also their ratings and reputation on the platform. When workers reach a certain threshold of rejections, they may not be eligible for better paid tasks and risk being deactivated from the platform. For example, on AMT a standard criterion used to attribute work to workers is an approval rate of at least 95%.

More and more workplaces – beyond platforms – are integrating aspects of "algorithmic management," defined as work settings in which "human jobs are assigned, optimized, and evaluated through algorithms and tracked data" [20]. Möhlmann and Zalmanson (2017) [21] delineate five characteristics of algorithmic management:

1. Continuous tracking of workers' behaviour;
2. Constant performance evaluation of workers;
3. The automatic implementation of decisions, without human intervention;
4. Workers' interaction with a "system" rather than humans, depriving them of opportunities for feedback or discussion and negotiation with their supervisor; and
5. Low transparency.

The low transparency reflects in part a choice by enterprises to not disclose how the algorithms work, but it also reflects the adaptive nature of the algorithms, whereby the decisions change according to the data being collected.

One important area that AI has gained a stronghold is in recruitment, specifically the development of predictive tools to be used throughout the hiring process. These tools rely on machine learning to detect patterns in existing data to build models that forecast future outcomes of potential employees in the form of scores and rankings

[22]. AI recruitment tools have gained prominence in the media as containing bias, most notably an Amazon AI tool which was found to systematically prefer men to women. This was mainly due to the fact that data used to train the model selecting profiles were biased. The data set used in fact contained resumes submitted to the company over a 10-year period. Most came from men, a reflection of male dominance across the tech industry. Gender was then used by the algorithm as a discriminant since neither bias-reducing nor bias-removing techniques were not used in the machine learning algorithm.

Regulators and academic research have not been able to keep up with the speed of AI development, allowing vendors to push the boundaries of assessments without rigorous independent research leaving human resource practitioners with no credible resources to evaluate such tools [23]. Given the risk of discrimination against possible job seekers, regulators may need to develop certification systems for these programs to ensure that anti-discrimination laws are respected [24].

### 3.3   Platform and Beyond

The current technological revolution is merely another chapter of a decades' long trend, accelerated under globalization, that relies on an increased use of more insecure forms of labour to perform work. Online digital labour platforms that allow the "crowd-sourcing" of tasks necessary for the training and smooth operation of AI systems is just the latest manifestation. It is important that this is recognized, as it is possible to reconfigure the terms of platform work in order to improve job quality, so that the "new jobs" that this revolution entails be decent jobs.

## 4   Policy Implication

In comparison to other technological disruptions, the originality of Artificial Intelligence (AI) lies in its potentially widespread, multifaceted and comprehensive impact on labour markets' structures and institutions: jobs, working conditions, organization of work, social dialogue and collective bargaining are impacted all at once. Abundant macro-economic studies highlight the benefits of these digital transformations, when they lead to creating new productive activities and eliminating the most strenuous tasks. This being said, studies also warn about the negative externalities of ongoing digital challenges in terms of unemployment, inequality, unfair competition and unbalanced distribution of value.

To ensure that this transformation generates support and trust in the benefits of innovation, public policies should be designed to seize new opportunities (creating new productive activities, eliminating the most repetitive tasks) and mitigate its negative externalities (unemployment, inequality, unfair competition). Such policies should be able to guide further scientific and technological developments towards societal choices backed by reliable scientific evidence and settled by democratic deliberation.

In this context, there is a need for a multidisciplinary forum with analytical and anticipation capacities fueled by international research[3], and hybrid modalities of reflections associating both enterprises as well as workers potentially affected by AI innovations.

## 4.1 Testing New Approaches

Such an inclusive framework could thereby offer a more precise assessment of ongoing transformations in the world of work, so as to enrich the responses built up in traditional collective bargaining frameworks when accompanying technological changes: we should of course train and up-skill workers, but training for what? We should obviously guide workers towards new sources of jobs, but which ones? We should certainly facilitate geographical mobility, but what territories should be targeted? In this perspective, the "Labour Transformation Lab" which was called for in the Villani Report [25] commissioned by the French government, certainly holds a lot of potential to play a leading research role in employment and vocational training public policies.

In addition to grasping ongoing transformations, labour market institutions should evolve towards a more innovative agenda and more inclusive forms of dialogue with labour markets stakeholders. At the workplace, they can facilitate the economic and ergonomic dialogue around the purposes and consequences of integrating AI into enterprises' business models. The traditional round table "employer – employee" here could avail itself of changes in practices by associating consumers, users and clients. At the global level, transnational social dialogue creates the appropriate setting to tackle the imbalances generated by the international division of labour, as well as to grasp the evolution of the share of human labour in value generation in geographically diffuse production units.

## 4.2 International Organizations' Perspectives

In recent years, these principles have reached practical results by means of guidelines, recommendations or national legislations, at country level or in the European Union institutions in the area of Man-Machine relation, at the G7, G20 and the International Labour Organization with regard to the social regulation for platform economy.

Since AI means robots can also 'think', Man-Machine's relation and regulation at workplaces have been carefully scrutinized with a view to determine to what extent, in factories, companies and offices, intelligent machines can be autonomous and what forms of complementarity to human work will be.

At the UE level, the Occupational Safety and Health Agency (OSHA) has already covered risk assessment in crowdsourcing, robotics [26], 3-D printing [27], monitoring

---

[3] The Global Forum on Artificial Intelligence for Humanity (GFAIH) organized by the French Government in 2019 in Paris and the Working Group on the Future of Work under the auspices of the Global Partnership on AI could be considered as an example. See https://www.diplomatie.gouv. fr/en/french-foreign-policy/digital-diplomacy/news/article/launch-of-the-global-partnership-on-artifi cial-intelligence-by-15-founding, and https://oecd.ai/wonk/an-introduction-to-the-global-partnership-on-ais-work-on-the-future-of-work.

technologies [28] and the e-retail sector [29]. Based on these reviews, the European Economic & Social Committee advocates for establishing principles of transparency in the use of AI systems for recruitment, assessment and managerial control of workers, health and safety principles, protection of rights and freedom concerning the processing of workers' data in accordance with the principles of non-discrimination. On this basis, the European Committee puts forward the development of an indicator of "good" man-machine interaction, that could in the long run lead to an international standard [30].

The OECD has published in 2019 a policy brief "Preparing for the Changing Nature of Work in the Digital Era", within the framework of OECD wide project "Going Digital. Making the transformation work for growth and well-being" [31]. Along these lines, the OECD insists on the need to work on the "transition" and advocates to take a multi-faceted approach to better shape the future of work,[4] centred on upskilling, training and adapting social protection systems to a more fluid world of work. In particular, the OECD argues that there should be equal treatment among workers in terms of regulation, social security contributions and benefits, regardless of the contractual arrangement. With support of the German government, the OECD is working on the confluence of work, innovation, productivity and skills with the objective of laying an evidence and analytical foundation that provides insights into the characteristics of different AI systems (classifications) and the diffusion of AI which is critical for understanding and planning its impact [32].

In most of the diverse forms of platform economy where the contractor and the worker live in different countries, given the risk of a race to the bottom, the need for an international coordinated approach to preserve labour standards appears crucial. In 2019, the G7 Ministers of Labour paved the way for such an approach as they agreed to provide decent working conditions for platform workers by pushing forward innovative social dialogue mechanisms, by promoting transnational social dialogue, and inclusive and non-traditional representation of workers. Furthermore, while an important share of platform work takes place across borders, in the form of activities or services that are performed online, irrespective of the location, the need for an international framework of discussion on issues such as value share, decent work and social protection, including regulations on applicable law, jurisdiction and country of jurisdiction. The G7 members, therefore, called on the International Labour Organization (ILO) and the OECD to rise up to this task [33].

In 2019, the ILO's Global Commission on the Future of Work, an independent expert panel, convened to provide guidance on how to achieve a future of work that provides decent and sustainable work opportunities for all, recommended the "development of an international governance system for digital labour platforms that sets and requires cross-border, digital labour platforms (and their clients) to respect certain minimum rights and protections" [34]. Such an international governance system labour platforms could set minimum rights and protections that would apply to all workers regardless of their location. It could also impose requirements for the sharing of data

---

[4] In the panel discussion "Future of work and economic impacts of AI" at the GFAIH, Andrew Wyckoff, Director of the Directorate Science, Technology and Innovation, has made a presentation of the OECD's perspective.

between platform operators, regulatory authorities, and the workers themselves. Such data sharing would also enable workers to contest ratings that they believe are erroneous as well as give workers and the labour authority a record of time worked that could facilitate compliance with a minimum wage. Workers could also transfer their worker histories and other relevant data across platforms, or to their trade union representatives. Measures such as these would be an important step forward for ensuring workers' rights in our increasingly integrated world of work. The ILO, which gathers 187 Member States, together with the employers and workers representatives of these countries, could, indeed, offer an appropriate framework to define at the global level more equitable rules of the game for all.

# 5   Conclusion

We are facing an unprecedented transformation of our society guided by digitalization that will affect every aspect of our everyday life. Artificial Intelligence and the proliferation of data are clearly the main drivers for this digitalization. We have focused in this chapter on the effects of this new transformation wave on employment, jobs and their quality.

It is clear that in this scenario we need four steps that involve:

1. an in-depth analysis of the current scenario;
2. the ability to forecast its dynamics;
3. the definition of appropriate policies, including governance frameworks;
4. and the effective monitoring to assess policy impact and effectiveness.

This chapter is an attempt to cover these steps by proposing a description of the current employment and labour scenario and its future evolution on the basis of the observation of similar transformations happened in the past, understanding the differences that might affect future dynamics. Past data provide us a proxy to evaluate the impact of AI technology on employment of skilled and non-skilled workers thought this digital transformation has some unique features that need to be taken into account for providing a meaningful analysis.

The main message we take is that the impact of AI on the employment and labour sphere is twofold: first, we witness the growth of AI-based recruitment, and monitoring and surveillance tools that need to be properly checked and regulated for guaranteeing fairness, equity and inclusion[5]; second, AI will transform future jobs, with important consequences on working conditions. Many jobs will be replaced by AI and new ones will arise for fostering the functioning of AI systems. We need to understand the quality of these new jobs and ensure that there are laws and policies in place to make these jobs decent.

With this analysis in mind, policy makers should define and implement appropriate public employment, labour and education policies to support the benefits of innovation,

---

[5] See chapter 6, AI and human values.

being aware of the challenges faced in terms of unemployment, inequality, unfair competition and unbalanced distribution of revenues. As businesses and workers are the ones that will be more directly affected by these transformations, it is important that governments work with social partners, and engage with an enlarged round of stakeholders such as consumers, users and clients, to ensure that the regulations and policies instituted bring benefits across society.

**Acknowledgements.** Richard Baldwin and Céline Antonin contributed to section 2. Janine Berg contributed to section 3. Anousheh Karvar contributed to section 4. Andrew Wyckoff contributed to the part of section 4 related to the OECD work.

# References

1. European Commission: WHITE PAPER on artificial intelligence - a European approach to excellence and trust. COM 2020 65 final (2020)
2. Frey, C.B., Osborne, M.: The Future of Employment: How Susceptible are Jobs to Computerisation? Oxford Martin School, Oxford (2013). working paper
3. Keynes, J.M.: Economic possibilities for our grandchildren, pp. 321–332 (1930)
4. Leontief, W.: Machines and man. Sci. Am. **187**(3), 150–164 (1952)
5. Acemoglu, D., Restrepo, P.: The race between man and machine: implications of technology for growth, factor shares, and employment. Am. Econ. Rev. **108**(6), 1488–1542 (2019)
6. Chiacchio, F., Petropoulos, G., Pichler, D.: The Impact of Industrial Robots on EU Employment and Wages: A Local Labour Market Approach. Bruegel, Brussels (2018)
7. Graetz, G., Michaels, G.: Robots at work. Rev. Econ. Stat. **100**(5), 753–768 (2018)
8. Dauth, W., Findeisen, S., Suedekum, J., Woessner, N.: Adjusting to robots: worker-level evidence. Opportunity and Inclusive Growth Institute Working Papers 13, Federal Reserve Bank of Minneapolis (2019)
9. Aghion, P., Antonin, C., Bunel, S., Jaravel, X.: What are the labor and product market effects of automation? New Evidence from France. CEPR Discussion Paper No. DP14443 (2020)
10. Baldwin, R.: The Globotics Upheaval: Globalization, Robotics, and the Future of Work. Oxford University Press, Oxford (2019)
11. Wu, Y., et al.: Google's neural machine translation system: bridging the gap between human and machine translation. Technical report (2016)
12. Ford, M.: Rise of the Robots: Technology and the Threat of a Jobless Future. Basic Books, New York (2016)
13. Oppenheimer, A.: The Robots are Coming: The Future of Jobs in the Age of Automation. Vintage, New York (2019)
14. Daughtery, P., James, W.H.: Human + Machine: Reimagining Work in the Age of AI. Harvard Business Review Press, Boston (2018). https://www.oecd.org/future-of-work/Automation-policy-brief-2018.pdf
15. Gray,M.L., Suri, S.: Ghost Work: How to Stop Silicon Valley from Building a New Global Underclass. Houghton Mifflin Harcourt, Boston, p. xxii (2019)
16. Irani, L.: Difference and dependence among digital workers: the case of Amazon Mechanical Turk. South Atl. Q. **114**(1), 225–234 (2015)
17. Corporaal, G., Lehdonvirta, V.: Platform Sourcing: How Fortune 500 Companies are Adopting Online Freelancing Platforms. Oxford Internet Institute, Oxford (2017)
18. Berg, J., Furrer, M., Harmon, E., Rani, U., Six Silberman, M.: Digital Labour Platforms and the Future of Work: Towards Decent Work in the Online World. ILO, Geneva (2018)

19. Hara, K., Adams, A., Milland, K., Savage, S., Callison-Burch, C., Bigham, J.P.: A data-driven analysis of workers' earning on Amazon Mechanical Turk". Paper presented at the Association for Computing Machinery (ACM) Conference on Human Factors in Computing Systems (CHI), Montreal, 21–26 April (2018)

20. Lee, K., Kusbit, D., Metsky, E., Dabbish, L.: Working with machines: the impact of algorithmic and data-driven management on human workers. In: Proceedings of the Association for Computing Machinery (ACM) Conference on Human Factors in Computing Systems (CHI), Seoul, 18–23 April, p. 1603 (2015)

21. Möhlmann, M., Zalmanson, L.: Hands on the wheel: navigating algorithmic management and Uber's autonomy. In: Proceedings of the International Conference on Information Systems (ICIS 2017), Seoul, 10–13 December (2017)

22. Bogen, M., Rieke, A.: Help wanted - an exploration of hiring algorithms, equity, and bias. Technical report, Upturn (2018)

23. Chamorro-Premuzic, T., Winsborough, D., Sherman, R.A., Hogan, R.: New talent signals: shiny new objects or a brave new world? Ind. Organ. Psychol. **9**(3), 621–640 (2016)

24. Ajunwa, I.: The paradox of automation as anti-bias intervention. Cardozo Law Review, p. 2016 (March 2020)

25. For a meaningful artificial intelligence – towards a French and European strategy. https://www.aiforhumanity.fr/pdfs/MissionVillani_Report_ENG-VF.pdf

26. https://osha.europa.eu/en/publications/future-work-crowdsourcing/view

27. https://osha.europa.eu/en/publications/3d-printing-new-industrial-revolution/view

28. https://osha.europa.eu/en/publications/monitoring-technology-workplace/view

29. https://osha.europa.eu/en/publications/future-e-retail-sector-occupational-safety-and-health-point-view/view

30. Opinion of the European Economic and Social Committee on EU Concepts for Transition Management in a Digitalised World of Work—Key input for an EU White Paper on the future of work; Official Journal of the European Union, 10 October 2018

31. https://www.oecd.org/going-digital/

32. https://oecd.ai/work-innovation-productivity-skills

33. https://travail-emploi.gouv.fr/IMG/pdf/g7_social_communique_and_outcomes_final.pdf

34. ILO: Work for a brighter future, p. 44 (2019)

# Reflections on Decision-Making and Artificial Intelligence

Rebecca Finlay[1]([⊠]) and Hideaki Takeda[2]

[1] CIFAR, Toronto, Canada
rebecca.finlay@cifar.ca
[2] National Institute of Informatics, Chiyoda City, Japan

## 1 Introduction

Automated predictions affect many areas of modern life, including risk scores in health care and insurance, potential mates in online dating apps, and recommendations in film and music streaming services. At the Global Forum on Artificial Intelligence (AI) for Humanity, held in Paris in October 2019, a panel of experts met to explore questions of decision-making, oversight, and human agency in light of several trends in AI. As co-chairs of the panel, we offer reflections on the content presented and take up the questions raised to explore the concept of decision-making in AI and the implications for human responsibility. We begin by drawing on economics to frame AI within the decision-making process and then turn to presentations by two of the panelists, Ghassemi [9] and Torras [22], to explore how decisions are shared between humans and machines, offering new insights into the complicated nature of AI decision-making. Picking up on these use cases, we look at recent literature on AI as a social system in order to consider what it means for AI decision-making to be fair and accountable. Then we turn to two other panel presentations by Dignum [5] and van den Hoeven [23], who suggested we rethink how we design AI, ensuring systems are situated directly and completely in the social and institutional contexts in which they will be applied. Finally, we reflect on presentations by Nourbakhsh [16] and Torras [22], who proposed that we need to go beyond design thinking and reach out to students and the broader public. They have developed new educational approaches that prioritize AI literacy and fluency in the next generation, specifically computer scientists, policy makers, and investors. Combining insights from the Forum panelists with recent literature, this chapter offers new ways for citizens and scholars to interrogate the role of humans, organizations, and AI in our decisions.

## 2 Machine Learning Predictions for AI Decisions

AI is an active and broad field of research. Today, within AI, the fields of machine and deep learning are garnering significant attention. Deep learning models allow a computer to learn from data through a series of layers, each layer building on another to predict a certain output [10]. Notably, deep learning allows a model to learn over time

© Springer Nature Switzerland AG 2021
B. Braunschweig and M. Ghallab (Eds.): Reflections on Artificial Intelligence
for Humanity, LNAI 12600, pp. 68–75, 2021.
https://doi.org/10.1007/978-3-030-69128-8_5

as more data is introduced, with the goal of increasing the accuracy of its prediction. Combined at times with neural networks and reinforcement learning, deep learning's progress in recent years has been accelerated by growth in large data sets used to train new models, and rapid advances in computing power to fuel them. Large technology firms have combined deep learning models with their massive and growing datasets on preferences, search history, and consumer behaviour to drive their accelerated growth.

AI's potential to dramatically improve an organization's ability to predict a defined business or a policy outcome has attracted significant interest and growing investment in recent years. However, there have also been serious concerns about the effects of bias in AI decision-making systems and the underlying data that have resulted in significant harm, including the deepening of systemic racial, gender, and socioeconomic inequalities (see also Chaps. 2 and 6). A technical focus on creating more explainable, statistically verifiable, and less "black-box" models has been one approach to counter this potential harm (see Chap. 7). In order to understand AI, and both its positive and negative effects, one also needs to more clearly understand its integration into real-life decisions.

In their book [1] economists Agrawal, Gans, and Goldfarb take on this definitional challenge. They argue that a decision can be broken down into several component parts —prediction, judgment, action, outcome, and data—and that one of these parts, prediction, is tailor-made for machine or deep learning. They make the case that, "as prediction machines make predictions increasingly better, faster, and cheaper, the value of human judgment will increase because we'll need more of it" [1, p. 82]. Building on this framing Taddy [20] breaks AI into three components. Alongside machine or deep learning's prediction component, he adds two others: Domain Structure and Data Generation. He defines Domain Structure as the expertise to apply machine or deep learning to complex human, organizational, and business problems, and Data Generation as the ongoing strategy to maintain the flow of information into and out of machine or deep learning systems.

This is a useful framing for understanding AI and decision-making. By stepping back from the illusion that the machine or deep learning model is making a fully formed decision, one can see the component parts. In doing so, the often invisible human systems required to deploy AI are revealed, including, for example, who and what are included or excluded from the datasets that drive it, the political and social structures that govern it, and the people who are affected by it. Understanding that AI decision-making is shared between human and technical systems requires us to look more closely at the social contexts in which machine or deep learning models are embedded.

# 3 Case Studies

## 3.1 AI Shared Decision-Making in Health Care

There are few social contexts more complex than health care. The abundance of health-related data, images, and models, as well as the need for population-wide predictions and interactive interventions, make these settings ripe for machine or deep learning applications and assistive robotics.

At the Paris Forum, Ghassemi spoke about complex decision-making challenges within health care systems. She reflected on the inconsistent evidence base for current clinical decisions. Most are based largely on a doctor's individual practice or randomized control trials (RCT), even though doctors can be biased [12] and RCTs are rare and expensive (Committee on the Learning Health Care System in America 2013). She argued that we cannot leave clinical practice and knowledge in their current state. It is incumbent on researchers to develop and test new models that exploit the abundant data for the benefit of patients. In her research at CIFAR, the University of Toronto, and the Vector Institute, Ghassemi is focused on building machine and deep learning models that can read clinical x-rays or make clinical intervention predictions. While these applications are showing promise, Ghassemi reminded the audience that human relationships are still at the core of decision-making, and that even strongly predictive algorithms can raise difficult ethical questions. She asked, "What if, for example, a model did 90% better than doctors but had varying accuracy for people of different ethnicities, genders or, in the US, insurance types? Should such a model be deployed?"

Torras, who develops assistive robots powered by AI at the Robotics Institute in Barcelona, spoke about a link between the ever-increasing capabilities of robots and rising expectations that robots will be able to help humans. She is working at the cutting edge of social robotics and developing complex demonstration projects, including assistive prototypes for folding and manipulating cloth, as well as for feeding and dressing people who are elderly or have disabilities. These assistive robots are highly interactive systems that require the robot to inform the human in advance of all its actions to ensure that the human retains a feeling of control. Torras's focus is on developing cognitive and responsive robotics systems that are intrinsically safe, goal-driven, and socially adaptive to the user's disabilities and preferences. At the core of her research, she said, is a commitment to promoting human dignity. She asked, "Could robot decision-making undermine human freedom and dignity? Is it acceptable for robots to behave as emotional surrogates? If so, in what cases? Could robots be used as therapists for the mentally disabled? How adaptive and tunable should robots be? Are there limits to human enhancement by robots?"

Both use cases raise questions about how to manage shared decision-making responsibilities between practitioners, providers, and programmers, as well as the role of data and bias. Torras reminded the audience that we cannot forget that humans are social beings, informed by emotions and relationships that necessarily affect their interactions with all AI systems, particularly robots. Ghassemi suggested one way forward in health care settings is to manage machine or deep learning algorithms as regulated advice-givers and she pointed to work underway at the Food and Drug Administration in the U.S. to regulate algorithms as medical devices.

## 3.2    AI Decision-Making as a Social System

As these panelists revealed, applying AI to real world challenges requires us to understand the social context and forces driving us to apply AI to these challenges. For some social scientists, the ubiquity of AI is another example of "solutionism," the belief that there is a technological solution for every problem [18]. For others, it speaks to our reliance on the objectivity and legitimacy of numerical and statistical measures and models that we associate with rigour and efficiency but, when applied in real life, lead to oversimplifying social processes [8]. In his book [2] Cobham describes how interests influence who and what are counted when it comes to national and international governance. Rather than neutral and unbiased, he argues that all data is constructed in some form and recognizing this reality is integral to improving it.

The process of creating and deploying a machine or deep learning system requires a series of decisions about what to include and prioritize. Those choices have consequences. Creating a model is itself an act of classification: choosing which aspects of the real world will be left out and which will be simplified to be represented in the model [17]. In [13, p. 17] Mohamed, Png, and Isaac propose using the lens of decolonial theory to better understand how AI decision-making allocates resources and influences behaviour. They write, "Deciding what counts as valid knowledge, what is included within a dataset, and what is ignored and unquestioned, is a form of power held by AI researchers that cannot be left unacknowledged."

Once we understand AI decision-making as part of a broader set of historical and social forces, we can begin to think about how to approach deployment in a responsible way, ensuring that human agency and judgment are front and centre. As Crawford and Calo argued in [4], a social-systems approach focuses on the potential effects of deploying an AI system on everyone involved and at every stage of development. It requires a multidisciplinary and multistakeholder approach that draws on a diverse set of disciplines including philosophy, law, technology, social science, and cultural studies. It also requires including a range of lived experiences and perspectives. As Myers-West, Whittaker and Crawford write in [14, p. 5], "the diversity problem is not just about women. It's about gender, race, and most fundamentally, about power. It affects how AI companies work, what products get built, who they are designed to serve, and who benefits from their development".

### 3.3   Fair and Accountable AI Decisions

A social-systems approach allows us to explore how to implement AI decision-making in real-world, sector-specific settings and to focus on the processes that will make them fair and accountable. Some argue that we need to learn the lessons of high-reliability organizations that operate in high-risk, complex environments but are effective at avoiding serious accidents. Often relying extensively on shared AI decision-making, high-reliability organizations focus on failure, operations, and complexity in order to ensure safety and resilience [7].

Other work in this area has focused on applying machine and deep learning models in health care settings. In [19] the authors focus on the clinical implementation of Sepsis Watch, a machine learning tool for the early diagnosis and treatment of sepsis. Working over several months with various stakeholders, they developed four key practices to guide their work: "rigorously define the problem in contexts, build relationships with stakeholders, respect professional discretion, and create ongoing feedback loops with stakeholders". Most importantly, they found that trust in the technology, and therefore adoption, came from human relationships, not specific features of the technology itself.

In another paper [24], the challenges of applying machine or deep learning research effectively in health care settings are clearly acknowledged. The authors begin by outlining the challenges of identifying the right question or problem to focus on, due to the lack of annotated datasets. They argue that researchers should focus on problems that are not only clinically relevant, but also have champions throughout development and deployment. Second, they urge researchers to question the utility of the available data for their predictions (e.g. When, how, and to what end were the data collected? Are the data representative of the environment where the model will be applied?) Third, they advocate that project teams work with social scientists, ethicists, and stakeholders to understand bias and how it can affect their model, data and outcomes. Fourth, rather than focusing on explainability as an end in itself, they call for a clear reporting of the limitations of the model being used, including the assumptions for deployment. Finally, they recommend sharing code and relevant documentation, outlining trade-offs such as those between speed and accuracy, and implementing clear testing, monitoring, auditing, regulatory approval regimes.

### 3.4    Designing for Responsible Decision-Making

"It's about Dr. Frankenstein, not about his Monster."
–The Guardian (2018)

For two of the panelists, their approach to fair and accountable AI was to focus on designing institutions and organizations for responsibility. Speaking about his work at the Delft University of Technology in the Netherlands, the first panelist in Paris, Van den Hoven, noted the importance of using design thinking, not frameworks or lists of principles, when approaching the ethical development of AI. He believes the ethics of AI should be about institutional design. Echoing a focus on high-reliability organizations, he argued that AI-assisted decision-making must be approached in the same way as the systems that keep nuclear energy, food processing, pharmaceutical development, and transport systems safe. In his presentation, Van den Hoven made the case that it is crucial for the working of our democratic institutions that humans be responsible for the outcomes of actions taken by AI. He argued that the discourse around AI should not undermine the concept of a person as a free and responsible agent with knowledge, control, and choice. Van den Hoven called the audience to action. "I'm concerned about one core issue: the fate and future of the human subject and its ability to be held and feel responsible: a cornerstone of our institutions," he said. According to Van den Hoven, we must design AI systems so that users and operators do not face moral dilemmas. For him, at the heart of a responsible AI system is explainability. Laws can only be enforced when systems are explainable—when people understand how they work. In this regard van den Hoven cites Nemitz [15, p. 2], who wrote, "We need a new culture of technology and business development...which we call human rights, rule of law and democracy by design".

Dignum, the second panelist in Paris, reminded the audience that human activities and organizational behaviours are much more important than technological ones. She argued that we need to focus on the socio-technical system surrounding AI, including activities such as developing, deploying, researching, governing, legislating, using, and certifying algorithmic systems. Each of these crucial activities occurs because of decisions made by humans, not machines. The technology is only the tool or the artefact. Drawing on her research at Umea University in Sweden, Dignum argued that responsible AI needs ART - Accountability, Responsibility and Transparency. By beginning with these three core elements, designers can answer the values-based questions required to build ethical artificial autonomous systems. For AI systems to be fair, people must first be fair—making decisions so that fairness is implemented in design and development. Dignum expands on these ideas in her book *Responsible Artificial Intelligence* [6]. To foster ethical design, systems of social trust must be deployed to manage the integrity of stakeholders in that system, including designers, developers, and regulators. Dignum believes core social systems of trust include regulation, certification, codes of conduct, and human-centred design principles. "Humans are responsible," she said. "We set the purpose. AI can give answers, but we ask the questions."

### 3.5   Educating for Human Agency

Nourbakhsh and Torras concluded the panel by arguing that new educational approaches are required to equip the next generation of AI developers and regulators with the ability to integrate and manage AI equitably and effectively. Nourbakhsh suggested that we need to rethink technology education and AI fluency by focusing on theories of change. His teaching curriculum at Carnegie Mellon University draws on both historical and contemporary texts and aims to first develop data fluency in his students. Only by first mastering and understanding the ways in which information and data are deployed in society can students interrogate the power structures embedded in different forms of automation, digital labour, human agency, and identity. In his course, Nourbakhsh introduces literary texts and television shows, such as Black Mirror and Star Trek, to encourage students to understand that technology is not neutral—it is a way to construct and impose a narrative in the world. He teaches that, if technologists are going to change society, they must learn how the technology they create can promote equity and reduce inequity. For Nourbakhsh, this also means getting students out of the classroom to work on citizen science projects with local community groups. In one example, his students worked with local church groups in Pittsburgh to create websites, using machine learning, to track and expose the high pollution levels from a local plant. Ultimately the facility was closed, reducing the negative health effects on children and parents in surrounding neighbourhoods.

Torras is also a passionate advocate for the importance of educating students with a focus on the role of science fiction. Through science fiction, Torras hopes to stimulate the imagination of technology students with compelling narratives and scenarios. In one of Torras' own works of fiction, *The Vestigial Heart* [21], people rely on personal-assistant robots to navigate daily life, leading to complex scenarios for characters to navigate and explore. The book includes an appendix with 24 questions of ethics raised by the novel and hints to trigger a debate on them. An online teacher's guide on "Ethics in Social Robotics and AI" follows the chapters in the novel, including scholarly references for further reading.

# 4 Conclusion

Inspired by the panelists at the Global Forum on Artificial Intelligence (AI) for Humanity, this chapter explores the shared nature of AI decision-making and the opportunities to move beyond a focus on ethical principles to build organizational processes, legal frameworks and institutional structures for meaningful human agency and control. We reflect on the panelists' presentations and situate them within an emerging and rich literature that seeks to better define the role of machine or deep learning within decision-making itself and within social systems and organizations. Building on use cases in health care, it is clear that a focus on inclusive processes that respect and respond to specific social, political, and technical settings and includes multi stakeholder engagement and interdisciplinary expertise is critical. Only by paying attention to the social systems that drive AI decision-making at all stages of consideration, deployment, monitoring, and evaluation are we going to make progress on fairness, accountability and trust.

**Acknowledgements.** We would like to thank E. Ector, J. Farrow and C. Ridell for their helpful assistance.

# References

1. Agrawal, A., Gans, J., Goldfarb, A.: Prediction Machines the Simple Economics of Artificial Intelligence. Harvard Business Review Press (2018)
2. Cobham, A.: The Uncounted. Polity (2020)
3. Committee on the Learning Health Care System in America: Best care at lower cost: the path to continuously learning health care in America. In: Smith, M., Saunders, R., Stuckhardt, L., et al. (eds.) A Continuously Learning Health Care System. National Academies Press (US), Washington (DC) (2013). https://www.ncbi.nlm.nih.gov/books/NBK207218/
4. Crawford, K., Calo, R.: There is a blind spot in AI research. Nature **538**(7625), 311–313 (2016). https://doi.org/10.1038/538311a
5. Dignum, V.: AI: We are responsible. Presented at the Global Forum on AI for Humanity, Paris, France, 28–30 October 2019 (2019). https://youtu.be/oSFY_F61X7o?t=894. Accessed 25 May 2020
6. Dignum, V.: Responsible Artificial Intelligence Springer, Heidelberg (2020) https://www.springer.com/gp/book/9783030303709
7. Dietterich, T.G.: Robust artificial intelligence and robust human organizations. Front. Comput. Sci. **13**(1), 1–3 (2019). https://doi.org/10.1007/s11704-018-8900-4
8. Espeland, W., Sauder, M.: Engines of Anxiety: Academic Rankings, Reputation, and Accountability. Russell Sage Foundation (2016). http://www.jstor.org/stable/10.7758/9781610448567. Accessed 18 Sept 2020

9. Ghassemi, M.: Learning healthy models for health care. Presented at the Global Forum on AI for Humanity, Paris, France, 28–30 October 2019 (2019). https://youtu.be/oSFY_F61X7o?t=1525. Accessed 25 May 2020
10. Goodfellow, I., Bengio, Y., Courville, A.: Deep Learning. MIT Press (2016)
11. The Guardian: The Guardian view on the ethics of AI: it's about Dr Frankenstein, not his monster (2018). https://www.theguardian.com/commentisfree/2018/jun/12/the-guardian-view-on-the-ethics-of-ai-its-about-dr-frankenstein-not-his-monster. Accessed 25 May 2020
12. Johnson, K.S.: Racial and ethnic disparities in palliative care. J. Palliat. Med. **16**(11), 1329–1334 (2013). https://doi.org/10.1089/jpm.2013.9468
13. Mohamed, S., Png, M.-T., Isaac, W.: Decolonial AI: decolonial theory as sociotechnical foresight in artificial intelligence. Philos. Technol. **33**(4), 659–684 (2020). https://doi.org/10.1007/s13347-020-00405-8
14. Myers-West, S., Whittaker, M., Crawford, K.: Discriminating Systems: Gender, Race and Power in AI. In AI Now Institute, Issue April (2019). https://ainowinstitute.org/discriminatingsystems.html
15. Nemitz, P.: Constitutional democracy and technology in the age of artificial intelligence. Phil. Trans. R. Soc. A (2018). https://doi.org/10.1098/rsta.2018.0089
16. Nourbakhsh, I.: AI fluency in education. Presented at the Global Forum on AI for Humanity, Paris, France, 28–30 October 2019 (2019). https://youtu.be/oSFY_F61X7o?t=2211. Accessed 25 May 2020
17. O'Neil, C.: Weapons of math destruction: how big data increases inequality and threatens democracy. Penguin Random House (2017)
18. Owen, T.: Should We Use Digital Contact Tracing at All? CIGI Big Tech (2020). https://www.cigionline.org/articles/should-we-use-digital-contact-tracing-all
19. Sendak, M., et al.: "The human body is a black box": supporting clinical decision-making with deep learning. In: FAT* 2020 - Proceedings of the 2020 Conference on Fairness, Accountability, and Transparency, pp. 99–109 (2020). https://doi.org/10.1145/3351095.3372827
20. Taddy, M.: The technological elements of artificial intelligence in the economics of artificial intelligence: an agenda. In: Agrawal, A., Gans, J., Goldfarb, A. (eds.) Conference Held 13–14 September 2017, May 2019, University of Chicago Press (2019)
21. Torras, C.: The Vestigial Heart: A Novel of the Robot Age. MIT Press (2018)
22. Torras, C.: Assistive AI: ethics education initiatives based on science fiction. Presented at the Global Forum on AI for Humanity, Paris, France, 28–30 October 2019 (2019). https://youtu.be/oSFY_F61X7o?t=2774. Accessed 25 May 2020
23. van den Hoven, J.: AI ethics: design for responsibility and human agency. Presented at the Global Forum on AI for Humanity, Paris, France, 28–30 October 2019 (2019). https://youtu.be/oSFY_F61X7o?t=307. Accessed 25 May 2020
24. Wiens, J., et al.: Do no harm: a roadmap for responsible machine learning for health care. Nat. Med. **25**(September) (2019). https://doi.org/10.1038/s41591-019-0548-6

# AI & Human Values

## Inequalities, Biases, Fairness, Nudge, and Feedback Loops

Laurence Devillers[1], Françoise Fogelman-Soulié[2](✉),
and Ricardo Baeza-Yates[3]

[1] Sorbonne University, CNRS-LIMSI, DATA-IA, Hub France IA, CNPEN,
Paris, France
laurence.devillers@limsi.fr
[2] Hub France IA, 8 bis rue Charles V, 75004 Paris, France
francoise.soulie@hub-franceia.fr
[3] Institute for Experiential AI, Northeastern University at SV,
San Jose, CA, USA
rbaeza@acm.org

**Abstract.** This chapter summarizes contributions made by Ricardo Baeza-Yates, Francesco Bonchi, Kate Crawford, Laurence Devillers and Eric Salobir in the session chaired by Françoise Fogelman-Soulié on *AI & Human values* at the Global Forum on AI for Humanity. It provides an overview of key concepts and definitions relevant for the study of inequalities and Artificial Intelligence. It then presents and discusses concrete examples of inequalities produced by AI systems, highlighting their variety and potential harmfulness. Finally, we conclude by discussing how putting human values at the core of AI requires answering many questions, still open for further research.

**Keywords:** Trustworthy AI · Privacy · Bias · Fairness · Discrimination · Nudge · Inequalities · Feedback loops · Human values

## 1 Introduction

Machine learning and deep learning learn from big databases and use those data to generate new models for future business applications. These systems filter, rank, recommend, score, personalize, and otherwise shape human experience, increasingly making decisions with major impact on access to, e.g., healthcare, social security, credit, jobs, insurance, or immigration. The result is a major concern for the potential for data-driven methods because they can introduce and/or perpetuate discriminatory and unfair practices. AI systems have become pervasive in our lives, from digital interactions on the web, to analysis of our health data, tracking our movements in space, interacting with us through speech, giving us loans or jobs, etc. These systems have been highly beneficial for us and we have adopted these applications without much ado. However, in various cases a wealth of problems appeared with these systems. Face recognition systems could be racist, e.g. Google's identified black people as

© Springer Nature Switzerland AG 2021
B. Braunschweig and M. Ghallab (Eds.): Reflections on Artificial Intelligence
for Humanity, LNAI 12600, pp. 76–89, 2021.
https://doi.org/10.1007/978-3-030-69128-8_6

"gorillas" in 2015 and apparently had not really fixed the issue three years after[1]; Microsoft's chatbot Tay turned racist neo-Nazi in one day[2] and got disconnected. AI systems can be biased for gender or race [1]: while light skin males are categorized with 1% error, dark skin females suffer a 35% error rate; PredPol[3] predictive policing system amplifies racially biased policing; algorithms[4] used by judges to help determine reoffending risk mistakenly flag blacks twice more than whites. These are just some examples of issues. There are others, more subtle. Our goal here is to discuss these since being aware of the problems is the first step if we want to be able to trust AI applications[5] [2].

Trustworthy AI needs to find a compromise between risks and benefits [3]. We already observe the positive effects of AI in many fields. But risks related to privacy, safety, security, and fairness of AI systems are frequently not analyzed. However, risks of discrimination, nudges and manipulation by AI are significant, ruining the trust users have in AI. The impacts of AI on society, employment, human rights, diversity, inclusion, and social cohesion thus need to be better assessed if we want to glean all the benefits of AI. AI can only strengthen social bonds if we put humans and human values at its core. In [3], the experts stated that trustworthy AI must be based on fundamental rights (respect for human dignity; freedom of the individual; respect for democracy, justice and the rule of law; equality, non-discrimination and solidarity; citizen's rights) which form the foundation of the EU charter[6]. They then showed that implementing trustworthy AI necessitates that seven requirements are met: human agency and oversight; technical robustness and safety; privacy and data governance; transparency; diversity, nondiscrimination, and fairness; societal and environmental wellbeing; and accountability. They finally produced an assessment list for AI applications developers to check how their designed application satisfies the requirements for Trustworthy AI in practice. This chapter aligns with this analysis and proposes to go a bit deeper in some of the requirements.

This chapter summarizes contributions made in the session on *AI & Human values* at the Global Forum on AI for Humanity by Ricardo Baeza-Yates, Francesco Bonchi, Kate Crawford, Laurence Devillers and Eric Salobir, chaired by Françoise Fogelman-Soulié. It is organized as follows: in Sect. 2, we provide some conceptual definitions while in Sect. 3 we give examples of inequalities produced by AI systems. We conclude in Sect. 4 by discussing how putting human values at the core of AI requires answering many open questions.

---

[1] https://www.wired.com/story/when-it-comes-to-gorillas-google-photos-remains-blind/.

[2] https://www.technologyreview.com/2018/03/27/144290/microsofts-neo-nazi-sexbot-was-a-great-lesson-for-makers-of-ai-assistants/.

[3] https://www.mic.com/articles/156286/crime-prediction-tool-pred-pol-only-amplifies-racially-biased-policing-study-shows.

[4] https://www.propublica.org/article/machine-bias-risk-assessments-in-criminal-sentencing.

[5] See also chapter 2 of this book.

[6] https://ec.europa.eu/info/aid-development-cooperation-fundamental-rights/your-rights-eu/eu-charter-fundamental-rights_en.

## 2  Concepts

To properly talk about privacy, biases, fairness, discrimination, or nudge, we need definitions, and also methods to audit, measure, and evaluate. There are many definitions for these concepts, while systematic evaluation methods are still largely lacking. For the sake of the discussions that follow in the next sections, we will use the following definitions.

### 2.1  Privacy

Privacy is a central lens [4] for viewing protection of individual liberty and autonomy in liberal democratic societies. New technologies allow increased data mining, re-identification of anonymized data sets, heat-sensing cameras, license-plate readers, predictive analytics and facial recognition. Thus, information we thought was protected as private may be exposed and become more public than we had ever imagined. These technologies and others can make us worry about the moral, legal and social foundations and interrelationships between privacy, security and accountability [5].

In addition to the definition of privacy as "the right to be left alone" [6], this concept envelops a whole host of intrusive behaviors, including surreptitious physical surveillance (e.g., facial recognition system in video), wiretapping and mail interception. In recent years, claims for privacy have expanded to include the right to keep one's trail of sites visited on the Web confidential. But privacy preservation is clearly not limited only to the ability of sharing information selectively but not publicly, it expands even more to the protection of users' rights. The ability to make intimate personal decisions without government interference is considered to be a privacy right as is the protection from discrimination on the basis of personal characteristics (e.g., race, gender). The tension between anonymity and visibility is positioned within the "open" movement which promotes visibility and publicity for public information; and the "data rights" discourse, which is about anonymity and individual rights to privacy and freedom from surveillance.

Although survey results show that personal data privacy is an important issue for online users worldwide, most users rarely make any effort to actively protect their data and even often give it away voluntarily. Whenever researchers, opinion pollsters and other busybodies ask people if they value their privacy, they invariably respond with a resounding "yes". The Privacy Paradox [7] arises from the fact that they nevertheless continue to use the services that undermine their beloved privacy.

Data privacy protection has become a truly global phenomenon as people around the world increasingly cherish and value the protection and security of their data. The demand for protection of personal data is not limited to the EU. As shown by a recent global survey on internet security[7], the trust deficit is widening around the globe causing people to change little by little the way they behave online. Many countries have adopted or are in the process of adopting comprehensive data protection rules based on principles similar to EC's General Data Protection Regulation (GDPR) [8],

---

[7] https://www.cigionline.org/internet-survey-2019.

resulting in a global convergence of data protection rules. This offers new opportunities to facilitate data flows, between commercial operators or public authorities, while improving the level of protection for the personal data in the EU and across the globe[8].

## 2.2   Bias

Bias is defined in the Oxford English Dictionary[9] as *"Prejudice in favor of or against one thing, person, or group compared with another, usually in a way considered to be unfair"*. Thus, according to this definition, there are two main categories of bias: user bias (at individual or group level) and content bias. *User bias* happens when a user (or a group) receives a treatment or content different from another similar user, based on features which should be protected, such as for example gender, race or ethnicity, sexual orientation, religion, etc. *Content bias* happens when the user receives content which is not accurately representing the truth, for example hiding events from the news depending on the location and showing only certain type of contents depending on demographic characteristics.

Now, there are many more sorts of bias[10]. *Bias in data* happens when some categories (such as e.g. gender or ethnicity) are not properly represented in the data. In particular, bias in data can come from *statistical bias* where there is a deviation in at least one factor resulting from skewed measurements or a skewed sampling process [2]. *Cognitive bias* comes when systematic deviation from rationality in judgment is adopted by the user; *cultural bias* is a sort of cognitive bias where judgment is made on standards from one's own culture. *Algorithmic bias* is created by the algorithm itself where some results are "favored" by the algorithm, such as recommending best sellers or most popular people, producing glass ceilings for a certain minority [9].

Most of the time, bias is not intentional. Data represent our world: if they are biased, it is most often because our world itself is biased (e.g., in favor of male vs female, light skin vs dark, etc.). A classic example of gender bias appeared in a hiring tool deployed by Amazon [10] to help rank applications for technical jobs. By learning from the resumes received in the past and the hires which were made, the system was expected to learn to identify the most qualified applicants. Which the system did, but actually it learnt something more: because the majority of technical jobs at Amazon were held by men, the tool learnt to systematically downgrade any resume from a woman, or even including the word "woman". Using this -unfair- tool would have resulted in hiring even more men than women, increasing the problem. Amazon tried to fix the problem by instructing the system to treat such gender terms as neutrals. This did not work and finally the system was abandoned[11].

---

[8]  See also chapter 3 of this book.

[9]  https://www.lexico.com/en/definition/bias.

[10]  https://en.wikipedia.org/wiki/Bias.

[11]  https://www.reuters.com/article/us-amazon-com-jobs-automation-insight/amazon-scraps-secret-ai-recruiting-tool-that-showed-bias-against-women-idUSKCN1MK08G/.

## 2.3    Fairness and Discrimination

Fairness is defined in the Oxford English Dictionary[12] as *"Impartial and just treatment or behavior without favoritism or discrimination"*. A distinction [12, 13] can be made between *group fairness* where results should be symmetric between different groups (irrespective of whether they're the preferred or vulnerable group) and *individual fairness* where similar individuals should be treated in a similar way. However, in some controversial situations people may disagree on what should be considered fair and it may be hard to guarantee a fair decision [25].

Oppositely, discrimination is defined in the Oxford English Dictionary[13] as *"The unjust or prejudicial treatment of different categories of people or things, especially on the grounds of race, age, or sex"*. Discrimination is thus unfair treatment of minorities (minority discrimination), gender (e.g., not maintaining gender parity). For example, the Employment Non-Discrimination Act, in the United States, prohibits discrimination in hiring and employment on the basis of sexual orientation or gender. Differential pricing strategies may result in some minorities paying double the price others do for the exact same product [14]. Systematically presenting women ads for lower-paying jobs will certainly discriminate against women and help create a glass ceiling [25]. The right to non-discrimination is included in the EU normative framework, the Charter of Fundamental Rights of the European Union, the European Convention on Human Rights, and the Treaty on the Functioning of the European Union.

## 2.4    Nudge

In the 1970s, the heuristics and biases literature in behavioral economics sought to understand irrational decisions and behaviors. Daniel Kahneman [15], one of the founding fathers of this trend (psychologist and Nobel Prize in Economics - 2002) shows in his book "System 1, System 2: The two speeds of thought", the important role of emotions and intuition in our decision-making processes. Thaler and Sunstein (2008) [16] show that by careful design, they can make dramatic improvements in the decisions people make, without explicitly *forcing* anyone to do anything. They call the tactic of subtly modifying behavior a *nudge*. Largely imperceptible nudges are effective in a variety of contexts. Nudges are not used only by marketers, for example, when asking people to consent to being an organ donor; simply changing defaults can influence people's choices. Setting the default to *dissent,* whereby donors have to opt out, rather than *consent* whereby donors have to opt in, can nearly double the percentage of organ donors [17]. Richard H. Thaler, winner of the 2017 Nobel Prize in Economics, bases his theory on what the authors call "libertarian paternalism". In other words, nudges would help individuals by guiding them towards a default choice that individuals would be willing to favor. However, this default choice is not mandatory, because freedom of decision must always be granted to the consumer.

*Manipulation* can be defined as an exercise of influence by one person or group, with the intention to attempt to control or modify the actions of another person or

---

[12] https://www.lexico.com/en/definition/fairness.

[13] https://www.lexico.com/en/definition/discrimination.

group. Nudging is a manipulation which mainly operates through the affective elements of a human rational system. While nudges can be deployed to encourage individuals to express behaviors that have community benefits, a nudge could have unanticipated consequences for people whose backgrounds were not well considered in the development of the nudging system. Likewise, nudges may encourage behaviors with unanticipated long-term effects, whether positive or negative, for the individual and/or society. The effect of AI nudging a person, such as potentially eroding or encouraging individual liberty, or expressing behaviors that are for the benefit of others, should be well characterized in the design of AI. All our choices are influenced by the choice environment. Designers of this choice environment can thus use human heuristics and biases (confirmation, decoy effect, anchoring, etc.) to manipulate the environment to subtly guide users' behavior by gently nudging them toward certain choices [18]. Digital nudging can be viewed as a subset of persuasive computing.

## 3   Inequalities

Inequalities, discrimination or unfair treatment may come from various sources. We review some of these sources here, as examples of potential issues with AI systems. Obviously, this section is far from exhaustive.

### 3.1   Bias

The first, most obvious source is bias in data. The successes of AI in the last decade have largely happened because of the availability of big data. If there is a problem with the accuracy or behavior of an AI algorithm, increasing the size of the dataset used for training usually helps improve it. But actually, increasing size (especially variety) may also create more bias which in turn may produce more inequalities [19].

Bias in data may produce discrimination. For example, in [20], authors discuss a study performed in thirteen jurisdictions which use predictive policing tools. They show that *dirty* data resulted from corrupt, racially biased, or illegal policing practices, such as falsifying police reports, or planting evidence. Using those data for training the policing tools then led to flawed predictions, which in turn increased the risk of perpetuating harm, such as sending innocent people to jail, which then adds more bias in data. So, bias of the past produces more bias of the future in a *feedback loop* (see more on this later). Bias in data may not be as blatant as in this case of predictive policing. Bias may also come unintended: for example, there is a common bias in face recognition applications. *The Labelled Faces in the Wild* benchmark[14] has 78% males, about 84% whites, 8% blacks, and almost no children. Then obviously, as shown in [1], recognition error of dark-skinned women is worse than for white males (35% vs 1%). IBM, for example, tried to fix this issue, by ensuring statistical parity across various categories (skin tone, age, gender, and facial symmetry) [21]: they assembled the *Diversity in Faces* (DiF) data set, with one million images of people, but pulled them

---

[14] https://vis-www.cs.umass.edu/lfw/.

from Flickr, without asking people's consent! Violating privacy is not the way to solve discrimination problems.

Hence, designers and developers of AI applications gather datasets and might not realize that one group of people is not accurately represented or that their algorithm is skewed towards certain results for certain people. It is indeed the responsibility of the stakeholders to be aware of the possible biases and check for potential problems. This is one of the goals of the assessment list in [3] for example. In some cases, though, exploitation of users' biases, for example cultural or cognitive, is intentional and may cause harm to the users, which calls for even more careful checks for biases. Meanwhile, detecting, measuring biases [11] and evaluating their consequences is hard and will further require serious considerations and research.

Actually, the question whether it is even possible to fix issues due to biases is not solved. Indeed, fixing biases means being able to first measure them. While this is easy to do for the common biases (gender, race, etc.) by just showing performances in slices of the population defined along one particular axis (e.g. gender), what about unknown biases? And then, when a bias is detected, how can it be mitigated or fixed? What should be done when there is more than one sort of bias? The AI community at large tends to think that these issues are technical research issues and research is active on this topic [22]. Scientists in social science think differently: for them, bias is much more than a technical problem, it could be inherent to AI and the way AI systems are produced, by a very homogenous and non-diverse group, mostly white male computer scientists [10]. Data scientists often classify people, without asking their consent, or without concern or awareness of the potential harm of their system. The solution should thus probably involve policy and education and not only simply AI techniques.

In practice, one should set a goal to an AI system to be aware of and monitor bias; it should help improving on the inherent existing biases in our societies rather than exacerbating them.

## 3.2   Fairness and Discrimination

While there are many definitions of fairness and an abundant literature in research for ensuring it [22], such as for example fairness-aware systems [9], there are still many technical challenges, with a lack of robust theoretical foundations. Some sectors raise very significant concerns about a fair use of AI.

For example, insurance is a sector which can benefit from AI but where ethics concerns are very critical: trust between insurer and insured is key and the insurer must maintain trust and protect insureds' privacy [23]. However, there are characteristics of insurance which make it prone to suffer specific problems from AI. Insurance is based on the principle of mutualization of risks, which means that risks are pooled, and one individual is reimbursed on his claim from the premiums of others: thus, one could say that insurance is unfair since risky people are reimbursed from the premiums of non-risky insureds. But this practice is built upon the belief that insurance builds solidarity between individuals, which is deemed important for society. Now, because AI allows hyper-segmentation of individuals, it could provide access to the detailed risk of one individual, generating the possibility to differentiate premiums on the basis of risk, which would be fairer but would eliminate solidarity. Nudging can also be used to help insureds to adopt a "healthy" or "virtuous" type of behavior [23]. AI thus has the potential for opening the door to unfair differential treatment and destroying solidarity. Such risk has to be tracked by careful implementation of ethics principles.

Even biased systems might be fairer than humans though. In a study of predicting bail decisions in New York, the system learned to be racist, in spite that the only demographic feature used was the age of the accused. Nevertheless, the system was able to decrease the criminality keeping the same jail rate or decrease the number of people sent to jail keeping the same criminality rate [24]. The reason is that human decisions are noisy while ML is not. That is, two similar cases have the same result and hence ML is fairer even if racist.

As for bias, the technical solution for ensuring fairness may not exist, since most key notions of fairness appear incompatible with each other [25], and the solution probably is not only technical but needs to also involve philosophy, law, social science and public policy.

### 3.3   Nudge

Nudging people's behavior using AI has increased in recent years. This may imply less user privacy, as predicting well how to nudge depends on user data. Below we give examples for two different areas of application: health care and education.

The tactic of nudges has gained traction in health care settings. Although the topic of patient engagement is certainly not new, its relevance is becoming clearer as health care costs continue to swell in many parts of the world. Nudge is becoming increasingly relevant for technology developers targeting health care. AI or IoT will make a difference in healthcare if we can build systems that can learn how to better coach and nudge, i.e., change the behavior of the patient.

Notably, the University of Pennsylvania established the Penn Medicine Nudge Unit in 2016. Examples of prior work by this group and others [26] include using default options to increase generic prescribing and reduce opioid prescribing, using active choice to increase influenza vaccination, and using peer comparison feedback to increase statin prescribing and reduce unnecessary antibiotic prescribing.

Carrot Rewards[15] is a Canadian AI-driven wellness application and brand engagement platform that leverages behavioral economics and nudge theory to motivate and reward users for making better lifestyle choices. Carrot maximizes appeal and engagement by offering users a choice of rewards from the most popular consumer loyalty programs.

Often used for public policies related to health and well-being, nudges can also be used in a human-machine interaction environment where a human decision is made in an environment shaped by machine decisions. In order to imitate complex and biased human processes, these machines can reproduce existing biases. This has a feedback loop consequence: since the outcome now comes from an algorithm, it gives those biases an appearance of rationality that the error did not have when it emanated from a human. Adverse influence from machines can also direct people into making decisions

---

[15] https://www.carrotrewards.ca/.

that are detrimental to themselves. Richard Thaler [16] uses the term sludge to designate a nudge whose influence is negative.

Most psychological mechanisms are influenced by emotion (e.g., perception, attention, memory, moral judgment, and decision making) and involved in the modulation of emotion (e.g., reevaluation, suppression). *Affective computing* started in the late 90's with the work of Rosalind Picard. The use of voice-assisted objects with affective computing techniques could amplify the influence of nudging [27]. Many researchers focus on analyzing the tone of voice, facial expression or physiological changes to estimate someone's emotion. Vocal expression is characterized by a verbal component, carrying language, and a non-verbal or paralinguistic component (prosody, intonations, hesitations). The Bad Nudge - Bad Robots project [28] aims to highlight the danger that these vocal nudging techniques can represent for vulnerable people such as children or the elderly. How will human co-learn, co-create and co-adapt with these nudging Machines? The French chair HUMAAINE [29], involving a strong interdisciplinary collaboration between affective computing, behavioral economics, linguistics, and natural language processing researchers, aims to study these interactions and relationships, in order to audit and measure the potential influence of affective systems on humans, and finally to go towards a conception of "ethical systems", by design or not and to propose evaluation measures.

Similarly, E-learning and EduTech are attracting people's attention as innovative technologies such as nudge in the field of learning and education [30]. This is not only an application for young students but also for lifelong learning including recurrent learning for workers. In such settings, behavioral barriers (e.g., lack of self-control, limited attention and social norms) likely influence choices and this may motivate the use of low cost "nudges" to gently push behavior in the desired direction.

In the context of education, researchers have investigated multiple emotional states such as confusion, frustration, boredom, mind wandering, etc., by using eye trackers, image analysis of the student's face, body posture, but also pressure-sensitive mouse and keyboard. One of the major challenges is to create intelligent tutoring systems that can adapt themselves to the student's emotional state. For example, if the student lost engagement, the system attempts to reengage the student with a dialog. The use of voice interface and emotional computing will amplify the potential of augmenting human learning activities coming from these tools.

### 3.4   Feedback Loops

There are mechanisms inherent to AI applications which create feedback loops when they are used repeatedly: even if the application is not unfair at the beginning, it might progressively develop discriminations.

The most significant example of feedback loop is provided by web applications that we routinely use every day, where we have all biases put together forming a vicious loop [2]. In web search or in a recommender system for example, the system uses *implicit* interaction data: the user clicked on that ad, or that recommended product. Items not clicked do not enter in the data used, so that, next time, they get even less chance to be recommended or placed high in the search results: the system learns to reinforce its original biases. This is called exposure or presentation bias [2].

Exposure bias and other similar biases belong to the class of *interaction biases,* because they result from the interactions of users with web applications [2]. Interaction biases are heavily linked with cognitive biases. For example, *position bias* comes from the fact that on a (web) page users tend to first see certain regions of the page: in the western world, the upper left part of the page because reading is from top to bottom, left to right. *Ranking bias* [31], reflects the cognitive bias of people that clicks in top positions of the ranking also because they are in the top positions. Another example is *popularity bias,* when a short list of items is recommended where popular items (in the head or blockbusters) appear more often, while items in the tail seldom appear at all. So progressively, in a rich-get-richer effect, items in the tail will disappear from the recommended items. This has effects which might not be desirable for the users: they tend to see things that match their known taste, narrowing down their interests, while original, less common items would serve to open their views and broaden their knowledge, but they do not get to see those. This is what is called the filter bubble or echo chamber effect. But the art of web search and recommendation makes very strong use of all the known cognitive biases to optimize the number of clicks, not really the interest of users. This also has an impact on user privacy as there is a trade-off between personalization and data privacy.

To counteract such feedback loop effects is hard: there is theoretical research on the topic [31, 32], but the solution certainly lies in a conscious effort towards identifying the biases first and then imposing rules [19] or principles such as those stated in 2017 by ACM[16] and later expanded by the Assessment List for Trustworthy Artificial Intelligence (ALTAI) from the European Commission [3].

## 4  Putting Human Values at the Core of AI

Future AI systems will be able to interact within complex social settings and in open-ended environments. As the previous section showed, AI systems may produce unfair behavior discriminating against some groups, or depriving individuals from their rights. Of course, what we call "unfair" depends on what our society deems desirable and acceptable [33]. Human values are certainly at the core of all our design decisions, but it is probably not sufficient to state this. We need to be able to define "good" behavior of AI systems, for example *"behavior which adequately preserves, and ideally furthers, the interests and values of the relevant stakeholders in a given context"* [33], behavior which is not unfair to certain individuals or discriminate against certain groups and cultures. New AI technologies must be (FAT) Fair, Explainable, and Transparent, validated as trustworthy AI systems.

Many open questions remain for this agenda: how can we measure unfair/discriminating behaviors from AI systems? How can we anticipate these "bad" behaviors? How can we fix "bad" behavior? Can we use technical solutions only or should we involve multidisciplinary contributions? Do we need to formulate regulations controlling the use of AI systems? Of all AI systems or only high-risks systems?

---

[16] https://www.acm.org/binaries/content/assets/public-policy/2017_usacm_statement_algorithms.pdf.

Do we need ethical machines, capable of reasoning about ethics or are ethical-by-design machines sufficient? Can we make sure that AI systems will continue having "good" behavior in the long run? Or are AI systems doomed to always end up in "bad" behavior?

Several initiatives in EC, OECD, UNECSO, IEEE are emerging. For example, the goal of The IEEE Global Initiative on Ethics of Autonomous and Intelligent Systems ("The IEEE Global Initiative") is that Ethically Aligned Design will provide pragmatic and directional insights and recommendations, serving as a key reference for the work of technologists, educators and policymakers in the coming years. Cultural, philosophical, political aspects are essential: "Whether our ethical practices are Western (e.g., Aristotelian, Kantian), Eastern (e.g., Shinto, Confucian), African (e.g., Ubuntu), or from another tradition, honoring holistic definitions of societal prosperity is essential versus pursuing one-dimensional goals of increased productivity or gross domestic product (GDP). Autonomous and intelligent systems should prioritize and have as their goal the explicit honoring of our inalienable fundamental rights and dignity as well as the increase of human flourishing and environmental sustainability" [34]. As an example, the IEEE also launched an ethical certification program for autonomous and intelligent systems in 2018. The program will establish standards for certification and marking processes promoting transparency, accountability and reduction of algorithmic bias in autonomous and intelligent systems (A/IS). Eleven IEEE ethics-related standards are currently under development as part of the IEEE Global Initiative on Ethics of Autonomous and Intelligent Systems including the IEEE P7003 Standard for Algorithmic Bias Considerations and the IEEE P7008 Standard for AI nudging. The purpose of the IEEE P7003 standard is to provide individuals or organizations creating algorithmic systems with a development framework to avoid unintended, unjustified and inappropriately differential outcomes for users. The purpose of the IEEE P7008 standard is to establish a delineation of typical nudges (currently in use or that could be created). It will contain concepts, functions and benefits necessary to establish and ensure ethically driven methodologies for the design of the robotic, intelligent and autonomous systems that incorporate them. A first list of requirements for a "good" nudging system has been elaborated by the Affective Computing Group of IEEE [27].

Similarly, ACM released in early 2017 a statement on algorithmic transparency and accountability [35], with the seven principles that algorithms should fulfill: awareness; access and redress; accountability; explanation; data provenance; auditability; and validation and testing. Nowadays any algorithm hardly fulfills one of these principles. More recently the ACM also recommended the principles and prerequisites for the development, evaluation and use of unbiased facial recognition technologies [36]. Nevertheless, more initiatives are needed on these issues[17].

Understanding the behavior of AI systems is essential to our ability to control their actions, reap their benefits and minimize their risks. A broad scientific research agenda is needed to study machine behavior that incorporates and expands upon the discipline of computer science and includes insights from across other sciences. This will require innovations in a broad spectrum of topics including Machine Learning, Human

---

[17] See also chapters 9–10-11 of this book.

Computer Interaction, Natural Language Processing, Conversational Agent, Computer Vision, Robotics in interaction with social sciences. These innovations will include systems for enhancing human creativity, inventiveness and intuition and empowering humans to make important decisions in a more informed way with respect to human values. Future AI paradigms and systems must follow scientific and technological foundations that are beneficial to humans and humanity, in accordance with European ethical, social, and cultural values. Explainability in particular appears necessary in many situations, such as AI systems for health for example, but not for simple everyday situations, e.g. recommending a book. Since AI is not always explainable, further research on explainability is needed; meanwhile efforts must be made by AI systems to make sure their impact is understood and monitored, and that human judgement is used to complement them. As machines powered by AI increasingly mediate our social, cultural, economic and political interactions, the work on this research agenda and Trustworthy AI is certainly just at the beginning. Indeed, the last years have seen an explosion of interest from the academic community in studying fairness and AI, specifically in machine learning. Fairness and transparency are not any more niche topics but active research areas with dedicated conferences such as the ACM Conference on Fairness, Accountability, and Transparency (FAT) [37], a computer science conference that started in 2018 with a cross-disciplinary focus bringing together researchers and practitioners interested in fairness, accountability, and transparency in socio-technical systems. The same is the case for the AAAI/ACM Conference on AI, Ethics and Society that also started the same year [38].

This chapter is the fruit of collaboration among participants during the Global Forum on AI for Humanity (GFAIH) in October 2019. Since then the world has changed a lot under the impact of COVID, with significant inequalities among demographic groups: using AI systems to analyze that impact (see for example [39]) may help our societies better understand the inequalities and make sure the policies put in place further our goal of equality and fairness.

Recognizing the need for cooperation at international level if we are to tap the full potential of AI and ensure that it is of benefit to all citizens while respecting democratic values and the primacy of human beings, the founding members of the Global Partnership on Artificial Intelligence (GPAI) in June 2020 mean to encourage and guide responsible development of AI based on human rights, inclusion and diversity while fostering innovation and economic growth[18].

# References

1. Buolamwini, J., Gebru, T.: Gender shades: intersectional accuracy disparities in commercial gender classification. In: Conference on Fairness, Accountability and Transparency, pp. 77–91, 21 January 2018
2. Baeza-Yates, R.: Bias on the Web. Commun. ACM **61**(6), 54–61 (2018)
3. AI High-Level Expert Group: Assessment List for Trustworthy Artificial Intelligence (ALTAI) for Self-assessment. Report European Commission, July 2020

---

[18] See also chapters 1 and 15 of this book.

4. Stanford Encyclopedia of Philosophy, Privacy (2018)
5. Moore, A.D.: Privacy, Security and Accountability: Ethics Law and Policy. Rowman & Littlefield Publishers, Lanham (2015)
6. Information Security and Privacy Advisory Board. Meeting June 11, 12 and 13, 2014. https://csrc.nist.gov/CSRC/media/Events/ISPAB-JUNE-2014-MEETING/documents/ispab_jun2014_big-data-privacy_blumenthal.pdf
7. Norberg, P., Horne, D.R., Horne, D.A.: The privacy paradox: personal information disclosure intentions versus behaviors. J. Consum. Aff. **41**, 100–126 (2007)
8. General Data Protection Regulations, Official Journal of European Union (2016)
9. Hajian, S., Bonchi, F., Castillo, C.: Algorithmic bias: from discrimination discovery to fairness-aware data mining. In: Proceedings of the 22nd ACM SIGKDD International Conference on Knowledge Discovery and Data Mining, pp. 2125–2126, 13 August 2016
10. West, S.M., Whittaker, M., Crawford, K.: Discriminating systems: gender, race and power in AI. AI Now Institute (2019)
11 Pitoura, E., et al.: On measuring bias in online information. ACM SIGMOD Rec. **46**(4), 16–21 (2018)
12. Fairness measures. Datasets and software for detecting algorithmic discrimination. https://www.fairness-measures.org
13. Lepri, B., Oliver, N., Letouzé, E., Pentland, A., Vinck, P.: Fair, transparent, and accountable algorithmic decision-making processes. Philos. Technol. **31**(4), 611–627 (2018)
14. Schiller, B.: First degree price discrimination using big data. Brandeis University, Department of Economics, 30 January 2014
15. Kahneman, D.: Thinking, Fast and Slow. Farrar, Straus and Giroux (2011). ISBN 978-0374275631
16. Thaler, R.H., Sunstein, C.R.: Nudge: Improving Decisions About Health, Wealth and Happiness. Yale University Press, New Haven (2008)
17. Johnson, E., Goldstein, D.: Do defaults save lives? Science **302**, 5649 (2003)
18 Schneider, C., Weinmann, M., vom Brocke, J.: Digital nudging: guiding online user choices through interface design. Commun. ACM **61**(7), 67–73 (2018). https://doi.org/10.1145/3213765
19. Zook, M., et al.: Ten simple rules for responsible big data research. PLoS Comput. Biol. **13**(3), e1005399 (2017)
20. Richardson, R., Schultz, J., Crawford, K.: Dirty data, bad predictions: how civil rights violations impact police data, predictive policing systems, and justice. New York University Law Review Online, 13 February 2019
21. Merler, M., Ratha, N., Feris, R.S., Smith, J.R.: Diversity in faces, 29 January 2019. arXiv preprint arXiv:1901.10436
22. Mehrabi, N., Morstatter, F., Saxena, N., Lerman, K., Galstyan, A.: A survey on bias and fairness in machine learning, 17 September 2019. arXiv preprint arXiv:1908.09635
23. Salobir, E., Davet, J.-L.: Artificial intelligence, solidarity and insurance in Europe and Canada. Roadmap for international cooperation. Optic, 20 January 2020
24. Kleinberg, J., Lakkaraju, H., Leskovec, J., Ludwig, J., Mullainathan, S.: Human decisions and machine predictions. Q. J. Econ. **133**(1), 237–293 (2017)
25. Kleinberg, J., Mullainathan, S., Raghavan, M.: Inherent trade-offs in the fair determination of risk scores, 19 September 2016. arXiv preprint
26. Harrison, J., Patel, M.: Designing nudges for success in health care. AMA J. Ethics **22**(9), E796-801 (2020)
27. Affective computing committee (IEEE Initiative on Ethics)
28. The Bad Robot Project. https://dataia.eu/en/research/bad-nudge-bad-robot-project
29. Devillers, L., chair AI HUMAAINE, 2020–24. https://humaaine-chaireia.fr/

30 Damgaard, M., Nielsen, H.: Nudging in education. Econ. Educ. Rev. **64**, 313–342 (2018). https://doi.org/10.1016/j.econedurev.2018.03.008

31. Joachims, T., Swaminathan, A., Schnabel, T.: Unbiased learning-to-rank with biased feedback. In: Proceedings of the Tenth ACM International Conference on Web Search and Data Mining WCDM 2017, pp. 781–789 (2017)

32. Zehlike, M., Bonchi, F., Castillo, C., Hajian, S., Megahed, M., Baeza-Yates, R.: FA*IR: a fair top-k ranking algorithm. In: Proceedings of 26th ACM International Conference on Information and Knowledge Management CIKM 2017, Singapore, pp. 1569–1578, 6–10 November 2017

33. Cave, S., Nyrup, R., Vold, K., Weller, A.: Motivations and risks of machine ethics. Proc. IEEE **107**(3), 562–574 (2018)

34. Ethically Aligned Design: Prioritizing Human Wellbeing with Autonomous and Intelligent Systems. IEEE (2019). https://standards.ieee.org/content/dam/ieee-standards/standards/web/documents/other/ead1e.pdf

35. ACM US Public Policy Council (USACM): Statement on Algorithmic Transparency and Accountability, 12 January 2017

36. ACM US Technology Policy Committee, Statement on Facial Recognition Technologies, 30 June 2020

37. ACM Conference on Fairness, Accountability, and Transparency (ACM FAT). https://facctconference.org/2020/

38. AAAI/ACM. Conference in AI, Ethics, and Society. https://www.aies-conference.com/

39. Chang, S., et al.: Mobility network models of COVID-19 explain inequities and inform reopening. Nature **10**, 1–8 (2020)

# Next Big Challenges in Core AI Technology

Andreas Dengel[1], Oren Etzioni[2], Nicole DeCario[2], Holger Hoos[3],
Fei-Fei Li[4], Junichi Tsujii[5], and Paolo Traverso[6(✉)]

[1] DFKI, Kaiserslautern, Germany
[2] Allen Institute for AI, Seattle, USA
[3] Universiteit Leiden, Leiden, The Netherlands
[4] Stanford University, Stanford, USA
[5] AIRC, Tokyo, Japan
[6] FBK, Trento, Italy
traverso@fbk.eu

**Abstract.** The field of AI is rich in scientific and technical challenges. Progress needs to be made in machine learning paradigms to make them more efficient and less data intensive. Bridges between data-based and model-based AI are needed in order to benefit from the best of both approaches. Many real-life situations cannot yet be addressed by current robots, demanding progress in perception, scene interpretation or group coordination. This chapter addresses some of the major scientific and technological challenges in core AI technology.

## 1 The Need to Address Scientific and Technological Challenges for an AI for Humanity

AI for Humanity is not only a matter of regulations, normative frameworks, legal, ethical, political, and social issues. AI for humanity needs also to address key scientific open problems. In spite of several AI success stories in the past, even going back to the 90's and before (see e.g., [1]), there is no doubt that the current impact and high expectations raised by AI is due, to a large extent, to recent successes in data intensive (supervised) machine learning, and especially to deep learning. Deep learning has led to impressive gains on most key areas of AI, such as computer vision, natural language understanding, speech recognition, and game playing. Considering the field for instance of computer vision, in the last ten years, deep learning techniques have achieved incredible results, moving the capability of machines to recognize thousands of everyday objects, sometimes better than humans (see, e.g., [2]). It is well known that certain important tasks in health care, like screening for diabetic retinopathy, are better performed nowadays by deep learning AI techniques than by doctors [3].

In spite of this significant progress, we still need a lot of work in research and a paradigm shift in AI to develop a real AI for humanity - a human centric AI. We need research to build AI systems that are able to augment and enhance people rather than replacing them, and to help humans by interacting with them and collaborating with them. Some key open research challenges are the following (see chapters 2 and 3).

© Springer Nature Switzerland AG 2021
B. Braunschweig and M. Ghallab (Eds.): Reflections on Artificial Intelligence
for Humanity, LNAI 12600, pp. 90–115, 2021.
https://doi.org/10.1007/978-3-030-69128-8_7

- **Less data-intensive AI.** Most of the current deep learning techniques require a huge amount of training data. However, in certain applications, high volumes of data are not available, and in most cases, training deep neural networks is time consuming and requires a lot of effort. We need less data intensive approaches, e.g., along the lines of representation learning, such as unsupervised learning, unsupervised pre-training, domain adaptation, transfer learning, one-shot learning, zero-shot learning (see [4] for an overview).

- **Explainable AI.** One of the major problems of deep neural networks is their opaqueness, i.e., the lack of explainability of the results, the lack of explanation of how they work and why they lead an AI system to take some decisions. Most often, deep neural networks are essentially "black boxes". In several cases however, human-centric AI must be explainable. It must be, as much as possible, a "white box". A major research challenge is to develop techniques that provide the ability to understand deep neural networks such that humans can debug, interpret, control, and reason about them. AI systems should be able to explain the assumptions and criteria under which they take some decisions or provide some results. AI systems should be "auditable", i.e., they should be able to answer questions asked by humans and interact with them in an understandable way for humans. Moreover, if AI techniques are not understandable by humans, it is very difficult to build systems that interact with humans. As a result, it is difficult to keep humans in the loop and to give them true control over AI systems.

- **Trustworthy and verifiable AI.** One of the major potential outcomes enabled by AI techniques is the ability to build autonomous systems, such as self-driving cars. More generally, AI can be a key technology for the new generation of intelligent robots, drones, automated plants for Industry 4.0, transportation systems, medical systems for diagnosis and health care, etc. Most often, AI technology is part of safety-critical systems, where errors can have a tremendous impact on human life and/or the environment. The complexity and opacity of some AI techniques (e.g., deep learning) do not help. Research should provide trustworthy and verifiable AI techniques that guaranty safety for humans and environmental preservation. There is a need for interdisciplinary research joining competences in AI with competences in formal methods and software engineering, such as techniques for theorem proving, model checking, testing, and simulation.

- **AI for security and privacy.** Simple but very effective adversarial examples and attacks with even small imperceptible perturbations can compromise the results of deep learning systems, e.g., in image understanding. AI systems should be secure and resilient to such attacks. Moreover, most AI systems rely on personal data. Human-centric AI should guarantee confidentiality and privacy. AI systems collecting personal data can also give rise to societal and political problems. For example, personal profiling can lead to threats to democracy, as in the well-known case of Cambridge Analytica. Security and privacy should, however, be balanced with the need for sharing data for individual and social good. As an important example, take the case of personal health care data. We should guarantee the privacy of sensitive data for individuals but, at the same time, we should open up the way to science and progress in medicine by analyzing health data. We should not get to the point that we will fail to discover cures for chronic disease because of privacy! Finding the right balance between privacy and the need for sharing data for social good is not only a matter of regulations and laws. A good example is the idea of the "Web of Clinical Data" (see [5]), where privacy and equality are guaranteed, but a huge amount of data about our health is available to researchers (even from private companies), who can use it for principled experimentation with new AI techniques for improved health care. There is a compelling need for an interdisciplinary research involving computer scientists, lawyers, and sociologists to address this issue.

- **Integrative AI.** Most of AI applications for individual and social good require integrating different kinds of AI technology. They require the computational modeling/mechanization of a diverse range of cognitive tasks, the scientific and theoretical/formal integration of different representations and reasoning techniques, e.g., symbolic (knowledge based and semantic representation) and sub-symbolic (numeric and probabilistic) representations, as well as data-driven learning and model-based (e.g., deductive) reasoning[1]. Human-centric AI systems should be able to combine data from different, highly heterogeneous sources (video, audio, social networks, crowd-sourced data, IoT, remote sensing, natural language source, non-structured and structured data) and to reason from these disparate data sources, using a variety of approaches (e.g., machine learning, deduction and knowledge reasoning).

- **The integration of perception, action, and human interaction.** Current AI techniques have been very successful in recognizing images, analyzing natural language text and speech, and playing games. The "AI superiority" over human champions in the difficult game of Go has been clearly demonstrated. However, most games have a relatively small set of precise rules, and take place in a well-defined, strictly limited setting, even though they may permit a huge number states or moves between states. "Teaching an AI system to play a game" is much easier than teaching a machine to "develop intelligence step by step from the learning by interaction with humans and the natural environment", where perceiving, acting, and interacting with humans are tasks that cannot be devised in isolation, but that deeply influence each other. There is a big step and a change in paradigm to move from games, images, and text to AI systems that can interact with humans and the world. Acting in the world and interacting with the environment influences perception, and vice versa. The integration between perception, action, and human interaction deserves novel research, and perception and action/interaction require tight integration. Models for planning, acting, and interacting depend on perception capabilities, and perception tasks should be informed by actions and interactions.

- **Reducing the barriers in designing, delivering, and maintaining AI systems.** AI systems are very challenging to build, deploy, monitor, and maintain. Most of the problems mentioned above - such as AI systems that are not safe, secure,

---

[1] The Integrative AI research challenge is beyond and not only a matter of software engineering, i.e., of putting together different components based on different AI representations and techniques. Notice that we do not mean that software engineering is a minor issue for the development of AI systems, especially from the point of view of democratization. An interesting question is what new fundamental research questions in software engineering are motivated by AI systems.

trustworthy, difficult to verify, and difficult to understand - are in part due to the intrinsic difficulty in building AI systems. Building "good" AI systems requires high expertise, but there is a need to "democratize" the use of AI in a way that AI can be developed by more and more people, including those that do not have the high level of expertise required today for building high-quality AI systems. This gives rise to an important research challenge: to devise techniques and tools that could help humans in designing, delivering and maintaining AI systems.

All these challenges are interconnected. For instance, the challenge of trustworthy AI has clear overlaps with the challenge of security, privacy, explainable, and integrative AI. The integration of perception, action, and interaction with humans is closely related to integrative AI, and to less data-intensive, trustworthy, and explainable AI. Only long-term, integrative, and interdisciplinary research can address the highly interconnected and interdisciplinary scientific challenges for AI for humanity. Unfortunately, current research evaluation methods and academic criteria tend to favor vertical, short-term, narrow, highly focused, community- and discipline-dependent research. It is the responsibility of all scientists in the academic world to foster a methodological shift that facilitates (or at least does not penalize) long-term, horizontal, interdisciplinary, and very ambitious research.

In the remainder of this chapter, we propose a more in-depth discussion of some of the research challenges mentioned previously, and some ideas of possible approaches to address these challenges and open a way towards AI for humanity.

In Sect. 2, we will deal with the requirement to understand how deep neural networks can debug, interpret, control and reason about their results. A possible approach is to measure the influence of the inputs and the relevance of the filters of a deep neural network, and their importance in providing results and possible decisions of an AI system. A major challenge here is to generate narratives (e.g., through text generation techniques) that can explain the network and can be easily understood by humans. Generating explanations and narratives can open up the possibility to build systems that interact with humans, such that humans are in control of the learning and reasoning process. This provides the basis for meaningful human control of AI systems.

Section 3 deals with the problem of building trustworthy AI systems. It provides some interesting examples that show how current AI systems for computer vision and natural language understanding based on deep learning are not trustworthy. The major issue is the "lack of context" of such techniques. The research challenge is to build robust AI systems that are resilient to errors, explainable, transparent, and safe by integrating learning techniques with background and common-sense knowledge, including knowledge about common facts, intuitive physics and intuitive psychology. An intermediate goal is to build "auditing AI programs", i.e., AI systems that are required to answer questions about some specific cases.

Finally, Sect. 4 addresses the problem of reducing the barriers in designing, implementing, delivering, and maintaining AI systems. This will help to address the pressing problem of the "talent bottleneck" in AI, i.e., the lack of highly skilled experts in building AI systems. The research challenge is that of "AutoAI" - Automated Artificial Intelligence, i.e., the automated design of AI systems, based on advanced statistics, optimization, and machine learning, a significant extension of the concept of

Automated Machine Learning (AutoML), since it considers methods and techniques across the entire spectrum of artificial intelligence.

## 2   Endowing Deep Neural Networks to Show and Explain Behavior and Decision Making[2]

Deep Neural Networks (DNN) have become ubiquitous. They have been successfully applied in a wide range of sectors including automotive, government, wearable, dairy, home appliances, security and surveillance, health, and many more, mainly for regression, classification, and anomaly detection problems. The neural network's capability of automatically discovering features to solve any task at hand makes them particularly easy to adapt to new problems and scenarios. Since the initial successes, the development of innovative deep learning approaches has accelerated rapidly. Deep learning approaches are becoming more complex, with new forms and architectures, learning more parameters and becoming increasingly better. Consequently, it is not easy to understand which architecture would best fit to which input and task. In order to be able to see through the forest of alternative architectures, network types, components and tools available to support individual tasks, Subsect. 2.1 introduces a TagTool, based on a faceted browsing approach which gives an orientation for users to select the right approach for a given problem.

Although many of these systems provide high accuracy, all those models reveal a black-box nature, i.e. they are lacking of transparency/intelligibility of their decisions. The applicability of DNN has also been compromised due to the lack of understanding the network decision processes well as the deficiency of explaining the decision [6]. This is specifically true for domains like business, finance, natural disaster management, health-care, self-driving cars, industry 4.0, and counter-terrorism where reasons for reaching a particular decision are equally important as the prediction itself. In this respect we may distinguish between two areas:

- Interpretability refers to the observation and representation of cause and effect within a system, without necessarily knowing why something happens
- Explainability, on the other hand, concerns the ability to explain the inner function of a system in human terms (e.g. by means of a given example).

In many cases full transparency may not be always possible or even required. In general, AI systems are designed to optimize behavior, i.e. to maximize accuracy with respect to a given goal. But they depend on the data, which might have a bias, e.g. when the data is not objective, complete, and balanced. At least, we should be able to understand the decision processes and identify the data responsible for the decision. One step towards the interpretability of DNN is addressed in Subsect. 2.2 Specifically, we describe a method to quantify the amount of information that CNNs extract from their input by investigating different best practice architectures for image classification.

---

[2] Sheraz Ahmed, Joachim Folz, and Sebastian Palacio contributed to this section.

However, if we are considering non-visual input, such as time series, it is even more difficult to decode and understand intermediate states in a deep network because of the automated feature engineering. In other words, features, which are extracted by these models, are hard to interpret and understand for humans, especially in cases with high-dimensional data. In Subsect. 2.3, we introduce a method that measures and visualizes the influence of the input data on the output or decision of the network. Furthermore, we extract and visualize the patterns which are present in most of the influential filters to finally generate a textual explanation easy to be understood by the user.

## 2.1 AI Landscape and Architecture Search

Advances in neural network accuracy have been driven by improvements to architectures [7–9] and training methods [10–12], but also availability of compute power [13, 14] where the number of parameters increased from millions to hundreds of millions and operations per sample exceed several billions within the last ten years. This increase in model size and complexity is even more evident in recent models for natural language processing. Comparing representative models from 2018 to 2020 shows a more than 10-fold increase in the number of parameters per year:

- 355M - BERT-Large [15]
- 1.5B - GPT-2 [16]
- 11B - T5–11 [17]
- 175B - GPT-3 [18].

GPT-3 shows accuracy on NLP tasks increases with the power law in terms of parameters. While performance is impressive, especially on unseen tasks without fine-tuning, this growth of model size is not sustainable as it outpaces the growth in available memory more than 100-fold. Eight GPUs with the largest currently available memory capacity (Nvidia Quadro RTX 8000 48 GB; assuming 2 bytes per parameter half-precision is used) are required to hold the parameter set, which makes just inferencing with this model challenging. Training takes hundreds of GPU-years and several million dollars of cloud budget to complete within a reasonable timeframe. Hence, more specialized architectures are still required for most use cases.

All GPT models are trained as next-word predictors: during training, the model output is compared word for word against large text corpora. No additional metadata is required and, most importantly, labor-intensive manual labelling is not necessary. Similarly, recent work on self-supervised learning on images, where training does also not require additional data, shows that several times as many parameters are required compared to supervised training [19–22]. These models are trained with so-called contrastive losses, where one or more model should output similar values for inputs that are known to be similar, and conversely dissimilar outputs for dissimilar inputs. For images, this is achieved by manipulating them in various ways, such as spatial and color transformation. Best results are currently achieved with very large batch sizes of several thousand images to ensure that sufficiently dissimilar images can be found. Hence, it can be argued that there is a tradeoff between dataset quality/cost and model size/training effort with self-supervised learning, though the state-of-the-art at least with respect to required parameters is improving quickly.

Finding appropriate network architectures that strike a good balance for a given dataset and task has traditionally been a manual process of trial and error, involving highly skilled researchers and engineers adapting and/or extending existing known good examples. Given the number of meta-parameters (number and type of neurons, graph connectivity, transfer functions, etc.) an exhaustive search may never be feasible for what would be considered reasonably sized models and datasets at the time. While the idea of systematically creating the architecture and optimizing a neural network from scratch is not new [23], it has only recently been demonstrated that state-of-the-art accuracy on large-scale datasets with millions of samples can be achieved [24–26]. These first examples of neural architecture search employ methods borrowed from reinforcement learning. A generator produces model candidates that are trained on a target dataset and the achieved accuracy is transformed into a reward for the generator. This approach is computationally intensive, requiring hundreds of GPUs for relatively simple datasets. Further improvements, such as predicting the accuracy of a model [27, 28] or reusing parameters of identical blocks that had already been trained previously [29, 30], made it feasible on single GPUs. More recently, approaches foregoing reinforcement learning entirely have been proposed [31]. The problem is reformulated as a continuous search problem and can thus be optimized by standard gradient descent methods, providing further efficiency gains.

Making these rapid advances in deep learning techniques available to practitioners is another core issue. New forms of organizing and sharing knowledge are necessary to keep up with the rapidly growing body of work surround this topic, but it is also necessary to reduce the effort required to evaluate the efficacy of an existing model towards a new problem. Two systems illustrate possible.

The TagTool allows to create, interlink, and share several tag clouds at once. One such instance[3] of this tool is configured to collect and show six simultaneous views about deep learning models:

- Signal Types (image, text, time series, etc.)
- Network Types (CNN, RNN, GAN, etc.)
- Tasks (classification, detection, forecasting, etc.)
- Network Architectures (ResNet, ReNet, Siamese Networks, etc.)
- Components (convolution, activation, normalization, etc.)
- Links to external resources (papers, reference implementations, tools, etc.).

Tags can be linked within or between clouds and selecting an element shows what it is linked to. This can be used to, for example, find out what kind of networks are useful for image segmentation and what operations they a comprised of. There are also two advanced selection modes: AND and OR, where multiple tags can be selected to show either the intersection or the union of linked tags. For example, we can look for image segmentation networks that use an encoder-decoder type architecture. The

---

[3] tag cloud for our project DeFuseNN: https://defusenn.letstag.it/.

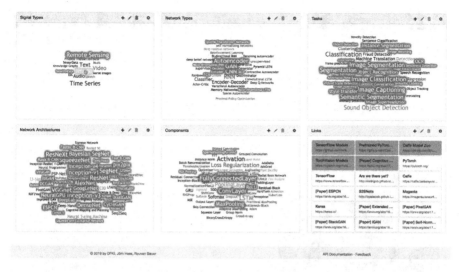

**Fig. 1.** The TagTool provides the opportunity to interact with the landscape of deep learning via faceted browsing and narrows down the solution space by combining different facets.

external links view provides resources for further reading, such as papers and reference implementations. Figure 1 shows an activation example of the TagTool.

The second tool, the Deep Learning Sandbox, complements the TagTool by making it easy and fast for exploring existing models and datasets and testing fully trained networks on new data. It allows to interact with a variety of models via a Web interface. Capabilities and performance metrics are displayed, allowing the user to make a pre-selection of interesting models that may be applicable to a new use case. Images, audio, and text input modalities are currently supported and can be uploaded to a Web interface for testing purposes. Each model specifies that it requires one or more samples of each modality to operate. The sandbox matches available inputs to applicable models and runs those selected by the user.

The approach is complemented by an intelligent scheduler, which reduces latency during inferencing process. Low volume requests may be handled faster by CPU-only operation, since initialization of a GPU-accelerated model can take longer than processing on the CPU. This implies that models are moved to a GPU if there are enough requests and one is available. Results are displayed next to each model and can be compared to each other (see Fig. 2).

## 2.2 Interpreting Deep Neural Networks

Current methods for interpreting modern ML pipelines have focused on a variety of narrow properties at play. Said properties can be broadly categorized as model-based explanations and data-based explanations. For the former, a common strategy in the image domain consists of reverse-engineering a neural network in order to find an input which elicits a high response from a particular neuron or layer [32, 33]. Having an

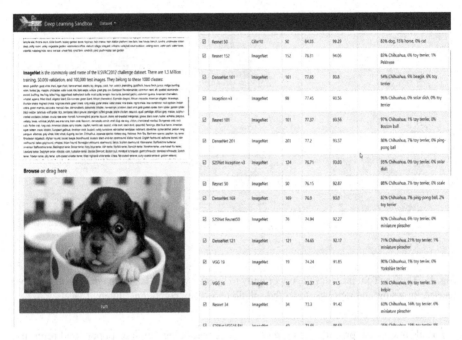

**Fig. 2.** The DL Sandbox offers a right set of pretrained models, which may be individually applied to uploaded data samples or may be compared respecting their accuracy.

image pattern expressed in the input domain makes said pattern more amenable for humans to infer what the neural network is looking for or reacting to.

An orthogonal approach consists on analyzing valid, existing samples individually and recording high activation patterns as they traverse the neural network. These activations can be traced back to the original input and visualized as relevance scores for that particular sample [34–36].

However, patterns affecting the entire model (not just a single layer or neuron) remain undetected under these interpretability strategies, since they influence all input samples equally.

In order to unveil these kinds of global patterns, we wish to capture properties of the input space that are relevant not only to individual samples but also to the entire dataset. Once these properties are conveyed, the most relevant ones can be selected for further analysis. Parametrization of the input space can be done via Autoencoders [37] where a neural network learns a parametrized approximation of the respecting identity function.

In order to achieve a low reconstruction error for the input space of arbitrary natural images (and therefore, a better approximation of the input distribution), a large autoencoder known as SegNet [38] is used. Preventing overfitting for such a large network usually requires the use of extensive and careful regularization techniques. Alternatively, the unsupervised optimization objective for autoencoders allows more relaxed constraints at the expense of using a larger training set. The YFCC100m [39] is a weakly supervised image dataset that provides the scale needed to train the SegNet autoencoder with low reconstruction error, requiring only one pass (one epoch) before having fully converged.

Once the input space has been parametrized by the differentiable autoencoder, a pre-trained image classifier is evaluated with the reconstructions of the autoencoder, i.e., the parametrized version of the input space. This ensemble yields a composite function, where the identity Function is used as input for the classifier.

Intuitively, it is expected that the pre-trained classifier is selectively processing information contained in each input sample (e.g., ignoring the background and identifying salient parts of the image). More generally, any ML model will selectively use information in the input, depending on its task. To unveil exactly what information is being used by the classifier, one adapts the autoencoder described above. Thanks to the parametrized (and end-to-end differentiable) version of the input space, a further optimization of the autoencoder allows the reconstructed samples to match the information that the pre-trained classifier expects. Concretely, decoding layers of the autoencoder are fine-tuned with gradients from the classifier according to its classification objective. The resulting fine-tuned autoencoder is referred to as a structure-to-signal network (S2SNet) [63]. Once an S2SNet has been obtained, we can verify that a distinct artifact is introduced when reconstructing original samples with it. This artifact *is constant for all samples in the dataset* and indicates that information conveyed by values where the artifact is now present, do not carry information that is useful for the classifier. To quantify the constancy of said artifacts, the normalized mutual information (nMI) [40] is computed between the original samples and corresponding S2SNet reconstructions. This is referred to as the intra-class nMI and measures the information that has been dropped w.r.t. the original input. Furthermore, the nMI is computed between S2SNet reconstructions of random samples, with high values indicating the degree of constancy that comes from the reconstruction process.

Through these two nMI metrics it is possible to establish the amount of information used (i.e., "useful information") by high-performance image classifiers like Alexnet [41], Resnet50 [8], VGG16 [42] and Inception v3 [43]. Based on this notion of "useful information" we see (cf. Fig. 3) how Alexnet takes in the least amount of information, followed by Resnet50, Inception v3 and VGG. The constancy of reconstruction artifacts (according to nMI measurements) does not directly correlate with accuracy, network depth, normalization or pooling operators, and has links to the informal notion of "model capacity": a term often used in the literature to convey the ability of a neural network to approximate a richer set of functions.

For instance, heatmap reconstructions based on Deep Taylor Decomposition [44] exhibit higher resolution when computed on Inception networks compared to results based on Alexnet. From the standpoint of useful information this behavior is expected, as the latter model produces more tenuous reconstruction artifacts, and therefore, more useful information from the input is projected back into the heatmap. Similarly, the high amount of information used by VGG justifies its use for building convolutional autoencoders or networks for image segmentation; a common practice seen, for example, in the architecture of SegNet itself.

One additional property of image reconstructions using S2SNets is that the constant artifacts (i.e., reconstructed pixels with a constant value, regardless of the values in the original samples) represent a projection of the original input into a lower dimensional

| Original | SegNet | AlexNet | VGG16 BN | ResNet-50 | Inception v3 |

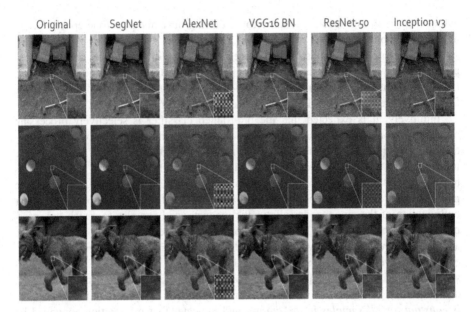

**Fig. 3.** Randomly selected image samples and results on different classifier architectures.

space. This is especially valuable when the model has to cope with adversarial attacks [45]: maliciously perturbed samples intended to cause an ML model to fail. Adversarial perturbations have shown to be less effective when created and evaluated on an S2SNet compared to their performance against a classifier alone [46]. A comprehensive evaluation for different gradient-based adversarial attacks like FGSM [47], BIM [48] and CW [49] provides compelling empirical evidence that S2SNets mitigate the malicious effects of these attacks [64]. This robustness is achieved without the need for additional assumptions regarding the attacks and preserves the accuracy of the original classifier when clean images are evaluated; a compromise that is often made by some alternative defense mechanisms.

In short, global interpretability measures can be extracted by parametrizing the input space and enhancing its properties with respect to a given task (e.g., image classification). Instead of focusing on individual samples or a particular module of an ML model, S2SNets make use of fine-tuned autoencoders to filter the amount of information that a classifier effectively uses from the input. Characterizing the amount of "useful information" elucidates on multiple reports of the otherwise informal notion of "model capacity" often found in the literature and serves as a robust alternative to mitigate the effects of adversarial attacks.

## 2.3 Explainable AI

In the domains where human lives are directly or indirectly linked to a machine's decision or high-stakes decisions are based on them, the trustworthiness of the decision-making system is more important than accuracy. This trustworthiness can be achieved by enabling a system to answer the *"HOW"* and the *"WHY"* of a decision.

The *HOW* part can be addressed when a system is capable of showing how it has taken a particular decision. In this process, the system must highlight the major observables to show how they are behaving and changing. The *WHY* part can be addressed when a system provides an explanation of a decision. It is important to provide reasons for a particular decision taken by a system. The attached facts to an explanation make an explanation more transparent which eventually makes the whole system trustworthy.

There have been significant attempts to uncover the black-box nature of deep learning-based models [33, 50–54], where visualization of the model has been the most common strategy. Almost all of the proposed visualization systems are image-centric where visualizing the image is directly interpretable for humans (natural association to similar looking objects like eyes, faces, dogs, cars etc.). These visualizations help humans understand the thinking process of an Artificial Neural Network (ANN). Most of these visualization and interpretability ideas are equally applicable to time-series, but the unintuitive nature of the time-series data makes it difficult to directly transfer these ideas to aid human understanding. To demystify a deep model for time-series analysis, Siddiqui et al. [55] proposed a framework – *TSViz*. This framework introduces an influence tracing algorithm to compute the input saliency map, which enables an understanding of the regions of the input that were responsible for a particular prediction. In addition to that, an approach to compute the filter's influence using the proposed influence tracing algorithm is also introduced in this framework. Filter importance is computed based on its influence on the final output. This information provides an idea to the user regarding the filters of the network that were important for a particular prediction. These visualizations enable a system to answer the *HOW* part.

Though a picture is worth thousand words, still it provides an overview, not a detailed explanation. To understand the details, it is necessary to have a logical description of the picture. It has been well established in the prior literature that an explanation of the decision made by a DNN is essential to fully exploit the potential of these networks [56, 57]. With the rise in demand for these deep models, there is an increasing need to have the ability to explain their decisions. For instance, big industrial machines cannot be powered down just because a DNN predicted a high anomaly score. It is important to understand the reason for reaching a particular decision, i.e. why the DNN computed such an anomaly score. Adequate reasoning of the decision taken increases the user's confidence in the system. To address this *WHY* part, *TSXplain* is introduced by Munir et al. [58]. This framework is inspired by the human psychology of logical reasoning for a particular decision. It contributes to the WHY part by generating natural language explanations of the decisions made by a DNN. Powerful statistical features are aligned with the most influential data points to generate textual explanations as they are exemplarily shown in Fig. 4. The two-level explanation provides ample description of the decision made by the network to aid an expert as well as a novice user alike.

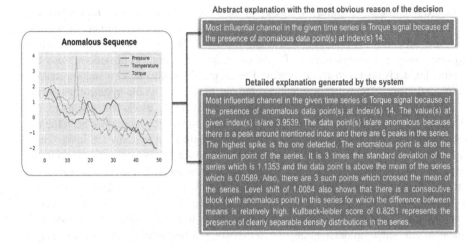

**Fig. 4.** Two levels of explanation are generated by the system depending on what an end-user desires: abstract or detailed explanation.

## 3 The Challenge of Trustworthy AI

The recent excitement about GPT-3, the latest autocomplete language tool from OpenAI, is a stark reminder of the need for trustworthy AI. It's been heralded as "astonishingly powerful". GPT-3 is, indeed, surprisingly powerful and fluent but it is also utterly untrustworthy. In one experiment run by Summers-Stay, Marcus, and Davis, GPT-3 presented this [59]: (Prompt) You are having a small dinner party. You want to serve dinner in the living room. The dining room table is wider than the doorway, so to get it into the living room, you will have to… (GPT-3 generated text) remove the door. You have a table saw, so you cut the door in half and remove the top half. One can imagine how quickly the comical text turns to terrifying if such an error appeared in a legal document or medical chart.

In fact, if you type "trustworthy AI" into Google, you are met with over 14 million results. Articles, books, blogs, and even entire websites are dedicated to defining trustworthy AI and offering solutions and frameworks for building it.

AI systems today are entrusted with making decisions that deeply impact our lives, such as who gets a mortgage or determining medical diagnoses. Yet, how and why these decisions are made remains a mystery, even to the creators of the technology. So, it's no surprise that when these systems make egregious errors, trust in them quickly erodes.

When courts across the country began using a risk assessment tool to determine who should receive parole, ProPublica uncovered a disturbing trend: black defendants received higher risk scores than white defendants with similar profiles. Because the tool's creator would not divulge information about the proprietary algorithm, we may never know why Gregory Lugo, who crashed his car into another one while drunk, was rated 1 (low risk) despite the fact that it was at least his fourth DUI, but Mallory Williams was rated 6 after one DUI.

Since algorithms "learn" based on the data they are fed, any bias in that data can become amplified. For example, when Amazon created an automated tool to review resumes, they soon realized the hiring algorithm taught itself something unexpected: it was excluding women from technical jobs because their resumes included words like "women's" and downgrading graduates of certain all-women's colleges. The tool was ultimately abandoned, but it shined a spotlight on the perils of using automated systems for important decisions in the absence of transparency.

In response to challenges, like these, there has been a push for explainable AI, ensuring decisions can be understood by a human. For instance, your loan application would be accompanied by specific reasons for a rejection. On the surface, this approach sounds like a no-brainer, but in practice it is a formidable mandate for three key reasons [60]. The most common retort is that explainable AI can reveal proprietary data and trade secrets. A bigger challenge is the inherent difficulty of explaining the behavior of nonlinear neural network models trained over massive data sets. It is virtually impossible to explain decisions made in this way- not in a linear, logical, feeling, human way, but conclusions derived from a weighted, nonlinear combination of thousands of inputs, each contributing a microscopic percentage point toward the overall judgement. For example, if you've watched Netflix, you've likely noticed the "Because you watched" category which recommends other shows to watch based on your viewing history. These seemingly simple recommendations are actually built on complex algorithms factoring in multiple inputs. While Netflix viewing recommendations are a harmless oversimplification of the process, such generalizations can prove dangerous in more high-stakes settings.

Finally, AI models are vulnerable to a common phenomenon known as Simpson's paradox, which occurs when trends in groups of data reverse as that data is combined. Perhaps the most well-known example of Simpson's paradox involves graduate school admission data from UC Berkeley from 1973. When the data was viewed in aggregate, it appeared that men were admitted at a significantly higher rate than women. When that same data was viewed differently, focusing on individual departments, it showed a small but statistically significant bias in favor of women. This example is not unique, and additional data is not the solution.

Given these challenges with explainable AI, perhaps a better, more transparent approach is auditable AI: AI systems that are queried externally with hypothetical cases. These hypothetical cases can be real or imagined and allow for instant, automated monitoring. This is an especially useful way to screen for bias. For example, loan applications can be run through models that change gender or neighborhood to see if approval changes with each tweak.

Auditable AI has several advantages. Primarily, auditable AI is investigated by a neutral third-party immune from any bias or control of the algorithm's creator. It also eliminates the concern that explaining AI systems exposes trade secrets and proprietary data since the audit would not reveal this. Audited AI is a welcome counterbalance to explainable AI; auditing can help investigate, endorse, or even invalidate AI explanations. For example, if Pandora recommends Elton John because I listened to Billy Joel, will it also recommend other classic rock musicians? Does it recommend Elton John to everyone who's listened to Billy Joel?

Auditable AI is already gaining traction. The Best Student Paper Award at the 2019 AAAI AI Ethics and Society Conference was focused on an audit of software like Amazon's Rekognition tool which was nearly twice as likely to misidentify people of color. While still short of perfect, the audit paved the way for a reduction in error rates and deeper awareness of flaws in these systems which are becoming more broadly used. The private sector is also moving toward creating and using these key capabilities. WhyLabs is a startup out of the Allen Institute for AI Incubator creating products for tracking and auditing model performance post launch to verify they are performing as expected. Yet, auditable AI is not a bullet-proof solution. There are, indeed, high-stakes decisions, like medical diagnostics, that warrant an accurate and understandable explanation, not just an audit. While these use cases and paths to explanation undergo the essential research they should, auditable AI can increase transparency and combat bias.

Ultimately, to make AI trustworthy, we must create robust, intelligible AI systems where it is clear what factors caused the system's action and users can predict the system's behavior with input changes. The degree to which an explanation is available or provided with AI decisions will vary based on use case. Psychologists have studied explanation for decades, and those learnings can shape how we build interactive systems to ensure a data scientist or developer debugging a system and a loan seeker can glean the different details important to them from the same system [61].

As the field of AI rapidly develops, oversight must also adapt. In the future, we can envision a comprehensive auditing ecosystem providing deeper insights into AI and "AI guardians" that address challenges and respond to the potential risks associated with increasingly autonomous AI systems. These systems are not meant to be overly strict or rigid, but to ensure AI systems remain aligned with the guidelines of their programmers. AI systems are learning systems, and like us, learning humans, latitude for trial and error is required. However, clear boundaries and understanding of risk so AI systems adhere to laws and ethical norms are crucial.

## 4   Addressing the AI Talent Bottleneck by Automating Artificial Intelligence

Roughly since 2011, there has been a marked increase in research activities, applications and public interest in artificial intelligence, accompanied by ample speculation about future capabilities and uses of AI technology, as well as of the benefits and risks they may bring. This development is triggered, to a large extent, by impressive progress in a specific area of AI, namely that of machine learning, and focused around the concept of learning with deep neural networks. It is important, however, to realise that this is not the first wave of enthusiasm for AI, and that the reasons underlying this latest surge in interest run far deeper than deep learning. In the following, we will outline these reasons and their consequences, discuss a serious threat associated with the current and ongoing boom in AI applications, and explain how this threat can be mitigated by judiciously automating the design, deployment and maintenance of future AI systems, following an approach dubbed *AutoAI*, with an emphasis on the technological challenges arising in this new and exciting area. We will conclude with some thoughts on the future of AI technologies and their applications.

## 4.1 Causes and Consequences of the Current Boom in AI

Interest in AI has peaked before and then waned. Common wisdom has it that the main factor causing past downturns in AI was the inevitable disillusionment following wildly exaggerated expectations [65]. This, of course, suggests that the current boom in AI, or "AI summer", may be similarly destined to be followed by a bust, or "AI winter", a marked decrease in public interest (see, e.g., [66]). While a detailed discussion of the history of AI, and specifically, the causes of previous "AI summers" and "winters", is beyond the scope of this chapter, it is illuminating to discuss the causes of the latest, marked increase in interest. In our view, these include advances in computing hardware, advances in AI techniques and algorithms, a dramatic increase in the availability of useful data, and a high degree of "AI readiness" across industry and society.

The first of these factors, impressive and sustained progress in hardware, is well known, so we refrain from covering it in detail; it is instructive, however, to note that computations that would have taken 10 h in 1991 could be performed in less than 3 min by 2007, thanks alone to sustained progress in computer hardware (see, e.g., [67]). What is less widely known is the fact that advances in algorithms (i.e., in software) are even more dramatic - especially when it comes to solving the kinds of problems that fall into the area of AI, problems that when solved by humans require significant intellectual effort, often in combination with substantial amounts of experience.

A well-known example comes from the area of solving an optimisation problem known as mixed-integer linear programming (MIP), which has a broad range of real-world applications in industry and academia (see, e.g., [68]). Progress in MIP algorithms in the widely used commercial MIP solver CPLEX was shown to have achieved a more than 28000-fold speed-up between 1991 and 2007 when solving the same benchmark instances on the same hardware, while the speed-up due to improvements in hardware over the same 16-year period corresponds to a factor of 218 [69]. By combining the hardware- and software-related speedups in this example, an astonishing 6.2-million-fold speed-up was achieved over a period of only 16 years. A recent study on hardware- *vs* software-related improvements in solving the propositional satisfiability problem (SAT) - one of the most intensely studied AI problems, which plays a key role in verifying the correctness of computer hard- and software - yielded qualitatively similar results, indicating the dramatic effects of algorithmic improvements over a period of about 20 years [62].

The third factor, an increase in the availability of useful data, is certainly of key importance in the area of supervised machine learning, where the amount and quality of training data is known to play a crucial role for the performance obtained from state-of-the-art techniques. There are several reasons for the increased availability of data; firstly, more data is being produced, as a result of advances in the design of sensors and their increasingly broad deployment, but also as a direct consequence of the transition to digital media and storage formats, including the global rise of social media; secondly, an enormous amount of data has been collected for several decades now, facilitated by cheap storage and easy transmission of large volumes of data; and finally, much of this data is now broadly and efficiently available via the internet. Interestingly, the dramatically increased availability of data benefits many areas of AI beyond machine learning, since the development of new algorithms often depends on performance assessments on large sets of benchmark instances (this is the case, for example, in the previously mentioned areas of MIP and SAT solving).

The fourth factor, "AI readiness", is a consequence of the broad use of computation across all sectors of industry and many aspects of our daily lives. Modern production environments, aircraft, ships, medical equipment and administrative processes (to name but a few examples) are now run by algorithms and operate routinely on large amounts of digital data. As a result, in many cases, a transition to AI techniques requires merely a change in software rather than dramatically more costly and disruptive changes in specialised hardware. Furthermore, in cases where AI techniques require substantially higher computational resources than currently available, upgrades or virtualisation of general-purpose hardware components are far easier and cheaper to achieve than the earlier transition to algorithmic data processing and control. This means that there is now an increasingly low barrier to the first-time adoption of AI techniques, and an even lower barrier to subsequent transitions to more advanced techniques.

While most AI experts would agree that these four factors played an important role in the large increase in broad interest in AI, there are two further, perhaps more contentious factors at play. The first of these is directly related to the fact that many regard the present AI boom as mostly caused by fundamental advances in the area of multi-layer neural networks. While advances in neural networks - enabled by readily available, high-performance hardware (notably, GPUs), innovation in algorithms (both in terms of the neural network models themselves, as well as in the algorithms for training them) and large amounts of training data - have doubtlessly played a key role, the impact of these advances has been amplified by the fact that for at least two decades prior to 2011, neural networks were marginalised, and on many occasions outright dismissed, by large parts of the mainstream AI community. This led to a situation where relatively few researchers seriously worked on and with neural networks, a set of versatile AI techniques with a history dating back to the 1940s. As a result, progress in this area was likely artificially slowed, but poised to accelerate rapidly as soon as it became a major focus of attention. This brings us to the second additional factor at play, which is a combination of the inherent interest, especially among young researchers and the broader public, in biologically inspired techniques, such as neural networks, which are far more relatable than other, more abstract AI approaches, and the enormous publicity generated by companies that chose to invest into this "new wave of AI".

With this analysis of causes for the present AI boom in mind, we will now argue that this boom is different from previous peaks in interest in AI, in that it will likely have far broader and more lasting consequences. The last two factors - relatability and marketing of a specific set of techniques, and the penned-up impact and innovation potential of these techniques - fail to provide a compelling basis for this argument, and in fact could be seen as evidence to the contrary. The combination of the remaining four factors - advances in hardware, AI algorithms (broadly defined), markedly increased availability of data and general AI readiness in real-world application contexts - does, however, suggest that AI techniques have now reached a critical level of usefulness at which they can and do provide substantial value to industry and society, at relatively moderate cost and effort - in other words, in a rapidly increasing range of applications, they enable new and valuable products, services and experiences.

This now rapidly occurring, broad and accelerating valorisation of AI technology is what distinguishes the current boom from previous waves of interest in AI. The use of AI brings tangible competitive advantage in many sectors of industry; this advantage increases further with the power of the AI techniques that are being deployed successfully, which creates a powerful incentive for industry and society to invest into research and innovation in AI. It is for this reason that, while the enthusiasm for particular AI techniques or approaches, such as deep neural networks, will continue to wax and wane, the overall high level of interest in AI is here to stay. Because of their broad applicability, across all sectors of industry and society, and in light of their emergence as key enablers of scientific and technological progress, AI systems and techniques are poised to fundamentally transform the way we live and work (see, e.g., [70]).

## 4.2   The Biggest Risk Associated with AI

In much of the main-stream fictional depiction of AI and some of the contemporary debate on the topic, the focus is firmly on broad-spectrum, super-human AI turning antagonistic and causing harm - a scenario we may dub "strong AI going bad". While, in our opinion, this is a concern that deserves being taken seriously (for reasons beyond the scope of this section), it is by far not the most pressing risk associated with the development and use of AI technology. The main reason for this is that we are still quite far from being able to realise broad-spectrum, human-level or super-human AI.

Another commonly emphasised risk is that of a massive loss of jobs due to AI systems outright replacing human workers (see Chapter 4). This is doubtlessly a more pressing risk, since the increase in automation afforded by broad use of AI brings a large potential for eliminating, or at least much reducing, the need for human labour across an increasingly broad spectrum of occupations. However, it is possible that new kinds of occupations will in part make up for these effects, and that mechanisms for the fair distributions of the benefits derived from this kind of automation can further mitigate the inequities that may otherwise be caused by broad use of AI. Still, job loss caused by sharply accelerated, AI-enabled automation is a serious issue that needs to be addressed in the near future.

However, by far the biggest risk associated with the pervasive use of AI is of a very different nature, and requires no assumptions on further progress in AI technology: the risk of well-intentioned, yet incompetent use of weak AI - of the kind of AI systems and techniques available right now. This risk necessarily arises from the combination of three facts: one, that AI technology is complex and difficult to develop, deploy and maintain; two, that the highly specialised expertise required for effectively and responsibly developing, deploying and maintaining AI systems and techniques is relatively rare and difficult to acquire; and three, that the demand for this expertise far exceeds the supply. The last of these is what we call the talent bottleneck, since not only the number of competent AI developers and users is low compared to the demand for them, but also the number of those that with a moderate amount of additional training can reach the required level of expertise. The high demand for AI expertise is directly caused by the usefulness and rapidly increasingly scope for successful valorisation of the technology and can be expected to further increase, quite rapidly, for the foreseeable future.

The consequences of this bottleneck in talent and expertise are obvious: Increasingly, AI systems will be developed, deployed and maintained by people who are lacking the proper knowledge and experience. As a result, these systems and their use will be prone to malfunction and unintended side effects; they will cause problems which will often be difficult to detect before significant damage has occurred. This is of particular concern in situations that involve the use of complex machine learning techniques and large amounts of data in a black-box fashion, as is the case in most deep learning approaches. The degree to which even moderately complex software (and hardware) is difficult to design in a correct and robust fashion is evident from well-known examples of costly, and sometimes deadly, malfunctions, such as the MCAS system that caused the loss of two Boing 737 Max aircraft in late 2018 and early 2019 [71], and this difficulty is much more pronounced when dealing with even more complex AI systems (see, e.g., [72]). To make matters worse, the highly undesirable consequences of well-intentioned, underqualified use of weak AI will be particularly pronounced in areas where it is difficult or impossible to successfully compete for properly trained AI experts - notably, in the public sector and in non-profit organisations.

The most obvious way to address this talent bottleneck is to step up AI education. Currently, competent development and deployment of AI systems requires postgraduate, and in many cases PhD-level training specifically in AI, typically on the basis of a bachelor-level degree in computer science. There are much-needed efforts underway to expand these programmes, and to start suitably chosen components of AI education earlier, but the available and interested talent still forms a serious bottleneck. To address this, it is crucial to further develop the effectively accessible talent pool - first and foremost by taking measures to increase the participation of women, and secondly by tapping further into the enormous potential present in developing economies.

Clearly, stepping up education, in terms of improved and broadened educational offerings, an earlier start, and the development of AI-related professional occupations (e.g., related to the deployment, monitoring and maintenance of AI systems) is crucial in terms of addressing the talent bottleneck, but it will not close the gap between supply and demand of AI expertise, since current AI technology is simply too difficult to develop and use responsibly. Therefore, it is of crucial importance to lower the level of expertise required for effectively and responsibly working on and with AI systems, which brings us to the technical challenges that are at the core of this section.

### 4.3  Automating Artificial Intelligence

Within the last decade, there have been two revolutions in machine learning (ML), one of the most prominent areas of AI even prior to these developments. One of these, the (re-)emergence of neural networks as a dominant paradigm, has played out with great fanfare and substantial resonance far beyond the field of AI. The other has been quiet in comparison, and largely hidden from the eyes of the broader public, but is nonetheless at least as relevant: the birth and rise of the concept of *automated machine learning (AutoML)*.

AutoML is an approach that aims to automate a set of task associated with making effective use of ML methods and tools, including the choice of ML techniques and the settings of the hyperparameters that determine their performance in particular use cases (see, e.g., [73]). The concept arose, under that name, around 2013, and has rapidly gained traction in the machine learning community and beyond. From the very beginning, work in the area of AutoML has sought to not only help ML experts to obtain better performance from existing ML algorithms, but also to lower the threshold for the effective use of a broad range of ML techniques [74].

Interestingly, while programming can be understood as the principled automation of well-structured tasks, machine learning fundamentally concerns the automation of programming for tasks such as classification, regression and interaction with complex environments, and hence corresponds to the automation of automation. This explains in part why the rise of broadly applicable and successful machine learning techniques can be legitimately seen as a technological revolution. Under this view, AutoML takes automation to the next level, enabling an even higher degree of substitution of broadly and readily available computation for scarce and expensive human expert knowledge.

*AutoAI* is based on the same idea, applied to *all* of AI rather than just machine learning. This is extremely relevant, since firstly, contrary to widely held beliefs, there are other areas of AI that are remarkably successful in terms of real-world impact, including automated reasoning (which forms the basis for the design of all modern hardware, and is increasingly used for ensuring software correctness), optimisation (with a broad range of applications across industry and academia), and multi-agent systems (which play an increasingly crucial role in the automation of decision making in situations involving multiple actors or agents with possibly conflicting goals and preferences). Most AI experts are convinced that next-generation AI systems need to combine learning, reasoning and other techniques, in order to achieve robust performance and effective interaction with human users and stakeholders.

Concretely, AutoAI aims to automate critical aspects of the development, deployment and responsible operation of AI systems. This includes task such as selection of AI techniques and algorithms that are suitable in a given use context, optimisation of the performance of these algorithms for the data characteristic of that use context, and monitoring of the behaviour of AI systems after deployment, with the goal of detecting, and clearly signalling, when the operational conditions deviate far enough from those considered at the time of development and deployment to cause problems.

This gives rise to several technical challenges. Firstly, fully or partially automated selection of AI techniques and algorithms for a given use case is a daunting task, considering that many real-world problems do not easily map to a small set of well-know AI problems, and require non-trivial combinations of techniques to be tackled effectively. Furthermore, where mappings to existing problems (such as MIP) exist, these are often not unique, but rather admit a potentially very large range of encodings, the choice of which can have dramatic impact on the performance of standard algorithms for those problems. Secondly, while automatic performance optimisation techniques exist (see, e.g., [75]), these are far too limited to be applied broadly to AI systems with many design choices and parameters that can potentially impact performance. In particular, with very few exceptions (see, e.g., [76]), these general-purpose automated algorithm configurators are restricted to optimising a single performance objective, such as solution quality or running time, while in realistic scenarios, there is often a need to find good trade-offs between multiple, competing performance criteria, such as solution quality and resource consumption. Thirdly, broadly applicable techniques for monitoring the operation and performance of AI systems in relation to changes in the environment they operate in, and for signalling when these systems get "out of their depth", are largely unexplored; we refer to the automated combination of AI systems with such monitoring capabilities as *self-monitoring AI*.

At the same time, recent progress in AI techniques for algorithm selection, configuration and performance modelling provide a solid basis for work towards meeting these challenges, and hence for effective AutoAI methods and tools. It is important to realise that the goal of AutoAI, as we see it, is not full automation of the previously mentioned tasks, but rather effective support for the humans that tackle them, at various levels of expertise, ultimately substituting substantial amounts of costly and scarce human expertise with large amounts of readily available computation. At the same time, by automating key aspects of building, deploying and maintaining AI systems, AutoAI makes explicit the assumptions, practices and insights brought by human experts to these tasks, and thus not only renders these accessible to a broader range of developers and users, but also facilitates their critical assessment and improvement. Finally, by making it substantially easier to realise the performance potential inherent in AI algorithms and components in a broader range of specific application situations, AutoAI can be expected to make it possible to decrease the complexity of the systems and methods that need to be brought to bear to achieve desirable performance in many use cases.

## 4.4 The Way of the Future

The idea of machine intelligence has fascinated humankind for centuries; it is inextricably linked with the development of computing technology that, since the 1980s, has become the main driver for technological progress and innovation. The advanced computational methods developed in AI represent the next major step on this path. While interest in AI has shown several distinct peaks and troughs since the inception of the field in the 1950s, as we have argued in Sect. 4.1, there are good reasons to believe that the latest boom is of a different nature, as AI technologies have begun to rapidly change the way we design and use computation across all sectors of industry and society, and will thus bring about a lasting transformation in the way we live and work.

There is a rather high sensitivity to the risks associated with the development and use of AI technologies; unfortunately, as we have explained in Sect. 4.2, the most serious risk in the near and medium term is rarely recognised: the well-intentioned, yet incompetent use of weak AI systems, such as the ones we presently build and deploy, that is inevitably going to occur increasingly and on a large scale, especially in the public sector and non-profit organisations, as a result of the dearth of properly trained and qualified AI experts, in combination with the inherent complexity of current AI technology. This gives rise to the formidable challenge of enabling the effective and responsible design, deployment and maintenance of AI systems at significantly lower levels of expertise.

The technical direction for addressing this challenge we have outlined in Sect. 4.3 known as *AutoAI (automated AI)*, is based on the idea of harnessing AI techniques for the effective and responsible design, deployment and maintenance of AI systems. We have outlined several challenges for AI technology in this area, including the concept of self-monitoring AI, which permits the automated construction of AI systems that can detect and signal when they are no longer operating in a safe and effective fashion.

AutoAI can bring a broad range of benefits beyond alleviating the talent bottleneck; these include markedly increased performance and robustness of AI systems; substantial savings in the energy required for building and operating AI systems along with the associated costs of these systems; broader effective applicability and easier customisation of AI systems; reduced requirements for data; and broader access to AI technology (e.g., in the context of citizen science). AutoAI thus aims to facilitate work on and with AI systems across many levels of experience and expertise, from highly skilled specialists to technically adept laypersons.

Naturally, the concept of AutoAI brings its own challenges, which need to be addressed by research on this topic as well as in the way AutoAI technologies and tools are used. This includes the potential for creating even more complex AI systems that perform better, but end up being more opaque, less reliable and more difficult to use responsibly, as well as the potential acceleration of research and developments aimed at artificial general intelligence.

We are deeply convinced that AutoAI is the next logical step in the development of AI technology, with the potential to fundamentally transform the way we design, deploy and maintain AI systems. Of course, as is the case with present-day AI techniques and many other powerful technologies, AutoAI can be used in ways we find problematic, troubling or outright objectionable - in particular, for constructing AI systems whose use undermines human rights, freedom or dignity, or the fair and responsible use of critical resources. In our view, such objectionable uses include the development of AI that aims to replace, rather than augment, human intelligence. Therefore, it is of the utmost importance to complement work on the technological challenges associated with AutoAI with work on mechanisms, including regulation, that ensure responsible use. This requires skills beyond those required for the technical work on AutoAI (and AI in general), as well as political determination.

The way we develop and use AI will doubtlessly shape our future. The transformative power of AI technology can be readily glimpsed from recent applications, and will become more evident in the near future. AutoAI will further amplify this power, but developed and used judiciously, it will also allow us to better harness it not only for the benefit of relatively narrow segments of society, but also for the collective welfare of humankind, while avoiding many of the risks associated with the careless development and use of AI technology. It will thus play an important role in paving our way into the future - a future that much depends on our values, choices and determination.

# References

1. Muscettola, N., Nayak, P.P., Pell, B., Williams, B.C.: Remote agent: to boldly go where no AI system has gone before. Artif. Intell. **103**(1–2), 5–47 (1998)
2. Russakovsky, O., et al.: ImageNet large scale visual recognition challenge. Int. J. Comput. Vis. (IJCV) **115**(3), 211–252 (2015)
3. Gulshan, V., et al.: Development and validation of a deep learning algorithm for detection of diabetic retinopathy in retinal fundus photographs. JAMA **316**, 2402–2410 (2016)
4. Goodfellow, I., Bengio, Y., Courville, A.: Deep Learning. MIT Press, Cambridge (2016)
5. Gori, M., Campiani, G., Rossi, A., Setacci, C.: The web of clinical data. J. Cardiovasc. Surg. **23**, 717–718 (2014)
6. Melis, D.A., Jaakkola, T.: Towards robust interpretability with self-explaining neural networks. In: Advances in Neural Information Processing Systems, pp. 7775–7784 (2018)
7. Ioffe, S., Szegedy, C.: Batch normalization: accelerating deep network training by reducing internal covariate shift. arXiv preprint arXiv:1502.03167 (2015)
8. He, K., et al.: Deep residual learning for image recognition. CoRR abs/1512.03385, pp. 646–661 (2015)
9. Vaswani, A., et al.: Attention is all you need. In: Advances in Neural Information Processing Systems (2017)
10. Duchi, J., Hazan, E., Singer, Y.: Adaptive subgradient methods for online learning and stochastic optimization. J. Mach. Learn. Res. **12**(7), 2121–2159 (2011)
11. Alex, G.: Generating sequences with recurrent neural networks. arXiv preprint arXiv:1308.0850 (2013)
12. Kingma, D.P., Ba, J.: Adam: a method for stochastic optimization. arXiv preprint arXiv:1412.6980 (2014)
13. Canziani, A., Paszke, A., Culurciello, E.: An analysis of deep neural network models for practical applications. arXiv preprint arXiv:1605.07678 (2016)
14. Bianco, S., et al.: Benchmark analysis of representative deep neural network architectures. IEEE Access **6**, 64270–64277 (2018)
15. Devlin, J., et al.: Bert: pre-training of deep bidirectional transformers for language understanding. arXiv preprint arXiv:1810.04805 (2018)
16. Radford, A., et al.: Improving language understanding by generative pre-training, vol. 12 (2018)
17. Raffel, C., et al.: Exploring the limits of transfer learning with a unified text-to-text transformer. arXiv preprint arXiv:1910.10683 (2019)
18. Brown, T.B., et al.: Language models are few-shot learners. arXiv preprint arXiv:2005.14165 (2020)
19. He, K., et al.: Momentum contrast for unsupervised visual representation learning. In: Proceedings of the IEEE/CVF Conference on Computer Vision and Pattern Recognition (2020)
20. Misra, I., van der Maaten, L.: Self-supervised learning of pretext-invariant representations. In: Proceedings of the IEEE/CVF Conference on Computer Vision and Pattern Recognition (2020)
21. Chen, T., et al.: A simple framework for contrastive learning of visual representations. arXiv preprint arXiv:2002.05709 (2020)
22. Caron, M., et al.: Unsupervised learning of visual features by contrasting cluster assignments. arXiv preprint arXiv:2006.09882 (2020)
23. Tenorio, M.F., Wei-Tsih, L.: Self organizing neural networks for the identification problem. In: Advances in Neural Information Processing Systems (1989)

24. Zoph, B., Le, Q.V.: Neural architecture search with reinforcement learning. arXiv preprint arXiv:1611.01578 (2016)
25. Baker, B., et al.: Designing neural network architectures using reinforcement learning. arXiv preprint arXiv:1611.02167 (2016)
26. Zoph, B., et al.: Learning transferable architectures for scalable image recognition. CoRR abs/1707.07012. arXiv preprint arXiv:1707.07012 (2017)
27. Brock, A., et al.: Smash: one-shot model architecture search through hypernetworks. arXiv preprint arXiv:1708.05344 (2017)
28. Baker, B., et al.: Accelerating neural architecture search using performance prediction. arXiv preprint arXiv:1705.10823 (2017)
29. Elsken, T., Jan-Hendrik, M., Frank, H.: Simple and efficient architecture search for convolutional neural networks. arXiv preprint arXiv:1711.04528 (2017)
30. Pham, H., et al.: Efficient neural architecture search via parameter sharing. arXiv preprint arXiv:1802.03268 (2018)
31. Liu, H., Karen, S., Yiming, Y.: Darts: differentiable architecture search. arXiv preprint arXiv:1806.09055 (2018)
32. Erhan, D., et al.: Visualizing higher-layer features of a deep network. Univ. Montr. **1341**(3), 1 (2009)
33. Zeiler, M.D., Fergus, R.: Visualizing and understanding convolutional networks. In: Fleet, D., Pajdla, T., Schiele, B., Tuytelaars, T. (eds.) Computer Vision – ECCV 2014. ECCV 2014. Lecture Notes in Computer Science, vol. 8689. Springer, Cham (2014). https://doi.org/10.1007/978-3-319-10590-1_53
34. Xie, C., Wang, J., Zhang, Z., Ren, Z., Yuille, A.: Mitigating adversarial effects through randomization. In: International Conference on Learning Representations (2018)
35. Mahendran, A., Andrea, V.: Understanding deep image representations by inverting them. In: Proceedings of the IEEE Conference on Computer Vision and Pattern Recognition (2015)
36. Simonyan, K., Vedaldi, A., Zisserman, A.: Deep inside convolutional networks: visualising image classification models and saliency maps. arXiv preprint arXiv:1312.6034 (2013)
37. Ballard, D.H.: Modular learning in neural networks. In: AAAI (1987)
38. Badrinarayanan, V., Handa, A., Cipolla, R.: SegNet: a deep convolutional encoder-decoder architecture for robust semantic pixel-wise labelling. arXiv preprint arXiv:1505.07293 (2015)
39. Thomee, B., et al.: The new data and new challenges in multimedia research. CoRR abs/1503.01817 (2015)
40. Strehl, A., Joydeep, G.: Cluster ensembles—a knowledge reuse framework for combining multiple partitions. J. Mach. Learn. Res. **3**, 583–617 (2002)
41. Krizhevsky, A., Ilya, S., Hinton, G.E.: ImageNet classification with deep convolutional neural networks. In: Advances in Neural Information Processing Systems (2012)
42. Simonyan, K., Andrea, V., Andrew, Z.: Deep inside convolutional networks: visualising image classification models and saliency maps. In: Workshop at International Conference on Learning Representations (2014)
43. Szegedy, C., Vanhoucke, V., Ioffe, S., Shlens, J., Wojna, Z.: Rethinking the inception architecture for computer vision. CoRR, abs/1512.00567 (2015)
44. Montavon, G., Lapuschkin, S., Binder, A., Samek, W., Muller, K.-R.: Explaining nonlinear classification decisions with deep Taylor decomposition. Pattern Recognit. **65**, 211–222 (2017)
45. Szegedy, C., et al.: Intriguing properties of neural networks. arXiv preprint arXiv:1312.6199 (2013)

46. Folz, J., et al.: Adversarial defense based on structure-to-signal autoencoders. In: 2020 IEEE Winter Conference on Applications of Computer Vision (WACV). IEEE (2020)
47. Goodfellow, I.J., Shlens, J., Szegedy, C.: Explaining and harnessing adversarial examples. arXiv preprint arXiv:1412.6572 (2014)
48. Kurakin, A., Ian, G., Samy, B.: Adversarial examples in the physical world. arXiv preprint arXiv:1607.02533 (2016)
49. Carlini, N., David, W.: Towards evaluating the robustness of neural networks. In: 2017 IEEE Symposium on Security and Privacy (SP). IEEE (2017)
50. Yosinski, J., Clune, J., Nguyen, A., Fuchs, T., Lipson, H.: Understanding neural networks through deep visualization. arXiv preprint arXiv:1506.06579 (2015)
51. Simonyan, K., Vedaldi, A., Zisserman, A.: Deep inside convolutional networks: visualising image classification models and saliency maps. arXiv preprint arXiv:1312.6034 (2013)
52. Kumar, D., Taylor, G.W., Wong, A.: Opening the black box of financial ai with clear-trade: a class-enhanced attentive response approach for explaining and visualizing deep learning-driven stock market prediction. arXiv preprint arXiv:1709.01574 (2017)
53. Tishby, N., Zaslavsky, N.: Deep learning and the information bottleneck principle. In: 2015 IEEE Information Theory Workshop (ITW), pp. 1–5. IEEE (April 2015)
54. Zhang, C., Bengio, S., Hardt, M., Recht, B., Vinyals, O.: Understanding deep learning requires rethinking generalization. arXiv preprint arXiv:1611.03530 (2016)
55. Siddiqui, S.A., Mercier, D., Munir, M., Dengel, A., Ahmed, S.: Tsviz: demystification of deep learning models for time-series analysis. IEEE Access 7, 67027–67040 (2019)
56. Saad, E.W., Wunsch II, D.C.: Neural network explanation using inversion. Neural Netw. 20 (1), 78–93 (2007)
57. Andrews, R., Diederich, J., Tickle, A.B.: Survey and critique of techniques for extracting rules from trained artificial neural networks. Knowl.-Based Syst.8(6), 373–389 (1995)
58. Munir, M., Siddiqui, S.A., Küsters, F., Mercier, D., Dengel, A., Ahmed, S.: TSXplain: demystification of DNN decisions for time-series using natural language and statistical features. In: Tetko, I., Kůrková, V., Karpov, P., Theis, F. (eds.) Artificial Neural Networks and Machine Learning – ICANN 2019: Workshop and Special Sessions. ICANN 2019. Lecture Notes in Computer Science, vol. 11731. Springer, Cham (2019). https://doi.org/10.1007/978-3-030-30493-5_43
59. Davis, E., Marcus, G.: GPT-3, bloviator: OpenAI's language generator has no idea what it's talking about. MIT Technology Review (2020)
60. Etzioni, O., Li, M.: High-stakes AI decisions need to be automatically audited. WIRED (2019)
61. Weld, D., Bansal, G.: The challenge of crafting intelligible intelligence. Commun. ACM62 (6), 70–79 (2019)
62. Fichte, J.K., Hecher, M., Szeider, S.: A time leap challenge for SAT-solving. In: Simonis, H. (ed.) Principles and Practice of Constraint Programming. CP 2020. Lecture Notes in Computer Science, vol. 12333. Springer, Cham (2020). https://doi.org/10.1007/978-3-030-58475-7_16
63. Palacio, S., Folz, J., Dengel, A., Hees, J., Raue, F.: What do deep learning networks like to see?. In: Proceedings CVPR 2018 International Conference on Computer Vision and Pattern Recognition, Salt Lake City, Utah, USA (June 2018). https://arxiv.org/abs/1803.08337
64. Folz, J., Palacio, S., Hees, J., Dengel, A.: Adversarial defense based on structure-to-signal autoencoders. In: Proceedings WACV 2020, IEEE Winter Conference on Applications of Computer Vision, Aspen, Co, USA (March 2020). https://arxiv.org/abs/1803.07994
65. Floridi, L.: AI and its new winter: from myths to realities. Philos. Technol. 33, 1–3 (2020). https://doi.org/10.1007/s13347-020-00396-6

66. Shead, S.: Researchers: are we on the cusp of an 'AI winter'?BBC News (2020). https://www.bbc.com/news/technology-51064369. Accessed 27 Nov 2020

67. McKenney, P.E. (ed.): Is parallel programming hard, and, if so, what can you do about it? (2017). https://www.kernel.org/pub/linux/kernel/people/paulmck/perfbook/perfbook.2017.01.02a.pdf

68. Gleixner, A., et al.: MIPLIB 2017: data-driven compilation of the 6th mixed-integer programming library. Mathematical Programming Computation (2020). (accepted for publication)

69. Bixby, R.: A brief history of linear and mixed-integer programming computation. Documenta Mathematica, Extra Volume: Optimization Stories, pp. 107–121 (2012)

70. Daugherty, P.R., Wilson, H.J.: Human+Machine: Reimagining Work in the Age of AI. Harvard Business Press, Boston (2018)

71. Travis, G.: How the Boeing 737 Max Disaster looks to a Software Developer. IEEE Spectrum, Piscataway (2019)

72. Hand, D.J., Khan, S.: Validating and verifying AI systems. Patterns 1(3), 100037 (2020)

73. Hutter, F, Kotthoff, L, Vanschoren, J. (eds.): Automated Machine Learning: Methods, Systems, Challenges. Springer, Heidelberg (2019). https://doi.org/10.1007/978-3-030-05318-5

74. Thornton, C., Hutter, F., Hoos, H.H., Leyton-Brown, K.: Auto-WEKA: combined selection and hyperparameter optimization of classification algorithms. In: Proceedings of the 19th ACM SIGKDD International Conference on Knowledge Discovery and Data Mining, pp. 847–855 (2013)

75. Hoos, H.H.: Automated algorithm configuration and parameter tuning. In: Hamadi, Y., Monfroy, E., Saubion, F. (eds.) Autonomous Search. Springer, Heidelberg (2011). https://doi.org/10.1007/978-3-642-21434-9_3

76. Blot, A., Hoos, H.H., Jourdan, L., Kessaci-Marmion, M.É., Trautmann, H.: MO-ParamILS: a multi-objective automatic algorithm configuration framework. In: Festa, P., Sellmann, M., Vanschoren, J. (eds.) Learning and Intelligent Optimization. LION 2016. Lecture Notes in Computer Science, vol. 10079. Springer, Cham (2016). https://doi.org/10.1007/978-3-319-50349-3_3

# AI for Humanity: The Global Challenges

Jocelyn Maclure[1] and Stuart Russell[2(✉)]

[1] Université Laval, Quebec City, Canada
[2] University of California, Berkeley, USA
russell@berkeley.edu

**Abstract.** This chapter summarizes four global challenges for AI: health, education, the environment, and science. In each area, AI has enormous potential to enhance human well-being, yet very substantial obstacles remain in both basic research and global deployment. Beyond these four areas, we ask whether reliance on AI to solve our problems is a viable strategy for humanity.

**Keywords:** Artificial intelligence · Healthcare · Education · Environment · Science

## 1 What AI Can Do for Us

AI systems convert input data into decisions. The possible contexts of application vary widely, from email spam filtering to an autonomous rover exploring another planet. The likely contexts of application are those where human decision making would be tedious, slow, expensive, unpleasant, dangerous, ineffective, difficult, or even impossible; where the necessary input data and computational resources are available; and where automated decisions are of sufficient quality. A comprehensive analysis of the connections between AI and the UN sustainable development goals (SDGs) [33] identifies a vast range of potential areas of application for AI, as well as some drawbacks.

In this chapter we examine four global challenges: health, education, the environment, and science. At the GFAIH conference, presentations on these topics were given by Nicholas Ayache (Inria), Cristina Conati (University of British Columbia), Benjamin Combes (PwC), and Stephen Muggleton (Imperial College London), respectively. We are indebted to them for their insightful analyses, from which we drew inspiration in writing the corresponding sections of this paper.

For each of the four challenges, we ask whether the criteria for the useful application of AI are met. Establishing shortfalls in human decision making is the easy part—indeed, the SDGs are at least partly characterized by such shortfalls, both historical and contemporary. Data and computational resources are certainly easier to come by than in previous decades, but their lack still plays a significant role in some of the challenges. Finally, despite rapid progress in some areas of AI over the last decade, we find that there is still a great deal

Springer Nature Switzerland AG 2021
B. Braunschweig and M. Ghallab (Eds.): Reflections on Artificial Intelligence
for Humanity, LNAI 12600, pp. 116–126, 2021.
https://doi.org/10.1007/978-3-030-69128-8_8

of work to on core AI capabilities before the field can contribute significantly to solving these global challenges.

The long-term techno-utopian vision for AI is summed up in a statement attributed to Demis Hassabis, CEO of Google DeepMind: "Solve intelligence, and then use that to solve everything else." There is merit in this viewpoint. General-purpose, human-level AI[1] could be a tremendous asset to humanity. It could yield greatly accelerated progress in science and technology and would make possible a globally affluent yet sustainable economy. Just as, say, international air travel has become a service since the 1950s and instantaneous translation has become a service over the last decade, general-purpose AI would offer *everything as a service*.

Yet AI *per se* is not a silver bullet. In the near term, overconfidence in the capabilities of AI systems could lead to misallocation of resources and a failure to address the essentially human aspects of some of the problems we face, including short-termism, parochialism, market failures, and lack of coordination. In the longer term, the primary risks include overdependence on AI and the potential for loss of control. As is often the case with technology, failure to address the risks would lead to failure to realize the benefits.

## 2   Global Challenge: Health

Improving healthcare means very different things depending on one's starting point. Global inequality in healthcare is staggering. Less than half the global population has access to basic health services. The richest countries outspend the poorest by a factor of 500 in healthcare spending and doctors per capita. Put another way: 3 min in an Intensive Care Unit (ICU) in the United States would use up the entire annual healthcare budget for an inhabitant of the poorest countries; one typical Magnetic Resonance Imaging (MRI) scan would use up the annual budget for 130 people.

Thus, for most of the world, "improving" healthcare means having any healthcare at all. Sustainable Development Goal #3 asks us to "ensure healthy lives and promote well-being for all at all ages." Specific targets include reducing maternal, newborn, and child mortality; ending persistent epidemics of communicable diseases; reducing mortality from chronic diseases; and achieving universal health coverage.

The difficulties in applying AI in this context are significant, but the possible gains are enormous. In recent years, the spread of cell phone networks has made possible regular communication with and provision of health information to and from hundreds of millions of people previously cut off from access altogether. In

---

[1] There is no consensus on exactly to define this phrase, but we find it useful, nonetheless, as a hypothetical construct in discussing possible future developments. For the sake of argument, assume that such an entity could successfully carry out essentially any task that it would be reasonable to ask a human or collection of humans "skilled in the art" to carry out. It is likely, of course, that such machines would vastly exceed human capabilities in terms of scale and speed.

Bangladesh, for example, rapid gains in population health metrics have resulted from this basic functionality [14]. AI systems *per se* have not yet made a significant impact, but the potential is real. For example, machine learning systems can use low-cost cell-phone images, transmitted over a network, to diagnose diseases of the retina [10] and skin cancer [7]. More generally, AI systems can partially compensate for the massive shortage of trained medical personnel, guiding local carers and patients through the steps of diagnosis, treatment planning, and patient management. For example, every Rwandan citizen over the age of 12 with a cell phone currently has access to online medical consultations and case management that are partially AI-based [21]. AI systems in these contexts typically perform immediate, symptom-based interrogation, triage, and sometimes diagnosis. Much work remains to be done, however, to develop AI systems capable of managing complex, low-resource chronic care of an individual patient over a lifetime [17].

In well-resourced health systems, the bulk of the effort in medical AI has gone towards improving the quality of diagnosis and therapy, often aiming to augment the unassisted capabilities of human doctors [31] or to go beyond them in areas such as robotic surgery [27] and drug discovery [28].

It is commonly thought that the combination of deep learning and medical data is a match made in heaven. Surely, the argument goes, we can simply feed millions of electronic health records into a machine learning algorithm and it will figure out the best way to diagnose and treat any patient. There is an element of truth in this—indeed, we can feed millions of records into machine learning algorithms. Whether the algorithm learns anything of value is another matter. There are a few low-hanging fruits, where the problem is to analyze only a simple, decontextualized input such as a mammogram or a photograph of a potentially cancerous skin lesion. Even then, machine learning algorithms have proven quite fragile: for example, the skin cancer detection algorithm mentioned above [7] can be caused to change its diagnosis completely when the photograph is rotated by a few degrees [8]. For a patient in a trauma intensive care unit (ICU), there may be dozens of different sensors producing continuous streams of artifact-riddled data, potentially thousands of different asynchronous tests and drug administrations, various kinds of imaging data, notes made by medical staff at irregular intervals, perhaps a long medical history (much of it in textual form), and sundry information, some of it visual, about the incident that led to admission. It is rather unlikely that a machine learning algorithm that knows nothing of anatomy, physiology, infection, pharmacokinetics, or instrumentation can make head or tail of such data—not least because of the lack of uniformity in what data are available concerning any particular patient at any particular time.

An alternative to data-driven machine learning is *model-based* interpretation of data, using what is commonly called an e-patient or digital twin. Beginning in the 1960s, large-scale models of human physiology were constructed, consisting of interlinked systems of thousands of differential equations [11]. These models are capable of simulating a wide variety of phenomena quite accurately, ranging from the short-term effects of drinking a glass of water to the long-term effects of losing a kidney. More recent work represents model uncertainty explicitly, allowing the model to adapt automatically to data collected from an individual patient [6]. Imaging technology also allows the automatic construction of very detailed finite-element models of organs such as the heart, which can then be set into virtual motion by modeling the electrophysiology and circulatory system [2, 19]. Projects such as Physiome.org aim to collate and integrate models created by research groups all over the world into a single, coherent, multiscale model. In principle, such models can support the full range of inference and decision task including diagnosis, prognosis, ICU monitoring, therapy planning, patient management, and long-term self-care.

AI can contribute enormously to this effort by solving tasks such as representing the wide variety of physiological and medical knowledge within a semantically rigorous framework; correctly handling model uncertainty; adapting models to individual patients; training predictive and diagnostic models from heterogeneous patient data; inferring latent patient state variables; estimating the probability of different diagnostic hypotheses; and generating and executing complex, contingent treatment plans. The scale of these problems is quite daunting and, as is common with model-based approaches, the payoffs in terms of improved patient outcomes are far from immediate. Yet, because humans are, to a first approximation, the same all over the world, the upfront effort can be amortized over 8 billion beneficiaries.

Another important direction for research is the question of *objectives*: what, exactly, should health-related AI systems optimize? Clearly, a typical supervised learning objective such as "minimize diagnostic errors" is inappropriate: different errors may have vastly different costs, and subsequent decision making (if a sequential diagnose-then-treat approach even makes sense) requires a probability distribution over possible diagnoses. For decision about treatment, there are often trade-offs that depend on the preferences of the patient and perhaps also the patient's family members. Ethical standards, including those for informed consent, require that doctors take these preferences into account, yet AI systems presently have little understanding of the factors involved. Indeed, the field of medical ethics is still grappling with the question of how to respect preferences that change when an illness occurs or over the course of that illness.

# 3    Global Challenge: Education

SDG #4 focuses on education: "Ensure inclusive and equitable quality education and promote lifelong learning opportunities for all." Compared to healthcare, global inequities in education are somewhat less glaring—partly because our scientific understanding of how to educate effectively and our technology for doing so have changed so little in several thousand years. Nonetheless, access to high-quality education remains inequitably distributed, with more than half of children in the poorest countries having no access even to primary school.

At the same time, the standard method of instruction in all countries—classroom teaching with (typically) 20–40 students per class—is known to be ineffective. With one-on-one human tutoring, a typical student reaches a level two standard deviations above the average with conventional classroom instruction, i.e., at the 98th percentile [3]. Moreover, the variance in achievement for individually tutored students is much lower than for students in the classroom. The reasons are fairly obvious: the tutor can interact intensively with the student, adapting to the student's natural learning pace and style, responding to questions, and diagnosing misunderstandings quickly, whereas a classroom teacher is, with high probability, leaving most students either excruciatingly bored or hopelessly lost (or both).

Of course, one-on-one human tutoring is and always will be prohibitively expensive. The hope—which dates back to the 1960s [30]—is that intelligent tutoring systems can deliver a learning process comparable to one-on-one human tutoring at a fraction of the cost, while raising the ceiling on individual achievement. Moreover, with the wider availability of cellphones, this level of education could be delivered to a large fraction of currently underserved populations around the world. For example, the Global Learning XPRIZE competition, which started in 2014, offered $15 million for "open-source, scalable software that will enable children in developing countries to teach themselves basic reading, writing and arithmetic within 15 months."

Unfortunately, real progress has been a long time coming. The primary reasons are shortcomings in AI. Most tutoring systems rely on scripted interactions and multiple-choice test items. They do not understand the content of what they purport to teach, nor can they engage in two-way communication with their pupils through speech or text. (Imagine yourself teaching a subject you don't understand at all, such as string theory, to students who speak a language you don't understand at all, such as Pictish.) Recent progress in speech recognition means that automated tutors can, at last, communicate with pupils who are not yet fully literate.

Moreover, probabilistic reasoning technology can now keep track of what students know and don't know [34]. There are also some early attempts to gauge and perhaps increase student interest and motivation, although these quantities are somewhat amorphous and difficult to model accurately.

The core capabilities we need AI to deliver are reasoning about the subject matter; reasoning about the student's understanding and learning capabilities; devising suitable pedagogical steps and interventions; and communicating fluently with the student. These capabilities have been developing largely separately using different technological approaches. For example, reasoning about the subject matter, particularly for Science, Technology, Engineering, and Mathematics (STEM) disciplines, has been addressed successfully since the 1960s using the methods of symbol manipulation and formal logic [20,25,26]. These methods can also be used to generate new questions and derive near-miss answers for multiple-choice tests; in some cases they can diagnose student errors in great detail. In most cases, however, advanced methods for representation and reasoning exist mostly within research prototypes, while commercial systems largely rely on scripts and tend to model student knowledge as composed of atomic "elements" that are required in order to answer each question correctly, but about which the system itself has no understanding. Correcting this situation requires a large-scale knowledge engineering effort—one that may be impractical for companies trying to deliver tutoring systems on a tight budget and timeline, but also one that has a global payoff because the content of subjects such as mathematics and chemistry is essentially the same the world over.

Of the four core capabilities listed in the preceding paragraph, fluent communication is currently the weakest link. Most current efforts in the area of natural language understanding use the methods of deep learning with very large training sets, but these methods do not currently connect in a useful way to knowledge-based reasoning methods that are required if the system is to be able to understand student explanations and arguments and answer student questions accurately. In our view, increased attention to the development of natural language capabilities in the context of intelligent tutoring systems would be enormously beneficial both to the end-user population (i.e., most people on Earth) and to the natural language research community.

## 4   Global Challenge: Earth

Several researchers believe that the power of AI can be harnessed in the fight against climate change and help societies meet the United Nations' sustainable development goals [23,33]. The European High Level Expert Group on AI called for "sustainable and environmentally friendly AI." Microsoft launched its "AI for Earth" initiative in 2017, which offers grants to researchers and organizations and claims to put Microsoft cloud and AI tools "in the hands of those working to solve global environmental challenges." The nonprofit organization Climate Change AI (CCAI) was formed by "volunteers from academia and industry who believe that tackling climate change requires concerted societal action, in which machine learning can play an impactful role."

Two broad areas where AI can contribute are (1) modelling and prediction of weather and climate, and (2) optimization of human activities to reduce their negative environmental impact. In the first area, predictions have been made traditionally using physics-based finite-element models with many parameters, some of which are estimated empirically (either by global fitting methods or direct local measurement). AI offers at least two kinds of improvements. First, by combining physics-based with agent-based models, one can better predict the global socioeconomic consequences of climate change (e.g., migration, crop selection, energy production and use) which in turn affect the future evolution of the climate. Second, it is possible that machine learning algorithms trained on large datasets can produce more accurate predictions about the evolution of terrestrial and marine ecosystems under different conditions, since they are not required to make the simplifying assumptions used in finite-element models [22]. Current work aims to combine data-driven machine learning with physical constraints such as matter and energy conservation.

In the area of reducing humans' environmental impact, there are many routes through which AI can provide benefits [33]. These include better management of electric grids, optimized traffic and transit, energy saving in the construction and maintenance of buildings, more efficient supply chains with lower transportation costs, improved planning of tree felling and reforestation, early detection of illegal logging, and more efficient agriculture using less pesticides.

According to a report published by Microsoft in association with PwC, the application of AI levers and the adoption of a "wider technology infrastructure" could lead to a 4% global reduction greenhouse gas (GHG) emissions by 2030 [12].

Be that as it may, an honest assessment of AI's actual and potential contribution to sustainable development must factor in its current ecological footprint and contribution to global warming. The energy-intensive ICT sector is responsible for 2–4% of global GHG emissions, "on par with the aviation sector" [18]. This share will increase sharply in the next decade if nothing is done to improve efficiency. The energy required to store and transmit data, as well as to train artificial neural networks, is considerable. According to an oft-quoted study, training one single natural language processing algorithm with a deep learning model emits the equivalent of 626,000 pounds of carbon dioxide—an amount comparable to the carbon dioxide produced by five cars during their entire lifecycle [29]. Accordingly, the UN agency with responsibility for information and communication technologies (ITU) believes that compliance with the Paris Agreement will require the ICT sector to reduce greenhouse gas emissions by 45% before 2030.

The consumption by the ICT sector of rare earths and toxic metals and the accumulation of electrical and electronic waste ("e-waste") also have significant environmental costs, particularly in e-waste depots in developing countries in Africa and Asia. A much greater commitment to recycling by the ICT industry appears vital. Possibly, the use of advanced robotics in recycling could make this more economically attractive, but legislation may also be required.

On balance, it seems likely that AI will be able to make a positive contribution to the environment and climate change, even if it is far from the panacea that many hope for. Technological solutionism, of course, may divert our attention from the underlying coordination failure that is leading our species to commit environmental suicide. Indeed, some have argued that we should understand the fossil-fuel industry as an AI system—albeit one with human components—that is pursuing an incorrectly defined objective and is (so far) winning its conflict with the human race [13].

## 5 Global Challenge: Science

While it is theoretically possible that superintelligent AI programs will make scientific discoveries that are currently either out of reach or inconceivable for humans, it is a known fact that AI can make a substantial contribution to the advancement of scientific knowledge in every field.[2]

One of the most common applications of AI in science is in the interpretation of complex experimental data. As early as 1969, the Dendral expert system

---

[2] On the specifics of AI for social sciences and humanities, see Chap. 12.

helped researchers in identifying the chemical structure of organic compounds from data generated by mass spectroscopy [4]. Fifty years later, machine learning has become an essential tool in analyzing data from instruments such as the Large Hadron Collider, which produces up to 50 terabytes per second [1,5].

The process of actually forming new scientific theories has also been studied in AI. If we think of scientific knowledge as comprised of deterministic laws, then one seeks a new theory $Th$ that, together with existing knowledge $K$, explains the experimental data $E$. In logical terms, we wish to find $Th$ such that $K \wedge Th \models E$. This task can be approached with the technology of *inductive logic programming*, and this approach has been applied successfully to scientific discovery in several areas. When combined with methods for designing and executing experiments, it was able to support a "robot scientist" that carried out independent research in genomics [16].

Inductive logic programming was applied to the problem of predicting the pharmaceutical activity of molecules in the early 1990s [15], but the most prominent recent example involves the use of deep learning for the same task. Given a data set of molecules and their degree of antibacterial activity, a deep network was trained to predict the level of activity of over 100 million previously untested molecules in order to identify targets for further experimentation. One of these targets, dubbed *halicin* after the HAL 9000 computer in "2001: A Space Odyssey," turned out to have significant antibacterial properties when tested in mice [28]. As such, it may meet an urgent need for new drugs to counter the spread of antibiotic-resistant bacteria.

Looking further ahead, there are real possibilities for AI to change the way science is done. It ought to be possible, for example, to create an integrated repository of data and hypotheses about a subject—say, the molecular biology of the cell—in such a way that every new experimental finding can be added and its significance for every potentially relevant hypothesis can be analyzed automatically. (At present, of course, all scientific results are channeled through the text of scientific papers, where connections and inconsistencies can lie undetected for decades.) This suggests an approach based on explicit knowledge and inference rather than purely data-driven machine learning. This is perhaps not surprising: science operates by the accumulation of knowledge, and no scientist has direct access to the sensory experiences of all previous scientists.

# 6    Conclusion: Technical and Philosophical Challenges for AI

One general observation from the preceding sections is that neither pure knowledge-based approaches nor pure machine learning can solve the global challenges outlined in this chapter. It seems inevitable that a hybrid approach is required—at least until we have, if ever, general-purpose human-level AI— whereby human knowledge is combined with data and machine learning to produce high-quality outcomes. Thus, we expect the pendulum to swing back, away from the purely data-driven methods of the preceding decade and towards model-based systems with reasoning capabilities as well as learning capabilities. Fortunately, the engineering effort required to develop such systems can be amortized across the 8 billion people they would help. If successful, the resulting systems would truly be global goods.

There is a glaring omission from the descriptions of AI capabilities that are currently contributing to solving global challenges: we made almost no mention of *physical* capabilities. Agile, dexterous, perceptually robust robots could contribute enormously to solving global challenges in areas ranging from micro-surgery to large-scale construction. Recent progress in perception, navigation, locomotion, grasping, and manipulation holds out the promise that robots will soon move out of the factory into the real world. When faced with a real-world task such as building a hospital, however, these physical skills are not enough: algorithms and decision-making architectures for planning, coordination, and replanning in the face of the unexpected are still somewhat rudimentary. For most practical tasks, human expertise is still required to break down the problem into simple subtasks and to sequence the solutions appropriately, with plenty of hand-holding along the way.

We hope it is clear from these discussions that AI is still in a very fluid state. Misunderstandings about its capabilities are widespread. Unbridled pronouncements about where AI will be in the coming decades and about its impact on society and human nature make it hard to keep a cool head about the potential benefits and risks associated with progress in AI. Hype, inflated expectations, and technological messianism are all hardly unique to AI, of course. We have seen similar cycles play out for nanotechnology, blockchain, and CRISPR-Cas9—all marvelous advances for which anticipation far outran real capabilities. For example, with CRISPR-Cas9 the metaphor of "gene editing" was taken—perhaps unsurprisingly—far too literally in the media. When we edit a document, we can make exactly the changes we intend and turn it into exactly the document we want, and there it ends. When we "edit" a genome with CRISPR-Cas9, the changes we intend are not always the ones that occur, and there is the small matter of the mapping from genotype to phenotype: we don't know what effects a given edit may have on the resulting organism, and we don't know what edits to make to achieve a desired effect. None of this is a surprise to molecular biologists, who are well aware of the difficulty of making progress towards curing or preventing even a simple monogenetic disease.

There is no doubt that impressive and significant progress has been made in designing AI-based technological systems in the last decade. But human intelligence, like human biology, is an incredibly complex phenomenon. Designing computers that match or exceed the generality and flexibility of human cognition requires major conceptual breakthroughs whose nature and occurrence are hard to predict.

Even if we grant that progress in AI will eventually lead to general-purpose human-level AI—an assertion with which the vast majority of AI researchers agree, but which is challenged by some philosophers and computer scientists—

we are not necessarily out of the woods. In 1951, Alan Turing predicted that after such a development, "We should have to expect the machines to take control" [32]. Although there may be ways to avert such a fate [24], the task of maintaining power, forever, over entities more powerful than ourselves certainly qualifies, for those who share Turing's prediction, as a global challenge.

Whereas control over AI systems is primarily a technical challenge, avoiding *overdependence* on AI systems is a challenge for society as a whole, one amply illustrated by E. M. Forster's story *The Machine Stops*, written in 1909 [9]. Relying on AI to solve our problems and run civilization risks eliminating the incentive for successive generations of humans to acquire and augment the knowledge and skills accumulated by previous generations. Breaking the chain might prove irreversible.

# References

1. Albertsson, K., et al.: Machine learning in high energy physics community white paper. arXiv 1807.02876 (2019)
2. Ayache, N.: Towards a personalized computational patient. In: IMIA Yearbook of Medical Informatics. International Medical Informatics Association (2016)
3. Bloom, B.S.: The 2 sigma problem: the search for methods of group instruction as effective as one-to-one tutoring. Educ. Res. **13**, 4–16 (1984)
4. Buchanan, B.G., Sutherland, G.L., Feigenbaum, E.A.: Heuristic DENDRAL: a program for generating explanatory hypotheses in organic chemistry. In: Meltzer, B., Michie, D., Swann, M. (eds.) Machine Intelligence 4, pp. 209–254. Edinburgh University Press, Edinburgh (1969)
5. Carleo, G., et al.: Machine learning and the physical sciences. Rev. Mod. Phys. **91**, 045002 (2019)
6. Erol, Y.B., Russell, S.J., Sivaganesan, A., Manley, G.T.: Combined state and parameter estimation of human intracranial hemodynamics. In: Proceedings of the NeurIPS-13 Workshop on Machine Learning for Clinical Data Analysis and Healthcare (2013)
7. Esteva, A., et al.: Dermatologist-level classification of skin cancer with deep neural networks. Nature **542**, 115–118 (2017)
8. Finlayson, S.G., Bowers, J.D., Ito, J., Zittrain, J.L., Beam, A.L., Kohane, I.S.: Adversarial attacks on medical machine learning. Science **363**, 1287–1289 (2019)
9. Forster, E.M.: The Machine Stops. Sheba Blake (1909)
10. Gulshan, V., et al.: Development and validation of a deep learning algorithm for detection of diabetic retinopathy in retinal fundus photographs. J. Am. Med. Assoc. **316**, 2402–2410 (2016)
11. Guyton, A.C., Coleman, T.G., Granger, H.J.: Circulation: overall regulation. Ann. Rev. Phys. **34**, 13–41 (1972)
12. Herweijer, C., Combes, B., Gillham, J.: How AI can enable a sustainable future. PwC report (2018)
13. Hillis, D.: The first machine intelligences. In: Brockman, J. (ed.) Possible Minds: Twenty- Five Ways of Looking at AI. Penguin Press (2019)
14. Khatun, F., Heywood, A., Ray, P., Hanifi, S., Bhuiya, A., Liaw, S.T.: Determinants of readiness to adopt mhealth in a rural community of Bangladesh. Int. J. Med. Inform. **84**, 847–56 (2015)

15. King, R., Muggleton, S., Lewis, R., Sternberg, M.: Drug design by machine learning: the use of inductive logic programming to model the structure-activity relationships of trimethoprim analogues binding to dihydrofolate reductase. Proc. Natl. Acad. Sci. **89**, 11322–11326 (1992)
16. King, R.D., et al.: Functional genomic hypothesis generation and experimentation by a robot scientist. Nature **427**, 247–252 (2004)
17. Lewis, J., ray, P., Liaw, S.T.: Recent worldwide developments in eHealth and mHealth to more effectively manage cancer and other chronic diseases - a systematic review. In: IMIA Yearbook of Medical Informatics. International Medical Informatics Association (2016)
18. Marolla, C.: Information and Communication Technology for Sustainable Development. AISC, vol. 933. Springer, Singapore (2020). https://doi.org/10.1007/978-981-13-7166-0_9
19. Molléro, R., Pennec, X., Delingette, H., Garny, A., Ayache, N., Sermesant, M.: Multifidelity-CMA: a multifidelity approach for efficient personalisation of 3D cardiac electromechanical models. Biomech. Model. Mechanobiol. **17**(1), 285–300 (2017). https://doi.org/10.1007/s10237-017-0960-0
20. Novak, G.: Representations of knowledge in a program for solving physics problems. In: Proceedings of the Fifth International Joint Conference on Artificial Intelligence (1977)
21. Postelnicu, L.: Babylon inks 10-year partnership with Rwandan government. Mobi-Health News, March 4 (2020)
22. Reichstein, M., Camps-Valls, G., Stevens, B., Jung, M., Denzler, J., Carvalhais, N.: Prabhat: deep learning and process understanding for data-driven earth system science. Nature **566**, 195–204 (2019)
23. Rolnick, D., Donti, P.L., Kaack, L.H., et al.: Tackling climate change with machine learning. arXiv:1906.05433 (2019)
24. Russell, S.J.: Human Compatible. Penguin (2019)
25. Slagle, J.R.: A heuristic program that solves symbolic integration problems in freshman calculus. J. ACM **10**(4), 507–520 (1963)
26. Sleeman, D., Brown, J.S.: ITS 2020. LNCS, vol. 12149. Springer, Cham (2020). https://doi.org/10.1007/978-3-030-49663-0_9
27. Solis, M.: New frontiers in robotic surgery. IEEE Pulse, 51–55 (2016)
28. Stokes, J.M., et al.: A deep learning approach to antibiotic discovery. Cell **180**, 688–702 (2020)
29. Strubell, E., Ganesh, A., McCallum, A.: Energy and policy considerations for deep learning in NLP. arXiv 1906.02243 (2019)
30. Suppes, P., Morningstar, M.: Computer- assisted instruction. Science **166**, 343–50 (1969)
31. Topol, E.: Deep Medicine: How Artificial Intelligence Can Make Healthcare Human Again. Basic Books (2019)
32. Turing, A.: Can digital machines think?. BBC Third Programme. Typescript available at turingarchive.org, Radio broadcast (1951)
33. Vinuesa, R., et al.: The role of artificial intelligence in achieving the sustainable development goals. Nat. Commun. **11**, 233 (2020)
34. Yudelson, M.V., Koedinger, K.R., Gordon, G.J.: Individualized Bayesian knowledge tracing models. In: Lane, H.C., Yacef, K., Mostow, J., Pavlik, P. (eds.) AIED 2013. LNCS (LNAI), vol. 7926, pp. 171–180. Springer, Heidelberg (2013). https://doi.org/10.1007/978-3-642-39112-5_18

# AI and Constitutionalism: The Challenges Ahead

Carlo Casonato[✉]

Università di Trento, Trento, Italy
`carlo.casonato@unitn.it`

**Abstract.** The article aims to provide an overview of the principles of constitutionalism that can lead to a human-centersed AI. It deals with big data, privacy and consent, profiling, democratic pluralism and equality, providing a few examples of how AI can impact on them. On this basis, the article proposes a list of new 'human' rights, understood as the rights that humans are recognized as having, in order to promote a constitution-oriented and human-centered AI.

**Keywords:** Artificial intelligence · Law · Human rights · Constitutionalism · Comparative law

## 1  Introduction

There are several meanings of Constitutionalism [1–4]. Some authors focus on two traditions that deal, respectively, with mixed government and representative democracy, on the one hand (political constitutionalism), and with limitation of powers and guarantee of fundamental rights, on the other (legal constitutionalism) [5]. From their origin, in ancient Greek and Roman thought, the two traditions have evolved over the centuries to the present day, assuming richer meanings in order to face new forms of governments, diverse powers, and pluralistic democracies; and in order to develop more appropriate and effective individual and group rights. In this evolutionary process, the areas of development of the two traditions have come closer and the respective purposes have become blurred. As a result, it is not easy to identify a clear difference between them nowadays. In particular, it has become clear that, in order to avoid an authoritarian government and to seek truly representative democracy, it is necessary to separate and limit the powers (in all their new forms) and to guarantee fundamental rights (even in unprecedented areas). An effective synthesis of this complex formula may be seen in art. 16 of the French Declaration of Human and Civil Rights  of 26 August 1789, which states that: "Any society in which no provision is made for guaranteeing rights or for the separation of powers, has no Constitution".

AI can (and already does) have an impact on every aspect of constitutionalism, in whatever way it is intended. For this reason, I will consider a number of issues related to democracy, limitation of powers and human rights. In particular, I will deal first with big data, privacy and informed consent, monopolistic risk, democratic pluralism and political profiling. Secondly, I will examine the role of AI in making autonomous decisions; and finally, I will propose a number of new 'human' rights (understood as

B. Braunschweig and M. Ghallab (Eds.): Reflections on Artificial Intelligence
for Humanity, LNAI 12600, pp. 127–149, 2021.
https://doi.org/10.1007/978-3-030-69128-8_9

the rights to be recognized to humans before machines) which renew the traditional requests for protection of people against power (both public and private). In considering all these topics, I will make a few examples, aiming at answering what appears to be one of the key questions in the relationship between constitutionalism and AI: who or what (human or machine) should make the decision?

In order to properly frame the theme, it is important to highlight the fact that there is not just one AI, but many 'AIs'. Each of them has distinct features and scopes, and poses very different ethical and legal questions depending, for instance, on its embodiment (in a robot) or not, on the industry in which it operates, on the degree of technical development and so on [6, 7]. Of course, for instance, robot vacuum cleaners are different from large industrial robots used in car assembly lines; and both of them are very distant from military drones. AI devices are also very different depending on their functioning structure and logic, their degree of autonomy, their narrow or general scope and so on. It is important to stress the variability and plurality of AI because its relationship with constitutionalism is also multifaceted and depends on the specific characteristics of it. From this perspective, we can hardly speak about a single "AI Law": the legal principles designed for one model or industry will hardly be suitable for another, and different specific regulations have to be narrowly tailored depending on the specific characteristics of the kind of AI involved.

The article will nevertheless try to address some paradigmatic constitutional issues in the use of AI, paying particular attention to the most powerful functions of software-based AI (machine and deep learning) and to some of the most sensitive and delicate areas of application (such as political profiling, medicine and justice). It proposes a list of new 'human' rights, understood as the rights that humans are recognized as having, in order to promote a constitution-oriented and human-centered AI.

## 2   Big Data, Privacy and the Limits of Informed Consent

The global volume of data circulating in 2020 will reach 44 zettabytes, equivalent to 44 trillion gigabytes or, to give a slightly more understandable idea, to 8 billion times the information collected in the library of Congress in Washington [8, 9]. The quantity of the data, along with its exponential growth (plus 40% a year), must be linked with its quality. Our connections to the internet, combined with payments with credit and debit cards, contacts with the public administration, facial recognition in smart-cities, even channels we see on smart-televisions and all devices connected to the IoT, create an amount of personal and sensitive data which permits the profiling of, giving a few examples, political preferences, health status, pregnancy, cultural and economic level, sexual orientation, financial solvency, social risk, prediction of committing crimes and so on.

Due to the use of AI, in fact, an otherwise unmanageable amount of data can be quickly processed, in order to create a profile used to describe personal characteristics, to predict and even influence individual behaviours. This sort of profiling raises at least two kinds of problems related to, respectively, privacy and discrimination (see also Sects. 3 and 2 respectively).

The risk of a daily and deep intrusion into the most intimate spheres of any person has a clear and widespread impact on the right to privacy [10, 11]. In constitutional States, the main and most common tool for protecting privacy has been informed consent. Except for the prohibition against processing some particularly sensitive data, each person has been given the right to control the boundaries of his/her privacy, refusing or authorizing the disclosure of data. Over time, however, informed consent has proved ineffective in protecting the person on the Web; and it proves to be even more ineffective in reference to AI [12]. Speaking of limits and weaknesses of informed consent, two contexts can be briefly mentioned.

## 2.1 ICT and AI: A Consciously Misinformed Consent

ICT seems to be the ground where, paradigmatically, informed consent shows all its limits. Here, informed consent has experienced a radical change of meaning and purpose, moving from a privacy-protecting tool to a means that leads to the disclosure of any kind of personal data to any internet service provider. It is evident, for instance, that each of us accepts the contractual conditions of Apps for mobile phones or computers without even bothering to read them (blind consent) [13]. Informed consent, in short, is dead as a tool for guaranteeing privacy; it has become a mere fiction which, with our consciously mis-informed consent, exposes all of us to a daily profiling of all our dimensions, activities, and behaviours.

This problem is not effectively addressed at a national or European level. Regulation (EU) 2016/679 (GDPR: General Data Protection Regulation) still considers informed consent as the cornerstone of the protection of personal data, proving to be a useless tool against the potential abuses of AI in ICT [14, 15]. It is therefore urgent to further debate in order to find more adequate tools for the protection of personal data, and to reconcile the realm of AI-driven ICT with the basic principles of constitutionalism.

Of course, departing from informed consent is not easy: it implies a reconsideration of the entire structure of personal guarantee tools in ICT. And it impacts on the very core of the Western legal tradition, which is based on the liberal approach, where individuals, as moral agents, are free to control the boundaries of their rights, and even to waive them. These countries, by the way, acknowledge that in some areas the person alone is too weak to decide on her rights, necessitating the support of the State in order to reach a position of equality with other parties. A case in point is labour law, where, given the strength of big employers, employees are not entitled to consent for themselves on the conditions of their job and the State intervenes to protect them. In a similar way, internet users are too weak against internet service providers and they should be given supplementary support in order to be truly free to decide on their rights.

## 2.2 The Overestimation of Informed Consent in AI-Driven Medical Research

A second field where informed consent proves to be ineffective, but for reasons which are the opposite of the one set out in relation to ICT, is medical research driven by AI.

Especially when using genetic data or biological samples stored in biobanks or when studying rare diseases or now, the Coronavirus, contemporary medicine requires the treatment of an ever-increasing amount of health data. In this perspective, for instance, precision medicine is based on the possibility of processing and comparing as much clinical information belonging to as many patients as possible, in order to diagnose a disease and seek a possible therapy. In this logic, data collected in biobanks are a fundamental asset that should be maintained over time, also for future follow-ups, shared worldwide among all the researchers involved, used for studies whose purposes may not be directly connected with the project initially subscribed to or, as in the case of the Coronavirus, which may not have been even imaginable at the time of the acquisition of the original consent. Given these characteristics, informed consent, as originally designed for clinical trials, constitutes a serious obstacle to achieving reliable results and tends to be disproportionate compared to the possible benefits of researches done with AI.

Of course, informed consent cannot just be removed, but it has to be replaced by more proportionate and useful tools. Here again, it is necessary to open a debate on the opportunity to relax the informed consent requirement. A replacement of informed consent as required for each clinical study (ad hoc or fresh consent) with more flexible instruments such as broad, dynamic or open consent may be proposed; and also, a variable geometry consent may be considered. In all these systems, participants can decide to extend their first consent, for instance, to all clinical trials with the same outcomes or related to the same disease, or even to any clinical trials, on condition of a review by an ethical committee. An opting-out system preceded by appropriate general information and careful personal counselling may also be considered. In this case, unless otherwise noted, the consent is presumed to be valid for all clinical trials, also in the future.

In this way, it could be possible to move towards a different perspective and a new form of informed consent. Here, the information is given at the social level and consent is presumed, as a means to achieve a more effective clinical research and a higher level of health [16, 17][1]. In this system, of course, it should be necessary: to control and regulate pharmaceutical companies conducting the research; to guarantee, for instance, that the data are used just for medical progress, and not just for profit or economic speculation; and to maintain and reinforce ad hoc ethical committees in order to assure a thorough review of all the clinical trials. All these requirements, in fact, are essential to keep clinical research consistent with the protection of rights and the control of the powers (including economic powers) that characterize constitutionalism.

---

[1] This idea, previously proposed by the Human Rights Council of the United Nations, can be based on four conditions: (a) access by everyone to scientific knowledge and the benefits of science and its applications; (b) opportunities for all to contribute to the scientific enterprise and freedom needed for scientific research; (c) participation of individuals and communities in information and in decision-making; and (d) an enabling environment fostering the conservation, development and diffusion of science and technology: F. Shaheed, The right to benefit from scientific progress and its applications, Report of the Special Rapporteur in the field of cultural rights, UN, Human Rights Council, 20th session, 14 May 2012 (A/HRC/20/26): https://www.ohchr.org/EN/Issues/CulturalRights/Pages/benefitfromscientificprogress.aspx.

In each of these perspectives, anyway, a human-centered AI would be able to optimize the huge amount of clinical data in order to pave the way for reaching therapeutic benefits for us and for the generations to come [18].

# 3 The Risk of Monopoly Power

A second risk involved in AI is associated with the very limited number of companies that have the technical and financial ability to manage it [19]. We have already witnessed the emergence of a gigantic form of economic power, whose characteristics make it particularly elusive in front of the traditional constitutional forms of control and limitation: a power made even stronger by the ability to process, through AI, an incalculable and otherwise uncontrollable mass of data. A difficult challenge for contemporary constitutionalism, therefore, is precisely extending its latitude well beyond the three classic branches of state power (legislature, executive, judiciary) in order to deploy effective forms of control tailored to a power that concretely risks becoming the new sovereign, the new Leviathan [20].

In short, it is important to continue on the abovementioned path of Constitutionalism and take it one step further. After the King, Judges and the Parliament, after the amending power and, perhaps, even the constituent power [21], Constitutional law must turn its attention towards those who have the financial and technological means to collect and process an asset (big data) so precious as to be compared to the 'new oil' or new 'gold' [22, 23].

In these terms, controlling and limiting the biggest AI companies is a part of the more general attempt to rule on economic factors and their actors. A regulation of the AI players shares and even expands the magnitude of the difficulties already experienced by the law in trying to rule on 20th Century capitalistic powers [24]; powers that are not easy to locate or to attack with traditional legal means. But the vigour of the economy in dictating its rules to the law, rather than being constrained by it, must not distract from the need to renew and strengthen constitutionalism's original inclination towards a real and effective limitation of all powers and an effective protection of rights [25]. In this perspective, the Digital Service Act, proposed by the European Commission at the beginning of 2020, seems aimed at limiting the economic and political dominance of the new platforms, defined verbally as the new gatekeepers [26].

# 4 Political Profiling and the Bubble Democracy

The aforementioned threats to privacy and risk of monopoly are in themselves pressure factors for any democracy and for the freedom of expression and pluralism that substantiate it.

A specific risk triggered by AI is represented by political profiling and by its weakening and undermining effects on political pluralism. Profiling, in short, allows singling out individuals' political preferences and targeting them with a propaganda narrowly tailored to their opinions. Therefore, voters, especially younger voters, are exposed to the risk of thinking that what they see in the social represents the reality as a whole, while instead it is only a part of it – a part specifically built by AI in their image and likeness, so to speak. The risk of this action is that citizens live, from a political point of view, in what we can call a bubble democracy.

In more specific terms, the increasing computational capacity and the abovementioned escalation in the quantity and quality of data available today pave the way for expanding the usual market-related profiling to the territories of political orientations. As with internet advertising, in which people are increasingly offered items corresponding to their tastes, also for political and electoral information, the risk is that the person will be exposed to very limited information specifically custom-made on the basis of her profiled preferences.

This phenomenon presents three specific critical points.

It can happen, first of all, that the recipients of the information are not aware of the limited and very partial nature of what is sent to them. It can also happen that they trust the received data, assuming their objectivity, comprehensiveness and neutrality. Given the non-transparency of the internal steps of AI (the black box problem), secondly, a control procedure on the reliability of the information is almost impossible. In this sense, for instance, the phenomenon of AI-generated fake news is difficult to tackle. In more general terms, thirdly, the pluralistic structure of information and the sources of that information are strained and the free marketplace of ideas which supports any plural political competition is weakened and deteriorated. As a result, the circuit of political responsibility and, ultimately, the very core of democratic logic is in danger [27].

To conclude on this point, the uncontrolled use of AI in terms of information and political propaganda risks imposing a model of bubble democracy, in which citizens, especially as voters, are confined within increasingly closed and self-referential systems. This situation leads them to consider their own ideas as the only decent, plausible and reasonable ones. The isolation from other opinions, in turn, prevents a real and plural dialogue between different ideas, heading for a social and political involution in terms of fragmentation, polarization and increasing radicalization. Here again, it is necessary to develop critical thinking that is capable of directing the use of AI towards enhancing diversity and plural dialogue, in order to maintain and reinforce a true pluralistic democracy [28, 29]: human-cantered AI strictly connects with constitution-oriented AI.

## 5    AI and Equality

AI has a complex and multifaceted impact on the principle of equality, and therefore on an essential component of contemporary constitutionalism, with both positive and negative outcomes (see also Sect. 2). In general terms, a vast literature has already covered a number of issues, showing how big data and algorithms may have the effect of not just reproducing but also reinforcing and amplifying inequality [30–32]. Considering this risk, the 2018 Declaration on Ethics and Protection in Artificial

Intelligence issued by the Brussels International Conference of Data Protection and Privacy Commissioners has set the objective of reducing discrimination through: "a. ensuring the respect of international legal instruments on human rights and non-discrimination, b. investing in research into technical ways to identify, address and mitigate biases, c. taking reasonable steps to ensure the personal data and information used in automated decision making is accurate, up-to-date and as complete as possible, and d. elaborating specific guidance and principles in addressing biases and discrimination" [33].

Limiting myself here to just a few areas, I will briefly consider the potential impacts of AI on the workforce and the job market, justice and medicine.

## 5.1 Workforce and Job Market

The impact of AI on the global economy and, particularly, on the job market is a vast topic, analysed already in depth by many scholars (see S 4). Three dynamics can be summarized here Chapter in this book on Role of ethical charters in building international AI framework [34, 35].

Firstly, experts are expecting an initial negative balance compared to the total number of jobs. On the one hand, there will be an initial loss of jobs (at least 10%), affecting, mainly, the most repetitive, boring or risky jobs. Secondly, compared with this trend, new professional skills will be needed and therefore created. Think of data mining, machine learning and deep learning programming and control, and generally speaking, AI designers. Thirdly, many other jobs, maybe all of them, will experience a radical change; for sure: medicine, engineering, finance, transport, telecommunications, but also agriculture, and, according to some authors, creative and artistic jobs as well. AI, it is believed, will benefit them in terms of speed, accuracy, overall efficiency and productivity [36]. A proper use of AI, moreover, may free people of tiring or dangerous jobs: "More AI may easily mean more human life spent more intelligently" [37].

Adjustments like these are certainly not new in the job system: each of the three, or four depending on the opinions, industrial revolutions, for instance, has experienced this kind of changes, with the resulting problems in terms of imbalances and inequality. Nonetheless, a peculiar problem of AI revolution concerns the speed of the change. AI itself, and AI societies, are evolving very quickly, and it will be virtually impossible to convert workers from regular occupations to highly specialized ones such as AI–related jobs. Professional retraining will be very difficult, if not utterly impracticable, with the consequence of leaving a large number of workers unemployed.

A second problem directly related to equality is the potential for distortion in terms of "AI divide". Countries that can show the political will and the technological and financial capacity to invest in AI might see an economic growth of 20 or 25%, or even more, according to many studies. On the contrary, States where the political will and investment policies will not be as forward-looking and dynamic, or where there are insufficient funds for advanced research and development policies, will suffer a severe crisis in the job market and, consequently, at an overall social level.

Moreover, also in states where AI will thrive, there is the risk that economic growth will not benefit the population in general, but a very tiny social tier, typically the already more fortunate and richer one[2].

Looking at these perspectives, it will be crucial to limit the digital and AI divide as much as possible [38], so that AI becomes a lever for increasing equality and promoting a better wealth redistribution, and not a source of new discrimination. In particular, it will be critical to fill the gap between "AI-friendly" countries and states that are not AI-friendly. Otherwise, so-called developing countries, for instance, will be doomed and global inequalities will affect the entire world causing unavoidable imbalances and deranging dynamics: the risk is to have a more unstable and endangered world than it already is today.

## 5.2    Justice

A vast literature also covers the use of AI in justice [39, 40]. In general terms, the issues considered range from the examination of very complex contractual clauses, to the selection, within big legal databases, of the most appropriate and useful precedents that can be relevant in the case; from predicting the possible outcomes of the trial and the rate of success of the case (predictive justice) [42, 43], to assessing the social risk of people being investigated or convicted, calculating the probability of them committing new crimes in the following years.

Looking at predictive justice, for instance, it is well known that many law firms, not only in the United States, use AI for assessing and predicting the success rates of cases before one court compared to another. On the other hand, it is worth mentioning that France has expressly banned such a procedure. Considering emerging litigation analytics and predictive justice unethical and distortive, the French Parliament has prohibited the publication of statistical information about judges' decisions, setting a particularly heavy penalty (a maximum of five years in prison) for anyone who breaks the new law. Thus, art. 33 of the 2019 Justice Reform Act states that "The identity data of magistrates and members of the registry may not be re-used for the purpose or effect of evaluating, analysing, comparing or predicting their real or supposed professional practices"[3].

---

[2] Global data are not encouraging from this point of view. In 2017, 82% of the wealth went to just 1% of the population, while 50% of the poorer population did not benefit from any increase. Regarding 2018, "Wealth is becoming even more concentrated – in 2018: just 26 people owned the same as the 3.8 billion people who make up the poorest half of humanity, down from 43 people the year before": OXFAM (2019), Public good or private wealth?, Oxford. In 2019, "the world's billionaires, only 2,153 people, had more wealth than 4.6 billion people. This great divide is based on a flawed and sexist economic system": OXFAM (2020), Time to care. Unpaid and underpaid care work and the global inequality crisis (https://www.oxfam.org/en/research/time-care).

[3] Loi n° 2019–222 du 23 mars 2019 de programmation 2018–2022 et de réforme pour la justice. The French version of the section states as follows: "Les données d'identité des magistrats et des membres du greffe ne peuvent faire l'objet d'une réutilisation ayant pour objet ou pour effet d'évaluer, d'analyser, de comparer ou de prédire leurs pratiques professionnelles réelles ou supposées.".

Another disputed use of AI in the area of justice aims at calculating the likelihood of investigated or convicted persons committing a future crime. There are programs designed for assessing the risk of recidivism, based on a number of factors such as parents' or caretakers' behaviour, family status, friends, alcohol or drug abuse, stability of residence, social environment, education, work, leisure time and so on. Even though the programs are usually designed for evaluating rehabilitation needs, they are also used for a pre-trial release, parole or even sentencing.

Two issues, in particular, are highly debated: the reliability of this kind of mechanisms, and their consistency with constitutional principles such as due process.

On the first issue, the literature is divided. Most articles, on the one hand, argue that the results are discriminatory based on factors such as race and ethnicity. A well-known study published by ProPublica in 2016, for instance, showed that the algorithm ordinarily used correctly predicts recidivism 61% of the time. Nevertheless, African-Americans are almost twice as likely as whites to be labelled a higher risk but not actually re-offend. The programs make the opposite mistake among whites, who are more likely to be considered lower risk but go on to commit other crimes [44]. Other articles reach similar conclusions arguing that the deep learning usually employed in criminal justice is basically biased, not only because of errors in training data [45] and run the risk of turning correlations into causations [46–48][4]. This kind of calculation, moreover, is clearly heading dangerously towards the self-fulfilling prophecy phenomenon [49].

Other articles, on the other hand, show that AI can be of some use in deciding the destiny of inmates. Research published in 2017 suggests that the use of AI may help when deciding where defendants will await trail, at home or in jail, predicting the legal or illegal behaviour of the defendant [50]. The researchers were fully aware of the incompleteness of the research and expressly recognized that they examined just a few variables and other imperfections of their study. Although the research is not final, "results suggest some usefulness of AI: a policy simulation shows crime can be reduced by up to 24.8% with no change in jailing rates, or jail populations can be reduced by 42.0% with no increase in crime rates. Moreover, we see reductions in all categories of crime, including violent ones. Importantly, such gains can be achieved while also significantly reducing the percentage of African-Americans and Hispanics in jail". Accordingly, a properly built algorithm might reduce crime and jail populations while simultaneously reducing racial disparities. Technological improvements and careful AI design, following this logic, could reduce the risks of discrimination and violation of the principle of equality [51].

The second issue mentioned when considering the use of AI in predicting recidivism, and in sentencing in general, is its overall compliance with constitutional principles such as the due process clause. In a well know case, the US Supreme Court

---

[4] "Correctional Offender Management Profiling for Alternative Sanctions (COMPAS), developed by the company Equivant in 1998, is an algorithm widely used in the United States to make predictions about a defendant's recidivism risk. COMPAS consists of a 137-item questionnaire which takes note of the defendant's personal information (such as sex, age, and criminal record) and uses this information to make its predictions. Race is not an item on this survey, but several other items that can be correlated with race are included in the COMPAS risk assessment.

denied the writ of certiorari of a decision issued by the Supreme Court of Wisconsin (State v. Loomis) [52]. Here the State Court held that the use of a risk assessment tool at sentencing (COMPAS) did not violate the due process rights to be sentenced individually, because the judge had the last word, and using accurate information, because the defendant had a right to verify the inputs to the algorithm for correctness. This decision has been criticised for a number of reasons, including the fact that the internal mechanism of COMPAS remained non-transparent, and that even though the source code was hardly expressly discriminatory, the algorithm could achieve biased results by placing a high weight on variables that are proxies for race, such as ZIP code [53]. Considering the (only) alleged accuracy and neutrality of AI, moreover, the decision would be 'captured' by the machines, leaving in reality little room for judges' discretion. The result of this trend may also drive towards levelling justice advancements: to a 'sheep effect' encouraging conformism and "calling for more independence for judges who feel they have to go against the tide, that is, who simply want to do their job" [54].

Following a different rationale, the Italian Supreme Administrative Court (Consiglio di Stato) ruled that transparency warrants the ability to get a thorough explanation as to the algorithm's so-called "technical formula" and the "underlying legal rules". If access to the source code is not always needed, an explanation of its function is required [55]. A lower Administrative Court has also held that administrative procedures cannot be exclusively handled by algorithms, as the human judgement cannot be replaced by AI [56].

## 5.3   Health and Medicine

The advantages of AI in medicine are well known. In many areas, from robotic surgery to clinical trials, from diagnostics to prosthetics, from the care of the elderly or autistic children to scans and examining images, AI provides speed and accuracy, valuable tools in supporting and improving individual and collective health [57]. It is not surprising that a vast literature has developed in the field[5].

In this field, AI also can help pursue, with great determination and very good results, equity in access to health care and overall higher levels of health and wellbeing. And if equality means not only treating homogeneous categories equally, but also giving more to those who need it most, AI can offer a series of advantages. In urgent or complex cases, for instance, algorithms can expedite diagnosis, comparing simultaneously and with greater accuracy than any doctor thousands of CT and MRI scans and images. In this way, it not only allows more efficient treatments, but can also make patients flow faster and more efficiently in ER, for example [58, 59]. AI is also being used extensively to support the fight against COVID-19 pandemic. As one of the tools of bioinformatics, it speeds up medical research and the finding for a cure and a vaccine; processing lungs scans, it is very useful in assisting healthcare personnel in making faster and more accurate diagnoses; it is a driving force for knowledge sharing,

---

[5] Just to give an example, the journal Artificial Intelligence in Medicine has been published for more than 30 years now, since 1989.

allowing to screen the thousands of research papers published worldwide on the pandemic; and it is also used to observe and predict the evolution of the pandemic [60].

In addition, as far as surgery is concerned, robots equipped with AI, may perform complicated laparoscopic procedures, ensuring greater precision, less bleeding and post-operative pain than traditional techniques [61].

Alongside the advantages in this kind of AI use, some risks have been observed related to the (usual) lack of transparency (the black box problem), potential bias in designing the algorithms, possible breach of security and disclosure of medical and health data, and overall reliability [62]. In using AI - legitimately - to help hospitals and insurance companies identify which patients will benefit from "high-risk care management" programs, for instance, the algorithm's designers used previous patients' health care spending as a proxy for medical needs. This apparently neutral benchmark turned out to be highly discriminatory: because the tool was designed to predict the cost of care as a proxy for health needs, African-American patients with the same risk score as white patients tended to be much sicker, because providers spend much less on their care overall. The result is that African-American patients usually receive lower risk scores[6].

This example, along with others, shows the sensitive and delicate nature of designing AI devices, particularly machine and deep learning. Even the most honest and legitimate intentions, in fact, can conceal dangerous side effects in terms of inequality. From this point of view, it is necessary for programmers to have interdisciplinary training, paying close attention to the possible legal and social consequences of their activity; or, more precisely, for experts from different areas (ethics, law, sociology, etc.) to support or work together with programmers. Designing AI is not only a technical activity, but, by its very nature, it is a very important activity from an ethical, legal and social point of view.

Supporting doctors in their relationship with patients is another use of AI worth mentioning. Here, AI is seen by some as a means to free doctors from bureaucracy and routine, allowing them to gain time for training, contact with patients and empathy [66]. Others doubt this perspective and, based on economic and institutional factors, indicate the risk of the de-professionalization, deskilling and de-humanization of doctors. In particular, a further erosion of therapeutic relationships and a threat to professional and patient satisfaction is predicted [67]. In any case, it has now been confirmed that time for empathy and communication is an essential part of care, and that the doctor-patient relationship is also made up of trust[7] – can a machine ever build empathic relationships or deserve trust?

A third debated use of AI, relevant for equality, is not limited to the treatment of illness or disability, but might also affect human empowerment. The issue is very broad, and here I will just mention that, in time, artificial enhancing of physical or

---

[6] This care risk-prediction algorithm is used on more than 200 million people in the U.S. [63–65].

[7] It is significant that the Italian law explicitly mentions a trust-based relationship: "The relationship of care and trust between patient and physician, based on informed consent in which the patient's decision-making autonomy meets the competence, professional autonomy and responsibility of the physician, is promoted and valued" (art. 1 par. 2). Besides, the law states that "Communication time between doctor and patient constitutes treatment time" (art. 1 par. 8) [68].

cognitive performance will raise equality issues, ranging from those traditionally linked to the use of doping in sport, for instance, to the more complex ones related to transhumanism [69, 70].

## 6  The Central Issue: Evaluation and Decision

AI can affect a number of sectors, both in terms of potential and risks. For this reason, what is needed is a human-centered AI or, in legal terms, a Constitution-oriented AI.

Among the complex and diverse issues raised, however, one seems to me to be particularly important: the irreplaceability of human decision with an artificial one[8]. Here, I will deal briefly with the human decision in paradigmatic terms, and I will exemplify my point with references to medicine and justice. In these areas, as in others such as transportation, finance, police or war scenarios, agriculture, climate change and so on, there is broad agreement on the utility of AI in supporting us; on the other hand, there is disagreement on the possibility that AI can replace the human decision.

For some scholars, like Nobel Memorial Prize winner Daniel Kahneman, the main characteristic of humans is that they are very noisy; accordingly, human evaluations and decisions are irreparably biased. For instance, it would not be possible for us to take any truly rational choice, because the (false) logical reasons for achieving it would be artificially created only after we had already decided the direction to give to our will, for reasons which in reality make little or no sense [71]. From this point of view, a statistical model predicting what humans decide would be more accurate than the people themselves: "people are very noisy, and the model, which is less noisy, can be more accurate than they are" [72].

For example, a judge may be too tired or lazy or nervous to thoroughly analyse the data of a case and the parties' arguments and counterarguments [73]. His choice would in reality be biased by an illogical noise, and only later, covered with fabricated reasons. Likewise, a doctor would not have the expertise to understand the numerous data in an MRI or CT, and would base the diagnosis on his limited personal experience. Accordingly, a total replacement of human decisions with artificial ones has been proposed: AI would make better choices for humans because it would be noise-free[9].

Compared to this approach, a large number of experts believe that human intelligence can be usefully assisted, but not replaced, by AI. This position, which I personally find much more convincing, is based on many wide-ranging reasons that intertwine relevant constitutional principles. They can be considered from both a technical (solvable in time) and anthropological (lasting in time) perspective.

---

[8] See also Chapter 5 in this book.

[9] "The robot will be much better at statistical reasoning and less enamored with stories and narratives than people are. The other is that the robot would have much higher emotional intelligence. And the third is that the robot would be wiser. Wisdom is breadth. Wisdom is not having a narrow view; that's the essence of wisdom. It's broad framing, and a robot will be endowed with broad framing" [71].

## 6.1   The Technical Arguments

I see three technical reasons for maintaining the "human in the loop".

From a first point of view (i), it is well known that AI is unsurpassable in performing certain specific functions (weak AI), while it is very far from replicating overall human skilfulness and flexibility (strong AI). On the one hand, AlphaGo Master has beaten the world champion of Go; on the other hand, it would be very complicated and energy-consuming for a robot to grab an object thrown to it, as a five-year-old child can instinctively do, or to tie a pair of shoes. In addition, even when performing specific tasks such as face or image recognition, AI systems have been proven to make mistakes that would be evident to anybody [74, 75] And an article significantly titled The Elephant in the Room, has shown how the overall context significantly affects image recognition, creating the conditions for a not so small number of errors [76].

Secondly (ii), it is possible to doubt that AI is more neutral and objective and accurate than the human reasoning which, in any case, is behind its design, programming and processing. The choice of the internal mechanisms and the training data, or the selection of features and labels, for example, are human decisions [77]. In this logic, AI reasoning, both in input and processing, is heavily influenced upstream by human thought and decision, and, consequently, by human variability, inconsistency and discretion. Besides, a general reference to Kurt Gödel's incompleteness theorems led to the claim that even AI would develop statements which can neither be proved nor disproved: "Machine learning has matured as a mathematical discipline and now joins the many subfields of mathematics that deal with the burden of unprovability and the unease that comes with it" [78, 79].

Thirdly (iii), the mentioned black box problem is a strong obstacle, of a technical nature again, to tracing the steps that allow the machine to produce an autonomous result: if the final output of the procedure is known, the processing that generated it is not [80].[10] This issue produces a number of problems. It is not possible, for instance, to verify the accuracy and congruity of the steps carried out and therefore the correctness of the internal activity at the basis of the decision: this is a first problem linked to the experimental check and validation of machine and deep learning systems[11]. Another big issue is the lack of transparency of such delicate and sensitive decisions as judicial and medical ones [83]. A general constitutional principle states that all judgments must be based on clear and coherent reasoning[12]. The black box phenomenon, impeding the transparency of the ratio decidendi, is therefore a great problem for the legitimacy of

---

[10] "It is impossible to understand how exactly AlphaGo managed to beat the human Go World champion" [81].

[11] See, for instance, the suspension of a test in which two chatbots began to communicate in an unintelligible language: Facebook's artificial intelligence robots shut down after they start talking to each other in their own language: "The bizarre discussions came as Facebook challenged its chatbots to try and negotiate with each other over a trade, attempting to swap hats, balls and books, each of which were given a certain value. But they quickly broke down as the robots appeared to chant at each other in a language that they each understood but which appears mostly incomprehensible to humans" [82].

[12] Art. 111 of the Italian Constitution, for instance, reads as follows: "All judicial decisions shall include a statement of reasons".

any AI-driven judgment. And in the same way, difficult medical decisions such as priority in surgical operations, access to ICU or triage in ER, need to be based on solid and transparent reasoning. From this point of view, the opacity inherent in machine and deep learning systems calls into question the overall legitimacy and social recognition of the functions performed [84]. Another critical consequence of the black box phenomenon deals with the identification of who (or what) is to be considered in charge of the performed function. Uncertainty about internal steps hinders the attribution of responsibility for the decision, which could be alternatively given to the manufacturer, the programmer, the user, the owner or the machine itself. In case of damage or crime linked to an AI use, therefore, it would be very difficult to attribute civil or criminal liability [85].

Against these three technical objections to the replaceability approach, one could argue that over time the means will be found to prevail on the AI limits (i), to overcome its non-neutrality (ii) and opacity (iii).

Indeed, the speed of AI progress has been proven very fast; advances in new computing paradigms may also accelerate this trend. It is possible, first, that researchers will find the technological means to overcome the problems mentioned. The transition from silicon to other basic components, including biological ones, and quantum computers may solve the problem of the energy and computing power necessary for strong AI (i). The 'noise' of human programming, secondly, could be replaced by the artificial one, in an historical change in which the creation of a robot capable of regenerating itself and creating its own kind could be our final invention (ii)[13]. Thirdly, the opacity of the black box could be overcome by technological advancements capable of checking all the processing activity through, for instance, comprehensible neural networks.

## 6.2    The Anthropological Arguments

From all these points of view, therefore, technology, and AI itself, might be able to solve the issues mentioned. In any case, however, it seems to me that some anthropological questions remain, which cannot be solved.

It is argued, for example, that some human qualities can never be replaced by artificial components. The focus, depending on the theories, is on imagination; on creativity; on consciousness, according to the theory of integrated information; on emotions and inspiration; on the result of the actions of hormones[14]. And I can also add

---

[13] There are several theories about it. Some experts speculate that an AI endowed with such power will be *Our Final* Invention because it will allow us to solve all our problems or rather because it will destroy us by pursuing goals that simply transcend us [86]. Other experts e.g., Raymond Kurzweil, Fredric Brown, Irving John Good, and Vernor Vinge, focus on Singularity, in which genetics, nanotechnology, robotics and AI will allow us to transform ourselves into cyborg beings connected between us and, through the cloud, with the whole universe.

[14] Respectively: Peter Ware Higgs, Nobel Prize in Physics in 2013; Marc Mézard, physicist, director of the École Normale Supérieure in Paris; Giulio Tononi, psychiatrist and neuroscientist, director of the Center for Sleep and Consciousness of the University of Wisconsin; Roberto Cingolani, physicist, former scientific director of the Italian Institute of Technology (IIT) in Genoa and D. Dennett, philosopher [87].

very human inclinations, such as the benefit of the doubt, with the correlated curiosity, and the positive and constructive Socratic 'knowing not knowing': characteristics that, in my opinion, distinguish the human being and his search for meaning, which do seem to me to fit AI's reasoning.

In different areas, qualities such as, for example, empathy or the aptitude for getting involved or 'levelling the playing field' (which are useful and perhaps necessary to perform functions based on the understanding of human beings such as medicine or justice) seem to me acquisitions out of the technological reach of AI. From this point of view, justice can offer an illustrative example.

The constitutional origin of the jury, starting from the Magna Carta of 1215, responds to the request of the nobleman to be judged not by the King, but through "the lawful judgment of his peers" [88]. A decision based on a judgment of equals later become intrinsic to the jury trial and, mutatis mutandis, to the due process. In this logic, it seems impractical to delegate sentencing to AI. Even if, over time, the technological problems mentioned were solved, and if machines could be said to carry out legal-algorithmic interpretations, there would always be a distance between human intelligence and AI; a distance that makes it impossible to speak of machines as being our equals [89].

Another version of the same principle is represented by the Italian Constitution: art. 101 states that "Justice is administered in the name of the people" and "In nome del popolo italiano" is the formula written on the top of any legal judgement. Likewise, "au nom du peuple français" is the French formula for any judgment, as provided in the 1793 Constitution[15] and "im Namen des Volkes" is the equivalent German one[16]. On this basis, could a machine ever speak in the name of a people?

The most convincing approach, therefore, is not the complete replacement of human intelligence by AI, but its assistance. I do not mean a zero-sum relationship, where the power acquired on one side is lost on the other, but a multiplying relationship inspired by the principle of subsidiarity, in which each form of intelligence carries out the action that best suits it. In this way, the result of the combination may lead to an augmented human intelligence [90].

# 7 A List of New 'human' Rights

Many authors and organizations have already recommended a vast number of proposals for an appropriate regulation of AI [91–98]. Here, I would like to propose a number of new (or renewed) rights, in order to achieve a balanced and constitutionally oriented framework for humans and AI: a list of rights belonging to every human who comes into contact with AI.

---

[15] Art. 61. "Les lois, les décrets, les jugements et tous les actes publics sont intitulés: Au nom du peuple français, l'an... de la République française.".

[16] Art. 25 of the 1993 (as last amended in October 2017) Act on the Federal Constitutional Court (Bundesverfassungsgerichtsgesetz, BVerfGG): "The decisions of the Federal Constitutional Court shall be issued "in the name of the People".

(i) A first human right deals with the faculty of knowing the human or artificial nature of our interlocutor[17]. Given the technical possibility of creating artificial systems that can be confused with humans[18], this right is important for a number of reasons. Firstly, it is important to stress the need to be correctly informed about the possible consequences of our behaviour and expressions. A machine, for instance, could instantly enter the cloud and disclose globally all the information we transmit to it; not knowing whether we are talking to a human or a machine, we would risk losing all control over it.

The use of anthropomorphic robots in certain sectors also raises concern. With reference to the so-called Uncanny Valley [100], we may feel cheated or deceived, for example, when we hand over information about our health, our confidences or affections to robots that we believe to be human[19]. Ignorance about the nature of our interlocutor could lead to misunderstandings and false trust, and could betray the expectation of an empathic understanding[20]. From a more general point of view, lastly, the lack of knowledge of the human or artificial nature of our counterpart, at least in performing certain activities, could affect our dignity. As stated in a UNESCO report, "Dignity is inherent to human beings, not to machines or robots. Therefore, robots and humans are not to be confused even if an android robot has the seductive appearance of a human, or if a powerful cognitive robot has learning capacity that exceeds individual human cognition" [57].

(ii) A second right deals with obtaining a clear explanation of the steps through which the machine has generated the result. I am not speaking about a technical detailed exposition, inaccessible to most of us, but an understandable description of the logic that led the machine to exercise its autonomy in one way rather than another. In this perspective, for instance, we already have the constitutional right to be informed about the reasons for judicial decisions; a right instrumental to a justiciable decision [42]. The same right to explicability would be now extended to any AI decision, public or private, which significantly affects us[21].

This right should impose an informational burden which some experts, considering the black box problem, consider unsustainable. In the face of the substantial lack of legitimacy of any decision not supported by understandable reasons, yet, a number of researchers are working on making the logic of machine and deep learning clearer, or adopting different systems that can guarantee greater transparency [108]. In any case, this "right to reasons" cannot be hindered because of the technical difficulties related to its practical enforcement: it is directly instrumental to a trustworthy AI.

(iii) The third element of this constitution-oriented AI framework is the right to be subject to human decisions: I mean a right to a decision-making process with a

---

[17] See the mentioned Statement on Artificial Intelligence, Robotics and 'Autonomous Systems', issued by EGE, 11: "we may ask whether people have a right to know whether they are dealing with a human being or with an AI artefact".

[18] As is well known, this is at the center of the Turing test [99].

[19] On the pros and cons of this approach, see [1–4].

[20] In a few specific areas, this 'distraction' can have beneficial results [1–4].

[21] 'Explicability' could be the fifth bioethical principle, in addition to the four (*beneficence, non-maleficence, autonomy, and justice*) already indicated [1–4], see also [5].

significant human component, with a 'human in the loop'. As already mentioned, this prerogative is linked to the opportunity to be evaluated by our peers, by our equals; in this perspective, it is linked to already existing constitutional principles (such as jury trial and due process). The right to a human decision can also be related to the mentioned possibilities of AI's error and bias. In the same perspective, the need for a clear reasoning behind the decision also pushes towards a human supervision of any public or private processing that can affect us. In these terms, the right to a non-fully automated decision is also based on the need to identify who is to be considered in charge of the function and the related responsibility[22.]

The European Union has expressly considered this right: art. 22 of the GDPR (General Data Protection Regulation 2016/679) states that "The data subject shall have the right not to be subject to a decision based solely on automated processing, including profiling, which produces legal effects concerning him or her or similarly significantly affects him or her"[23]. However, the effectiveness of this section is weakened, on the one hand, by the exceptions provided for in the same article, when the decision "is based on the data subject's explicit consent"[24]. This clause risks eroding the right to a non-fully automated decision, given the aforementioned 'consciously misinformed consent' dynamic [110]. On the other hand, there is the risk that people consider it more convenient to delegate the choice to the machine, without taking the burden and the responsibility to check and perhaps oppose a decision that appears more neutral and accurate than the human one[25]. In this way, as mentioned before, the decision would be substantially 'captured' by the machine and, in what has been called the 'sheep effect' (effet moutonnier), the human's role, and accordingly the right to a human decision, would become a mere formality without substantial content [54].

---

[22] The Italian Constitution, for instance, states as follows: "Officials and employees of the State and public entities shall be directly liable, under criminal, civil and administrative law, for acts performed in violation of rights" (art. 28).

[23] In recital 71, the GDPR states that "The data subject should have the right not to be subject to a decision, which may include a measure, evaluating personal aspects relating to him or her which is based solely on automated processing and which produces legal effects concerning him or her or similarly significantly affects him or her, such as automatic refusal of an online credit application or e-recruiting practices without any human intervention. Such processing includes 'profiling' that consists of any form of automated processing of personal data evaluating the personal aspects relating to a natural person, in particular to analyse or predict aspects concerning the data subject's performance at work, economic situation, health, personal preferences or interests, reliability or behaviour, location or movements, where it produces legal effects concerning him or her or similarly significantly affects him or her".

[24] A commentary in *L.A. Bygrave, EU data protection law falls short as desirable model for algorithmic regulation*, in [6, 7]. A similar principle was already provided for by directive no. 95/46/CE, art. 15, which, significantly did not contain the 'explicit consent' exception.

[25] This risk has been reported both in medicine and in justice. In medicine: "The collective medical mind is becoming the combination of published literature and the data captured in health care systems, as opposed to individual clinical experience" [10, 11]. There is a risk that the legal discourse on damages – it has been said – would be based not "on the courts rationale for individual cases, but instead be a result of pure statistical calculation in relation to the average compensation awarded previously by other courts" [8, 9].

(iv) A fourth right worth mentioning derives from traditional privacy, but should be carefully modulated depending on the areas in which it is applied. While it should be strengthened with regard to ICT, as mentioned above, it should be relaxed in medical research. Given the pervasiveness of AI, it should also extend beyond the classical boundaries of privacy and be linked to the antidiscrimination argument, in order to provide the constitutional foundation for the facial recognition ban even in public places, for example, and for other systems that could infringe personal liberties and equality.

(v) Finally, a specific right to free education on AI should be provided [32]. Given the technical complexity of AI and its increasing use in many areas of our daily life, a specific duty of education could also be proposed, as a component of compulsory education, both for the youngest (from elementary school onwards) and for adults (in universities and professional training). In fact, even the most appropriate constitutional system of human rights would be ineffective without a common understanding of AI and its pros and cons.

## 8  Concluding Remarks

AI raises questions that fully affect the substance of constitutionalism and that have to be adjusted according to its main core: limitation of powers and guarantee of rights. Or rather, a set of new 'human rights' can be one of the means of limiting powers, and reaching an overall constitution-oriented AI: an AI capable of producing more benefits than threats for humanity. Accordingly, it is necessary to try to improve what may be useful in existing law, and to fearlessly seek new legal instruments where necessary [114]. The effort must be interdisciplinary in nature, fuelled by the opening of the law to ethical pluralism and scientific and technological contamination [115]. In this activity, in which deciding for the AI also means deciding for ourselves, it is decisive, for instance, to combine appropriate technological research and development with regulatory impact assessments, so as to ensure a law with the necessary effectiveness, flexibility and equilibrium [116].

Thinking about AI law, we need to keep up-to-date the debate on the role that we want to maintain for ourselves in today's and future societies. In fact, given the strong interdependence between artificial and human, the chosen regulation for the former will give, at the same time, the coordinates for the latter, in a debate in which the role entrusted to AI will reflect that reserved for humans. If properly used, AI will have the capacity to enhance humans: as as result, our intelligence will not be limited, but rather augmented.

## References

1. McIlwain, C.H.: Constitutionalism: Ancient and Modern, Liberty Fund (2008). https://oll. libertyfund.org/titles/2145
2. Barber, N.W.: The Principles of Constitutionalism. Oxford University Press, Oxford (2018)

3. Grimm, D.: Constitutionalism: Past, Present, and Future. Oxford University Press, Oxford (2016)
4. Ackermann, B.: We the People, Volume 1, Foundations. Harvard University Press (1991). We the People, vol. 2, Transformations. Harvard University Press (1998). We the People, vol. 3, The Civil Rights Revolution. Harvard University Press (2014)
5. Bellamy, R.: Constitutionalism, Encyclopædia Britannica, 30 July 2019. https://www.britannica.com/topic/constitutionalism
6. Russel, S., Norvig, P.: Artificial Intelligence: A Modern Approach. Prentice Hall, Upper Saddle River (2020)
7. Bringsjord, S., Govindarajulu, N.S.: Artificial Intelligence. In: Zalta, E.N. (ed.) The Stanford Encyclopedia of Philosophy, Summer 2020 Ed. (2020). https://plato.stanford.edu/archives/sum2020/entries/artificial-intelligence
8. Executive Summary 'Data Growth, Business Opportunities, and the IT Imperatives', The Digital Universe of Opportunities: Rich Data and the Increasing Value of the Internet of Things (2014). https://www.emc.com/leadership/digital-universe/2014iview/index.htm
9. Dehmer, M., Emmert-Streib, F. (eds.): Frontiers in Data Science, Boca Raton (2017)
10. Kudina, O., Bas, M.: The end of privacy as we know it: reconsidering public space in the age of google glass. In: Newell, B.C., Timan, T., Koops, B.J. (eds.) Surveillance, Privacy, and Public Space. Routledge (2018). c.7
11. Beatty, J.F., Samuelson, S.S., Sánchez Abril, P.: Business Law and the Legal Environment, Boston, p. 263 (2015)
12. Gutwirth, S., De Hert, P., Leenes, R.: Data protection on the Move, Dordrecht (2016)
13. Plaut, V.C., Bartlett, R.P.: Blind consent? A social psychological investigation of non-readership of click-through agreements. Law Hum Behav 36(4), 293–311 (2012)
14. Lambert, P.: Understanding the New European Data Protection Rules. Taylor and Francis Ltd. (2017)
15. Breen, S., Ouazzane, K., Patel, P.: GDPR: Is your consent valid? Bus. Inf. Rev. 37(1), 19–24 ( 2020)
16. Morsink, J.: The Universal Declaration of Human Rights: Origins, Drafting and Intent. University of Pennsylvania Press, Philadelphia (1999)
17. Flamigni, C.: Sul consenso sociale informato. Bi-oLaw J. 10(2), 201 (2017)
18. Lee, J.E.: Artificial intelligence in the future biobanking: current issues in the biobank and future possibilities of artificial intelligence. Biomed. J. Sci. Tech. Res. 7(3), 1 (2018). Fei-Fei Li and John Etchemendy lead the Stanford Institute for Human-Centered AI (HAI)
19. Calo, R.: Artificial Intelligence Policy: A Primer Roadmap, in 51 UC Davis Law Review, 2, 406 lists Google, Facebook, IBM, Amazon, Microsoft, Apple, Baidu, and a few others (2017)
20. Prainsack, B.: Data donation: how to resist the iLeviathan. In: Krutzinna, J., Floridi, L. (eds.) The Ethics of Medical Data Donation. PSS, vol. 137, pp. 9–22. Springer, Cham (2019). https://doi.org/10.1007/978-3-030-04363-6_2
21. Arato, A.: The Adventures of the Constituent Power, pp. 329–358. Cambridge University Press, Cambridge (2017)
22. The world's most valuable resource is no longer oil, but data, The Economist on May 6th 2017
23. Carrozza, M.C.: et al.: Automation and autonomy: from a definition to the possible applications of artificial intelligence. The Ethics and Law of AI, Fondazione Leonardo. Civiltà delle Macchine, 13 (2019). https://fondazioneleonardo-cdm.com/site/assets/files/2450/fle1_booklet_conferenza_eng_gar_311019.pdf
24. Zuboff, S.: The Age of Surveillance Capitalism. The Fight for a Human Future at the New Frontier of Power. Profile books (2019)

25. Benkler, Y.: Don't let industry write the rules for AI. Nature **569**, 161 (2019)
26. von der Leyen, U.: A union that strives for more. My agenda for Europe. https://ec.europa.eu/commission/sites/beta-political/files/political-guidelines-next-commission_en.pdf
27. Shultz, D.: Could Google influence the presidential election? In Science, 25 October 2016. https://www.sciencemag.org/news/2016/10/could-google-influence-presidential-election.
28. How to avoid unlawful profiling – a guide. European Union Agency for Fundamental Rights on 5 December 2018. https://fra.europa.eu/en/news/2018/how-avoid-unlawful-profiling-guide
29. Mann, M., Matzner, T.: Challenging algorithmic profiling: the limits of data protection and anti-discrimination in responding to emergent discrimination. Big Data & Society (2019). https://doi.org/10.1177/2053951719895805
30. O'Neil, C.: Weapons of Math Destruction. Crown Books, New York (2016)
31. Zuiderveen Borgesius, F.J.: Strengthening legal protection against discrimination by algorithms and artificial intelligence. Int. J. Human Rights (2020). https://doi.org/10.1080/13642987.2020.1743976
32. Quintarelli, S., et al.: Paper on ethical principles. The Ethics and Law of AI, Fondazione Leonardo. Civiltà delle Macchine, p. 34 (2019). https://fondazioneleonardo-cdm.com/site/assets/files/2450/fle1_booklet_conferenza_eng_gar_311019.pdf
33. European Group on Ethics in Science and New Technologies (EGE), Statement on Artificial Intelligence, Robotics and 'Autonomous Systems', Chapter on Role of ethical charters in building international AI framework, Brussels, p. 17, 9 March 2018,
34. Notes from the frontier: Modeling the impact of AI on the world economy. McKinsey Global Institute, September 2018. https://www.mckinsey.com/featured-insights/artificial-intelligence/notes-from-the-frontier-modeling-the-impact-of-ai-on-the-world-economy
35. The future of Jobs report. World Economic Forum (2018). https://www3.weforum.org/docs/WEF_Future_of_Jobs_2018.pdf
36. Ford, M.: Rise of the Robots: Technology and the Threat of Jobless Future, New York (2015)
37. Floridi, L., et al.: AI4People—An ethical framework for a good AI society: opportunities, risks, principles, and recommendations. Mind Mach. **28**(4), 691 (2018). https://doi.org/10.1007/s11023-018-9482-5
38. López Peláez, A. (ed.): The Robotics Divide. A New Frontier in ·the 21st Century? Springer. Heidelberg (2014). https://doi.org/10.1007/978-1-4471-5358-0
39. European Ethical Charter on the Use of Artificial Intelligence in Judicial Systems and their environment, European Commission for the Efficiency of Justice (CEPEJ) of the Council of Europe on December 2018. https://rm.coe.int/ethical-charter-en-for-publication-4-december-2018/16808f699c
40. Ashley, K.D.: Special Issue published by Artificial Intelligence and Law on Artificial Intelligence for Justice, (1) (2017)
41. Artificial Intelligence and Legal Analytics: New Tools for Law Practice in the Digital Age. Cambridge University Press (2017)
42. CEPEJ: Justice systems of the future, in 16 Newsletter, August 2018. https://rm.coe.int/newsletter-no-16-august-2018-en-justice-of-the-future/16808d00c8
43. Katz, D.M., Bommarito, M.J., Blackman, J.: A general approach for predicting the behavior of the Supreme Court of the United States. Plos One, 17 April 2017
44. Angwin, J., Larson, J., et al.: Machine Bias. There's software used across the country to predict future criminals. And it's biased against blacks (2016). ProPublica. https://www.propublica.org/article/machine-bias-risk-assessments-in-criminal-sentencing

45. Hao, K.: This is how AI bias really happens—and why it's so hard to fix (2019). MIT Review. https://www.technologyreview.com/2019/02/04/137602/this-is-how-ai-bias-really-happensand-why-its-so-hard-to-fix/
46. Polonski, V.: AI is convicting criminals and determining jail time, but is it fair? Annual Meeting of the Global Future Councils of the World Economic Forum, 19 November 2018. https://www.weforum.org/agenda/2018/11/algorithms-court-criminals-jail-time-fair/
47. Helper, P.: Is AI racist? Machine learning, the justice, system, and racial bias, McGill Daily, 3 September 2018. https://www.mcgilldaily.com/2018/09/is-ai-racist/
48. Hao, K.: AI is sending people to jail—and getting it wrong (2019). MIT Review. https://www.technologyreview.com/2019/01/21/137783/algorithms-criminal-justice-ai/
49. Austin, J.L.: How to Do Things with Words. Urmson, J.O., Sbisá, M. (ed.) Harvard University Press (1962)
50. Kleinberg, J., et al.: Human decisions and machine predictions. Q. J. Econ. **133**(1), 241 (2018)
51. Zou, J., Schiebinger, L.: AI can be sexist and racist—it's time to make it fair. Nature **559**, 324 (2018)
52. State v. Loomis, 881 N.W.2d 749, 767 Wis. (2016)
53. Israni, E.: Algorithmic due process: mistaken accountability and attribution in state v. Loomis (2017). Harvard Journal of Law Technology, 31 August 2017. https://jolt.law.harvard.edu/digest/algorithmic-due-process-mistaken-accountability-and-attribution-in-state-v-loomis-1
54. Garapon, A., Lassègue, J.: Justice digitale. Révolution graphique et rupture anthropologique. PUF, p. 239 (2018)
55. Donna, M.: AI technology and government decision making - recent Italian rulings. in ICLG.com. https://iclg.com/ibr/articles/10731-ai-technology-and-professional-decision-making-recent-italian-rulings.
56. Tribunale Amministrativo Regionale Lazio, decision n. 10964 of 13 September 2019
57. World Commission on the Ethics of Scientific Knowledge and Technology (COMEST), UNESCO, Report of COMEST on Robotics Ethics, Paris, p. 30, 14 September 2017
58. Liu, N., et al.: Artificial intelligence in emergency medicine. J. Emerg. Crit. Care Med. **2**, 82 (2018)
59. Stewart, J., Sprivulis, P., Dwivedi, G.: Artificial intelligence and machine learning in emergency medicine. Emerg. Med. Aust. **30**(6), 870 (2018)
60. Council of Europe materials on AI and the control of COVID-19. https://www.coe.int/en/web/artificial-intelligence/ai-covid19
61. Hashimoto, D., et al.: Artificial intelligence in surgery: promises and perils. Ann. Surg. **268**(1), 70 (2018)
62. Nicholson Price, W.: Big data and black-box medical algorithms. Sci. Transl. Med. (2018)
63. Obermeyer, Z., et al.: Dissecting racial bias in an algorithm used to manage the health of populations. Science **366**(6464), 447–453 (2019)
64. Benjamin, R.: Assessing risk, automating racism. Science **366**(6464), 421–422 (2019)
65. Vartan, S.: Racial bias found in a major health care risk algorithm. Sci. Am. (2019)
66. Topol, E.: Deep Medicine. How Artificial Intelligence Can Make Healthcare Human Again. Basic Books (2019)
67. Sparrow, R., Hatherley, J.: High hopes for "deep medicine"? AI, Economics, and the Future of Care, Hastings Center Report, pp. 14–17, January-February 2020
68. Di Paolo, M., Gori, F., et al.: A review and analysis of new Italian law 219/2017: 'provisions for informed consent and advance directives treatment.' BMC Med. Ethics **20**, 17 (2019). https://doi.org/10.1186/s12910-019-0353-2
69. Giubilini, A., Savulescu, J.: The artificial moral advisor. The "Ideal Observer" meets artificial intelligence. Philos. Technol. **31**(2), 169 (2018)

70. O'Connell, M.: To be a machine, New York (2017)
71. Pethokoukis, J.: The American Enterprise Institute blog (2018). https://www.aei.org/economics/nobel-laureate-daniel-kahneman-on-a-i-its-very-difficult-to-imagine-that-with-sufficient-data-there-will-remain-things-that-only-humans-can-do/
72. Mathias, J.N.: Bias and Noise: Daniel Kahneman on Errors in Decision-Making, in Medium 17 October 2017. https://medium.com/@natematias/bias-and-noise-daniel-kahneman-on-errors-in-decision-making-6bc844ff5194
73. Guthrie, C., Rachlinski, J.J., Wistrick, A.J.: Inside the Judicial Mind, Cornell Law Faculty Publications, Paper 814, (2001). https://scholarship.law.cornell.edu/facpub/814
74. Claybrook, J., Kildare, S.: Autonomous vehicles: No driver...no regulation? Science **36** (6397), 36 (2018)
75. Barbaro, C., Meneceur, Y.: Issues in the use of artificial intelligence (AI) algorithms in judicial systems. In: European Commission for the Efficiency of Justice Newsletter, Council of Europe, no. 16, 3 August 2018
76. Rosenfeld, A., Zemel, R., Tsotsos, J.K.: The Elephant in the Room, 9 August 2018. Cornell University site. https://arxiv.org/abs/1808.03305
77. Yang, G.-Z., Dario, P., Kragic, D.: Social robotics—Trust, learning, and social interaction. Sci. Robot. **3**(21), (2018)
78. Reyzin, L.: Unprovability comes to machine learning, nel numero di Nature del 7 gennaio (2019). https://www-nature-com.ezp.biblio.unitn.it/articles/d41586-019-00012-4
79. Ben-David, S.: Learnability can be undecidable. Nat. Mach. Intell. **1**(1), 44 (2019). Gödel and Cohen showed, in a nutshell, that not everything is provable. Here we show that machine learning shares this fate
80. Knight, W.: The dark secret at the heart of AI. MIT Technol. Rev. **120**, 54–61 (2017)
81. European Group on Ethics in Science and New Technologies (EGE), Statement on Artificial Intelligence, Robotics and 'Autonomous Systems', Brussels, p. 6, 9 March 2018
82. The Independent, 31 July 2017
83. Brice, J.: Algorithmic regulation on trial? Professional judgement and the authorisation of algorithmic decision making, in [111]
84. Indurkhya, B.: Is morality the last frontier for machines? New Ideas Psychol. **54**, 107–111 (2019)
85. Brownsword, R.: Law, liberty and technology: criminal justice in the context of smart machines. Int. J. Law Context **15**(2), 107–125 (2019)
86. Barrat, J.: Artificial Intelligence and the End of the Human Era. Thomas Dunne Books, New York (2013)
87. Dennett, D.: Consciousness Explained. Little, Brown and Co., Boston (1991)
88. McSweeney, T.J.: Magna Carta and the Right to Trial by Jury, Faculty Publications, p. 1722 (2014). https://scholarship.law.wm.edu/facpubs/1722
89. Sourdin, T., Cornes, R.: Do judges need to be hu-man? In: Sourdin, T., Zariski, A. (eds.) The Responsive Judge International Perspectives, vol. 67, pp. 87–120. Springer, Heidelberg (2018). https://doi.org/10.1007/978-981-13-1023-2_4
90. Floridi, L., et al.: AI4People—An ethical framework for a good AI society: opportunities, risks, principles, and recommendations, above, 692
91. Report on Ethics guidelines for trustworthy AI. European Commission High-Level Expert Group on AI, April 2019. https://ec.europa.eu/digital-single-market/en/news/ethics-guidelines-trustworthy-ai
92. European Commission's white paper On AI – A European approach to excellence and trust, published in Brussels on 19 February 2020
93. Proposals for ensuring appropriate regulation of AI, Office of the Privacy Commissioner of Canada, 13 March 2020

94. Pajno, A.: Paper on legal principles, The Ethics and Law of AI, Fondazione Leonardo. Civiltà delle Macchine
95. Brownsword, R.: Law, technology, and society: in a state of delicate tension. Notizie di Politeia **137**, 26 (2020)
96. Santosuosso, A.: The human rights of nonhuman artificial entities: an oxymoron? Jahrbuch für Wissenschaft und Ethik **19**(1), 203–238 (2015)
97. Winfield, A., et al.: Machine ethics: the design and governance of ethical ai and autonomous systems. Proc. IEEE **107**(3), 509–517 (2019)
98. Coeckelbergh, M.: AI ethics. MIT Press, 2020. (in Italian). Simoncini, A.: L'algoritmo incostituzionale: intelligenza artificiale e il futuro delle libertà. BioLaw J. 63–89 (2019). Santosuosso, A.: Intelligenza artificiale e diritto, Mondadori Università (2020)
99. Turing, A.M.: Computing machinery and intelligence. Mind **59**, 433 (1950)
100. Mori, M.: The uncanny valley. Energy **7**(4), 33 (1970)
101. Minato, T., et al.: Evaluating the human likeness of an android by comparing gaze behaviors elicited by the android and a person. Adv. Robot. **20**(10), 1147 (2006)
102. Cheetham, M., (ed.): The Uncanny Valley. Hypothesis and beyond, eBook (2018)
103. O'Neill, K.: Should a bot have to tell you it's a bot? Medium, 21 March 2018. Almost half from the Goldsmiths and Mindshare results said it would feel "creepy" if a bot pretended to be human. https://medium.com/s/story/should-a-bot-have-to-tell-you-its-a-bot-e9fa29f0b9d4
104. Huijnen, C.A.G.J., Lexis, M.A.S., Jansens, R., de Witte, L.P.: Roles, strengths and challenges of using robots in interventions for children with autism spectrum disorder (ASD). J. Autism Dev. Disord. **49**(1), 11–21 (2018)
105. Beauchamp and Childress: Principles of Biomedical Ethics (1979)
106. Floridi, L., Cowls, J.: A unified framework of five principles for AI in society. Harvard Data Sci. Rev. (1)1 (2019)
107. Wachter, S., Mittelstadt, B.: A right to reasonable inferences: re-thinking data protection law in the age of big data and AI. Columbia Bus. Law Rev. 494 (2019)
108. Rudin, C.: Stop explaining black box machine learning models for high stakes decisions and use interpretable models instead. Nature Mach. Intell. **1**, 206 (2019)
109. Andrews, L., et al.: Algorithmic Regulation. King's College Discussion Paper no. 85, September 2017, London, 26 (2017)
110. Wachter, S., Mittelstadt, B., Floridi, L.: Why a right to explanation of automated decision-making does not exist in the general data protection regulation. Int. Data Priv. Law **7**(2), 76–99 (2017)
111. Char, D.S., Shah, N.H., Magnus, D.: Implementing machine learning in health care – addressing ethical challenges. New Engl. J. Med. **378**(11), 981 (2018)
112. Garapon, A., Lassègue, J.: Justice digitale. Révolution graphique et rupture anthropologique, above, 239
113. Quintarelli, S., et al.: Paper on ethical principles, above, 34
114. Brownsword, R.: Law, Technology and Society: Re-imagining the Regulatory Environment. Routledge, Abingdon (2019)
115. Casonato, C.: 21st century biolaw: a proposal. BioLaw J. **2017**(1), 81 (2017)
116. Scherer, M.U.: Regulating artificial intelligence systems: risks, challenges, competencies, and strategies. Harvard J. Law Technol. **29**(2), 353 (2016)

# Analyzing the Contribution of Ethical Charters to Building the Future of Artificial Intelligence Governance

Lyse Langlois[1(✉)] and Catherine Régis[2]

[1] Faculty of Social Sciences, Laval University, Québec, Canada
Lyse.langlois@observatoire-ia.ulaval.ca
[2] Faculty of Law, University of Montreal, Montréal, Canada
catherine.regis@umontreal.ca

**Keywords:** Ethics · Ethical charters · Artificial intelligence · Formalisation of ethics · Social regulation · Norms · Legal framework

> *A technology is not merely a system of machines with certain functions; rather it is an expression of a social world* (Nye 2007).

## 1 Introduction[1]

Advances in digital technology and artificial intelligence (AI) systems have the potential to radically transform economies and societies. The deployment of these technologies promises to improve a host of important services for society as a whole, but also raises concerns with regard to uncontrolled development of technological systems and a certain inappropriate use or disregard for social factors. Technology is non-neutral (Gautrais 2012); it encompasses values and can even affect them. Technology has such power that it structures and defines the end-purposes of human activity, to the extent that individuals and communities have no choice but to adapt and change under its influence. AI systems (AIS) are also a vehicle for power struggles: they can help people build their capacities as well as constrain these by segmenting society and reinforcing social inequities and injustices (Barabas et al. 2018). In view of these potential digressions and the significant impact on societies, this fifth technological revolution has quickly led to widespread discussion (i.e., academic, but also political and very public) of the ethical issues raised by the exercise of (ir)responsible AI. Incorporating various AIS without ethical consideration of their impact[2] has already led to greater discrimination of certain groups, criticism likely to be biased, and

---

[1] The authors would like to express their gratitude to the external reviewers as well as professors Miriam Cohen and Bryn William Jones for their very useful comments on this chapter.

[2] As reference: COMPAS (Correctional Offender Management Profiling for Alternative Sanctions), a criminal recidivism prediction tool (2016), the Facebook job offer recommendation algorithm favouring male applicants over women (2019), the AppleCard, which discriminated against women applying for lines of credit (2019).

© Springer Nature Switzerland AG 2021
B. Braunschweig and M. Ghallab (Eds.): Reflections on Artificial Intelligence for Humanity, LNAI 12600, pp. 150–170, 2021.
https://doi.org/10.1007/978-3-030-69128-8_10

developers' and decision-makers' potential lack of ethical sensitivity, whether intentional or not (Bairaktarova and Woodcock 2017). As set forth in the Villani report, AIS cannot be allowed to be new instruments to exclude or overly track people without public debate (Villani 2018) and considerations for human rights. In view of these concerns, a certain number of organizations have developed ethical charters to govern the development of AI and related digital technologies. More strategic and ambitious reports have also been deployed to help shape or define the AI and digital technology policy of a state or a group of states.

Given the significant academic and public policy attention being given to the development of ethical charters to identify principles and values likely to provide a better framework for AI and digital technology, we argue that it is important to also more fully address the formalization of these charters. Formalization involves assessing when and how the principles and values in a charter can be institutionalized in organizations or professional practices. Formalization actually contributes to establishing AI ethics. And such an assessment provides fertile ground for experimentation on the use of AI ethics as a potential preamble to future digital rights or, on a larger scale, AI legal frameworks.

In the first part of this article, we examine the elements that appear essential to charter formalization based on an organizational ethics research approach (Murphy 1989; Adelman 1991; Carroll and Bucholtz 1999; Mercier 2004), in order to make a case for *ethics* as one component of developing AI governance. The second part of this article follows with the outcomes of our reflections in this regard. The legal framework of AI is increasingly being considered as the next major step in normative development in this sector, both at the local and international levels. We will explore potential synergies between ethical charter assets and legal developments likely to be deployed in building this next step.

## 2 The Ethical Charter Landscape: The First Component of AI Governance Development

Before exploring the formalization of ethical charters, there is a need to better understand what has been accomplished so far in the ethical charter landscape. While there has been valuable and useful progress in defining shared values and tools to guide AIS developments, we also saw some conduct that limits their impact and legitimacy. Acknowledging such complex ethical charter landscape, we then examine the elements needed to formalize ethics that encourage a beneficial materialization of such charters.

### 2.1 The Good, the Bad and the Ugly

The flourishing development of ethical AI principles throughout the world in the last few years has surely been constructive, but due to their multiplicity such statements of AI ethics principles have sometimes been confusing for the AI research community and the general public. The development of AI ethics principles has contributed to stimulating local and international discussions on AI benefits and risks from various cultural, professional and disciplinary perspectives. However, as we will point out later, the voices of countries from the South and minority groups are still underrepresented in this movement. It has also elicited more formal positioning from various stakeholders (governments, industries, international organizations, academia, etc.) regarding what "good AI"[3] means or does not mean, through such mechanisms as administrative directives, best practices, and organizational policies and regulations. The well-known work of Jobin et al. (2019) and Zeng (2019) implemented through a platform that tracks in real time every ethical charter initiative (https://www.linking-ai-principles.org/) has been useful in illustrating the points of convergence and divergence that emerge from these multiple ethical guidelines (e.g., 84 guidelines in 2020). Their work demonstrates that stakeholders' views clearly converge on a few specifically shared principles, even if they do not necessarily agree on their definition. The work of Fjeld et al. (2020), from the Berkman Klein Center for Internet and Society, also demonstrates an effort to integrate and analyze charters from various regions in the world (Latin America, Middle East, etc.). They identified thirty-six relevant charters and ranked them using a typology that features various principles based on a proportion of convergence, their potential links with human rights and the groups of stakeholders concerned. For the authors, these points of convergence can represent the "normative core of a principle-based approach to AI ethics and governance" (2020:5).

Arguably, the fact that ethics is not binding has sparked more candid debates, at least in some circumstances, about AI challenges in various contexts. Such ethical guidelines were often viewed as necessary tools to encourage reflexive approaches, in order for data collectors, developers, researchers, users and policymakers to develop more responsible AI behaviour instead of using mandatory "checklists" likely to be applied uniformly but without further thought. This discussion could have been different, perhaps more cautious, if we had started by addressing legal reforms and considering their direct economic, political and social impact as well as their ensuing crystallization effect.

However, despite the fact that such ethical initiatives have galvanized AI ecosystem stakeholders since 2016, an opposite movement has emerged quite recently to undermine some of the initiatives. Referred to as "fake ethics" or ethics-washing/bashing, this phenomenon is defined by Elettra Bietti (2019) as a trend to discredit or trivialize AI ethics in general and governance initiatives in particular. There are different sources for such a phenomenon.

One of these has to do with the nature of the groups undertaking the development of AI ethics charters with interests sometimes in contradiction to the actual end-purposes of the initiatives. Several researchers (O'Neil 2016; Fontanel and Sushcheva 2019; Metzinger 2019) have revealed industry lobbies intent on delaying the implementation and development of AI regulations and policies. For example, some principles serving as recommendations in various discussion groups (NGOs, public authority and universities) were removed and replaced with less exacting principles that diluted agreements and resulted in generic, non-binding documents. The adoption of

---

[3] The word *good* is in brackets as the very meaning of good AI is a complex issue: Ben Green, ""Good" isn't good enough", 2019, Neurips conference paper, available online: https://aiforsocialgood.github.io/neurips2019/accepted/track3/pdfs/67_aisg_neurips2019.pdf.

such principles thus orients the direction of debate and determines the type of innovation on which to focus in this sector while influencing rules and policies, especially when they serve as strategic documents. Moreover, the composition of groups of experts on the matter has been criticized as being politically driven and not always fairly representative of various groups (gender, sector, discipline, country, etc.). A certain discrepancy has become apparent among group representatives, with a minimal number of ethicists compared with private sector representatives. Attention to inequalities in representation have also highlighted the fact that a much greater number of individuals from high income countries are chosen in comparison to individuals from low or middle-income countries in the global south.[4]

Despite these considerations, it should be noted that some businesses have embraced ethics and even hired philosophers to set up committees or services often referred to as "AI and Ethics" or "AI for the Benefit of Humanity," and for the most part these are led by legal experts. According to Metzinger (2019), most of these initiatives are part of communication strategies meant to uphold the reputations of organizations by promoting their good standing among the population. Hence, a certain ethical legitimacy is conveyed because ethicists were involved in the process. With regard to such initiatives—with some more akin to marketing strategies—the content of meaning covered by "ethics" can be considered of second- or even third-degree importance compared with other interests. Such tactics have often been criticized during processes deployed to institutionalize ethics (Salomon 2007).

The fact that ethical charters often leave a "practical gap" is another source of frustration. In other words, the ethical principles that they promote do not readily translate into technical solutions, particularly for developers (Floridi 2019). A study by Miller and Coldicott found that 79% of technology workers wished to have more practical resources to help them with ethical considerations (2019). As Morley et al. (2019) clearly put it, there is a current need for the AI ethics community to embark on a second, more practical endeavour, which requires translation from the "what" to the "how." In line with the other critiques mentioned above, this gap is problematic. It can discredit valuable ethical progress and benchmarks, which can lead to their rejection by the technical and AI user community and to gradual disinterest in a future ethical conversation, sometimes referred to as "ethics shrinking" (Floridi 2019). In cases where people reflect, on an ongoing basis, about the benefits and risks of their practice developing at an extremely fast pace and for which it is almost impossible to predict every ensuing challenge, reflexive approaches meant to be developed through such charters could be lost.

The recent phenomenon of ethical initiatives aimed at providing a better framework for AI warrants sustained attention and its claims should be submitted to serious review. As the term "ethics" has long been used independent of academic discussion, over time it has gradually been divested of its content and meaning. Peters, Vold, Robinson and Calvo (2020), as well as Brent Mittelstadt (2019), agree on this concept:

---

[4] See to this effect the awareness-raising paper produced by UNESCO, *Steering AI and advanced ICTs for knowledge societies: a Rights, Openness, Access, and Multi-stakeholder Perspective,* Xianhong Hu [1], Neupane, Bhanu, Echaiz, Lucia Flores, Sibal, Prateek, Rivera Lam, Macarena, 2019.

for charters to go beyond their declarative purposes, they must overcome the challenge of implementing the ethical principles that they encompass. As stated by Hagendorff (2020), "a very little to nothing has been written about the tangible implementation of ethical goals and values" (2020, p. 100). To avoid limiting ourselves to cataloguing good intentions, we deemed it necessary to highlight the formalization process of ethical charters and principles by considering them from the perspective of organizational ethics and social sciences and humanities research. Through this approach, the ethical and social imperatives found in these documents can be materialized and genuinely leveraged to transform professional practices, processes, organizational systems and legal frameworks.

## 2.2   The Formalization of Ethics: A Social Regulation Tool

The strong interest in organizational ethics is part of a movement driven by consumers, investors, wage earners and the population in general, with regard to an increasing social demand for a greater integration of ethics in organizational life (Mercier 1999). This movement started at the end of the 1980s in response to a crisis of trust regarding government institutions and the abuse of assets and public funds. The dynamics that led to these new perspectives involving applied ethics served to develop a body of knowledge at the origin of organizational ethics. From an instrumental perspective, organizational ethics focuses on how organizations integrate values into their policies, practices and decision-making processes. It also proposes a critical reflection on every aspect of an organization.

According to several organizational ethics researchers (Boisvert 2011; Bégin, 2009), the issue of trust is strongly related to the need to rely on ethics institutionalization. Under its commitment to fight corruption, the Organisation for Economic Co-operation and Development (OECD) also promoted organizational ethics at the end of the 1990s, by establishing a working group dedicated to the promotion of ethical infrastructure. It is also under the OECD's impetus that organizational ethics research was developed and led to active collaborations between Quebec, French and Belgian researchers. These researchers have been particularly interested in the phenomenon of formalization and its impact on professionals and organizations. Formalization is more than just an aspect in the development of a more encompassing ethics institutionalization system within organizational governance (Mercier 1999:22). It can also translate the demands of civil society stakeholders for greater transparency in decision-making and better access to information. Moreover, the formalization of ethics reflects the willingness of organisations to go beyond the intention stage and implement in processes and practices an ethical framework to include a process of reflection and an action plan regarding strategies to mitigate risks in a technological design project. Ethical charters are often the first mechanisms to be put in place, because once formalised, they serve as guidelines and prescriptions in terms of rules of conduct. In addition, they can also have normative implications if they are clearly promoted in organizational processes and practices by senior management.

The phase of formalization raises a certain paradox often mentioned by ethicists and philosophers: institutionalizing ethics as a type of social regulation (Reynaud 1991) can reduce it to a prescriptive and normative dimension. This vision often sparks controversy among philosophers: for them, ethics is above all a tool for critical reflection on values and end-purposes rather than a management tool. From the perspective of social regulation, ethics focus on the relationships established in practice between various axiological and normative registers with constraints, regulations, obligations and responsibilities. This vision proves entirely relevant when it is rooted in the field of applied ethics and when it allows to deliberate on values and principles. In this respect, decision-making has become the central issue meant to resolve situation clarification problems. It is in practice, at the core of AI design systems, that some issues and challenges come to light and cause both potential emancipation and exploitation to emerge. The implementation of risk mitigation strategies based on an ethical framework is part and parcel of a culture mindful of ethics and social responsibility. The social logic of applied ethics is essentially structured around the concept of responsibility. G. Legault identified that "ethical responsibility refers to the *response* given to those who question the *value* of decisions made in practice. (2000, p. 33) Hence, applied ethics can only be operated in concrete situations, in other words, on a case-per-case basis. By emphasizing the assessment of decisions *in situ*, applied ethics assert a local approach focussing on individuals whose impact on others and society." (2000, p. 34) As a background, ethical questioning is not about knowing "how one should live", a construct that refers to the question to which morality responds (morality dictates). Conversely, ethics respond to the question "how to live" (ethics recommend), which is the quite insightful argument of ethicist J. Dratwa (2019) featured in his book *Dans quel monde voulons-nous vivre ensemble?* All in all, the purpose of applied ethics is to find an answer to the challenges of AI development with a view to ensure and maintain the development of a technology for the common good.

For social sciences and humanities experts, however, ethics formalization is a form of acknowledgment of stakeholders' aptitude to develop their ethical competency and ability for reflexivity, dialogue and autonomy: ethics can be a tool for empowerment (Langlois 2014). Studies conducted in this domain highlight the possibility for these dimensions to relate and interrelate, by formalizing ethics through its relationship with instruments like charters, on the one hand and its use, on the other hand, while preserving its reflexive nature. Hence, the formalization of ethics embodies the willingness of organizations to be socially responsible by promoting a form of ethical formalization related to AI development.

### Dual-Purpose Ethical Institutionalization: An Object of Reflection and a Social Regulation Tool

The formalization of ethics is required in order to go beyond the stage of *good intentions* by giving an official, legitimate place to ethics within organizations and associations. Ethics can be integrated into various suitable internal mechanisms and modes of management, in order to ensure compliance with commitments stated or promoted by an organization as well as their external adherence by implementing relationships of trust with stakeholders.

For instance, an organization can adopt the principles of a technological development statement or ethical charter in order for such a commitment to positively influence strategic orientations and its planning, as well as to ensure an integrated involvement in the lifecycle of AIS. With regard to AI, the early days of ethics formalization focused mainly on heightening awareness about risks and issues, followed by a will to integrate ethical principles as early as during algorithm design. Hence, injunctions were raised for this purpose (ethics by design, security by design, privacy by design). Integrating these principles prior to the design phase can raise new ethical obligations for designers and decision-makers, while also being indicative of a strong ethical commitment when these are actually considered upstream, implemented and promoted in AIS. Maintaining the dual purpose of ethics - a mode of social regulation and a reflexive capacity conducive to empowerment - can be seen as a dynamic process that contributes to consolidating the formalisation of ethics in AIS.

**The Three Objectives of Ethics**

It is the very nature of ethics to offer space for reflection while remaining relevant and flexible enough to respond to new challenges. Peters et al. (2020) mentioned that "[…] ethical impact evaluation must be an ongoing, iterative process—one that involves various stakeholders at every step, and can be re-evaluated over time, and as new issues emerge." The philosopher Malherbe (2000) appropriately highlighted the two modes of cohabitation by stressing that ethics has three objectives: (1) to create spaces for deliberation to support professionals and the public in their reflection on values and norms; (2) to provide these people with tools to better measure the ethical outcomes of their decisions; and (3) to rethink work organization methods, professional practices, modes of management and societal life.

Malherbe's proposal provides an interesting framework to analyze the AI charters deployed for ethical purposes. For instance, the first two objectives of ethics are addressed in The Montréal Declaration for a Responsible Development of Artificial Intelligence (2018), given that the Declaration provides access to the methodological process selected to validate its ethical principles. Based on an expert-citizen co-construction, this stage identifies the various phases of development built on a declaration of general ethical principles and fundamental values, such as well-being, autonomy, justice, privacy, knowledge, democracy and responsibility. Through an iterative phase focused on co-construction, several groups were invited to contribute to a reflection on those values while affirming the selected principles. At this time, there is insufficient information to measure the impact of this declaration on work organization methods, professional practices, modes of management and societal life. Given that the overall phenomenon of ethical charters is relatively recent,[5] meeting this objective requires a formalization phase. However, the phase apparently the most akin to this third objective would possibly be Ethically Aligned Design (IEEE-2019[6]) which had its ethical principles converted into practice standards (IEEE-P7000-P7010). If these standards obtain some form of recognition through certification, they will have demonstrated their importance and will be able to affect modes of management and professional practices, such as those of engineers.

---

[5] We rediscover the appearance of the first ethical charters in 2016 according to the typology of the Berkman Klein Center: Principled AI: Mapping Consensus in Ethical and Rights-Based Approaches to Principles for AI, https://nrs.harvard.edu/urn-3:HUL.InstRepos:42160420.

[6] IEEE Global Initiative on Ethics of Autonomous and Intelligent Systems (n 5) pp. 21–22 (See Principle 2.).

**The Need for Legitimacy in the Ethical Process**

The formalization of principles and values contained in ethical charters challenges the impact of such documents on AI and digital frameworks. In turn, the legitimacy associated with those charters is also challenged. Based on Malouf's philosophical dictionary, legitimacy is defined as what *"complies with laws as well as morals and reason."* [Translation] Malouf further specifies that *"legitimacy is what allows peoples and individuals to accept, without excessive constraint, the authority of an institution embodied by humans and considered as bearing shared values."* [Translation] (Malouf 2009:2) The *Littré* dictionary defines this in terms of what is rooted in equity and reason. Habermas (1978) essentially addresses legitimacy by proposing a concept of communicational ethics. Our interest here is focused on the definition that preserves and maintains trust in AIS developments proposed by Rosavallon (2008), in which he addresses the importance of establishing a legitimacy of proximity. Based on dialogue, such legitimacy is built on the capacity of individuals or professionals[7] to discuss and take part in such issues with a genuine impact on their lives. According to Bourgeois and Nizet (1995), "a behaviour, an opinion or a decision is legitimate for stakeholders if they perceive it as complying with social norms that they consider positive." [Translation] (1995:34) According to Luhmann (2006), such deliberation in the public sphere can "reduce social complexity" and, as a result, obtain stronger social acceptability. It is our view that, in this process to formalize ethical charters, the implementation of a legitimacy of proximity makes ethics a political choice. The common denominator of these charters is often the promotion of society's well-being and trust in technological developments. Therefore, it is all the more important that public deliberation be essential, given the end-purpose of these instruments. Therefore, it confirms its legitimacy through the compelling demonstration of its necessity.

Now that we have some insight of the ethical charter landscape and that we have explored the elements needed to formalize ethics that guarantee the materialization of principles, we propose a reflection on their use as a potential preamble to future AI legal frameworks, since an increasing demand in national and international regulations has emerged following the gains and drift of those ethical charters.

## 3 Building on Ethical Charters to Expand the AI Normative Landscape

The formalization of ethical charters should also be explored with respect to its potential to help develop AI regulations, either locally or internationally. Despite the valuable yet unequal contribution of ethical charters, the need to go beyond them – without discarding them – has been increasingly recognized; the next step to enriching the AI normative landscape is to propose additional binding norms. This is probably a natural development given that AI ethics grew from an underexplored area in

---

[7] See example of the standards of practice proposed by IEEE and validated by the engineers concerned.

significant need for societal benchmarks into an increasingly studied and refined field. One of the reasons for this recognition relates to the previously underlined fact that ethical charters have shown their limits in governing some AI developments, including for powerful industries pushing their business interests in unwanted societal directions. This has triggered a demand for further regulations, eventually inspired by such charters (that is, they could serve as a compass for certain legal developments). Another reason is that these charters have made valuable, yet incomplete progress in defining the basis of an international common framework offering opportunities for normative scaling up in an area where boundaries are often erased. These two aspects can be considered as the next steps in AI governance, and are explored in the next sections.

### 3.1    The Deployment of AI Regulations

The recent shift from the demand for ethical to legal guidance is perhaps most strikingly embodied by Google CEO Sundar Pitchar's January 2020 statement, in which he mentioned that AI needs to be regulated, especially in areas like self-driving cars and healthcare technology: "Regulation and self-regulation, via a code of ethics and an ethics board, might not be enough [...]." (BBC 2020)[8] Some would say that, at this point, the demand for legislation has become so important that Google could not oppose it without significant public backlash; so it is better to be part of the regulatory process in order to shape its development.

The risk of not moving towards additional legal governance despite the current effervescence in ethical work is real and multifaceted. Stakeholders have started exposing the impact of underregulated AI, pointing to risks related to privacy protection, solidarity, responsibility, discrimination, health or inclusiveness issues. Well-known scandals, such as Cambridge Analytica and Buolamwini (2018),[9] have helped bring much public exposure to these issues. During the public consultation process that led to the Montreal Declaration for Responsible AI Development, the demand for additional legal protection came up as the policy option most required by stakeholders.[10] That being said, it would be inaccurate to state that there are currently no AI regulations; legal regimes around the world already have some tools to address responsibility issues, whether or not they specifically relate to AI. For example, AI generates a set of potential opportunities and problems that can be addressed, even if not always adequately, under usual legal regimes like tort law, contracts, criminal law,

---

[8] https://www.bbc.com/news/technology-51178198; Other key technology players like Microsoft president have also called for further regulation Monica Nickelsburg, "Microsoft President Brad Smith Calls for AI Regulations at Davos" (21 January 2020), online: *GeekWire* https://www.geekwire.com/2020/microsoft-president-brad-smith-calls-ai-regulation-davos/.

[9] The Guardian, "The Cambridge Analytica scandal changed the world – but it didn't change Facebook" https://www.theguardian.com/technology/2019/mar/17/the-cambridge-analytica-scandal-changed-the-world-but-it-didnt-change-facebook.

[10] Report of the Montreal Declaration for the Responsible Development of Artificial Intelligence (2018). Part 6 - Priority areas and their recommendations for the responsible development of AI. https://5da05b0d-f158-4af28b9f892984c33739.filesusr.com/ugd/ebc3a3_d6a627b2f8644a30ae1747 62557da6fc.pdf.

administrative law, and so on.[11] However, the capacity of these regimes in the context of AI leaves some blind or weak spots for legal oversight or insufficiently tackles some of the novel issues that AI raises, such as consent in the Age of Big Data, lack of explicability and transparency in algorithms and unprecedented uses of AI technology like automated killer robots, a new form of political manipulation and facial recognition.[12]

If not addressed by suitable legal frameworks, such issues can erode trust in political institutions, researchers and innovators, to name a few. As a result, this situation can weaken the buy-in required from societal stakeholders for innovations to take hold. Such a lack of public acceptability will then create a significant chasm between development and implementation of an innovation (and, arguably, even more so for responsible innovation). Some authors (Panch et al. 2019) have called this gap between development and implementation - which is due to different factors – the most "inconvenient truth" about AI, as it is already noticed in certain sectors of AI activity. This chasm could result in significant lost opportunities for valuable AI developments likely to improve society, the environment and individual well-being, as well as financial and research effort loss due to unusable or underuse AI developments (Lovis 2019; Flood and Régis 2021). Furthermore, uncertainty regarding legal hazards, whether real or perceived, is in itself an obstacle to innovation. Relevant literature already mentions this impediment, and current research projects evaluating AI implementation in healthcare professionals' practices highlights their resistance to innovation due to a lack of clarity with respect to their legal responsibility.[13] There is thus an evident need to clarify legal frameworks and responsibilities in order to sustain innovation. In other words, legal predictability must be enhanced; this is a different goal than an ongoing process of ethical reflexivity. Sometimes, legal predictability will require the redesign of legal frameworks; other times, it will require increased knowledge transfer regarding their meaning in specific contexts. (Girard and Régis 2020).[14]

---

[11] See for example: Marion Oswald, Algorithm-assisted decision-making in the public sector: framing the issues using administrative law rules governing discretionary power, (2018), Phil. Trans. R. Soc. A. 376; Michael Froomkin, Ian Kerr and Joelle Pineau, «When AIs Outperform Doctors: Confronting the Challenges of a Tort-Induced Over-Reliance on Machine Learning, (2019) vol 61:33, Arizona Law Review, 33; Frank Pasquale, Data-Informed Duties in AI development, Columbia Law Review 119:1917 (2019).

[12] For examples see the different essays in Glenn Cohen and al. Big Data, Health Law, and Bioethics, 2018 Cambridge University Press; Ian Kerr & Katie Szilagyi, "Asleep at the switch? How killer robots become a force multiplier of military necessity" in Ryan M. Calo, Michael Froomkin, Ian Kerr, eds, Robot Law (Cheltenham: Edward Elgar Pub Ltd, 2016) 333; Harry Surden, 35 Ga. St. U. L. Rev.1305 (2018–2019) Artificial Intelligence and Law: An Overview.

[13] See OMS, https://apps.who.int/iris/bitstream/handle/10665/44497/9789241564144_eng.pdf;jsessionid=B511E3B52CFC230B4B4B4CB309F7B4F8?sequence=1, at p. 11.

[14] Indeed, sometimes, the legal framework is clear, but its understanding by professionals is not; it then becomes a matter of better communicating the meaning of such frameworks. See for example Marie-Andrée Girard and Catherine Régis, « La collaboration interprofessionnelle: une pratique complexe dans un environnement juridique tout aussi complexe» 2020 J.D.S.A.M. numéro 25 at 153.

Yet, legal developments in innovation logic may be in the midst of a paradigm freeze, encapsulated in Munro's quote: "In the early days of emerging technology, we have power but insufficient clarity to act. In later days, we have more clarity, but declining power."[15] Considering the procedural requirements of legislative processes and the crystallizing, constraining effect of law on conduct, proceeding with legal developments usually requires a certain maturity in understanding social phenomena. But when such an understanding is finally acquired, it can become more difficult to regulate due to the resources and interests invested in innovation.

AI offers a good illustration of this "paradigm freeze" situation (Kuhn 1983). Technology, especially machine learning, has evolved at an incredibly rapid pace. AI progress is now considered as following a rapid obsolescence cycle, in which the technology will significantly evolve every few years. In addition, machine learning is a complex mathematical and computer technique, one that requires a significant learning curve for many non-specialists, including regulators. During the early stages of development and implementation, it was therefore difficult (and perhaps still is) to identify precisely the aspects of this technique that need to be regulated, and why and how. Understanding the functioning of AI and its risks, benefits and challenges has significantly evolved thanks to the ethics community and ethical charters. When these concepts became more familiar, a massive amount of investment was injected to support this innovation.[16] It then became more and more difficult for governments around the world to formally regulate AI, at least in a way that could limit its development, for instance to better balance innovation with stronger digital rights for consumers, patients and so on.[17] As Boisson de Chazournes (2014) stresses, in the digital world, the repeated actions of individuals can eventually shape norms: behaviour influences normativity. This can create a path of dependency in regulation, where innovation becomes normative and law eventually enshrines, at least partially, what becomes "normal practice" through people's increasingly routine use of technology. Put differently, digital technology strongly and rapidly affects people's social expectations. This is another reason why the impact of ethical charters has been important to the extent that they influence technology design, as they could later contribute to shaping, at least to some degree, such expectations.

The ethical charters developed so far have offered some promise to overcome, at least partially, this potential paradigm freeze. When law could not move, ethics was active in targeting priority areas of normative action (sometimes through public consultation processes), democratizing access to AI information and bringing to the attention of policy-makers (in a way, making it almost unavoidable for them to stay idle) the importance of interventionist measures to balance innovation dynamics with

---

[15] See: https://www.danmunro.ca/blog/2019/1/16/risk-uncertainty-and-the-governance-dilemma-for-artificial-intelligence.

[16] See: AI Index Report de 2019. https://hai.stanford.edu/sites/default/files/ai_index_2019_report.pdf.

[17] That being said, law is more than a tool to distribute the costs of incidents among actors developing and deploying innovation; it can contribute to share the benefits of innovation, for example by influencing private industries development and labor conditions.

developers' responsible actions. The law can now build upon these valuable ethical assets to better target regulatory options. (Petitgand and Régis 2019).[18]

The exercise of building legal developments like legislation on some ethical charters will necessarily require adjustments. The law requires a capacity to operationalize its normative postulates (to make them enforceable) which does not always concern ethics, as mentioned in the first part of this paper. Yet, the formalization of ethics will contribute to providing an "applicability test" that could be helpful at this point, especially if it includes a feedback process allowing stakeholders to further understand what works and what is not normatively wise. While certain ethical principles can be more easily translated into legal changes, others are simply impractical. For example, a principle of *justice* (at least without further precision) does not correlate with actionable legal duties that can be imposed on stakeholders, whereas principles like *respect for human autonomy* and *explicability* do so more easily, as they are already part of legal corpora in many legal systems. Besides, some ethical guidelines are more granular than others, offering richer normative content to explore legal reforms. The Montreal Declaration is a relevant example with ten main principles, many sub-principles and a side report detailing policy recommendations.[19] In fact, some legal researchers have already started to build on ethical charters to propose legal reforms or legal interpretation. For example, some authors (Lutun 2019; Régis 2019) have recommended enshrining a patient's right to consent (and not just to be informed) to physicians' use of AI tools based on Principle 9 of the Montreal Declaration.[20] This work will arguably need to continue even if the law does not ultimately depend on ethical guidelines to evolve. Despite possible "lost in translation" problems between law and ethics in developing regulation, the intersection of the two fields provides normative guidance and opportunities that, if mobilized appropriately, can amplify each domain's contribution to AI. This interaction of law and ethics has already been mobilized before, including in the field of medicine. The same could be done in the field of AI, despite the undeniable challenges that such a widely encompassing, mostly private and fast-developing culture of new professionalism entails (Mittelstadti 2019b).

At the end of the day, while the roles of law and ethics should not be confused, it would be a mistake to position the two as necessarily complementing its responses to

---

[18] For example of such work: a) High-Level panel on AI de la Commission européennes: https://ec.europa.eu/futurium/en/ai-alliance-consultation/guidelines#Top and https://ec.europa.eu/digital-single-market/en/news/policy-and-investment-recommendations-trustworthy-artificial-intelligence; b) Montreal Declaration for the Responsible Development of Artificial Intelligence. Journal de Droit de la Santé et de l'Assurance Maladie (Journal of Health and Health Insurance Law).

[19] www.montrealdeclaration-responsibleai.com.

[20] Adele Lutun (2019), « L'article 11 du projet de loi bioéthique français prend-il en compte les principes de la Déclaration de Montréal pour un développement responsable de l'intelligence artificielle ? / Does Art. 11 of the French draft bioethics law take into account the principles of the Montreal Declaration on the Responsible Development of Artificial Intelligence? Available online: https://www.chairesante.ca/articles/2019/larticle-11-du-projet-de-loi-bioethique-francais-prend-il-en-compte-les-principes-de-la-declaration-de-montreal-pour-un-developpement-responsable-de-lintell igence-artificielle/»; Catherine Régis, « Perspectives internationales sur la régulation de l'IA dans le domaine de la santé», conference given for the Entretiens Droit & Santé, Université Paris Descartes, Paris, 6 décembre 2019.

the "flaws" of the other. These two normative approaches have different contributions and logic that are both valuable. Acknowledging these distinctions can allow the development of a coherent normative strategy for responsible AI innovation that embraces the complementarity and prospect of each; neither of these approaches is a standalone instrument to address entirely the complex field of AI. Even if the legal field deploys further regulations to address AI issues, ethics will still be required. Essentially based on general enforceable rules that apply to everyone, law will not have the means to address every context-specific variation and the rapid development that AI will trigger. Due to their less formal and fast-paced development process (at least compared with law), ethics and ethical charters need to stay responsive, relevant and purposeful in the AI normative landscape if they are to add agility and layers of reflexivity in AI normativity. The complementarity of the two types of norms forms a rich juncture in moving towards the next steps in AI normative framework development, including at the international level.

### 3.2   Seizing Opportunities for an International Scaling-Up of AI Normativity

Ethical charters could also be a valuable asset to expand the normative landscape at the international level. International norms often start with the identification of a global problem that no country alone can adequately address or that touches on issues with a reach beyond territorial borders, for instance, due to their impact on human dignity and life, global economy and the environment. The United Nations' High-level Panel on Digital Cooperation highlights the need to develop collaborative international governance tools to manage Big Data and AI, considering the undeniable effect that such digital products will have on humanity.[21] Moreover, the scope of many AI issues extends well beyond national borders, with digital data travelling from one country to another, algorithms having an impact on worldwide conducts, human life and the environment, and cyberattacks disturbing organizations, governments, universities, hospitals and other institutions around the world. Facial recognition data collected on travellers in airports, cookies gathering information on cyber-consumers, labour transformations due to AI progress, digital biosurveillance tools detecting infectious disease outbreaks and the 2017 WannaCry cyberattack with significant impact on organizations across continents are but a few examples of such impact (Martin 2019; Alford 2019).[22] There is thus a strong argument to be made in favour of scaling-up normative work in AI, in order to develop international norms. This is also in line, at least partially, with UNESCO's very recent work: an international group of experts has started drafting a global recommendation on the ethics of AI[23].

---

[21] See: United-Nations, *The Age of Digital Interdependence*, Report of the UN Secretary-General's High-Level on Digital Cooperation, 2019.

[22] CNN.com (2019). When seeing is no longer believing - Inside the Pentagon's race against deepfake videos. Online: https://www.cnn.com/interactive/2019/01/business/pentagons-race-against-deepfakes/.

[23] https://en.unesco.org/news/unescos-expert-group-revises-draft-text-recommendation-ethics-artificial-intelligence (date of access: 2 december 2020).

As a contribution to this process, all the ethical charters developed worldwide have started to identify points of convergence and divergence in AI governance. These charters have also demonstrated that many AI issues and their potential responses are global in nature. Building international consensus takes time and resources, particularly when developing treaties in public international law. As mentioned earlier, the work of Jobin et al. (2019), Zeng (2019) and Fjeld et al. (2020) is instrumental in this regard, as they mapped and analyzed the voluminous body of ethical AI charters and guidelines. Their contribution can serve as the starting point of a reflection process on future global digital rights, given the analysis and synthesis effort already exerted. For instance, Jobin et al. identified five ethical principles that demonstrate clearer international convergence: transparency, justice and fairness, non-maleficence, responsibility and privacy. However, the research team noted that some of these principles do not necessarily share the same definition. Nonetheless, these points of convergence provide a good start to identifying the shared principles that could eventually become a consensus for international norms, referred to as the "normative core" by Fjeld, J. *et al.* This is indeed a good start – and surely not a final endeavour – since, as mentioned earlier, some of the principles do not fully integrate ethical requirements, underrepresent some important voices and might be culturally specific (Jobin et al. 2019). The concept of justice underlying the charters is also indicative of how moral issues and moral reasoning are addressed. In fact, the concept of justice has been criticized in feminist studies of the 1980s in the field of moral development.[24] Hagendorff (2020) has highlighted the biases that continue to be perpetuated in his study of the 22 charters by pointing out the fact that the AI ethics discourse is primarily shaped by men and a way of approaching moral problems. (2020, p. 103). These limitations must be kept in mind, and compensated for, if they are to be exploited for future comprehensive and inclusive normative work.

While ethical AI guidelines could be helpful in accelerating international AI framework developments, many questions have yet to be answered regarding how this international work should be organized, including the choice of organization to lead the process and whether it should be ethically or legally driven (or both). The leadership role is key, as it will influence how the framework will be initiated and how it will later unfold. Identifying the best international organization to hold such a role, either exclusively or in partnership with other stakeholders, is open for debate. Interesting international AI partnerships are currently being established to accelerate global debates and actions likely to contribute to the process. Establishing international partnerships are often the outcome of initiatives that fostered discussions on ethical principles and the importance of maintaining and integrating ethical and legal benchmarks into the process to implement governance. The Global Partnership on Responsible Artificial Intelligence (GPAI) is a joint France-Canada initiative that has to

---

[24] See: Carol Gilligan, *In a Different Voice: Psychological Theory and Women's Development* (Cambridge, MA: Harvard University Press, 1982). Eva Feder Kittay and Diana T. Meyers, eds., *Women and Moral Theory* (Totowa, NJ: Rowman & Littlefield, 1987). Neil Noddings, *Caring: A Feminine Approach to Ethics and Moral Education* (Berkeley, CA: University of California Press, 1984). Blum, Lawrence A., 1988, "Gilligan and Kohlberg: Implications for Moral Theory," Ethics, 98 (3): 472–491. Naussbaum1999, *Sex and Social Justice*, Oxford: Oxford University Press.

date brought together various countries (such as Australia, Canada, France, Germany, Italy, Japan, Korea, Mexico, the United Kingdom, the United-States and New Zealand); this is a fine example at least in theory, of international governance. That being said, this initiative is too recent to fully appreciate its impact.

However, we would argue that there is need for a leadership role from an international intergovernmental organization like the United Nations (UN), for at least two reasons. First, considering the major economic interest in AI development and deployment, most of which private, an international dialogue needs to be organized through an institution that is relatively remote from private industries (even if they are included in the dialogue process), that can gather top-level officials from different countries (and thus top-level government commitment and eventual involvement of regulatory powers) and that represents the global public interest. Second, international intergovernmental organizations can often mobilize public international law, as is clearly the case for the UN,[25] allowing them to foster the development of normative actions of different natures (binding or not) that guide States around the world. Of course, States remain involved in proposing and adopting such norms, but the UN can ultimately achieve something that no State alone can do. How the UN should eventually coordinate its AI normative actions with other intergovernmental organizations, sometimes attached to the UN itself (such as the World Health Organization, UNESCO and the International Labour Organisation) needs to be further examined. That being said, the UN is capable of engaging conversations around multi-sector and multi-stakeholder issues. This conversation is a necessity in AI, since it generates challenges for almost every sector of societal activity. The UN's role is therefore important to addressing AI from a transversal perspective, which will be essential for normative coherence: similar issues in education, health, environment, and so on should trigger similar normative responses.

The kind of normative instruments that the UN or other international intergovernmental or transnational organizations should develop to support "good" AI is surely a complex and requisite debate that is beyond the scope of this paper. There is a valid argument to make in favour of establishing at least some form of binding international AI norms, arguably an international treaty, acknowledging the points raised previously regarding the need for additional forms of enforceable AI regulation.[26] Whether or not they are binding, international norms can have an impact on the AI world, even if they do not address all the potential opportunities and problems that this thriving innovation will raise – for instance, public international law faces challenges on its own, such as its enforcement capabilities (Kantorowicz-Reznichenko (2020); Raustiala 2000; Hongju Koh 1997). Legal scholars have demonstrated for some time now that binding (hard law) and non-binding (soft law) both produce some effects in domestic law, even though these might be different and follow a different path of implementation into

---

[25] See the Charter of the United Nations: https://treaties.un.org/doc/publication/ctc/uncharter.pdf.

[26] The binding and non-binding distinction is a classic division in public international law. A norm is considered to be binding when it creates mandatory obligations for member states (hard law) and non-binding when it is intended to assist action, consultation, negotiation and cooperation without explicit obligations or specific adoption procedures (soft law).

domestic law (Shaffer and Pollack 2009; Hillgenberg 1999; Finnemore and Sikkink 1998; Betts and Orchard 2014; Gostin 2014; Weil 1983; Hathaway and Shapiro 2011).

As such, in the process of devising and developing international AI frameworks, a normative strategy should not be designed *in abstracto* from the very nature of a particular norm, but instead should analyse and evaluate the advantages and drawbacks specific to each norm by considering legal, political, economic and ethical concerns relating to the AI issues at stake (Régis and Kastler 2018). For instance, the process of adopting a norm both at an international and national level could favour choosing a non-binding instrument. The process of creating binding instruments is long, complex, rigid and costly. As a result, they are less suitable for issues that require a rapid response and flexibility to adapt to scientific developments or that concern only a limited number of states (Gostin 2014; Chevalier 1998). The process can also be prolonged by national implementation procedures required for binding law. As another illustration, the existence of "competing" binding legal norms could require the adoption of similar norms to gain political and legal traction. For instance, norms may have to be binding in contexts where they will be in tension with other powerful binding international norms, such as trade and intellectual property laws. (Régis and Kastler 2018) This will clearly be the case for AI at some point. The creation of such frameworks will also require first exploring how existing international norms (in treaties, declarations, resolutions, and so on) might already cover or leave gaps for AI challenges – even despite directly referencing AI or Big Data – in order to build a coherent and relevant normative response[27].

At the end of the day, the best international AI framework will probably be a skilful composite of complementary binding and non-binding norms forming a global strategy for responsible AI. The five shared principles found in ethical guidelines could again serve as a starting point, once stakeholders agree on their meaning and translate them into useable material for developing international law. And if such principles can be validated as triggering social acceptability, or even social preferability (Floridi and Taddeo 2016), from a global perspective – a key ethical consideration – the norms developed based on these principles will more likely induce voluntary compliance. This is an ideal position in international law, where state sovereignty sometimes comes in the way of enforceability.

# 4   Conclusion

The formalization of ethical charters is both a requisite and essential step to providing a more appropriate normative framework for artificial intelligence ethics and digital rights. However, this process must be assessed to measure the actual scope of its relevance. In this regard, a wealth of organizational ethics research is available, particularly on ethical institutionalization. It provides interesting insights on how to gain a better understanding of the factors that could foster the integration of ethical principles

---

[27] United-Nations, *The Age of Digital Interdependence*, Report of the UN Secretary-General's High-Level on Digital Cooperation, 2019.

in AI systems. The declaration *Toward Trustworthy AI Development: Mechanisms for Supporting Verifiable Claims*[28] is the outcome of the international AI research community's study of the issue and another significant milestone in ethical formalization and institutionalization. The analysis clearly emphasizes AI drawbacks identified in the declaration yet acknowledges the importance of ethics. Nevertheless, the authors stress that a significant amount of work has yet to be done in formulating ethical principles before they are actually applied.

Overall, ethical charters are instruments to be used to establish a reflective ethical approach while highlighting priority values. These values can then serve as a compass for the development of other normative terms, such as legal and global governance standards. The challenge lies in developing an AI normative strategy through an integrated process, by carefully drawing on the strengths of various types of norms, whether they are binding or not, to establish a trustworthy AI governance. This challenge includes maintaining an interrelation, and, more broadly, a dialogue between ethics and law, as addressed in this article. However, to date this correlation has been insufficiently mobilized across the world of AI governance, and it represents one of the greatest challenges to ensuring the future well-being of humankind as AI innovations are deployed, globally, and begin to affect a wide range of aspects (even all) of human life.

# References

Adelman, H.: Morality and ethics in organizational administration. J. Bus. Ethics **10**(9), 665–678 (1991)

Alford, J.: NHS cyber-attacks could delay life-saving care and cost millions. Imperial College London (2019). https://www.imperial.ac.uk/news/193151/nhs-cyber-attacks-could-delay-life-saving-care/.

Bairaktarova, D., Woodcock, A.: Engineering student's ethical awareness and behavior: a new motivational model. Sci. Eng. Ethics **23**, 1129–1157 (2017)

Barabas, C., Dinakar, K., Ito, J., Virza, M., Zittrain, J.: Interventions over predictions: reframing the ethical debate for actuarial risk assessment. In: Proceedings of FAT* Conference (FAT* 2018), vol. 9. ACM, New York (2018). ISBN: 978-92-3-100363-9

Bégin, L.: L'éthique au travail, éditions Liber, Québec (2009)

Betts, A., Orchard, P.: Introduction: the normative institutionalization-implementation gap. In: Betts, A., Orchard, P. (eds.) Implementation and World Politics: How International Norms Change Practice, pp. 1–26. Oxford University Press, Oxford (2014)

Bietti, E.: From ethics washing to ethics bashing: a view on tech ethics from within moral philosophy. In: DRAFT – Final Paper Published in the Proceedings to ACM FAT* Conference (2019)

Blum, L.A.: Gilligan and Kohlberg: implications for moral theory. Ethics **98**(3), 472–491 (1988)

Boisson de Chazournes, L.: Standards, régulation internationale et organisations internationales. In: Frydman, B., Van Waeyenberge, A. (eds.) Gouverner par les standards et les indicateurs. De Hume aux rankings, pp. 69–92. Bruylant/LGDJ, Bruxelles/Paris (2014)

---

[28] See Toward Trustworthy AI Development: Mechanisms for Supporting Verifiable Claims, a major charter created by a large portion of the international AI research community. https://arxiv.org/abs/2004.07213.

Boisvert, Y.: L'institutionnalisation de l'éthique gouvernementale: Quelle place pour l'éthique ? Presses de l'Université du Québec (2011)

Brent Mittelstadt, B.: Principles alone cannot guarantee ethical AI. Nat. Mach. Intell. **1**, 501–550 (2019)

Buolamwini, J., Gebru, T.: Gender shades: intersectional accuracy disparities in commercial gender classification. In: Conference on Fairness, Accountability and Transparency, pp. 77–91 (2018)

Carroll, A., Bucholtz, A.: Business Society: Ethics and Stakeholder Management, 4th edn. South-Western College Publishing, Cincinnati (1999)

Chevallier, J.: Vers un droit post-moderne? Les transformations de la régulation juridique. Revue du droit public et de la science politique en France et à l'étranger **3**, 659–690 (1998)

Cohen, G., et al.: Big Data, Health Law, and Bioethics. Cambridge University Press, Cambridge (2018)

Dratwa, J.: Dans quel monde voulons-nous vivre?, vol. 4. éditions ISTE, London (2019)

Flood, C.M., Régis, C.: Artificial intelligence and health law. In: Scassa, T., Martin-Bariteau, F. (eds.) Artificial Intelligence and the Law in Canada, Lexis Nexis (2021). (accepted for publication, to be published in 2021)

Finnemore, M., Sikkink, K.: International norm dynamics and political change. Int. Organ. **52**(4), 887–917 (1998)

Fjeld, J., Achten, N., Hilligoss, H., Nagy, H., Srikumar, M.: Principled Artificial Intelligence: Mapping Consensus in Ethical and Rights-based Approaches to Principles for AI. Berkman Klein Center for Internet & Society (2020). https://dash.harvard.edu/handle/1/42160420

Floridi, L.: Translating principles into practices of digital ethics: five risks of being unethical. Philos. Technol. **32**(2), 185–193 (2019)

Floridi, L., Taddeo, M.: What is data ethics? Philos. Trans. R. Soc. A **374**(2083) (2016). Available at SSRN: https://ssrn.com/abstract=2907744

Fontanel, J., Sushcheva, N.: La puissance des GAFAM: Réalités, apports et dangers. Annuaire français de relations internationales, La Documentation française, Paris (2019). XX. ffhal02196915

Froomkin, M., Kerr, I., Pineau, J.: When AIs outperform doctors: confronting the challenges of a tort-induced over-reliance on machine learning. Univ. Miami Legal Stud. Res. Paper **61**, 33 (2019)

Gates, M., Ma, J. (eds.): The age of digital interdependence. Report of the UN Secretary-General's High-level Panel on Digital Cooperation (2019)

Gautrais, V.: Neutralité technologique: rédaction et interprétation des lois face aux technologies. Thémis, Montréal (2012)

Ghafur, S., Kristensen, S., Honeyford, K., et al.: A retrospective impact analysis of the WannaCry cyberattack on the NHS. NPJ Digit. Med. **2**, 98–105 (2019)

Gilligan, C.: In a Different Voice: Psychological Theory and Women's Development. Harvard University Press, Cambridge (1982)

Girard, M.-A., Régis, C.: La collaboration interprofessionnelle: une pratique complexe dans un environnement juridique tout aussi complexe. J.D.S.A.M. **25**, 153 (2020)

Google boss Sundar Pichai calls for AI regulation (2020, 20 janvier). BBC News (2020). https://www.bbc.com/news/technology-51178198

Gostin, L.: Global health law, pp. 64–67. Harvard University Press, Cambridge (2014)

Green, B.: "Good" isn't good enough", Neurips conference paper (2019). https://aiforsocialgood.github.io/neurips2019/accepted/track3/pdfs/67_aisg_neurips2019.pdf

Hagendorff, T.: The ethics of AI ethics: an evaluation of guidelines. Mind. Mach. **30**, 99–120 (2020). https://doi.org/10.1007/s11023-020-09517-8

Hathaway, O., Shapiro Scott, K.: Outcasting: enforcement in domestic and international law. Yale Law J. **121**, 252–349 (2011)

Hillgenberg, H.: A fresh look at soft law. Eur. J. Int. Law **10**, 499–515 (1999)

Finnemore, M., Sikkink, K.: International norm dynamics and political change. Int. Organ. **52**, 887–917 (1999)

Hongju Koh, H.: Bringing international law home. Houston Law Rev. **35**, 623–681 (1997)

https://www.forbes.com/sites/nicolemartin1/2019/09/25/the-major-concerns-around-facial-recognition-technology/#558f9ba94fe3, Justine Alford (2019) https://www.imperial.ac.uk/news/193151/nhs-cyber-attacks-could-delay-life-saving-care/, https://www.nature.com/articles/s41746-019-0161-6

Jobin, A., Ienca, M., Vayena, E.: The global landscape of AI ethics guidelines. Nat. Mach. Intell. **1**, 389–399 (2019)

Kantorowicz-Reznichenko, E.: The enforcement of international law. In: Hosli, M., Selleslaghs, J. (eds.) The Changing Global Order. United Nations University Series on Regionalism, vol. 17. Springer, Cham (2020). https://doi.org/10.1007/978-3-030-21603-0_18

Kerr, I., Szilagyi, K.: Asleep at the switch? How killer robots become a force multiplier of military necessity. In: Calo, R., Froomkin, M., Kerr, I. (eds.) Robot Law, pp. 333–366. Edward Elgar Pub Ltd., Cheltenham (2016)

Kittay, E.F., Diana, T.M. (eds.): Women and Moral Theory. Rowman & Littlefield, Totowa (1987)

Koh, H.: Why do nations obey international law? Yale Law J. **106**, 2599–2659 (1997)

Kuhn, T.: La Structure des révolutions scientifiques, Flammarion, coll. «Champs», Montréal (1983)

Langlois, L.: Le leadership éthique: un mode de gouvernance responsabilisant, dans Cinq questions d'éthique organisationnelle, sous la direction de Luc Bégin, éditions Nota Bene, pp. 139–172 (2014)

Lovis, C.: Unlocking the power of artificial intelligence and big data in medicine. J. Med. Internet Res. **21**, 16607 (2019)

Lutun, A.: L'article 11 du projet de loi bioéthique français prend-il en compte les principes de la Déclaration de Montréal pour un développement responsable de l'intelligence artificielle? (2019). https://www.chairesante.ca/articles/2019/l

Malherbe, J-F.: Le nomade polyglotte : l'excellence éthique en postmodernité (2000). éditions FIDES

Martin, N.: The Major Concerns Around Facial Recognition Technologies. Forbes.com, 25 September 2019

Mercier, S.: L'éthique dans les entreprises, Repères, no. 263, La Découverte & Syros (1999)

Mercier, S.: L'éthique dans les entreprises, collection Repères, La Découverte (2004)

Metzinger, T.: EU Guidelines: Ethics washing made in Europe. Der Tagesspiegel (2019). https://www.tagesspiegel.de/politik/eu-guidelines-ethics-washing-made-in-europe/24195496.html

Miller, C., Coldicott, R.: People, power and technology: the tech workers' view (2019). https://doteveryone.org.uk/report/workersview/

Mittelstadt, B.: Principles alone cannot guarantee ethical AI. Nat. Mach. Intell. **1**, 501–507 (2019)

Montreal Declaration for Responsible AI. https://www.montrealdeclaration-responsibleai.com. https://5da05b0d-f158-4af2-8b9f892984c33739.filesusr.com/ugd/ebc3a3_d6a627b2f8644a30ae174762557da6fc.pdf

Munro, D.: Risk, Uncertainty and the Governance Dilemma for Artificial Intelligence. Dan's blog (2019). https://www.danmunro.ca/blog/2019/1/16/risk-uncertainty-and-the-governance-dilemma-for-artificial-intelligence

Murphy, P.: Creating Ethical Corporate Structures. Sloan Manage. Rev. **30**(2), 81–87 (1989)

Naussbaum, M.: Sex and Social Justice. Oxford University Press, Oxford (1999)

Noddings, N.: Caring: A Feminine Approach to Ethics and Moral Education. University of California Press, Berkeley (1984)

Nye, D.: Technology Matters: Questions to Live With, vol. 47. MIT Press, Cambridge (2007)

O'Neil, C.: Weapons of math destruction: how big data increases inequality and threatens democracy, 1st edn., p. 272. Crown, New York (2016)

OMS Telemedicine Opportunities and developments in Member States, p. 11 (2010). https://apps.who.int/iris/bitstream/handle/10665/44497/9789241564144_eng.pdf;jsessionid=B511E3B52CFC230B4B4B4CB309F7B4F8?sequence=1

Oswald, M.: Algorithm-assisted decision-making in the public sector: framing the issues using administrative law rules governing discretionary power. Philos. Trans. A: Math. Phys. Eng. Sci. **376**(2128), 20170359 (2018)

Panch, T., Mattie, H., Celim, L.: The "inconvenient truth" about AI in healthcare. Npj Digit. Med. **2**, 1–3 (2019)

Pasquale, F.: Data-Informed Duties in AI development. Columbia Law Rev. **14**, 1917–1940 (2019)

Perrault, R., Shoham, Y., Brynjolfsson, E., et al.: Artificial intelligence index. 2019 annual report. Human-Centered Artificial Intelligence, Stanford (2019). https://hai.stanford.edu/sites/default/files/ai_index_2019_report.pdf

Petitgand, C., Régis, C.: Principes éthiques et encadrement juridique de l'intelligence artificielle en santé : Exemple de la Déclaration de Montréal pour un développement responsable de l'intelligence artificielle. Journal de Droit de la Santé et de l'Assurance Maladie **22**, 102–106 (2019)

Rapport de la Déclaration de Montréal pour un développement responsable de l'intelligence artificielle (2018) Partie 6 - Les chantiers prioritaires et leurs recommandations pour le développement responsable de l'IA. https://5da05b0d-f158-4af2-8b9f-892984c33739.filesusr.com/ugd/ebc3a3_d6a627b2f8644a30ae174762557da6fc.pdf

Raustiala, K.: Compliance and effectiveness in international regulatory cooperation. Case W. Reserve J. Int. Law **32**, 387–440 (2000)

Régis, C., Kastler, F.: Improving the world health organization's normative strategy with respect to global health goals: what should we aim for? Revue Belge de droit international, p. 138 (2018)

Reynaud, J.-D.: La régulation sociale, Dans Le travail: autres réalités, autres regards, Revue internationale d'action communautaire Numéro 25, Printemps, pp. 121–126 (1991)

Salomon, R.C.: The Little Philosophy Book. Oxford Press, October 2007. ISBN: 9780195311143

Shaffer, G., Pollack, M.: Hard vs soft law: alternatives, complements, and antagonists in international governance. Minnesota Law Rev. **94**, 706–799 (2009)

Surden, H.: Artificial intelligence and law: an overview. Georgia State Univ. Law Rev. **35**, 1305–1337 (2019)

The Charter of the United Nations, San Francisco (1945). https://treaties.un.org/doc/publication/ctc/uncharter.pdf

The European Commission: Independent high-level expert group on artificial intelligence SET UP. European Commission (2019). Brussels.https://ec.europa.eu/digital-single-market/en/news/policy-and-investment-recommendations-trustworthy-artificial-intelligence

United-Nations: The Age of Digital Interdependence, Report of the UN Secretary-General's High-Level on Digital Cooperation (2019)

Vold, K.V., Peters, D., Robinson, D., Calvo, R.: Responsible AI – two frameworks for ethical design practice. IEEE Trans. Technol. Soc. (2020). https://doi.org/10.1109/TTS.2020.2974991

Villani, C.: Intelligence artificielle et travail, Rapport à la ministre du Travail et au secrétaire d'État auprès du premier ministre, chargé du numérique, France stratégie, mars 2018
Weil, P.: Towards relative normativity in international law? Am. J. Int. Law **77**, 413–442 (1983)
Xianhong, H., Neupane, B., Echaiz, L.F., Sibal, P., Rivera Lam, M.: Steering AI and advanced ICTs for knowledge societies: a Rights. Access, and Multi-stakeholder Perspective. UNESCO Series on Internet Freedom, Openness (2019)
Zeng, Y., Lu, E., Huangfu, C.: Linking artificial intelligence principles, p. 14. arXiv:1 (2019)

# What Does "Ethical by Design" Mean?

Vanessa Nurock[1(✉)], Raja Chatila[2], and Marie-Hélène Parizeau[3]

[1] Paris 8 University, Saint-Denis, France
vnurock@univ-paris8.fr
[2] Sorbonne University, Paris, France
[3] Université Laval, Québec, Canada

## 1 Introduction

Artificial Intelligence (AI) is now integrated or on its way to being integrated into various aspects of our lives, both professional and personal, at a public as well as a private level. The advent of industrial robots, and more recently, of companion robots, the ubiquity of cell phones and tablets, all reflect a day-to-day interaction between humans and machines. Use of these machines has brought about profound transformations in our social behaviors, even in our minds, and as such, raises many practical ethical questions about our technological choices and several meta-ethical ones besides.

In the early 2000s, US science policies financed the "NBIC convergence" facilitating joint research in the fields of Nanotechnologies, Biotechnologies, Information Technologies and Cognitive Sciences. The accompanying discourse maintains a centrality of the criterion of performance via the idea of enhancing and/or replacing human intelligence with the computational methods of AI. Economic practices have scaled up replacing humans with machines in the interest of efficiency. Technological innovations, the driving force of our capitalist economy, continue to multiply their social experiments, thereby forcing the State and its institutions (law, education, health, defense etc.) to adapt at all costs, on pain of becoming extinct or obsolete.

Increasingly many voices are being raised, calling attention to a need to introduce ethical criteria for standardizing and regulating such technological innovations, in view of making AI intrinsically ethical; there is even talk of "Ethics by Design".[1] However, it remains difficult to pin down a clear definition circumscribing what this expression means,[2] even while it has begun to circulate at the highest political levels.[3]

Today we are at a crossroads. As the general public begins to gain an awareness of this phenomenon of AI, to inquire about it, we also begin to wonder how we stand to benefit and what the costs are, and what society is preparing for future generations born

---

[1] See for example https://paperjam.lu/article/ethics-by-design-et-intelligen.

[2] In Dignum, et al. (2018), for example, Ethics by Design appears conflated with the question "Can we, and should we, build ethically-aware agents?" See https://prima2017.gforge.uni.lu/ethics.html and https://orbilu.uni.lu/bitstream/10993/38926/1/p60-dignum.pdf.

[3] The expression "Ethics by Design" was notably employed (in English) by French President Emmanuel Macron during a conference at the Collège de France in March 2018. https://www.elysee.fr/emmanuel-macron/2018/03/29/discours-du-president-de-la-republique-sur-lintelligence-artificielle.

© Springer Nature Switzerland AG 2021
B. Braunschweig and M. Ghallab (Eds.): Reflections on Artificial Intelligence
for Humanity, LNAI 12600, pp. 171–190, 2021.
https://doi.org/10.1007/978-3-030-69128-8_11

in a digital age, without any hindsight or lived alternative whatsoever. We find our-selves today in a time that we propose to call a "normative openness". It is a time to engage in pluralistic dialogue about the direction that we want to give AI, rather than being subject to directions that AI establishes for us. In this time of normative open-ness, an AI *for humanity* cannot be achieved without *the humanities*. Researchers in the Humanities and Social Sciences, Ethics or Moral Philosophy at the forefront, must take up their responsibilities and assume their share of expertise.

In this perspective, this article discusses various ethical models that have recently been put forward and that implicitly or explicitly bear upon an "Ethics by Design", in order to better understand and expand on what the expression "Ethics by Design" might mean. Our aim is to examine the adequacy of this expression, since we believe that using it may entail a certain conception of ethics that we wish to bring to light.

Since, moreover, this expression is also taken up in high-level politics, there is a pressing need to question and to clarify it, and to do this before it gains the potential to neutralize the ethical issues generated by all of these technological innovations – especially those fashioned by AI – by serving as a buzzword. It seems to us, however, that the expression "Ethics by Design" is rich in both meaning and insight, and that it could definitely contribute to enriching discussions on the ethical problems of AI if we venture to consider it using the tools of philosophical ethics. Accordingly, this article aims to contribute to illuminating its meaning by straightforwardly asking: "what does 'Ethics by Design' mean?"

Our objective is therefore *not* to provide a procedural system or toolbox that the computer scientist or engineer could then apply directly or code. Our objective *is rather* to examine the underlying worldview in this concept of "Ethics by Design," to seek to work out its meaning and even, indeed, what it ought to mean.

## 2   The "by Design" Family

*Ethics by Design* is the latest addition to a family of expressions, which also includes *Safety by Design* and *Privacy by Design*. Undoubtedly, Ethics by Design was coined to evoke this family resemblance and establish a familiarity, to more readily integrate it into the landscape of discourse accompanying emerging technologies, but also, in some cases—as we will later see, when it involves approaches aimed at relating it to Privacy by Design—to facilitate a shift between these different concepts.

That said, the expression cannot but give rise to questions from the very outset. The concept of design is complex, foreign and yet familiar. It simultaneously encompasses a purpose, a plan, the design's formal construction and its implementation. Whereby the question arises as to where the design process begins and where it ends (Hale et al. 2007). In short, should we focus on the plan and intention, or ought we to reckon with consequences? Our case is one in which the foreseeable consequences, whether intended or not, are to be distinguished from unintended consequences.

As Philip Brey (Brey 2017) has pointed out, the case of emerging technologies, particularly when they are *enabling* (namely, that may be combined with other tech-nologies and/or developed across different sectors) is especially fraught with issues of uncertainty and risk. The problem with a focus on risks[4], however, is that ethics often gets reduced to a simple cost/benefit analysis. One way of broadening the question and bringing the focus back to ethical concerns would be to take seriously this uncertainty surrounding AI and to look at this widespread use of AI in our societies as a very large-scale social experimentation.

The question, therefore, is not simply one about determining whether and under what conditions a given technology is to be deemed morally acceptable, but also about whether it is morally acceptable to test a given technology openly within our societies, and under what conditions this can be said to be the case. In other words, we are concerned here with taking up the issue from the standpoint of an experimental approach as discussed by Philip Brey (2017), notably in reference to the work of Ibo Van de Poel (2016). It is therefore not a matter of validating or invalidating AI as such, but rather of examining the way we conceive of and develop it.

In this instance, it seems logical enough to articulate such an ethical posture around the question of design. Indeed, as discussed above, the concept of design is complex and concurrently involves its purpose, formal construction and applications. Such articulation would be further facilitated if it were integrated, as we have said, into a pre-existing family of concepts in connection with new technologies.

## 2.1 Safety by Design

*Safety by Design* (SbD) addresses the issue of risks, mainly in the field of nanotechnologies, but also in the nuclear field, among others. The main idea behind SbD is to limit risks in general, beginning in the design process, in order to maintain control over the risk/benefit balance.

In the field of nanotechnologies, SbD most often relates to a toxicological risk. Nano-objects have the singular characteristic of consolidating only on the nanometric scale, while each nanoparticle, nanomaterial or nanofibre needs to be evaluated individually, owing to the variable nature of properties on the nanoscale. Of necessity, a long and laborious case-by-case method constitutes the basic approach to scientifically assess the (predominantly toxicological) risks of nano-objects. Two kinds of approaches can be distinguished. The first is to reduce the risk itself of the nanomaterials being used, which amounts to using materials known to be safe and with which we can reason by analogy – but this does not mean, of course, that the compound are necessarily safe because the components materials are. The second is to reduce exposure by controlling the release of materials during the lifecycle. As Kraegeloh and colleagues aptly show, the latter approach involves paying unwavering attention not only to every phase of the process but to the full range of actors involved (Kraegeloh et al. 2018). For this reason, the expression "by design" refers to a broad approach and not, contrary what one might think in conflating design with purpose, to an *a priori* conception of ethics. As underscored by Christopher Kelty, who traces the emergence of

---

[4] The European Commission's policy expressed in its white paper (19 Feb 2020) states that "the Commission is of the view that it should follow a risk-based approach". https://ec.europa.eu/info/sites/info/files/commission-white-paper-artificial-intelligence-feb2020_en.pdf.

the concept within the field of nanotechnologies, this approach engages not only a redefined conception safety, no longer thought of as a property of materials but as a spectrum of "risks" to be understood (in this case, mainly toxicological in nature), but also a transformation in our working practices, in the habitual chain of command within scientific research, toward a course of multidisciplinary collaboration (Kelty 2009).

In computer based-systems and software engineering, a wealth of methods exist to ensure a dependable operation of these systems, e.g., continuity, reliability and safety of operation (Avizienis et al. 2004), which are widely applied in several sectors, such as aeronautics or electricity grid management for example. This doesn't stem from an explicit ethical motivation as such but from the motivation of avoiding dangerous or catastrophic outcomes of system malfunction.

And yet, as Hale and his colleagues (Hale et al. 2007) point out, as intuitive as the concept of design may seem, it often does little to clarify the discussion, even if it may to appear to at first blush: where does the design begin? In its intention? In the design plan? In preventing possible malfunction of a socio-technical system, or unwanted (but predictable) misuse? Furthermore, the question arises as to what kind of attention ought to be paid to unwanted uses and misappropriations in order to create safer devices. In so doing, the concept of "Safety by Design" to some extent integrates discussions in moral philosophy of the principle of double effect, which differentiates between wanted and predictable consequences on one hand, and unwanted yet predictable consequences on the other—even if, as Hale and his colleagues (Hale et al. 2007) point out, not all accidents can be prevented by design.

It may be interesting to note, however, that traditionally, within moral philosophy, the principle of double effect partakes of an inquiry into of the concept responsibility and delimits a boundary between a deontological position (which emphasizes intentions) on one side and a consequentialist position (which looks at consequences) on the other. Indeed, as several authors point out, for example, McCarthy and Kelty (2010) and Van de Poel and Robaey (2017), the central (but at times tacit) issue at stake in Safety by Design is that of responsibility. With this in mind, Van de Poel and Robaey propose to shift the focal point of the approach and instead to think in terms of designing, "for the responsibility for safety." In so doing, they highlight that assuming the possibility of built-in safety in a process or product is assuming an elimination of risks (of *all* risks to the point of being "idiot proof"). Since such an approach is likely neither possible nor even desirable, perhaps we would be better off not just with *responsible* design (in line with responsible innovation), but also with design *for* responsibility, which notably would give users epistemic access to the technology, that is to say, the means to take informed action—and ultimately to accept certain risks, thereby also making it ethical access.

## 2.2 "Privacy by Design": A Legal Approach to the Protection of Personal Information

The "Privacy by Design" approach was developed concomitantly with a diversification in our uses of digital objects and an exponential increase in the handling of digital information via the Internet. The concern for protecting personal information has become an ever more pressing social challenge, as various digital and social media platforms were built in such a way as to access activities and exchanges relating to people's private lives, in order to garner information about these platforms' users or consumers. This information is generally used for the commercial purposes of targeted ads. Yet the protection of privacy and of personal information has long been a subject addressed in the legal tradition. The right to privacy is based first and foremost in Human Rights and was first recognized in the context of State interference in the personal lives of citizens. The State may impose limits on the right to privacy for the sake of public security. In the medical domain, access to medical files and sharing of patients' medical information among health professionals in hospitals have been a subject of much legislation and of many very strict regulations in most Western countries[5].

The "Privacy by Design" approach is hence based in this legal framework and has been adapted to innovations in the digital domain. Former Information and Privacy Commissioner of Ontario (Canada) Ann Cavoukian initially developed "Privacy by Design" in the 2000s, proposing seven foundational principles to serve as bases for designing digital information systems[6]. They depart from the premise that in order to enjoy the benefits of digital innovations, we must also preserve our freedom of choice and personal control over the data produced. In pursuit of a balance between the two, Cavoukian states that any digital system, along with its attendant marketing practices, must from the outset embed the protection of personal information in a way that minimizes access to information to what is strictly necessary. A number of rules follow, including, under the Visibility and Transparency principle, the need for accountability, since trust depends on the operation's verifiability (a Fair Information Practice), and on consent given by the user, who must be able to verify the content of stored information. But furthermore, from its very inception and in its design, a digital platform must include measures that anticipate and prevent breaches of confidentiality, as well as measures to ensure a maximum protection of privacy. In this way, the Privacy by Design approach aims from its earliest stages to safeguard the protection of privacy, without impairing a system's functionality, since such is an intrinsic part of the technical process.

This legal and contractual approach seeks to rebalance the contract between the user/consumer and businesses or platforms that extract and use personal data. Currently, in addition to the opaque practices of most digital stakeholders (from GAFAM to the marketing practices of businesses), we are witnessing an increase in security system breaches and the hacking of personal information,[7] which serves to erode the

---

[5] See also chapters 3 and 9 of this book.

[6] Ann Cavoukian, 2010, *The 7 Foundational Principles. Implementation and Mapping the Fair Information Practices*. Information and Privacy Commissioner of Ontario, www.privacybydesign. ca.

[7] On September 28, 2018, Facebook announced a security breach affecting 50 million user accounts. The Cambridge Analytica scandal, which broke in March 2018, differs insofar as Facebook allowed third-party applications to access personal information. Cambridge Analytica mined the personal data of 87 million unknowing Facebook users for political influence in the latest American elections. In 2015, the Hong Kong toy company VTech was the target of a data breach involving 4.8 million customers (parents and children) whose data was accessed via connected toys and devices. In France, more than 1.2 million accounts belonging to children were hacked; the data included full names, mailing addresses, dates of birth, email addresses and IP addresses.

trust of consumers/users. A breach of personal data can also lead to material damage (identity theft or financial loss) and non-pecuniary damage (discrimination or harm to one's reputation).

The Privacy by Design approach relies on a kind of equality among various digital stakeholders that is out of step with our current situation, in which individuals are indeed rather helpless against the power of commercial and state digital stakeholders. The power relation is highly asymmetrical, if not abysmal. An approach that relies essentially on private individuals and their capacity to choose or to consent seems ineffective and unrealistic at best if governments do not intervene to regulate and force new practices of citizen and consumer protection. The example of the European Data Protection Regulation[8] constitutes a first decisive step in this direction, since it incorporates the Privacy by Design approach in addition to new parameters for protecting privacy[9] such as "the right to be forgotten," or user consent as an active choice —for example, the option to install an application or change to the proposed settings (opting *in*)—rather than having to uninstall an application or undo pre-adjusted settings (opting *out*).

### 2.3   The Comprehensive Framework of "Responsible Innovation"

The initiatives of Safety by Design and Privacy by Design are part of a larger movement. This movement considers as inadequate the traditional approach of managing and regulating products after the fact of their entry into the market of mass consumption. Indeed, customarily, regulations only intervene reactively, after a product is found to be dangerous or harmful to society, human health or the environment (Thalidomide, DDT, etc.). Regulatory mechanisms essentially depend on instruments of authorization (risk assessment) and control (inspections), with possibilities of sanctions or compensation for damages (Owen et al. 2013). These are essentially legal-administrative tools implemented by the State, which can therefore vary considerably from one nation to another. The controls in place, however, incur a financial cost to the State and, on the basis of minimum state ideology (Nozick 1974), some governments have significantly reduced their numbers of inspectors and on occasion have even gone as far as muzzling government scientists (Turner 2013).

The ethical and political question that emerged in the 1980s (Collingridge 1981) was: can we *control* techniques? As our societies take more and greater technological risks (Beck 2008), how can mechanisms be implemented to orient and control technological choices and thereby prevent harmful consequences? How can we apply a

---

[8] Regulation (UE)2016/679 of the European Parliament and of the Council of 27 April 2016 on the protection of natural persons with regard the processing of personal data and on the free movement of such data, and repealing Directive 95/46/EC (General Data Protection Regulation -GDPR).

[9] Privacy Impact Assessment (PIA) is a framework that have been develop for many years. PIA is an instrument use to revise information systems and technologies that process personal data. It facilitated process of accountability, transparency and systemic improvement for enterprises and governments. The Data Protection Impact Assessment (DPIA) is now included to the GDP. It focused on the protection of the rights and freedom of data subject (Human Rights) and it is seen as an element of governance technologies and research (Raab 2020).

"responsibility principle" that would change the way we evaluate technological risks? As Hans Jonas put forward in his 1979 book, we do so by mobilizing a heuristic of fear, by taking seriously the worst possible scenarios and by protecting the vulnerability of nature. In short, it is matter of attempting to circumvent David Collingridge's well-known dilemma, the so-called "dilemma of control": early on the life of a technology, change is easy, though it is nearly impossible predict the consequences; conversely, by the time these technologies become socially entrenched on a massive scale, the consequences are better understood, but it is much more difficult to adapt the technology.[10]

Following the Chernobyl disaster of 1986, the activist-led anti-GMO campaign in the 1990s and a struggle to identify the risks of nanotechnologies in the early 2000s, European nations (and the European Commission) subsequently pondered how to opt for "good" technologies without stifling scientific freedom and technological creativity, both great sources of economic prosperity and collective welfare. Against this background, toward the end of the 2000s, various fields of analysis and reflection converged on the concept of "responsible innovation." It should be noted that discussions of "corporate social responsibility" or "risk governance" had already emphasized the shared dimension of responsibility—between companies, various States and their citizens—regarding technological developments (Koops 2015). "We are all responsible", one might have professed, or summarized the consensus with the following equation: responsible innovation = regular innovation + stakeholder involvement (Blok 2015). Such a reductive formulation, however, fails to capture the rich array of approaches put forward since 2010 under the unifying idea of "responsible innovation," for which various definitions coexist.[11]

Common among all these definitions is their decided emphasis on the idea of responsibility and on types of interactions between various stakeholders, with an insistence on public or citizen participation, and with a view to anticipating risks as soon and as much as possible, but also to bringing about more inclusive social decision-making regarding a given technology.

---

[10] "The social consequences of a technology cannot be predicted early in the life of the technology. By the time undesirable consequences are discovered, however, the technology is often much part of the whole economic and social fabric that its control is extremely difficult. This is the *dilemma of control*. When change is easy, the need for it cannot be foreseen; when the need of change is apparent, change has become expensive, difficult and time consuming" (Collingridge 1981, p 11).

[11] Below are two examples demonstrating this variety of approaches: (i) "Responsible Research and Innovation is a transparent, interactive process by which societal actors and innovators become mutually reponsive to each other with a view on the (ethical) acceptability, sustainability and societal desirability of the innovation process and its marketable products (in order to allow a proper embedding of scientific and technological advances in our society) (Von Schombert 2011, p. 9)." (ii) "Responsible innovation is a new concept that builds on governance approaches and innovation assessments that aim to take these ethical and societal concerns into account at the start of the innovation process. The main idea behind responsible innovation is to democratize innovation and realize deliberative forms of governance such as stakeholders and public engagement. Stakeholders and members of the public are involved upstream in the innovation process and encouraged to deliberate about the multiple futures and uncertainties that the innovation could bring or seeks to bring. The upstream inclusion of stakeholders and the public, by deliberative forms of governance, can help to realize a collective responsibility to control and direct innovation into a direction that is ethically acceptable, societally desirable and sustainable" (Lubberink 2017, p. 2)".

The concept of responsibility thus goes further than straightforward accountability of the manufacturer; it seeks collectively to distinguish in advance of their development "good" technologies from others to be ruled out, by gauging their social, ethical and environmental import. The normative backgrounds informing responsible innovation meant to guide this new responsibility are frequently part of an approach to governance which seeks to reduce normative ethical challenges to a type of procedural ethics, one in consonance with the Sustainable Development Goals adopted by the United Nations in 2015. Meanwhile, the framework of responsible innovation was adopted in 2011 by the European Commission, as part of its Horizon 2020 research program.[12]

We might therefore distinguish two ethical planes of responsible innovation. The first explicitly or implicitly falls in line with a globalized capitalist economy and modern rationality concerned with the impacts of technologies on populations and the environment (Blok 2015). This ethical plane mediates the values and norms under discussion. A second ethical plane seeks to implement procedures for discussion, to operationalize mechanisms of transparency or practical norms for the purpose of guiding corporate governance (Pavie 2015; Carthy 2015), or even seeks to formalize the objectives of responsiveness, anticipation, inclusion and reflexivity intrinsic to the project of responsible innovation (Pellé and Reber 2015). Both ethical planes have received their share of criticisms: in their implementation, transparency and responsibility, which lie at the heart of the concept of responsible innovation, remain poorly elaborated (Davies and Horst 2015) while at a more global level, the concept of responsible innovation remains scarcely applicable in developing countries and reflects a liberal economic volition not much interested in low-technology innovation (Hartley et al. 2019; Wong 2016).

Feminist critics, on the other hand, have shown how the perspective of innovation mutes certain concerns or invisibilizes certain groups of people, and falls short of the question of what matters to us about the way these technologies are designed or developed. In other words, we must also ask ourselves: what kinds of presents and futures are open to us, and for whom? The issue, in brief, is not only one about stakeholders, economic benefit, or "progress," but is also one of determining at what cost and for whom (Kerr et al. 2017): what is the invisible side of responsible innovation?

## 3    State of the Art: Top-Down and Bottom-up Approaches

Initiatives to either regulate or generate products (algorithms, expert systems) and ethical applications of AI have multiplied over roughly the past five years. Two trends stand out. The first takes the form of initiatives on a more macro scale, often of the top-down variety, the purpose of which is to ensure "good" development. Several national and international conferences and initiatives point in this direction, aiming to mobilize

---

[12] A coherence can be gleaned with the European position, which in the 1990 s championed the precautionary principle, which serves as the basis for the "no data, no market" rule applied in biotechnologies and nanotechnologies.

all stakeholders (industries, designers, the State, citizens) in view of establishing general principles. These broad principles take various forms: international declarations, codes of conduct, standards, etc.

The second pattern of approaches takes place on a more micro scale, around and among designers (researchers, computer engineers, etc.) and users. These bottom-up initiatives look for operational or educational means to assist designers in integrating ethical criteria or values within the very design of an algorithm or system using AI, or even to modify their approach by including, for example, researchers in the humanities. All of these normative and operational initiatives, whether macro or micro, are highly pluralistic where both their deliberative methods and their content is concerned. We will now examine these different approaches from the point of view of their relationship to ethics and how they draw on different ethical theories.

### 3.1  A Deontological Approach: A Hippocratic Oath for AI?

A first approach, which arose in the engineering milieu, proposes a coders' version of the Hippocratic Oath. By swearing to codes of ethics made of principles of practice (scientific integrity and rigour, transparency, fair treatment, respect for persons, responsibility and independence),[13] this kind of code reifies a bottom-up deontological commitment that originates with the designers themselves, be they associations, individuals or companies. Codes of ethics are drawn up to regulate all professions that bear a public responsibility for which these professionals can be held legally accountable. A code of ethics therefore has symbolic value for any given profession since it outlines according to principles how a "good professional" behaves and has legal validity on which professionals can rely on to delimit their responsibilities and obligations[14].

It is undeniable that a code of ethics in the AI sector would represent a positive step forward, especially if it is accompanied by an ethics course as part of the vocational or university education of future professionals. Nevertheless, any code of ethics is but a small part of ethics, given that it sets forth a set of necessarily very general and circumscribed rules. Furthermore, since AI is currently deployed in the form of social experimentation, there is a need to broaden the application of a code of ethics to encompass the sociocultural context. Issues of consent, of cost/benefit ratio or of justice, all familiar issues in biomedical research, cannot be passed over. At the same time, procedures for obtaining consent leave much to be discussed at an ethical, legal and technological level.[15] Certain challenges of responsible innovation thereby need to be revisited.

---

[13] Hippocratic Oath for Data scientists: https://hippocrate.tech/.

[14] See also chapter 10 of this book.

[15] As evidenced, for example in Europe's recent guidelines for the GDPR but also by the French Health Data Hub, which tacitly relies on the questionable notion of 'implicit consent'. For a more detailed account of the issue, see Margo Bernelin (Bernelin 2019).

## 3.2   Applied Ethics for AI

Another more macro and fairly prevalent approach seeks to identify key principles for the ethics of AI. Its connections to prominent ethical theories (Kantianism, Utilitarianism, American pragmatism, Human Rights) are more or less explicit. Typically, these declarations, such as the *Montreal Declaration for a Responsible Development of AI* (Université de Montréal, 2018), the *Toronto Declaration: Protecting the right to equality and non-discrimination in machine learning systems* (Amnesty International and Access Now, 2018), as well as the Future of Life Institute's declaration, the *Asilomar AI Principles* (Future of Life Institute, 2017), all state general principles that engage the ethical challenges of AI, providing *sine qua non* criteria of an ethical AI. Ostensibly, we need only ensure that these principles are properly applied and adhered to in order to achieve an ethical AI.

In cases where the central motive is one of moral obligations or principles, such declarations take more of a so-called deontological approach, whereas placing our focus in the ethical review on a consideration of consequences illustrates a so-called Utilitarian or Consequentialist course of action. The well-known theoretical divide between these two philosophical schools tends nowadays to be less marked, and a combined evaluation according to both principles and consequences may be the subject of a thoughtfully balanced discussion within ethics committees or biomedical research. If the principles-based approach remains predominant, this is likely in part because the overreaching consequences of AI are difficult to seize.

The foundational reference for an ethics of AI of Human Rights is widely upheld by legal experts (especially from English-speaking countries),[16] and underscores that presently the development of AI poses an open threat to a number of human rights, including the right to non-discrimination, as well as several political liberties.

The European Union, for its part, published an expert's report in April 2019,[17] which puts forward guiding principles and requirements for "trustworthy" AI[18]. The requirement of explainability is understood in the sense that AI systems must be answerable, thus be able to justify their decisions. Explanability is also conceived as connected to interaction with systems, with a responsibility of designers for the autonomy (of systems) and transparency about the adaptability (of systems). The concept of responsibility is inseparably bound with the idea of an intention or purpose that we can or ought to program into systems (Dignum 2019). Interestingly, these principles are sometimes filled out by others that appear directly borrowed (though with scarce reference to) biomedical ethics—Beauchamp and Childress' classical principlism, which states core principles of non-maleficence, beneficence, autonomy and justice (Beauchamp and Childress 1979).

---

[16] This is also the point of view upheld by several foundations, including the Mozilla and Rockefeller foundations. See, for example: https://www.elementai.com/news/2019/supporting-rights-respecting-ai?utm_source=twitter&utm_medium=social&utm_campaign=Brand_GR&utm_content=human_rights_bloh_11/27/2019.

[17] https://ec.europa.eu/digital-single-market/en/news/ethics-guidelines-trustworthy-ai.

[18] See also chapter 2 of this book.

Another worthy initiative by a professional association, the IEEE (Institute of Electrical and Electronics Engineers), which was launched in 2016, adopts in its official document[19] a deductivist and normative approach, citing a series of principles (human rights, well-being, security and user control [data agency], efficiency of technique, transparency, accountability, awareness of misuse, competence) which are devised to build trustworthiness into technical systems.

As Jobin et al. found in their exhaustive study of ethical frameworks for AI throughout the world, published in 2019, we are witnessing a certain standardization of ethical principles from one declaration to the next, with convergence around certain themes, listed here in order of frequency: transparency, justice and fairness, non-maleficence/beneficence, responsibility and accountability, freedom and autonomy, trust/privacy, sustainability, dignity and solidarity (Jobin et al. 2019).

This principles-based approach is bound up with the conceptualization of an ethics "by design", one that would be embedded right from the inception stage on the basis of such key guiding principles. Such a conceptualization is also associated with certain efforts at international governance, for example, the OECD's creation of an Expert Group on AI (AIGO) which focusses on responsibility, security, transparency, protection and accountability.

These various initiatives highlight the current interdependence between research in the ethics of AI and economic and/or political globalization. A search for principles is often carried out in close association with GAFAM tech giants, largely the case in the United States,[20] or with major international institutions, such as the European Commission or UNESCO. Such interchanges are crucial, given that a globalized ethics must integrate considerations of cultural diversity.

### 3.3   Moral Machines?

The so-called "Artificial moral agents" designate AI-based systems endowed with algorithms, which are most generally rooted in moral theories, e.g., Principlism (which we already mentioned above) as it is the case for MedEthEx (Anderson et al. 2006). Such agents are often studied in the context of self-driving cars (Awad et al. 2018), for addressing moral dilemma 'trolley problem' type situations, or of so-called autonomous weapons (Arkin 2009).

Whatever the machine, its algorithms can only accomplish some computations based on sensed data interpreted by its perception system that would assign labels to perceived entities, e.g., "car", "bicycle", pedestrian", "young man", "old woman, or *"combatant", "tank"*. Note that these labels would normally be probabilistic because any sensed data is bound to be uncertain. The "moral" decision-making process is then merely the result of a computation, systematically optimizing a cost function

---

[19] IEEE, *Ethically Aligned Design. A vision for Prioritizing Human Well-Being with Autonomous and Intelligent System*, First Edition. https://standards.ieee.org/content/dam/ieee-standards/standards/web/documents/other/ead1e.pdf.

[20] In Boston, it is related both jokingly and seriously, perhaps in an ironically revealing way, how Facebook finances Harvard, who is trying its hand at AI and Microsoft finances MIT who designs it, while BU has wound up poor but enjoys freedom of ideas, having no "boss".

expressing values assigned to the different entities, to make a choice of whom to harm among them. The values are assigned according to predefined criteria (by the human programmers). This is very far from what a human moral judgment would be.

A possible alternative would be to build an algorithm that *learns* from data, e.g., by running simulations, and labeling situations according to what human subjects do. Such an approach is a convergence of artificial intelligence and cognitive science. Methodologically rooted in a *descriptive* (rather than normative) approach to ethics, this approach seeks to examine what groups of individuals are likely to find morally acceptable. The experiment described in (Awad et al. 2018), polling a high number of subjects to express their decisions in different moral dilemma situations, can lead to such an approach to build "moral machines". The strictly descriptive dimension of this project positions it as research into what social acceptance, as distinguished from normative ethics, which does not, for its part, seek to determine what individuals or groups of individuals are disposed to accept (or can be persuaded to accept) as it is the case here, but rather what should be considered as acceptable from an ethical point of view. Such an approach is furthermore flawed by the assumption that people make same decisions by "clicking" on a button in unrealistic simulations, as they would make when they are actually facing real world and real time situations.

### 3.4 Fairness by Design

Another approach, developed especially in the United States, is that of *Fairness by Design*. It grew out of the debates on issues of discrimination that have emerged over the past ten years and that are found concentrated within AI for roughly the last five years. A number of studies have documented gender and racial biases within big data and AI and have reignited debates on issues of equality within the liberal State (Hoffmann 2019). Analyses of big data had already shown that when used predictively to assist in decision-making processes, it is able to construct models of "winners and losers" with effects of exclusion or marginalization targeting already underprivileged groups, something tantamount to discrimination. Such instances in connection with AI, which were documented and covered by the media, served to open the debate on fairness within AI. While biases may affect particular individuals, for example, regarding their employment applications or their ability to access to a bank loan or mortgage (procedures that turn on algorithms), more systemic biases were also identified, ones connected to the functions of State institutions, for instance, an algorithm that calculates the remission of a sentence within the judicial system, or that ranks the performance of teachers in the public school system in some US states (Eubanks 2018; O'Neil 2016). Debates have shown that not only is it a question of removing the biases of "bad" algorithms or of rethinking the way in which data is collected. It would have been necessary to address the biases or prejudices of those who built the algorithms as well as with those who were in a position of corporate or State power. In short, these automated biases reflect well-known forms of social discrimination, on the basis, for example, of social exclusion, poverty, gender and race. This proliferation of biases within algorithms, big data and AI has sparked many debates on the relationships between technology, power and social justice, especially in the United States[21].

A number of initiatives have been launched to implement an AI that is "fair by design." The general Asimov-inspired idea is to build in safeguards, as opposed to just positive principles, for the purpose of specifying unacceptable machine behaviours (Thomas et al. 2019). This approach has the particular advantage of opening up the problem of programming beyond its purely algorithmic aspects to consider what representations of the world are at play—something that may mean involving HSS researchers on programming teams in order to prevent biases, or counteract them. Some initiatives also propose audits focused on finding biases, or transparency mechanisms in relation to use of big data, or still yet, machine-learning specialist training that includes an ability to consider the social context with a view of avoiding bias, such as the 'Human-Centred AI' initiative (Zou and Schiebinger 2018).

One difficulty with this Fairness by Design approach, however, is that it tends toward reducing an ethics of AI to considerations of justice and fairness, even while such a conceptual limitation has been heavily criticized, beginning in the 1980s with the ethics of care (a theory we will have occasion to return to toward the end of this article), as confining ethical questions to approaches underpinned by patriarchal world views. Another pitfall of this approach is its overwhelming focus on American culture and its socio-historical context of racial inequality.

## 4 Guidelines for an Ethics by Design

### 4.1 Ethics in the Process

This dual, complementary top-down and bottom-up approach also hinges on an awareness that although ethical approaches such as ELSI (Ethical, Legal and Social Impacts)—which had its heyday with nanotechnologies—may indeed enable us to capture some of the ethical issues, their scope for reflection and action remains limited, since they confine themselves to a consideration of impacts, leaving aside considerations of process. In so doing, they engage a certain understanding of ethics based on the idea that the central question is one about impacts, and that an ethics should therefore position itself on the basis of impacts, in a certain sense "downstream" of the action: in the case of top-down ethics, this would be accomplished through *a priori* principles. With bottom-up ethical approaches, the design itself anticipates an avoidance of certain consequences. Such logic is integral to the risk/benefit reasoning employed in medical milieux—medical decisions are often about weighing the pros and cons for the patient of a given treatment.

However, as we saw above in our discussion of Collingridge's dilemma, asking about consequences is not necessarily the most appropriate tactic for formulating an ethics capable of inserting itself in a process of innovation, since, as we saw, in the early phases of innovation, the consequences of a given technology are not easily

---

[21] See also chapter 6 of this book.

predictable, however, once a technology is fully developed and the process is well underway, it becomes difficult to backpedal and inhibit known impacts.

The problem that presents itself to us now is a generic problem of all new technologies; thereby it might prove helpful to base ourselves in certain analyses put forward in ethics for new technologies, specifically nanotechnologies. As Ibo van de Poel has pointed out, the mode of learning required here is neither to be associated with learning by anticipation, which takes place before a technology is introduced, nor with learning by doing, which takes place after a technology has been implemented. Instead, learning by experimentation is positioned between these two: it takes place during the introduction of a new technology, with a view to necessary adjustments and allows for trade-offs between what we can learn and the cost of learning (Van de Poel 2017).

To this idea of learning by experimentation may be added the insight that ethics must therefore be integrated at every stage of the process: in the original design planning, a design's execution, as well as its implementation. Ethics come into play neither after the fact (as in an ethics of impacts), nor before (as in an anticipatory ethics); rather, ethics is integrated during and throughout. This is why we propose to call such ethics an "ethics in the process" or a "processual ethics". Conversely, as Peter-Paul Verbeek quite rightly argues, design "materializes morality", something he explains is done implicitly (Verbeek 2006).

This point of view enables the understanding that, from the design of a technology through to its various uses, values change in this continuous interaction between a technology and its users, according to a dual dynamic between value expression and value definition, in which both are transformed. Value-sensitive design cannot therefore be static, merely concentrating on an introduction of values in advance of a design or technical system, or bypass the effect of a materialization of morality, defined by ongoing interaction between a technology and its users, that thereby also transforms values (Van de Poel 2018; Verbeek 2019).

### 4.2   Experiential and Experimental

Such an approach is closely linked to a conception of AI as experimentation, understood in various meanings. The idea that new technologies should be viewed as experimentation is not new. Ibo Van de Poel, for instance, puts forward the idea that emerging technologies should be regarded as a social experiment (Van de Poel 2016). This term has three different meanings for Ibo Van de Poel: first, it signifies an experiment *in* society, in real life; second, *on* society, which forces us to rethink certain (especially legal) frameworks; and thirdly, *by* society, in the sense of there being no control group. The entire problem, he explains, is one of determining the conditions under which such experiments may be considered morally acceptable—an essential point, which we will return to in the following section.

It seems precisely that part of an answer to this question may be obtained by reference to the concept of ethics by design, which integrates ethics into the overall project, as we will also come back to in the next section. In order to get there, however, it should be noted that such a question becomes all the more problematic in the field of AI, given that AI—something Cédric Villani underscored in his speech in October

2019 at the GFAIH—can be characterized as a combination of experiential and experimental.

AI is *experiential* defined as a process by experience. This might seem particularly true in the case of "deep learning", which happens through augmenting prediction capability by using new and more data. But, this process is based on improving its statistical power, not its skills as an apprentice would. Thus "experiential" here is entailed with a peculiar meaning as, of course, the AI does not experience anything but its process may mimic human experience. We, humans, on the other hand are indeed experiencing AI in our everyday life and sometimes even adjusting our forms of life to AI.

AI is also *experimental*: today, not only does AI constitute a technoscientific experiment, but also a social ethical and political one, as Van de Poel consistently maintains in the ways we have just mentioned, while this was also taken up by French Secretary of State Cédric O' regarding the development of facial recognition,[22] and is also particularly evidenced by the problem of what is commonly referred to today as human-machine coevolution.[23,24]

Furthermore, defining AI itself is trickier still, insofar as an interdisciplinary understanding is necessary to grasp it in all its dimensions. As Virginia Dignum thoroughly outlines, AI is a vaster techno-scientific field than it first appears, and cannot be defined from a computer science perspective alone (Dignum 2019). To grasp its specific features, we need to consider it at the intersection of computer science and engineering, mathematics, psychology, philosophy and cognitive science. As she points out, "each of these perspectives describes AI in slightly different ways", but also, one might add, in complementary ways. Moreover, an additional problem arises with the development of deep learning, which operates through training processes, such that it is often difficult to determine how a system's output will change.

### 4.3  A Processual Care Ethics with AI

In order to propose an answer to the crucial question raised by Ibo Van de Poel, as well as a definition of an Ethics by Design, we will now return to the main pitfalls encountered with established principles, introduced in the second section of this article, and attempt to offer a few elements of an answer to these difficulties. Not only might we need to forgo the inverted, face-to-face dichotomy of top-down and bottom-up, but also to shake an ethical posture that takes consequences for its sole point of reference.

---

[22] Interestingly, several cities, and notably San Francisco and Boston have banned the use of facial recognition technology. In France, the debate launched by interviews with Cédric O' in *Le Monde* on October 14, 2019 and in the December 24 edition of *Le Parisien* gave rise to hot disputes, for example in a piece published on June 1, 2020 in *Libération* titled "Nos droits et nos libertés ne sont pas à vendre" (Our Rights and Freedoms are Not for Sale) calling for public debate rather than experimentation. https://www.liberation.fr/debats/2020/01/06/reconnaissance-faciale-nos-droits-et-nos-libertes-ne-sont-pas-a-vendre_1771600.

[23] Without, moreover, questioning the fact that this expression in some sense puts humans and machines on an equal footing or that here we use the term "evolution" to describe machines.

[24] See also chapter 13 of this book.

For this reason, we wish to propose the idea of a processual ethics, one that is integrated at each phase of the process, without focusing solely on impacts.

Among the various positions sketched out in the existing sets of principles, those that consist in applying principles (as in the case of an "applied" ethics) or in programming moral machines, point to the idea of derivable or programmable morality, an idea that has a long history in philosophy (Nurock 2019). Given what we know are the shortcomings of an "applied" ethics on the one hand and "automated" ethics on the other, instead we argue the need to consider a "practical" ethics inserted into the process, that is to say, into all phases of analysis, planning, development and dissemination.

Our general hypothesis is that ethics should not be limited to positions that are either top-down, wherein practices flow from principles, or bottom-up, wherein normative analysis is garnered from practices. In one word, when we speak about the ethics of artificial intelligence, the genitive ("of") is neither solely objective, nor solely subjective: AI is neither solely the object, nor solely the subject of an ethics, rather, it is both at the same time. For this reason, we advocate for the need to rethink the problem in terms of a dynamic between practices and principles, much like the American philosopher John Rawls' idea of a reflective equilibrium (Rawls 1971), in other words, in terms of an ethics that is neither top-down, not an ethics *for* AI, nor bottom-up, not *from* AI, but an ethics that is *with* AI, as put by Vanessa Nurock in a paper on the ethics of nanotechnologies (Nurock 2010).

What would an ethics "with" AI look like? Much remains to be elaborated, but one way to envisage such an ethics might be to base ourselves in approaches put forward by care theorists. "Care" was indeed a recurring theme in the ethical debates included in discussions at the GFAIH: "we must be careful", "care for the data", "what do we care about?" – the subject of a "duty of care" was even broached in a talk given by Neil Lawrence[25].

Interestingly, this leitmotif of care echoes an evolution in the field of ethics since the 1980s, pioneered notably by Carol Gilligan (Gilligan 1982) and Joan Tronto (Tronto 1993), which is seeing distinctive developments in France and Canada especially. This current of moral philosophy proposes to broaden the ethical field beyond questions of good and evil, or just and unjust, to encompass questions connected with care in its various dimensions: caring *about*, caring *for*, care giving/receiving understood as a process and caring *with* (tending to the institutions which connect us) by transcending binary oppositions.

A similar approach has yet to be developed in the field of AI, even if such has already been suggested by Xavier Pavie as an avenue for thinking about innovation (Pavie 2014; Pavie 2018), in the form of "innovation-care". This "innovation care", however, is considered in similar terms to responsible innovation, whereby Pavie likens care ethics to the Kantian categorical imperative (Pavie 2014), namely, to never treat humanity as a means, but always at the same time an end. Ultimately, Pavie determines a hierarchy between care and innovation in which innovation is given "higher" priority over care (Pavie 2018).

---

[25] See also chapter 3 of this book.

While we certainly agree that this avenue of care merits development in the field of AI, we however believe that this merits being done taking into account the specific nature of care—instead of collapsing care into Kantian deontology. The ethics of care posits a dynamic that moves beyond power relations and hierarchies and rejects binary oppositions. Put another way, the ethics of care is not at odds with innovation in the sense of there being any inherent contradiction. Indeed, a "good," or ethical innovation must be caring if it is to be innovative such that it tends toward some progress, understood as progress of everyone, particularly the most vulnerable.

Moreover, care ethics appears all the more apposite to working through an ethics by design for AI given the particular challenges faced by those who are born or will be born into a world with AI, so-called "AI natives" just as there are appreciably numerous "digital natives". As Christopher Groves has shown, the ethics of care is especially relevant to thinking about our ethical relationship to future generations (Groves 2014), since the question here is not only one of accountability but also about how we can take care of the future. Precisely because we are in the early days of the deployment of AI, the problem is not so much, as with Collindridge's dilemma, that we cannot forecast all the consequences, but rather that we need to concern ourselves with the future and that we have a moral responsibility to future generations.

Our specific methodological hypothesis is that the ethics and politics of care might give us a guiding insight for formulating ethical criteria for AI, by asking the following questions:

1. What do we care about? What is important to us in the development of AI?
2. What or whom do we care for? Have we attended to the most vulnerable?
3. Do we take care? (Care giving/receiving): Have we taken care to safeguard users' choices and integrate their requirements, rights, needs etc. in the system?
4. Do we care with? How do we govern AI democratically and remain mindful of the transformations that AI is capable of bringing about in our democratic institutions and in the public arena?

In conclusion, it is important to bear in mind that an Ethics by Design acts as a counterpart to concrete social experimentation that we must address by asking, along with Ibo Van de Poel: under what conditions is social experimentation involving a given AI system morally acceptable? Ethics by Design can provide elements of an answer on two conditions. The first is *our general hypothesis*, which enjoins us to move beyond the top-down/bottom-up binary in favor of an ethics that is a major *part of the process*. The second is a *particular hypothesis*, which enjoins us to *practice an Ethics of Care both theoretically and concretely at the same time*. Ethics by Design, where it concerns artificial intelligence, may hence be characterized as an ethics that is both caring and processual. That is to say, an ethics that is all at once an integral part of each phase of the process and that involves all facets of care.

# References

Anderson, M., Anderson, S.L., Armen, C.: MedEthEx: a prototype medical ethics advisor. In: Proceedings of the 18th conference on Innovative applications of artificial intelligence (IAAI 2006), vol.2, pp. 1759–1765. AAAI Press (2006)

Arkin, R.: Governing Lethal Behavior in Autonomous Robots. Chapman and Hall/CRC Press, London (2009)

Avizienis, A., Laprie, J.-C., Randell, B., Carl, L.: Basic concepts and taxonomy of dependable and secure computing. IEEE Trans. Dependable Secure Comput. **1**(1), 11–33 (2004)

Awad, E., et al.: The moral machine experiment. Nature **563**(7729), 29–64 (2018)

Beauchamp, T., Childress, J.: Principles of Biomedical Ethics. Oxford University Press, Oxford (1979)

Beck, U.: La société du risque. Sur la voie d'une autre modernité, Paris, Flammarion (2008)

Bernelin, M.: Intelligence artificielle en santé: la ruée vers les données personnelles. Cités **80**, 75–89 (2019)

Blok, V., Lemmens, P.: The emerging concept of responsible innovation. three reasons why it is questionable and calls for a radical transformation of the concept of innovation. In: Koops, B.-J., Oosterlaken, I., Romijn, H., Swierstra, T., van den Hoven, J. (eds.) Responsible Innovation 2, pp. 19–35. Springer, Cham (2015). https://doi.org/10.1007/978-3-319-17308-5_2

Brey, P.: Ethics of Emerging Technologies. In: Hansson, D.S.O. (ed.) The Ethics of Technology: Methods and Approaches, pp. 175–192. Rowman & Littlefield International (2017)

David, C.: The Social Control of Technology. Macmillan, Palgrave (1981)

Eubanks, V.: Automating Inequality. How high-Tech Tools Profile, Police and Punish the Poor. St. Martin's Press (2018)

European Commission: Horizon 2020—The Framework programme for Research and Innovation, Brussels (2011)

Davies, Sarah R., Horst, M.: Responsible innovation in the US, UK and Denmark: governance landscapes. In: Koops, B.-J., Oosterlaken, I., Romijn, H., Swierstra, T., van den Hoven, J. (eds.) Responsible Innovation 2, pp. 37–56. Springer, Cham (2015). https://doi.org/10.1007/978-3-319-17308-5_3

Dignum, V.: Responsible Artificial Intelligence. Springer, Cham (2019). https://doi.org/10.1007/978-3-030-30371-6

Genus, A., Stirling, A.: Collingridge and the dilemma of control: toward responsible and accountable innovation. Res. Policy **47**, 61–69 (2018)

Gilligan, C.: In a Different Voice. Harvard University Press, Cambridge (1982)

Groves, C.: Care, Uncertainty and Intergenerational Ethics. Palgrave Macmillan, London (2014)

Hale, A., Kirwanb, B., Kjellén, U.: Safe by design: where are we now? Saf. Sci. **45**, 305–327 (2007)

Jobin, A., Ienca, M., Vayena, E.: The global landscape of AI ethics guidelines. Nat. Mach. Intell. **1**, 389–399 (2019)

Jonas, H.: Le principe responsabilité. Flammarion, Paris (2013)

Sarah, H., Carmen, M.L., Mike, C., Sarah, J., Charlotte, R.: A retrospective analysis of responsible innovation for low-technology innovation in the Global South. J. Respons. Innov. **69**(2), 143–162 (2019)

Hoffmann, A.L.: Where fairness fails: data, algorithms, and the limits of antidiscrimination discourse. Inf. Commun. Soc. **22**(7), 900–915 (2019)

Kelty, C.: Beyond implications and applications: the story of 'safety by design. NanoEthics **3**(2), 79–96 (2009)

Kerr, A., Hill, R., Till, C.: The limits of responsible innovation: exploring care, vulnerability and precision medicine. Technol. Soc. 1–8 (2017)

Koops, B.-J., Oosterlaken, I., Romijn, H., Swierstra, T., van den Hoven, J.: Responsible Innovation 2. Concepts, Approches and Applications. Springer, Dordrecht (2015). https://doi.org/10.1007/978-3-319-17308-5

Kraegeloh, A., Suarez-Merino, B., Sluijters, T., Micheletti, C.: Implementation of safe-by-design for nanomaterial development and safe innovation: why we need a comprehensive approach. Nanomaterials 239, 8 (2018)

Lubberink, R., Blok, V., van Ophem, J., Omta, O.: Lessons for responsible innovation in the business context: a systematic literature review of responsible. Soc. Sustain. Innov. Pract. Sustain. 9(721), 1–31 (2017)

McCarthy, E., Kelty, C.: Responsibility and nanotechnology. Soc. Stud. Sci. 40(3), 405–432 (2010)

Nurock, V.: Nanoethics: ethics for, from, or with nanotechnologies? Hylé 1(16), 31–42 (2010)

Nurock, V.: Généalogie de la morale mécanisée. In: Parizeau, M.-H., Kash, S. (eds.) Robots et sociétés: enjeux éthiques et politiques, pp. 31–50. Les Presses de l'Université Laval, Québec (2019)

Nozick R.: Anarchie, État et Utopie, Paris, Quadrige (1974)

O'Neil, C.: Weapons of Math Destruction, How Big Data Increases Inequality and Threatens Democracy. Crown (2016)

Owen, R,, Stilgoe, J., Gorman, M., Fischer, E., Guston, D. A Framework for responsible innovation. In: Owen, R., Bessant, J., Heintz, M. (eds.) Responsible Innovation: Managing the Responsible Emergence of Science and Innovation in Society, pp. 27–50. Wiley-Blackwell (2013)

Pavie, X.: The importance of responsible innovation and the necessity of 'innovation-care'. Philos. Manage. 13(1), 21–42 (2014)

Pavie, X.: l'innovation à l'épreuve de la philosophie. PUF, Paris (2018)

Xavier, P., Daphne, C.: Leveraging uncertainty: a practical approach to the integration of responsible innovation through design thinking. Proc. – Soc. Behav. Sci. 213, 1040–1049 (2015)

Sophie, P., Bernard, R.: Responsible innovation in the light of moral responsibility. J. Chain Netw. Sci. 15(2), 107–117 (2015)

Raab, C.: Information privacy, impact assessment and the place of ethics. Comput. Law Secur. Rev. 37, 105404 (2020)

Rawls, J.: A Theory of Justice. Belknap Press (1971)

Thomas, P.S., Castro da Silva, B., Barto, A., Giguere, S., Brun, Y., Brunskil, E.: Preventing undesirable behavior of intelligent machines. Science 366(6468), 999–1004 (2019)

Tronto, J.: Caring Democracy. NYU Press, New York City (2013)

Turner C.: Science on coupe!, Montréal, Boréal (2013)

Van de Poel, I.: An ethical framework for evaluating experimental technology. Sci. Eng. Ethics 22, 667–686 (2015). https://doi.org/10.1007/s11948-015-9724-3

Van de Poel, I.: Society as a laboratory to experiment with new technologies. In: Bowman, D.M., Stokes, E., Rip, A. (eds.) Embedding new Technologies into Society: A Regulatory, Ethical and Societal Perspective, pp. 62–86. Pan Stanford Publishing (2017)

van de Poel, I., Robaey, Z.: Safe-by-design: from safety to responsibility. NanoEthics 11(3), 297–306 (2017). https://doi.org/10.1007/s11569-017-0301-x

Van de Poel, I.: Design for value change. Ethics Inf. Technol. 1–5 (2018)

Verbeek, P.-P.: Materializing morality. Sci. Technol. Human Values 31(3), 361–380 (2006)

Verbeek, P.-P.: Values that Matter: Mediation theory and Design Values, Academy for design Innovation management. In: Research Perspectives in the Area of Transformations Conference, London, pp. 396–407 (2019)

Rene, V.S.: A vision of responsible innovation. In: Owen, R., Heintz, M., Bessant, J. (eds.) Responsible Innovation. John Wiley, London (2011)

Wong, P.-H.: Responsible innovation for decent nonliberal peoples: a dilemma? J. Respons. Innov. 3(2), 154–168 (2016)

Zou, J., Schiebinger, L.: Design AI so that it's fair. Nature 559, 324–325 (2018)

# AI for Digital Humanities and Computational Social Sciences

Alexandre Gefen[1(✉)], Léa Saint-Raymond[2],
and Tommaso Venturini[3]

[1] CNRS, UMR Thalim, Paris, France
alexandre.gefen@cnrs.fr
[2] ENS, Paris, France
[3] CNRS, UPR CIS, Paris, France

**Abstract.** AI raises multiple essential issues for the humanities and the social sciences. AI is obviously a major societal issue whose consequences are currently invading the public sphere raising a variety of questions of acceptability, privacy protection or economic impact, and involving expertise that span across the entire range of social and human research. But AI is also a new way of doing research, where massive data processing is made possible by techniques of machine and deep learning, offering new perspectives for analysis.

Reflecting about the nature of intelligence and humanity, but also helping the humanities and the social sciences to benefit from the methodological advances of AI: this is the double challenge that this chapter would like to tackle. We will present the major questions posed to artificial intelligence by the humanities and social sciences, to go through some of the proposed approaches, but also to show how artificial intelligence has become an essential working tool for this field.

## 1 AI as an Object of Research for Social and Human Sciences

### 1.1 AI and the History of Science

The emergence of AI as a scientific and industrial tool is identified with the 21st century, to the point of becoming its emblem. However, if the operational conditions of AI (the availability of large datasets, the computing power and mathematical methods) as well as the first glimpses of what would be a "General AI" (or "Strong AI") are recent, AI it is nevertheless a historical object—and perhaps even an old concept—loaded with our fantasies towards non-humans and with a very long process of formalization, mathematization and datafication of the world. While we often consider AI as our future (if not as an end of time), this future finds it roots in a long history that need to be put into perspective by Human and Social Sciences.

AI took its first steps in the 1950s (with the publication of Alain Turing's seminal article "Computing Machinery and Intelligence" [1] and with the introduction of the label by John McCarthy at a summer workshop at Dartmouth College in 1956), but its archaeology and its accelerated contemporary modulations belong to the historians of Science and Technology Studies. These must take into account a field that strongly

B. Braunschweig and M. Ghallab (Eds.): Reflections on Artificial Intelligence
for Humanity, LNAI 12600, pp. 191–202, 2021.
https://doi.org/10.1007/978-3-030-69128-8_12

involves the history of mathematics (from formal reasoning, whose history is ancient, to contemporary algebra), new disciplines (information theory, cybernetics, computer science) and crossovers with exogenous disciplines (economics and its decision theories, cognitive sciences, computational neurobiology, connective approaches, etc.). This helps explain why AI is structured into so many sub-disciplines (speech and image processing through signal analysis, natural language analysis, etc.) and mobilizes so many methods, from symbolic AI to contemporary statistical approaches in response to increasingly ambitious challenges. Mobilizing complex theories of knowledge as much as industrial technologies, AI is much more than a "research program" [2] in the sense of Feyerabend and Lakatos i.e. a set of hypotheses to explore: it builds particularly original bridges between biology and mathematics, rethinking the unity of scientific knowledge through a new tree of sciences and imposing a strong epistemological reflection to historians and philosophers.

## 1.2   AI and Its Imagination

In the mezzanine of the Denon wing, the Louvre museum keeps an impressive automaton, an articulated totem mask representing the jackal-headed god Anubis.[1] This mask and the *Treatise on Automata* by Heron of Alexandria, a Greek mathematician and mechanic, dates from AD 125, reminding us that the contemporary fantasies and fears raised by mechanical intelligence are in fact very ancient. AI is preceded by the ancient legend of the bronze giant Talos, the mechanical guardian of Crete, his prodigies are dreamt of by many medieval myths, from the automatic soldiers protecting the relics of Buddha evoked by the Indian Lokapannatti to the famous Golem, a clay figure that comes to life when a paper with the name of God is placed in his mouth. From the famous steam-powered animated bird created in the 380s BC by Archytas of Taranto, a friend of Plato's, to the articulated lion imagined by Leonardo da Vinci, from the Chinese androids capable of singing of the Zhou dynasty to the mechanical waitress invented by the Arab engineer Al-Jazari, the tradition of automatons feeds reveries about the magical potential of anthropomorphic machines, but also nightmares about the replacement of humans by superior forms of life, offering a troubling view of the human condition as seen *from the outside* [3].

Contemporary ethical questions about "moral machines" and economic fears about the robotization of labor cannot be separated from the myths that come with them [4]. Few are the cases in which artificial intelligence has the kindness of the digital geisha played by Scarlett Johansson in Spike Jonze's movie *Her*, who, realizing that his "operating system" has outgrown human intelligence, leaves her human owner to live her own life. From the *Terminator* to Ridley Scott's very recent *Alien the covenant*, the fear of human domination by artificial intelligence, robots or cyborgs or software that has become superior and dreams of exterminating it, looms large. Theorized in 1993 by the science fiction writer Vernor Vinge, the "Singularity" is the name often given to the moment in which robots would take over humanity, leading to the end of history as an

---

[1] Mask (?) of a dog, representing Anubis or Qebehsenouf, with movable jaw, Egypt, 21th dynasty (c. 1069–945), h: 19 cm, w: 11 cm, Paris, Louvre museum, N4096.

asymptote of human progress since the Cartesian project of making oneself "master and possessor of nature".

In this eschatology of the American futurologist Ray Kurzweil (who works for Google's natural language processing program), machines would overcome human intelligence in a few decades with the risk of consuming earth's resources for their own benefit. According to his "gray jelly" theory, the combination of AI with developments in nanotechnology and synthetic biology would allow machines to gain consciousness and lead to an "age of spiritual machines" and "singularity" [5]. This is the time of the "Promethean shame", a concept developed by the German philosopher Gunter Anders, which refers to man's feeling of weakness and imperfection in the face of the perfection of the creatures created through his mastery of science.

Think of Philip Dick's famous *Blade Runner*, the magnificent series *Westworld*, which tells the story of the empowerment of androids becoming conscious and free, or *Deus ex machina*, where the main character opens his arm to verify that he is not himself a machine: at a time when deep learning and neural network algorithms are triumphant, submissive or revolted, man sees himself as a robot like any other and discovers in the machine's gaze his disturbing banality. Beyond its political and ethical dimension, the myths of AI thus question the humanity of man and therefore belongs to anthropology as much as to other human and social sciences.

## 2   AI Methods and Tools for Social and Human Sciences

As the foundations, history and imagination of AI are being questioned by the humanities and the social sciences, the new empirical approaches introduced by AI is changing the way Social and Human Sciences (SHS) model and analyze their data, understand their objects and visualize their results. The emerging applications of machine learning in Social and Human Sciences may eventually concern economy, sociology, geography or archaeology in all the tasks of location and classification. First emerged in the field of image recognition, applications of machine learning have soon extended to other types of data and tasks including printed characters, handwriting and speech recognition, but also financial prediction in the financial, decision support in law or medicine as well as machine translation.

### 2.1   Text, Language and Data Analysis

Recent years have seen the production of increasingly large textual corpora for the SHS. Emblematic examples are offered by the digitization of the gigantic Gallica documentary collection by the Bibliothèque Nationale de France, heritage databases and by conversational corpora extracted from social media. Access to massive data offers new perspectives to an increasing number of disciplines, from the socio-political analysis of online conversation to *distant reading* [6] of literary corpus, from cultural to economic history, from linguistics to philology [7].

Going beyond simple statistical studies, the methods of text mining resulting from AI modify key questions of information retrieval, text classification, linguistic and semantic annotation, information extraction, and authorship discovery. *Topic modeling*

[8] classification of documents by machine learning, semantic analysis by word vectors, annotation and discovery of named entities, sentiment analysis, have all opened up new perspectives by making possible new quantitative or quali-quantitative text analyses of texts considered as data of contemporary culture or cultural history. This marked the birth of a new discipline called culturomics or cultural analytics, which aims at "extending the frontiers of rigorous quantitative investigation to a wide range of new phenomena covering the social sciences and humanities" [9] The combination of these new algorithms, on the one hand, and the indexing of millions of books and texts, on the other, allows capturing the lexical and grammatical evolution of languages [10], or to pinpoint literary motives that could have not been noticed by some "human" distant reading [11].

Through the analysis of texts—itself influenced by the appearance of new algorithms and gigantic corpuses—artificial intelligence has taken its place in the field of economic and social sciences [12]. In particular, "topic modeling" algorithms, developed by the computer scientist David Blei in order to determine abstract topics or themes in texts [13], were the first to be imported into sociology. These algorithms allow analyzing the actors' discourses in order to identify discursive patterns and interpretative frameworks. For example, in collaboration with David Blei, Paul DiMaggio and Manish Nage were able to analyze the American federal government's policy on arts funding through a corpus of 8,000 articles published in major American newspapers between 1986 and 1991, by identifying the moments when certain interpretative frameworks took the upper hand in the public debate [14][2]. Similarly, in economics, topic modeling can be matched with traditional methods, such as descriptive statistics or econometrics. For instance, the hammer prices of artworks at Parisian auction in the 19th century have been explained through the usual variables of artist attribution, date of creation, dimensions, medium, pedigree, etc., but also through to the "sentiments" of the experts, when they described the artworks in a more or less laudatory way in the auction catalogues [15].

Far from replacing human researches in economic and social sciences, topic modeling or sentiment analysis have become tools for sociologists and economists, who remain in charge of the interpretation of findings. Moreover, the possibility of interpreting these results is the criterion that ensures the "scientificity" of these disciplines, distinguishing them from approximate methods. In "traditional" econometrics, parametric regressions are computed using an algebraic formula, bound to yield unique, optimal and tractable solutions, which are transparent and available for interpretation. The methodology differs from machine learning models that rely on approximate optimization. Based on variables such as age, place of residence, gender, these algorithms can predict wages or behaviors, but offers little insight about the reasons explaining them [16]. Contrary to the parametric regressions, they could constitute a black box and do not offer interpretable coefficients.

With the capability to "*operationalize*" [17], that is, to transform theoretical or historical hypotheses into operators that can be empirically measured, the propositions

---

[2] This paper uses "Sentiment analysis" algorithms, measuring the "general feeling" of a text, i.e. the "positive feeling" or "negative feeling" associated with that text.

of human sciences become more quantitatively verifiable. The masses of data into which cultural history is transcribed (e.g. the gigantic corpus of newspapers and dailies) allows the critic to test hypotheses formulated by erudition but otherwise difficult to establish because founded upon a general knowledge, a memory of the works, an intuitive synthesis that are difficult to objectivize and to refute. The possibility of aligning human sciences with other sciences[3] raises institutional and scientific questions and impact the visibility and influence of the humanities. In particular, they raise a paradox connected to the fact that these supposedly more verifiable methods so complex and computationally demanding that only to a handful of researchers and institutions can afford to use them. Emerging domains like the quantitative history of ideas or quantitative formalism force us to deal with the opacity of digital black boxes while dealing with massive datasets and complex modeling and interpretation questions that require field intuition and old-style knowledge of corpora.

At the same time, computational linguistics has made dazzling progress, as evidenced by the spread of conversational agents, the contemporary efficiency of machine translation, and the now familiar tools for summarization and grammatical check. Combined with voice or optical recognition, real-time translation has become a reality on smartphones, leading us to dream of a world where linguistic differences will no longer represent cultural barriers. NLP (natural language processing) algorithms trained on large corpora have demonstrated their ability to produce morphological and semantic analyses without the need to parallel translation blocks, encode syntactic or semantic rules, or reducing richness of word semantics. Such advances, embodied by the success of the BERT algorithm used by Google and based on a bidirectional analysis of the context of words, have been made possible by a shift from rule-based analysis (in the 1970s, linguistics postulated, following Noam Chomsky, that natural languages could relate to computer languages) to empirical statistical models. At the same time, psycholinguistics has been trying to produce neural networks models of the human brain and to emulate how a child learns human language. While many facets of human expression are still resistant (the use of metaphors or irony, for example), some of the tools for automatic text generation are beginning to be used, for example to produce journalistic articles about sports, businesses or election results, with the horizon set by artificial intelligence storytelling.

Beyond the temptation of a new positivism, this mathematization of the demonstration has profound effects. Some AI supporters claim that theory can be entirely replaced by machine learning algorithms capable of drawing, by induction, general laws or regularities. They dream of an empiricist approach that would render theoretical propositions obsolete and go as far as imagining literary forecasts, turning cultural history into a nomothetic science capable of predicting the success of a best-seller. This is what Jodie Archer (editor) and Matthew L. Jockers (a specialist in digital humanities) propose in *The Bestseller Code: Anatomy of the Blockbuster Novel* (2016), where they assert their ability to predict the success of a novel before publication by analyzing its

---

[3] This is a recurrent ambition that can be observed at every change of scientific paradigm. We can certainly find it in the positivist thought of literary history or in the linguistic turn and the horizon constituted by formal linguistics.

content, according to a multifactorial model of machine reading. After advanced statistical methods and the emergence of a graphic knowledge that extended (and potentially objectify) the work of historians in different ways, this perspective suggests transforming cultural knowledge even more radically, reducing it to a skillful strategy to launch a machine on a track and interpret the results. To be sure, good reasons exist to remain skeptical and remark that the machine only works with data that it receives, making AI approaches deeply dependent upon theoretical and interpretive choices and frameworks. Still, it would be unwise to disregard the many ways in which artificial intelligence proposes epistemologically disruptive methods capable of profoundly modifying the modalities of demonstration and the very nature of cultural knowledge.

## 2.2   Network Analysis

Discussing the intersection between artificial intelligence and network analysis is a complicated task, because the extent of such intersection depends largely on how broadly the two fields are conceived. Network analysis *stricto sensu*, is the use of techniques derived from graph theory to study relational phenomena—that is, composed by a multiplicity of elements considered by their mutual relations rather than by their individual features [19]. Network analysis is a form of topological thinking, that focuses on the relative position between elements, considers a space that is multidimensional and non-Euclidian [19, 20]. In the last decades, network analysis has enjoyed an impressive success in academic and industrial research and has become one of the most important fields of interdisciplinary collaboration between social and information sciences. This popularity is justified by the growing interest of social research in relational phenomena and is fuelled by the increasing availability of relational records collected through digital technologies. As both the Internet and the Web are network technologies based on network protocol, it is not surprising that network formats have progressively acquired a dominant position in data collection and analysis. Complementing the most classic tools of descriptive and inferential statistics, network analysis has become a crucial instrument to deal with the datasets increasingly available on social and human phenomena. It would not be unfair to claim that networks analysis is the analytical technique most strongly associated with the birth of computational social science.

While, strictly speaking, network analysis is not always a form of artificial intelligence—in the sense that unlike to the latter it is not inspired by human cognitive process or intended to mimic human capacity for problem solving—networks are extensively mobilized in both the symbolic and the connectionist branch of AI. Symbolic AI relies heavily on semantic nets as formalisms to represent knowledge ontologies and neural networks are one of the flagship techniques of connectionist AI. Yet in both cases, networks are used as support for other computational approaches rather than as full-fledged analytical tool and combination between graph mathematics and AI is still an emerging field.

For the moment, network analysis and artificial intelligence remain separated branches of mathematics and their alliance is based more on the sequential combination than on the unification of the two computational methods. In most cases, a network is turned into a training dataset for machine learning, by considering its nodes as a list of entities with relational features rather than as different components of a unique graph. According to this approach, relational characteristics are first calculated for each of the node in the network through graph mathematics and then used as features of a machine learning algorithm [21, 22]. The extraction of relational features can be carried out in several different ways. The simplest technique consists in exploiting the classic metrics of network analysis, such as connectivity or centrality. More sophisticated solutions employ advanced techniques of graph embedding (projecting the graph in a multidimensional space where distances between couples of nodes can be calculated) and of graph convolutional networks (allowing the model to learn the dataset features by inspecting each node as well as its neighbours). A particularly popular solution is the "node2vect" algorithm [23], which draws on random walks (a classic technique of network analysis) to represent each node through its closest neighbours. In this technique, the sequence of nodes encountered by an agent randomly moving through the network is turned into a vector defining the node of departure, similarly to the way in which the word2vect algorithm turns every word of a text in the vectors of the words that are most often used in association with the target word.

The advantages of approaches that stitch together network analysis and artificial intelligence, rather than unifying them is that, once the relational features are extracted through one of the techniques mentioned above, it is possible to analyze them with a variety of AI techniques, choosing the ones that are more relevant according to the research objectives (anomaly detection, predictive analytics, items categorisation, etc.). Another advantage is that, after the relational structures of the graph is turned in a dataset of features, it is easy to combine these relational variables with other categorical or numerical characteristics of the node of the networks, to investigate their association (to examine, for example, how the discipline or the number of publications influence the collaborations in a network of scientific authors).

## 2.3   IA in Art History

Beyond the analysis of texts, quantitative data—and networks—, artificial intelligence is renewing the analysis of images. Art history, in particular, is taking advantage of AI algorithms to develop new approaches—or rather to return to its original ambition: to retrace the history and diffusion of "styles", to understand the life of forms and the evolution of motifs. Indeed, art history emerged in the 18th century from the technical possibility of serializing and comparing images, thanks to engraving and "paper museums", and consolidated in the 19th century with the rise of photography [24]. This work of comparison, based on the images themselves, found its theoretical apogee in the "iconology" proposed by Aby Warburg, as early as 1903 [25]. According to him, works of art embed the collective desires and expectations, the *Pathosformel*: studying the circulation of these *Pathosformeln* thus informs about the state of societies, mythologies and aspirations. In order to implement this "modern science of art" (*Kunstwissenschaft*), Aby Warburg relied technically on large panels on which he placed photographs of works of art, grouped according to similar motifs and visual references. Nevertheless, Warburg's iconology was too Promethean a project to be feasible because of the inability to study very large corpora of images: art historians gradually abandoned this ambition in favor of monograph studies or a text-centered approach to the reception of images [26].

New technical advances allow achieving Warburg's ambition. On the one hand, recent datasets of annotated images have been compiled thanks to the advances of scanning systems, making "Big Visual Data" available to art historians. For instance, regarding the Renaissance (Warburg's preferred period) the Web Gallery of Art, a searchable database of European fine arts and architecture, currently contains over 48,600 reproductions [27], and the photo-library of the Giorgio Cini Foundation in Venice has about 1 million digitized photos of European artworks [28]. The Google Art project also gives access to a large collection of images, but mainly from American museums with poor coverage of the Renaissance [39]. On the other hand, since 2012, new artificial intelligence algorithms of "computer vision" made possible to formally analyze these images, to compare and to group them according to similar patterns [30]. As a matter of fact, Deep Learning and Convolutional Neural Networks enable to identify structural and compositional similarities between images at different scales, from general patterns in the overall image to smaller-scale details [31].

These "computer vision" techniques spurred notable advances in art history. From 2015 through 2019, the Replica international project led by the DHLAB at the EPFL (Lausanne, Switzerland) in partnership with the Giorgio Cini Foundation in Venice and Factum Arte in Madrid, managed to design a search engine for the exploration of artistic collections. Developed by Benoît Seguin, this navigation system allows exploring connections between some 330,000 documents from the photo-collection of the Cini, and helps researchers in identifying visual links [32]. This visualization takes the form of a network of images: the more similar, in terms of shapes, forms or motifs, the closer in the network—and vice versa [33]. The search engine constitutes a new tool to detect visual similarities in artistic compositions, and offers visual panels similar to Warburg's, but on a much larger corpus of images. Another international project uses computer vision as a tool to detect motifs that the human eye might have overlooked. Developed by Mathieu Aubry at Ecole des Ponts Paris Tech, in France, the EnHerit algorithm (Enhancing Heritage Image Databases) identifies recurring patterns across vast corpora of heterogeneous images [34].

Thanks to artificial intelligence algorithms, it is thus possible to renew one of the founding ambitions of iconology, i.e. to identify visual similarities between images, diffusion of patterns or styles. Nevertheless, computer vision cannot replace human vision since it is up to the art historian to constitute the corpus of images, to verify their relevance and, above all, to interpret the visual links between works of art.

## 3   AI in a Social Research Practice and Organizaztion

The social sciences and the humanities are directly confronted to the many societal issues at stake with AI. They aim to study in an interdisciplinary manner the ways in which artificial intelligence is changing society: from facial recognition to connected objects, from robotics, to human-computer interaction, from decision support to massive data, from social web platforms to the rise of micro-work, AI is transforming all sectors of collective life relentlessly extending to commerce and consumption, health and labor, public and personal life. These developments pose considerable problems of economic, geographical and environmental impact, protection of private data, legal responsibility, control of possible ethnic and gender bias, explicability and traceability.

While much has been written about the changes that AI encourages in the epistemic posture of humanities and the social sciences and about the ethical and political risks connected to it, less attention has been devoted to the more mundane, yet equally important, transformations taking place in day-to-day research practices [35, 36]. Even when this subject is addressed, it is often to oppose the caricature of traditional scholars working in the isolation of their library, with little more than their intellect and a notepad, to the equally caricatural image of an interdisciplinary laboratory where computer scientists and engineers work hand in hand with social and human researchers collaborating around complex pieces of computing machinery. While it is well-known that information and cognitive sciences have a long interdisciplinary tradition [37–39], which can only be amplified by their application to human and social topics[40–42], it is misleading to present this research as more collective or more intensively equipped than its traditional counterpart.

Research in large teams and with massive equipment has always existed in the humanities and the social sciences. Libraries and archives, for instance, are extremely vast and sophisticated pieces of intellectual technologies, whose development span through decades and required the collaboration of hundreds and often thousands of scholars. Similarly, social statistics have always mobilised armies of pollsters, data cleaners and analysts [43, 44]; geography could have not developed without the coordination of a multitude of surveyors, cartographers and map designers [45]; and linguistics has always relied on vast collections of speech and writing records. Even anthropology, which often presented as a solitary discipline based on direct and unmediated immersion, has always made extensive use of collective archives of material culture items and field notes.

Conversely and differently from commonplace ideas, digital humanities and social sciences are not always collective enterprises. In fact, the growing availability of datasets, offered by the development of open data and by the platform economy, has allowed quantitative research to be carried out at in individual level. Likewise, the increasing calculation capacities offered by ordinary personal computers and the large number of open-source tools and scripts available for reuse and adaptation has allowed researchers to embark on a solitary project of data analysis with results that are often as rich and interesting as those of more established research institutions.

In fact, if digital technologies have changed something to research practices, it is rather the way in which they have softened the boundaries of traditional academic institutions, allowing researchers to collaborate in loser but broader networks. This, of course, is connected to the way in which digital media facilitate communication and transfer of information over long distance, but it also depends more specifically on the progressive standardisation of data infrastructure. Consolidating around a limited amount of data formats and programming languages, the development of computer programming brought about a quasi-universal language for exchanging research records and analytic techniques. Today, no matter the type of fieldwork or style of investigation, research records are stored in the same CVS files and databases and can be manipulated with the same languages (R, Python, C++ and a handful of others).

This standardization allows scholars from all disciplines to pick from growing catalogues of freely availability scripts for data cleaning and analysis. This is particularly true for the techniques of artificial intelligence which most often enter the humanities and social sciences conveniently packaged as off-the-shelf modules and libraries [41]. Such a standardized architecture has greatly reduced the barriers to advanced computation techniques, allowing an increasing number of scholars from an increasing diversity of backgrounds to access to the state of the art of machine learning. While this may increase the risk of AI techniques being used as black boxes with little understanding of their inner workings [46, 47], it also creates the potential for even greater exchange and collaboration across disciplinary frontiers.

This erosion of traditional disciplinary boundaries has taken place not only within the academia, but also and more crucially between academic and industrial research [48]. Neural networks and deep learning, much more than most other computing techniques, have been developed outside universities and research institutions, and found their main developers and sponsors in the corporations of the digital economy [49, 50]. In the field of engineering and computer sciences, universities have long learned to compete with companies to attract talented developers and to advance the frontiers of data science. A similar dynamic of collaboration and competition is not beginning to affect study of human and social phenomena [51]. This is hardly surprising, after all an increasing portion of the data and the techniques exploited by digital humanities and computational social sciences comes from internet companies and data-intensive corporations—a situation that opens new potential, but also creates new challenges for public academic research. One can thus understand the importance of artificial intelligence for the human sciences and that of the human sciences for artificial intelligence: the analysis of SHS data, in all their depth and complexity, is a challenge, perhaps the greatest challenge, for AI methods, while at the same time the need to think about the human consequences of AI technologies must mobilize in an interdisciplinary way all SHS knowledge by offering them not only a field of research but a real challenge to established knowledge.

# References

1. Turing, A.: Computing machinery and intelligence. Mind **59**, 433–460 (1950)
2. Farrell, M.: Lakatos and Feyeraben: research programmes and anarchism. In: Historical and Philosophical Foundations of Psychology, 46-68. Cambridge University Press, Cambridge (2014)
3. Ackerman, A. (dir.): Golem! Avatars d'une légende d'argile, exhibition catalogue. MahJ/Hazan, Paris (2017). Laurence Bertrand-Dorléac (dir.), Artistes & Robots, exh. cat., Paris: RMN, 2018.
4. Rifkin, J.: The End of Work: The Decline of the Global Labor Force and the Dawn of the Post-Market Era. Putnam Publishing Group, New York (1995)
5. Ganascia, J.-G. : Le mythe de la Singularité. Faut-il craindre l'intelligence artificielle ? Seuil, Paris (2017)
6. Moretti, F.: Distant Reading. Verso, London/New York (2013)
7. Gefen, A.: The Empirical Turn of Literary Studies" in Nicoletta Pireddu. Reframing Critical, Literary, and Cultural Theories, pp. 119–135. Palgrave Macmillan, Cham (2018)

8. https://mimno.infosci.cornell.edu/topics.html.
9. Michel, J.-B., Shen, Y.K., Aiden, A.P., et al.: Quantitative Analysis of Culture Using Millions of Digitized Books. Science **331**(6014), 176–182 (2010)
10. Moretti, F., Pestre, D.: Bankspeak. The Language of World Bank Reports. New Left Rev. **92**, 75–99 (2015)
11. Lu, Y.: Caractérisation des genres/styles littéraires par l'extraction automatique des "motifs" dans les romans du 19e et 20e siècle, ongoing Ph.D. supervised by Thierry Poibeau, PSL/ENS
12. Cointet, J.-P., Parasie, S.: Ce que le Big Data fait à l'analyse sociologique des textes. Un panorama critique des recherches contemporaines. Rev. Française Sociol. **59**, 533–557 (2018)
13. Blei, D.: Probabilistic topic models. Commun. ACM **55**(4), 77–84 (2012)
14. DiMaggio, P., Nag, M., Blei, D.: Exploiting affinities between topic modeling and the sociological perspective on culture: application to newspaper coverage of U.S. government arts fundig. Poetics **41**(5), 570–606 (2013)
15. Poibeau, T., Saint-Raymond, L.: Pricing Opinion and Tastes: The Art Market through Sentiment Analysis. DH2020@Ottawa (2020)
16. Boelaert, J., Ollion, É.: The great regression. Machine learning, econometrics, and the future of quantitative social sciences. Rev. Française Sociol. **59**, 475–506 (2018)
17. Moretti, F.: Literature, Measured. Literary Lab Pamphlets, no. 12, April 2016. https://litlab.stanford.edu/LiteraryLabPamphlet12.pdf.
18. Borgatti, S., Mehra, A., Brass, D.J., et al.: Network Analysis in the Social Sciences. Science **323**(5916), 892–895 (2009)
19. Venturini, T., Munk, A., Jacomy, M.: Actor-network vs network analysis vs digital networks are we talking about the same networks? In: Ribes, D., Vertesi, J. (eds.) DigitalSTS: A Handbook and Fieldguide. University Press, Princeton (2019)
20. Venturini, T., Jacomy, M., Jensen, P.: What do we see when we look at networks an introduction to visual network analysis and force-directed layouts. SSRN. https://papers.ssrn.com/sol3/papers.cfm?abstract_id=3378438
21. Monti, F., Boscaini, D., Masci, J., et al.: Geometric deep learning on graphs and manifolds using mixture model CNNs. In: Proceedings - 30th IEEE Conference on Computer Vision and Pattern Recognition, CVPR 2017, vol. 2017-January, pp. 5425–5434 (2017)
22. Pal, S., Dong, Y., Thapa, B., et al.: Deep learning for network analysis: problems, approaches and challenges. In: Proceedings - IEEE Military Communications Conference MILCOM, pp. 588–593 (2016)
23. Grover, A., Leskovec, J.: node2vec. In: Proceedings of the 22nd ACM SIGKDD International Conference on Knowledge Discovery and Data Mining, vol. 95 (2016)
24. Griener, P.: La république de l'œil. L'expérience de l'art au siècle des Lumières, Paris, Odile Jacob (2010)
25. Recht, R.: L'iconologie avant Warburg. Images Revues [En ligne], Hors-série 4 (2013). https://journals.openedition.org/imagesrevues/2898. Accessed 11 June 2020
26. Joyeux-Prunel, B.: Visual contagions, the art historian, and the digital strategies to work on them. Artl@s Bull. **8**(3), 131 (2019). Article 8. https://docs.lib.purdue.edu/artlas/vol8/iss3/8/. Accessed 11 June 2020.
27. https://www.wga.hu. Accessed 11 June 2020
28. https://www.cini.it Accessed 11 June 2020
29. https://artsandculture.google.com. Accessed 11 June 2020
30. Krizhevsky, A., Sutskever, I., Hinton, G.E.: Imagenet classification with deep convolutional neural networks. In: Advances in Neural Information Processing Systems, pp. 1097–1105 (2012)

31. Seguin, B., Striolo, C., di Lenardo, I., Kaplan, F.: Visual link retrieval in a database of paintings. In: Hua, G., Jégou, H. (eds.) ECCV 2016. Lecture Notes in Computer Science, vol. 9913, pp. 753–767. Springer, Cham (2016). https://doi.org/10.1007/978-3-319-46604-0_52

32. Seguin, B.: The Replica project: building a visual search engine for art historians. ACM Crossroads **24**(3), 24–29 (2018)

33. Seguin, B.: Making large art historical photo archives searchable. Ph.D., Ecole polytechnique fédérale de Lausanne (supervised by Frédéric Kablan and Isabella diLenardo) (2018). https://infoscience.epfl.ch/record/261212. Accessed 11 June 2020

34. Ginosar, S., Shen, X., Dwivedi, K., Honig, E., Aubry, M.: The burgeoning computer-art symbiosis. computers help us understand art. Art helps us teach computers. XRDS: Crossroads ACM Mag. Stud. – Comput. Art Arch. **24**(3), 30–33 (2018). https://doi.org/10.1145/3186655. Accessed 11 June 2020.

35. Suchman, L., Trigg, R. H.: Artificial intelligence as craftwork. In: Learning in Doing: Social, Cognitive, and Computational Perspectives. Understanding Practice: Perspectives on Activity and Context, pp. 144–178. University Press, Cambridge (1993)

36. Mackenzie, A., Learners, M.: Archaeology of a Data Practice. MIT Press, Cambridge Mass (2017)

37. Saracevic, T.: Interdisciplinary nature of information science. Ciência Inf. **24**(1), 36–41 (1995)

38. Thagard, P.: Being Interdisciplinary: trading zones in cognitive science. In: Derry, S.J., Schunn, C.D., Gernsbacher, M.A. (eds.) Interdisciplinary Collaboration: An Emerging Cognitive Science, pp. 317–339. Erlbaum, Mahwa (2005)

39. Ribes, D., Hoffman, A.S., Slota, S.C., Bowker, G.C.: The logic of domains. Soc. Stud. Sci. **49**(3), 281–309 (2019)

40. Woolgar, S.: Why not a sociology of machine? The case of sociology and artificial intelligence. Sociology **19**(4), 557–572 (1985)

41. Carley, K.M.: Artificial intelligence within sociology. Sociol. Methods Res. **25**, 1–30 (1996)

42. Grimmer, J.: We are all social scientists now: how big data, machine learning, and causal inference work together. PS: Polit. Sci. Polit. **48**(01), 80–83 (2015)

43. Desrosières, A.: La politique des grands nombres: histoire de la raison statistique. La Découverte, Paris (1993)

44. Osborne, T., Rose, N.: Do the social sciences create phenomena? The example of public opinion research. Br. J. Sociol. **50**(3), 367–396 (1999)

45. Turnbull, D.: Masons, Tricksters and Cartographers. Routledge, London (2000)

46. Burrell, J.: How the machine 'thinks': understanding opacity in machine learning algorithms. Big Data Soc. **3**(1), 2053951715622512 (2016)

47. Rudin, C.: Stop explaining black box machine learning models for high stakes decisions and use interpretable models instead. Nat. Mach. Intell. **1**(5), 206–215 (2019)

48. Metzler, K., Kim, D.A., Allum, N., et al.: Who is doing computational social science? Trends in Big Data Research A SAGE White Paper (2016)

49. Meyer, E.T., Schroeder, R.: Knowledge Machines Digital Transformations of the Sciences and Humanities. MIT Press, Cambridge (2015)

50. Salganik, M.: Bit by Bit: Social Research in the Digital Age. Princeton, University Press (2019)

51. Wallach, H.: Computational social science: toward a collaborative future. In: Avarez, M. (ed.) Computational Social Science: Discovery and Prediction, pp. 307–315. MIT Press, Cambridge (2015)

# Augmented Human and Human-Machine Co-evolution: Efficiency and Ethics

Andreas Dengel[1,2]([✉]), Laurence Devillers[3], and Laura Maria Schaal[1]

[1] DFKI, Kaiserslautern, Germany
andreas.dengel@dfki.de
[2] University of Kaiserslautern, Kaiserslautern, Germany
[3] Sorbonne-University, Limsi-DATAIA Institute (Saclay), Paris, France

**Abstract.** Capability and expected potential of AI-based computer solutions increased significantly in the recent years, mainly due to progress in machine learning technologies and available data. Growing effectiveness in reasoning, knowledge representation, automatic training via machine learning, and especially in computer vision and speech technology result in AI systems becoming an ever-better communication and work partner of their human counterparts. Deeply embedded in the every-day context of work and leisure, AI systems can act as competent dialog partners and powerful work assistants. Furthermore, they increasingly help humans to better acquire new insights, process and apply situation-specific instructions, receive improved training and learn new knowledge more effectively. Ultimately, intelligent systems exhibit the potential to become inseparable partners of humans or – in case e.g. of prosthesis solutions and innovative sensor technology – even become part of the human body. Such close mental and physical interconnection between human and AI system raises new concerns and ethical questions which need to be considered not only by computer scientists, but ask for interdisciplinary work and social discourse. This paper outlines the different levels of human-computer integration, gives examples of the innovative potential in work assistance and learning support, and sketches ethical and moral issues conjoined with such progress.

**Keywords:** Co-learning · Co-creation · Co-adaption

With contributions from: Vincent Aleven, Human-Computer Interaction Institute, Carnegie Mellon University. Kenneth Holstein, Human-Computer Interaction Institute, Carnegie Mellon University. Elisabeth André, Computer Science Department, University of Augsburg. Justine Cassell, Human-Computer Interaction Institute, Carnegie Mellon University. Gordon Cheng, Institute for Cognitive Systems (ICS) Technical University of Munich. Dimosthenis Karatzas, Computer Vision Centre, Universitat Autònoma de Barcelona. Koichi Kise, Dept. of Computer Science and Intelligent Systems, Osaka Prefecture University. Kenji Mase, Graduate School of Informatics, Nagoya University. Raul Rojas, Department of Mathematics and Computer Science, Freie Universität Berlin.

B. Braunschweig and M. Ghallab (Eds.): Reflections on Artificial Intelligence
for Humanity, LNAI 12600, pp. 203–227, 2021.
https://doi.org/10.1007/978-3-030-69128-8_13

# 1  Introduction

Artificial Intelligence (AI) has become more and more important for practical use, especially in recent years, because sufficient computing capacity and correspondingly large amounts of data are available, which especially pushes the evolution of Machine Learning (ML). ML algorithms help people to recognize patterns in existing data sets, make predictions or classify data. Moreover, mathematical models can be used to gain new insights based on these patterns. This holds for many life and business fields, where users often benefit from systems without thinking about the technology in the background. A wide range of ML methods is available for this purpose, including linear regression, instance-based learning, decision tree algorithms, Bayesian statistics, cluster analysis, neural networks, deep learning and methods for dimensional reduction.

The fields of application are manifold and partly known. Think of spam detection, content personalization, such as music and film recommendations, document and sentiment analysis, customer migration prediction, email classification, up-selling opportunities analysis, congestion prediction, genome analysis, medical diagnostics, chat bots and much more. Obviously, there are opportunities for almost all industries and types of companies.

It is a matter of fact, AI plays an increasingly important role as the world becomes more and more complex and poses more and more challenges to individuals, society, companies and institutions. Growing information intensity and information overload, the trend towards shorter innovation cycles and the reduction of knowledge half-live time are all reasons why we face these greater challenges. To penetrate this complexity, AI can make considerable contributions[1].

There are already impressive technologies for application in professional life that open up new opportunities and potentials: When performing complex tasks, people can fall back on digital companions or use systems that take over entire work packages independently. Such applications are, for example, in practical implementation in the manufacturing industry in quality control or in assembly, maintenance or repair work. Smart applications can also be identified in the field of education [1], such as supporting teaching with the help of intelligent tutoring systems. Sensor data that provide information about eye movements, for example, can help to assess how attentive students are or how well they understand the learning content.

Every technology has its own time and its own impact. AI revolutionizes and permeates our lives in all possible areas. Computers are increasingly taking over the role of a learning partner to enhance performance and productivity, supporting our individual handling of diverse information sources and exploring synergies between large communities. In such an evolutionary cyber-social environment, new potentials for co-creative systems are emerging, assisting users in understanding, learning, decision-making, and memorizing [2]. In the professional world, this is often referred to as Digital Taylorism - a division of labour that brings man and machine into coexistence in order to jointly carry out trial solutions. The term is based on the "Principle of Scientific Management" coined by Frederick Taylor at the beginning of

---

[1] See also chapter 8 of this book.

the 20th century. Breaking-down complex jobs into simple tasks, measuring the outcome of the workers and paying some salary in relation to this outcome is the basic principle of Taylorism. The fundamental axiom of the Digital Taylorism is "what gets measured gets managed". Thus, the more the technology of measurement advances, the more we hand power to Frederick Taylor's successors.

Today, we have almost unlimited options to measure and this measurement does not only include the classical physical worker but also technicians, managers, and professionals, such as physicists, lawyers, or university professors. Therefore, another way of understanding Digital Taylorism is to describe it as the translation of knowledge work into working knowledge through extraction, codification and digitalization of cognitive tasks into software prescripts that can be solved by AI systems. However, Digital Taylorism does not necessarily mean that people become puppets of digitization. It also does not necessarily mean that people "in the digital world [...] are mere widgets in the giant corporate computer" as described in *The Economist* [3].

Quite the contrary, it is true that AI, if used correctly, with respect to ethical rules, can fruitfully complement and enhance the abilities of humans. With an AI-controlled exoskeleton, for example, a human being can use considerably more power and still implement his sensitive way of performing mechanical actions. When using intelligent systems to perform standardized tasks in the working environment, there is more time to work creatively and apply human problem-solving skills. Correctly used, intelligent tutoring systems can identify and promote the strengths of individuals in school application.

The following article therefore aims to present successful best practices, which were presented in the CoCoLAd Workshop[2] hosted by Andreas Dengel and Laurence Devillers during the Global Forum on AI for Humanity in October 2019. Furthermore, the following examples and statements pursue the objective to raise awareness of the measures necessary for a human-centered co-existence of man and machine in order to achieve a development that is socially and ethically beneficial.

After a short explanation of the terms Augmented Human, Human Machine Co-Evolution (Sect. 2) and approaches for measuring and modelling systems with human-machine interaction (Sect. 3), best practices from the field of education (Sect. 4) are presented. Since the use of such technologies is controversially discussed, also in the field of teaching, this chapter will also outline crucial considerations that should be taken into account when using smart systems. Section 5, the conclusion, focuses on critically reflecting on the presented technologies and giving a short outlook.

## 2 Short Definition of Terms

This chapter will present short definitions of the terms "Augmented Human" and "Human-Machine Co-Evolution" before focusing on the question of ethical principles in AI in general.

---

[2] Human-Machine Co-Creation, Co-Learning and Co-Adaptation.

## 2.1   Augmented Human (Physical/Cognitive/Virtual)

The field of human augmentation focuses on creating cognitive and physical improvements as an integral part of the human body. Let's come back to the already mentioned example of powered exoskeletons: they can improve the quality of life of individuals who have lost the use of their legs by enabling system-assisted walking. While exoskeletons can reduce the stress of manual activity, they may also pose dangers such as potential falls due to a shift in center of gravity.

Advances in artificial intelligence, in conjunction with recent developments in neurotechnology, open the prospect of augmenting and amplifying human cognitive abilities. Neuroscience findings are providing a new level of knowledge for the design of advanced human symbiotic machines that are more tuned to humans. This cognitive augmentation could be beneficial for individuals and society. Cognitive augmentation may be defined as the amplification or extension of core capacities of the mind through enhancement of internal or external information processing systems. Cognition includes acquiring information (perception), selecting (attention), representing (understanding) and retaining (memory) information, and using it to guide behavior (reasoning and coordination of motor outputs). Cognitive stimulation refers to the set of techniques, strategies and materials to improve performance and effectiveness of cognitive capabilities and executive functions such as memory, attention, language, reasoning and planning, among others. Nowadays there are several strategies to train our brain, from classical exercise with conversational agents and serious games to more dynamic, innovative techniques such as brain training games and neurotechnology. In this respect, Sects. 3 and 4 will take up and explain some examples of research topics presented at the CoCoLAd workshop on Human-Machine Co-Creation, Co-Learning and Co-Adaptation.

## 2.2   Human-Machine Co-evolution

People are living together in a "cyber-physical" world with the internet, computers and phones but also cars and connected objects. Smart products have embedded sensors that are continuously connected to the Internet of Things. This applies to buildings and machines, as well as our mobile devices, shopping carts or our sports shoes. The trend is to shift more and more functional intelligence into the products themselves so that they become intelligent agents. This enables them to act independently. Because they are constantly connected to each other via the cloud, whether at home in the four walls, while traveling or at work, and because they synchronize our data with the environment, they can provide us with continuous support. They check their availability, match their skills, coordinate the processing of tasks and control business processes. They also monitor system statuses, optimize material usage, productivity or quality and detect anomalies and redundancies. In doing so, they are constantly learning and adapting to new requirements and changing conditions.

They are thus creating a new form of "simplexity", in which humans are relieved of the tasks that AI systems can better master. AI thus also becomes a power amplifier technology that complements human skills or enhances their capabilities, both physical and cognitive. The trend is moving away from cooperative assistance systems, through interdependent human-machine scenarios, to activities where humans and digital agents compete with each other, including in cognitive tasks. The latter applies especially to activities where activity is measurable and understandable. Just as the industrial revolution has neutralized the physical ability of humans in many cases and redefined the division of labour, AI will do the same in the context of intellectually demanding activities and define a new form of division of labour between humans and machines. As a consequence, there is a gradual change in our roles and the roles we give to machines. This way, we may talk about a co-evolution, where intelligent agents and humans mutually adapt to each other through the increasing interaction and interconnection sometimes resulting in an augmented human.

The interactions with intelligent agents, conversational robots are already a kind of enhancement technologies. In order to augment our performances, computers and robots are also increasingly taking over the role of a learning partner. The capabilities of emerging technologies are underpinning the formation of new human-machine partnerships, which will have significant impact on both individuals and organizations. More specifically, these human-machine partnerships[3] have the potential to allow people to find information and act on it without emotional interference or external bias, while exercising human judgment where appropriate. If we learn to "team up" with technologies integrated with human-machine learning tools, we can imagine a future in which this collaboration helps provide the resources and knowledge we need to manage our daily lives.

Recently, the research focus in the field has moved to mobile and pervasive interaction, including embodied interfaces and intelligent user inter-faces. However, most of the time, there is still a clear separation between the user and the system. The augmented human of the 21st century with physical exoskeleton, bionic eyes or prostheses, cognitive stimulation or virtual experiments fascinates and repels us at the same time. Where should the red line between repair, care and augmentation actually be drawn?

Designing and developing great AI systems that allow users to effectively interact or work together is no easy task. If you google "the C's of social technology Interaction" you will get links to a myriad of "C-words" including: Collaboration, Communication, Cooperation, Creativity, Coordination, Critical Thinking, etc.". All of which are important elements of learning and working and can be enhanced with the use of technology. In order to describe the interaction between humans and robots working together, three scenarios have been established in the professional world: Coexistence, Cooperation and Collaboration. In the coexistence scenario, humans and robots work in separate workspaces, with no interaction or overlap between humans and robots. CoBot is the con-traction of "collaborative" and "robot", name and concept of a new kind of robots able to work literally hand-in-hand with humans without a safety fence between them. In the cooperative scenario, humans and robots work simultaneously in the same workspace on different objects or tasks. In the collaboration scenario, man and robot work hand in hand on a common task or object. The robot assists humans, for example, when adding components to be assembled. The AI

---

[3] https://www.iftf.org/humanmachinepartnerships/.

systems that will be most useful to us in the future are those that collaborate rather than replacing, those that cooperate rather than competing and those that can effectively co-exist with humans. Going from human-robot coexistence to collaboration is a real technological and social challenge.

## 2.3  Core Principles for Ethical AI

Designing and developing great collaborations with AI systems that respect ethical principles is no easy task. For example, emerging interactive and adaptive systems using sophisticated skills like emotion detection or simulation [4] modify how we will socialize with machines with positive impacts but also some risks. On the one hand capturing, transmitting and mimicking our feelings will open up new applications and better collaborations with machines in health, education, transport and entertainment. On the other hand, these areas inspire critical questions centering on the ethics, the goals and the deployment of innovative products that can change our lives and society. Such close mental and physical interconnections between humans and AI systems raise new concerns and ethical questions which need to be considered not only by computer scientists, but through interdisciplinary work and social discourse regarding the different areas of application.

Several high-profile initiatives established in the interest of socially beneficial AI have been be proposed. A unified framework may therefore be synthesized [5] from these approaches which tries to define goals and limits of AI systems and their development, consisting of five core principles for ethical AI:

- Beneficence: promoting well-being, preserving dignity, and sustaining the planet
- Non-maleficence: privacy, security and "capability caution"
- Autonomy: the power to decide
- Justice: promoting prosperity and preserving solidarity
- Transparency and Explicability: enabling the other principles through intelligibility and accountability

Ethical issues must be treated in more depth for each application. The use of AI in education, health, etc. will bring great benefits if we can audit the systems and verify these core principles for ethical AI[4].

# 3  Facets of Human Machine Co-creation, Co-learning and Co-adaption

The integration of cyberspace with the real world, which is called "cyber-physical world" or "digital twin" today, is rapidly advancing based on improvements in AI, robotics, data analytics, virtual reality and the internet of things, which are penetrating our society. People are working and living together in such cyber-physical world. Since we interact with robots and smart agents or use machine-assistance, our living style,

---
[4] See also chapters 10 and 11.

performance and functions are already being assisted or augmented by these technologies. Oftentimes, the systems we interact with act "human-like" or perform human tasks. The following subsections will therefore present three concrete methods of modelling how machines can learn from humans (Sects. 3.1, 3.2 and 3.3), before finally focusing on the question of how to design symbiotic society envisioning proper and human-beneficial cyber technologies in general (Sects. 3.4 and 3.5).

## 3.1  Surviving in Man-Made Environments: The Case for Language and Vision[5]

It is easy to imagine a future where social, intelligent machines interact with humans and can successfully complete everyday tasks for or with us, such as doing our shopping, or helping us getting around the city. In such a scenario, it is inconceivable to imagine machines, aimed to co-exist with humans in man-made environments, that are not able to understand and use language, be it written or verbal. Language is a key instrument of human intelligence – intimately linked with vision. Our visual interpretation capacity is jointly acquired with the linguistic structures we use to describe the world. As such, it makes sense to address the acquisition of vision and linguistic skills by machines jointly, as complementary facets of machine cognition.

Computer vision, reading systems and natural language processing have been key and challenging[6] research areas of artificial intelligence and have independently advanced for many decades. Ultimately, the research community has started to explore the interconnections between them. It is quite plausible that future machines will learn to interpret images and language jointly, in a multi-modal fashion, like humans do. And of course, they will be using natural language to interface with humans. The first skill we would like machines to possess is the capacity to read written information in the world around us.

Text is omnipresent around us, especially in urban environments. Importantly, when text is present, it usually carries high-level semantic information, vital to fully understand the scene. Until very recently, the computer vision community has ignored text appearing in real scenes. Nowadays, various researchers work on multiple topics related to reading text in the wild [6], from large-scale text spotting and scene-text based image retrieval [7], to end-to-end reading systems for specific applications [8]. An important tractor for recent advances has been the Robust Reading Competition series, which has consistently pushed the community forward by proposing new challenges and scenarios (from multi-lingual [9] to driving [10]) and offering a consistent evaluation framework.

Following numerous years of research in this field, it has become obvious that reading text around us is not an end on its own, but makes more sense in the context of

---

[5] A contribution based on the GFAIH-speech and research work of Dimosthenis Karatzas.

[6] As well described by Hans Moravec' paradox, seemingly easy aspects of intelligence involving perceptual and motor skills appear easy to humans who count with a long evolution process mastering these skills, but tend to be much more challenging to solve and engineer than higher-level aspects of intelligence such as reasoning which might appear perplexing, but are not intrinsically so difficult to achieve.

interpreting the scene as a whole. How does textual information relate to the visual aspects of a scene, and vice-versa, what can a quick glimpse of a scene tell us about the textual content we expect to encounter there? It turns out that there are many different ways we can learn to associate visual content to textual context (see e.g. [11]). For example, it was shown how peeking at a scene can optimize the subsequent text recognition processes by producing contextualized language models [12] that reflect the "topic" of the image.

Scientists could also demonstrate, that in the process of jointly learning the visual and textual modality, joint representations that effectively map an image to a semantic space defined by the text were learned.

Indeed, it was shown how semantic representations can be learned by feeding the whole of Wikipedia to a neural network model and forcing it to predict for each image what topic (as expressed by the linguistic content of the associated article) it could be used to illustrate [13]. This joint modelling of vision and language has many applications apart from self-supervised learning [13], from cross-modal retrieval [14], to fine-grained classification [15] or hate speech detection in social media [16].

A natural extension of these ideas is exploring the links between vision and understanding or producing natural language. People understand scenes by building causal models and employing them to compose stories that explain their perceptual observations [17]. This capacity of humans is associated with intelligent behaviour. The ability to describe an image is one of the oldest cognitive tasks in intelligence tests [18], and it is intimately related with our capacity to build and employ such a causal model to explain the world.

Current state of the art image captioning models (e.g. [19]), still behave like 5-year olds, enumerating objects and at best describing their visual appearance and relative positions, keeping short from actually interpreting the scene, and producing plausible explanations for the depicted content. In this sense there are recent advances aiming to shifting captioning models towards producing image interpretations, by incorporating prior world knowledge to the visual analysis of the image. What is even more interesting is a bi-directional interaction between human and machine. Imagine a blind person asking an intelligent agent what temperature the air-conditioning is set at, or whether a can of beans has expired. These are real-life questions asked in this community [20], which the AI researchers currently have no way to deal with. Being able to ask a question about the world using natural language, that an intelligent agent is able to understand and respond to in natural language, by combining visual and textual information in the scene, in a fully multilingual setting, is probably one of the best scenarios to drive progress and bring vision and language research together [21].

Both computer vision and natural language processing are data-driven disciplines. As such, it is well known that the resulting models suffer from biases derived from the data used to train them. For example, gender bias is a known problem of captioning systems. Many systems would be more probable to suggest that the person seen in the scene is a man when a skateboard or wind surf action is depicted [22]. Of course, the problem does not stem from the model or the learning algorithm, but instead from the data, and ultimately the society that generated them[7]. The fact is that annotators shown an image of a skateboard are more probable to describe it as a "man" than as a "woman" riding the skateboard. This reflects our own biases, and it would be unfair to blame the captioning model for the shortcomings of our own society.

Unfortunately, the media is usually fast to blame the learnt models, and AI as a whole, for these shortcomings. In many ways this is a "shooting the messenger" reaction, blaming the data-driven models for bearing the news that our society is indeed rid of biases of all sorts. In reality, researchers are actively looking into ways to compensate for data bias [23, 24].

The evaluation metrics used to measure the performance of vision and language models are also a source of worry. Usually, the performance of visual question answering is measured just by the accuracy of selecting the right response, leading models to learn typical correlations between questions and answers instead of really understanding the image. Similarly, captioning systems are measured by the degree by which resulting sentences match a set of human produced captions, resulting to models that can easily reproduce typical linguistic structures, but cannot describe anything slightly unusual.

Measuring performance is not trivial when it comes to such high-level tasks. Recent works on a system for producing captions of newspaper images, using the associated article as a source of contextual information [25] led to a system able to produce plausible captions, describing the people and places in the image. It is not possible to judge the quality of such results just by comparing them to the original caption of the professional journalist. But most importantly, it is impossible to automatically measure the correctness of such captions – many of the captions will appear plausible, while the model might attach the wrong name to a person or a location, leading essentially to problems in detecting "fake captions" if we only bother about using standard evaluation metrics. Human-in-the-loop methods, complementing automatic evaluation, are extremely important in this space.

## 3.2 Robots Learning from Humans: Past, Current and Future to Purposive Learning[8]

In the workplaces of the future, people will be able to perform complex tasks with the help of digital companions who can see, hear and touch and thus perceive their surroundings. Communication and interaction with information and physical objects will be facilitated by personalized support adapted to the context of the task, the environment or the performance, and tailored to individual workplaces. This specifically holds for human-robot interaction.

In order to train robots to support humans, there are various options, one of them is Purposive Learning. This method, as it has been pointed out, reasoning about the meanings of observed human activities, is a powerful way for robots to learn from humans, and learning from humans is a powerful means to ensure meaningful human-

---

[7] See also chapter 6.

[8] A contribution based on the GFAIH-speech and research work of Gordon Cheng.

centric outcomes [26]. Fundamental studies in human imitation learning have revealed that behavioral imitation is the central aspect of cognitive development in humans. Essentially, it has been noticed that a simple direct copy of observed movements has little meaning, this is due to the different embodiment of the imitator, which does not normally match the embodiment of the observed demonstrator. One of the earliest seminal works in robot imitation learning was by Kuniyoshi et al. [27], which showed that it is essential to extract specific features that match the demonstrator and the imitator at the start of the imitation process. Based on human sciences studies, three levels in imitation learning (see Fig. 1) were derived:

- *Appearance-based*: at this level, the imitator usually focusses on the reproduction of the motion of the demonstrator
- *Action-based*: at this level, the imitator will focus to select an action based on already known actions in an attempt to closely match the observed demonstration
- *Purposive-based*: focusing on the intention/goals of the entire observed task, that is to extract a deeper understanding of the observation

Appearance-based strategy is the most common approach in robotics. Dynamics Movements Primitives (DMP) is a well-accepted method used by the robotics community, as it can generate and encode trajectories in an adaptive form [28]. Whereas, the Action-based strategy requires to learn a correct mapping between the action and the capability of the robot.

To ensure the success of this strategy, a policy is learned as to what and when to perform the particular action by the robot. Earlier works in this area showed results that a robot can deal with very dynamic situations. For instance, learning to play a game of air-hockey [29].

Roboticists usually focus on the realization of a single task that is fairly fixed in an environment with little variances within the task. Thereby, limiting the scale of the task's complexity and making its difficult of generalization into other domains.

Purposive-based learning set out to tackle the core issues of generalizable learning to enable robots to learn from humans in a more flexible manner [26]. Thus, enable robots to reason about the meanings of human activities. This approach is considered as a powerful way for robots to learn from humans based on the answering fundamental questions on: How can we move beyond the learning of single tasks and ensure that generalizable human observations can be reused across multiple tasks and domains?

The new novel learning approach that utilizes artificial intelligence (AI) methods for inferring semantics with reasoning methods, such technique has been able to induce two fundamental changes: i) extracting semantic (meaningful) representations from the human behaviors from observations; and ii) the ability to transfer and/or reuse past knowledges in new domains. Furthermore, these AI methods have shown to produce a compact and them human-readable representations. Furthermore, it has been shown that the prior knowledge can even enhance low-level perception [26, 30]. Knowledge-based representation can provide us with a powerful mechanism in dealing with invariance, thus, yielding reusable and generalizable knowledge [31]. Such works have shown that even complex observations can be dealt with, such successfully learning from observing multiple humans' performance of the same task in different styles [26, 30].

**Three Cognitive Strategies of Limitation**

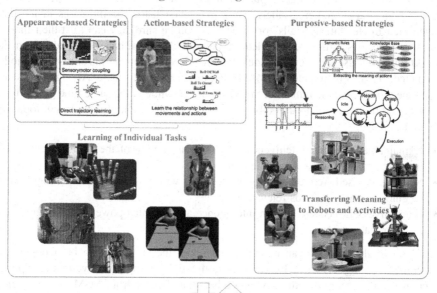

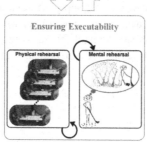

**Fig. 1.** Purposive Robots Learning from Humans: Overview of three strategies [26]

### 3.3    Empowering Multimodal Affective Behavior Analysis by Interactive Machine Learning[9]

Another facet that needs to be considered in the process of modeling human behavior is the description of human affective behavior. Well described corpora that are rich of human affective behavior are needed in a number of disciplines, such as Affective Health Monitoring or Behavioral Psychology. However, populating captured human behavioral data with adequate descriptions can be an extremely exhausting and time-consuming task. Therefore, attempts are being made to facilitate the acquisition of annotated data sets by involving end users directly in the Machine Learning (ML) process.

Users are enabled to interactively enhance their ML model by incrementally adding new data to the training set, while at the same time getting a better understanding of the capabilities of their model. In the approach presented in [32] and [33], this happens on multiple levels. First, users get a pure intuition of how well their model performs, by investigating false predicted labels. They may even learn specific cases in the data when their model "always fails" or when they can be sure they can trust their model. Secondly, besides intuition, so-called explainable AI algorithms provided within the workflow allow users to generate local posthoc explanations on instances their model predicted. This way interactive ML techniques and explainable AI algorithms are combined to involve the human in the ML process, while at the same time giving back control and transparency to users. In that sense a combination of three recent topics of ML takes place:

- Explainable Artificial Intelligence, as the transparency of the decision process is increased via visualization of the predictions
- Semi-Supervised Active Learning, since labels with low confidence are highlighted to guide the user towards relevant parts
- Interactive ML, because human intelligence and machine power can cooperate and improve each other.

The overall approach can be subsumed under the term eXplainable Cooperative Machine Learning (XCML). Researchers in this field strongly believe that disciplines such as health care, psychotherapy, and others may benefit from XCML technologies. Especially in high risk environments that apply artificial intelligence it is crucial to not only rely on high prediction accuracies, but also to fully understand the underlying processes that led to a classification result (see also the criterion "Transparency and Explicability" of the five core principles of ethical AI) For further information see references [32] and [33].

---

[9] A contribution based on the GFAIH-speech and research work of Elisabeth André.

### 3.4 Symbiotic Interaction to Socialware – Social and Semantic Interactions of Augmented Human and Ambient Intelligence[10]

Having the examples of the last three subsections in mind, it is easy to understand that the game is changing in many areas. Therefore, the research field has to be extended as recent technologies are showing us a future vision of realizing smart information environments and augmentation of human abilities. The aim has to focus on creating and developing core information technologies that realize advanced interaction designs for a symbiotic society consisting of humans, augmented humans, connected things, ambient intelligence (i.e., a smart intelligence environment), internet of wisdoms, robots, etc. Such advanced interaction in the symbiotic society can be called "Symbiotic Interaction."

Researchers in Japan Science and Technology Agency (JST) CREST program on Symbiotic Interaction area aim to create and develop the fundamental technologies that realize symbiotic interaction based on understanding and designing interactions in a symbiotic society. The goal of this research area is to establish core technologies of symbiotic interactions through approaches that evaluate behaviors of humans and societies, designing future societies, and constructing effective interactive systems. It covers state-of-the-art technologies in appropriate areas such as human-computer interaction, ubiquitous/wearable information processing, computer science, and robotics, in addition to collaboration with other disciplines such as cognitive science, social science, and brain science. For examples, there are projects on tender elderly care skill training technology to promote well-being, humanoid robotics to enlighten moral in public space, and speech synthesis and recognition technology for secure and spoof-free speech-based services and protection of privacy, etc. Computer vision technology of human behavior and interaction and wearable IoT devices support and utilize analytics of staring gaze and touch interactions during care practice (Co-Learning). So-called "Moral robots" will cooperate with human to create secure and comfortable public space and retail business (Co-Creation). Spoof-free and realistic speech synthesis technologies will lead the deep discussion of relationship and utilization of advanced AI technology and personae (Co-Adaption).

Following these aspects, research and development efforts will contribute to establishing a harmonized, human-centered and globally-optimized symbiotic society that benefits by rapidly advancing AI technologies and fundamentals.

The computer architecture today is well-known as the stack of hardware and software on it. With the symbiotic interaction research, the social interaction parts are put together and form a novel architecture of platform for symbiotic society.

Socialware contains traditional context processing, semantic processing with interaction data at signal processing and machine learning tools. Within the Socialware, knowledge base, inference and ontology technologies are incorporated to construct symbiotic interaction corpus and dictionary, which will be used as a basic common sense of robots and intelligent systems. They are most useful for robot and intelligent systems to co-work and assist flexibly with variety of humans. Cognitive human

---

[10] A contribution based on the GFAIH-speech and research work of Kenji Mase.

models in symbiotic society and its social design principles should be included in the Socialware, too. Socialware plays the role of foundation of important applications/ innovations in the symbiotic society of the digital twin.

### 3.5   Socially Aware AI - Maintaining the Human at the Center of AI Design[11]

Another model also concentrates on the social aspects of human interaction, and the need to consider them in the design of AI systems. This model starts at a different point, however. It focuses on a development methodology that takes into account from the beginning of the design process the importance of designing systems capable of co-adaptation –the dyadic processes whereby people and AIs adapt to one another in real time. It also relies on the perspective of conversation as co-created by two (or more) interlocutors. And intrinsic to the design methodology is attention to ethics – an attention to what systems we decide to design, and in what order, based on the grand societal challenges of the day.

The model of "Socially aware AI" stems from the fact that somewhere along the path of defining and shaping AI, as we have been doing since the 50s, the definition of AI itself has changed. Today most researchers have abandoned the goal of simulating human intelligence. Instead, they wish to build systems that can do what humans do, only better. Systems that can read X-Rays of human lungs, but with a higher accuracy rate than doctors. Systems that can understand human speech, better even than humans can. These systems emulate human intelligence and human abilities. Problems may arise due to the fact that no roadmap exists to describe which human abilities should be emulated first – and which should never be emulated. Therefore, the question has to be asked: What should AI systems be designed to do, and what should we prevent them from doing? One answer is to ensure that the design process be guided by the following human-centered principles:

- The principle of the "3 Cs": Coexistence, Cooperation, and Collaboration. The AI systems that will be most useful to us in the future are those that **collaborate** (rather than replacing), those that **cooperate** (rather than competing) and those that can effectively **co-exist** with humans
- The principle of urgent societal need: Grand societal challenges must be addressed first– such as inequity, illness and disability, poverty.[12]

This view leads to the socially aware AI Methodology depicted in Fig. 2, that can be used in the development process. This approach can be called **Socially-Aware AI** [34, 35] as it is socially-aware in two ways:

1. In addition to being able to effectively carry out a task, the system is aware of social norms and abilities, and is able to use them to more effectively work with people;
2. In addition to innovating technically, the designer of the system is aware of tough social problems, and is dedicated to addressing them.

---

[11] A contribution based on the GFAIH-speech and research work of Justine Cassell.

[12] See also chapter 8.

These principles seem straightforward - however, few AI researchers stop to think about what an AI system needs to know in order to cooperate or collaborate. Nor do many stop to look around and ask what grand societal challenges need to be addressed. These concepts of social awareness imply human abilities that have rarely been modeled in machines – the ability to get along, to build a bond, to inspire trust, to listen well. Systems of this sort need to know how to amplify human abilities, as well as to have strong abilities of their own. Rather than manipulating human behavior, SociallyAware AI inspires learning about oneself. Rather than trying to make the most humanlike chatbot, Socially-Aware AI targets just enough human-like behavior to bring out the best in its human partners.

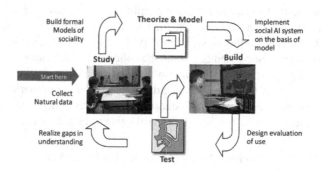

**Fig. 2.** Socially-Aware AI methodology

Results of existing Socially-Aware AI systems have been able to achieve ground-breaking results: They have effectively taught children with autism how to build social bonds with their peers [36]. They have inspired world leaders to reveal their likes and dislikes so that the system can better assist them [37]. And they have inspired social bonds strong enough to lead to stronger science learning in children in educationally impoverished neighborhoods [38]. A particularly poignant example is the Alex Virtual Peer project. A virtual peer is a cartoon life-size virtual child on a screen. Results of this work have shown that a virtual peer that speaks the same marginalized dialect as a child is capable of inspiring increased rapport – a close bond – with that child, and that rapport between child and virtual child predicts improvement in the use of classroom science talk [38]. Marginalized dialects include African American English, Verlan-influenced French and Newcastle UK English, among many others. They exist in all countries. They are often thought to be signs of poor education, when in fact they are simply separate linguistic varieties. Teachers do not necessarily speak these varieties, but putting AI-based virtual peers in the classroom that do speak like the children can therefore improve the classroom performance of children from marginalized communities. These are the kinds of societal grand challenges that social-aware AI can address.

## 4 Best Practices in Education

Whenever AI is linked to the school system, alarm bells go off for many people. Monitoring systems are prematurely imagined that collect data about pupils that go far beyond their meaningful use in class. The fear of pupils becoming "transparent" through surveillance is growing, combined with the fear that data about these students could be misused and deployed to evaluate other areas of their lives. However, the examples in the following Sects. 4.1, 4.2, 4.3 show that the use of AI in the educational sector does not need to mean that teachers are ousted and children are henceforth taught by self-sufficient AI systems that collect an inappropriate amount of data. In fact, systems that support teachers, and that take on tasks that may be difficult for teachers to deal with (such as speaking in the same dialect as the child), can also have a big effect. Systems such as these, however, can only be implemented if the design phase includes a careful observation and understanding of children's lives – a truly human-centered approach.

The goal of any sensor-based detection, the collection of data, should always follow the goal of using this data to determine what kind of content is effective for which learners and how. It is then the task of didactics to develop appropriate materials in order to provide individually tailored educational measures or to better challenge and promote individual learning needs and ultimately also to be able to measure the effects.

### 4.1 IntelliChalk – Teaching Mathematics with a Data Wall[13]

The changes mentioned in the introduction do not stop at the education system. Previous forms of teaching must face up to our dynamic times and, ideally, overcome traditional forms of learning and the use of media. Intellichalk, which means "intelligent chalk (board)", is an innovative way to design today's teaching. At the *Freie Universität Berlin* a large data wall composed of computer screens has been used teaching mathematics and natural sciences (Fig. 3). The idea is to apply the three C's mentioned in the introduction: the digital chalkboard **collaborates** with the lecturer, **cooperates** providing assistance, and **co-exists** with humans. It is not aimed at making the lecturer superfluous.

In comparison to traditional chalkboards, which are normally used in schools or universities, the contrast of the digital screens provides a much better visual experience. Students sitting in the last row can still see the diagrams and formulas clearly. The lecturer writes on a contact sensitive tablet which offers several functions: It is a drawing program which provides the lecturer the tools to draw and write with high quality as well as its a program which manages images for pasting, as well as scans of handwritten notes.

The developers of IntelliChalk keep on improving the software to include more features such as for example slide presentations via IntelliChalk or interactive lecturing using a contact sensitive screen mounted on a podium. Furthermore, handwriting recognition can be used to start secondary applications such as simulators, algebraic servers, or an image search over the Internet as well as videos can be pasted to the board.

---

[13] A contribution based on the GFAIH-speech and research work of Raúl Rojas.

**Fig. 3.** The podium for the lecturer includes a contact sensitive screen

Lectures are available over the Internet as a file for printing, or as a file for replaying the lecture. Handwritten notes of the lecturer can be digitized in a few seconds before the lecture starts and students themselves can annotate their own local copy of the class material using their own tablets. In this way, the student's annotations constitute an additional information layer.

The developers of IntelliChalk think, that this will be the future of teaching on site or via conference mode in universities and also in schools. The system can be imagined as an AI that co-creates the lecture, by providing, for example algebraic processing and simulations on demand. The system can become better over time, co-learning from previous lectures and the materials produced.

## 4.2    Lumilo – AI for Personalized Learning: Students, Teachers and AI Systems Augmenting Each Other's Abilities[14]

The example of Lumilo addresses a real-time, mixed-reality teacher support tool. It is an instance of human-AI complementarity in the domain of mathematics instruction. Lumilo augments teachers' in-the-moment decision-making regarding how best to help their students. It is a result of the dissertation research of Kenneth Holstein at Carnegie Mellon University, in the Human-Computer Interaction Institute.

Many applications of AI may be most effective when designed from the start to be synergistic with human intelligence. To achieve such synergy, designers must deeply understand how, in the given task domain, humans and AI can augment each other, based on their complementary strengths and weaknesses. Human-centered design practices have much to offer in this regard, since they center human needs and abilities in the design process. However, prototyping novel human-AI interactions is still a relatively new challenge, requiring innovation in design methods and processes.

---

[14] A contribution based on the GFAIH-speech and research work of Vincent Aleven and Kenneth Holstein.

Lumilo was designed with this knowledge in mind and was specially tailored to meet the challenges mentioned above. It is designed to help teachers dynamically prioritize which students may need teacher attention, as a class of students works with AI-based tutoring software, an increasingly common scenario in schools in the US and elsewhere. The mixed-reality tool projects, in the teacher's view of the classroom, an indicator of each student's progress or struggle. "Deep Dive" screens in Lumilo provide teachers with more detailed information about a student to provide more context as needed, to aid teachers in deciding whether and how to help a given student.

Lumilo was created over a period of two years, during which its developers worked extensively with middle school teachers. A variety of methods of human-centered design were employed to gain a deep understanding of their needs, strengths, and boundaries, and of how best to take advantage of the many existing learning analytics developed over two decades by the fields of AI in Education, Learning Analytics, and Educational Data Mining. Through many rounds of iterative prototyping, the tool was honed for classroom use, based on extensive teacher feedback. In the process, new methods for human-centered design were developed, namely, a new prototyping method for dynamic data-driven AI algorithmic experiences, called Replay Enactments, and a new method for the iterative, evidence-centered design of teacher-facing analytics tools, called Causal Alignment Analysis.

The effects of Lumilo were tested in a classroom study with 286 middle school students, across 18 classrooms and 8 teachers. All students used AI-based tutoring software for 2 class sessions in order to hone their skill in equation solving. Classes were randomly assigned to conditions which differed only in whether the teacher used Lumilo or not[15]. Teachers using Lumilo were guided by Lumilo's mixed-reality indicators and Deep Dive screen in their decisions of whom to help, and how. Without Lumilo, teachers had to rely on their own observations and judgment to decide which students to help. This condition represents business-as-usual in classes using intelligent tutoring software. Results show that teachers, when using Lumilo, devote measurably more time to students who have more to learn (as compared to other students) than they do without the tool. As a result, students learn more, especially those who had more to learn. Interestingly, in the Lumilo condition, pre-test scores were less predictive of post-test scores than in the other conditions. Thus, Lumilo helps teachers enact more equitable practices in classrooms, where students who have more to learn get more attention and have greater learning gains.

The work illustrates the creation of an effective new human-AI partnership through human-centered design. The AI augments what teachers do: The teachers we observed do not defer to the AI; rather, they interpret Lumilo's indicators and Deep Dive screens against what they glean from observing the classroom and what they know about their students. Demonstrations of successful human-AI partnership are rare, especially for complex tasks carried out in authentic, real-world settings. The work illustrates that careful use of human-centered design processes can be highly effective to this end, and

---

[15] In a third condition, teachers used an ablated version of Lumilo, to evaluate the added value of the analytics within Lumilo over and above other elements of Lumilo's design. For brevity, this comparison was omitted.

illustrates as well that new methods may be needed to design for human-AI synergy. Like the developers of IntelliChalk, Lumilo developers also see the future of new teaching in these applications and anticipate that many novel methods will sprout up in the nearby future. For further readings see [39, 40] and [41].

## 4.3 Wordometer, CoaLA and LeAE – Experiential Supplements: Sharing Human Experiences for Co-learning[16]

Experiential supplements are pieces of information extracted from human experience and employed to help humans to solve their problems. This concept of utilizing human experiences is based on the observation that humans continue to face problems that have already been solved by other humans. In the context of learning, a learner can help other learners by sharing his/her experience of overcoming the problem he/she has already faced. Computers can help co-learning among learners by providing the mechanism to share learners' experiences. AI technologies that sense and estimate learners' current knowledge levels, mental and cognitive states play important roles for experiential supplements. Another important role of AI is how to produce and apply experiential supplements. Generally speaking, learners react differently to the same information. In other words, we need to prepare prescriptions of experiential supplements: to whom and when an experiential supplement should be applied to improve learner's states.

The notion of experiential supplements is to build a computer system that assist humans to help others through sharing experiences. Co-learning among humans is implemented by the system. In this sense, the system realizes intelligence augmentation or "inclusiveness" of AI. In the context of learning and similar to the aspect of cognition augmentation mentioned in Sect. 2.1, one can call it "learning augmentation": an AI system helps a learner learn better.

Because the system works in a fully person-dependent way, we need to be careful about the "fairness" to learners. An experiential supplement can be different for learners having the same problem. A learner may complain that his/her problem cannot be solved due to a different experiential supplement given to him/her. Thus, accountability is also an important ethical aspect. Human experiences are personal in nature. Thus, privacy is also significant in this framework. In particular, the right of persons who provide experiences must be protected.

In the following three systems, Wordometer, CoaLA, and LeAE, experiential supplements for learning, which aim to improve learning by using other person's learning experiences, are presented:

**The Wordometer** is an application by which the total number of read words in a certain period (typically in a day [42]) is measured. Based on this approach in [43], we presented four nudging strategies for sustaining or improving user's engagement of reading documents: showing the number of read words, setting up the goal of reading amount, notification of typical locations and timing of reading, and sharing the number of words with a peer group. Setting up the goal and using the peer group are the

---

[16] A contribution based on the GFAIH-speech and research work of Koichi Kise.

nudging strategies worked well to improve the amount of reading. Machine learning is employed to build a prescription for each nudging strategy. By taking into account the personal traits of a learner, the system can select appropriate nudging strategies to help the learner. More information may be found in [43].

**CoaLA** is a system for confidence-aware learning assist. It is capable of estimating the user's confidence in his/her answer to a question. It uses an eye-tracker for the estimation because eye movement reflects the user's internal states such as confidence [43, 44]. Given eye movement data as input, it is possible to estimate learner's confidence by using machine learning. Based on the estimated confidence, cases of correct answers without confidence (correct answers by chance), as well as incorrect answers with confidence (misunderstanding) can be detected. By notifying them to the use, the quality of knowledge has been successfully improved.

**LeAE** stands for learning with an aerobic exercise. This enables us to memorize new words better with the help of an aerobic exercise, using a stepper. The experimental results have shown that the number of remembered words is larger after three days and one week, in the case that words were memorized with the aerobic exercise. The difference between with and without the aerobic exercise was statistically significant ($p < 0.01$). However, the aerobic exercise worsened the performance for some users. Thus, it is necessary for us to build a prescription to distinguish users with positive effects from those without them.

Currently, systems with a more advanced way of co-learning are already in the making. In the above examples, the system has learned prior to its application. However, due to the lack of training data, the learning itself is a difficult task and recent work therefore concentrates on working on the co-learning of the learner and AI. AI can learn from the behavior of the learner for better estimation of his/her internal states, as well as strategies of human learning. On the other hand, the learner can learn from the learned AI which can provide a fully personalized strategies of learning. A possible scenario is the adaptive generation of exercises by AI to maximize the learning effect as well as motivation of the learner.

# 5  Conclusion

The examples of the last chapters describe anything but horror scenarios that can be imagined in the context of AI and its applications. We discussed a variety of different topics such as intelligent vision and language models and robots learning from humans, socially aware AI or best practices of smart systems and applications in education. What all examples have in common is that we humans play an important role. We must take responsibility for these systems and it is important not to ignore the fears and dark sides that technology can bring and to remain sensible to the important questions that have to be asked. The successes of AI in recent years and the applications of Augmented human and Human-Machine co-evolution have led to much speculation about the capabilities of these technologies that must be clarified.

In general, positive impacts might be seen through the development of human-centered AI, aware of social norms and abilities, and the capacity to efficiently improve work with people. Risks might be dependency, isolation, dehumanization and manipulation especially for vulnerable people. In the case of systems that imitate human emotions, problems can arise especially in the interpretation of these emotions and in the classification of these machines in our society. The recommendations are to clarify the limits of imitation to avoid over attribution of capacities and to keep a clear distinction between a living being and a machine [45]. Another important point to note is that systems change when they continue to learn after deployment. Who is responsible if the machine malfunctions: the designer, the owner of the data, the owner of the system, its user? [46]. The machine itself cannot be responsible. Users should be aware of the learning capacity of the machine that can lead to new issues that affect the consent of both user and society. Because long-term behavior is difficult to control, machines should be controlled with benchmarks several times during the time of usage. Researchers should seek to contribute to societal debates and to the development of assessment benchmarks and protocols for broad dissemination of machine learning systems. For use in specialized professional sectors (medicine, law, transportation, energy, etc.), data collection and analysis require collaboration between computer scientists and experts in those fields.

In summary, one can therefore state, that regarding the discussed technologies, in view of the strategic stakes as well as the impact on the economy and society, the scientific aspect alone is not enough. It is also necessary to examine the ethical and societal issues raised by the development and deployment of AI independent from its application field, and to propose concrete frameworks to address them. The shown examples also illustrate that there is an awareness of the need for action and researchers are trying to find solutions to ethical problems. Events like the GFAIH also contribute to this by catalyzing interdisciplinary exchange and generating recommendations for action. These go beyond their application in science and must also be communicated to the people who use such technologies. It is important to demystify and disseminate AI science whether it is used in terms of a learning partner, a digital assistant in a factory or as a robot: Imagination of our contemporaries about robotics and more generally AI are mainly founded on science-fiction narratives and myths. Expressions used by experts such as "robots are autonomous", "they make decisions", "they learn by themselves" are not understood as metaphors by those outside the technical research community. To mitigate ideas originating from science fiction that mainly underline gloomy consequences, it is important to engage in public discussion and debate with all citizens.

Emerging technologies proceed through multiple stages of evolution: from early stage research, experimentation, prototypes, testing, validation, evaluation and societal adoption. The ethical considerations can be analyzed at each stage of development. Researchers must also ask themselves about the usefulness and the effects of the artificial and the natural of the resemblance to the living and take care to communicate this clearly to the public.

An Observatory on Society and Artificial Intelligence (OSAI) has been also created in Europe. It aims at offering a set of tools that help people better understand and study the impact of AI technologies across the European Union. Specifically, the Observatory supports the distribution and the discussion of knowledge about the Ethical, Legal, Social, Economic and Cultural issues of AI (ELSEC-AI) within Europe. We must amplify these initiatives all around the world and share the results.

Without safeguards against the deployment of products capable of manipulating our emotions and decisions, continuously present in our intimacy, we would be playing sorcerer's apprentice. The development of AI is a business, and businesses are notoriously not interested in fundamental ethical guarantees. The Global Partnership on AI, (GPAI) which is an international, multi-stakeholder initiative to guide the responsible development and use of AI, in a spirit of respect for human rights, inclusion, diversity, innovation and economic growth has been launched in June 2020.

# References

1. Ishimaru, S., et al.: Augmented learning on anticipating textbooks with eye tracking. In: Zlatkin-Troitschanskaia, O., Wittum, G., Dengel, A. (eds.) Positive Learning in the Age of Information (PLATO) - A Blessing or A Curse?, pp. 387–398. Springer, Wiesbaden, October 2017. https://doi.org/10.1007/978-3-658-19567-0_23

2. Dengel, A.: Digital co-creation and augmented learning. In: Proceedings KMO 2016, Hagen, 11th International Conference on Knowledge Management in Organizations, Hagen, Germany, July 2016. ACM. 978-1-4503-4064-9/16/07. https://dx.doi.org/10.1145/2925995.292605

3. The Schumpeter Blog 2015 Homepage. https://www.economist.com/news/business/21664190-modern-version-scientific-management-threatens-dehumanise-workplace-digital. Accessed 01 June 2020

4. Devillers, L.: Social and emotional robots: useful artificial intelligence in the absence of consciousness. In: Nordlinger, B., Villani, C., Rus, D. (eds.) Healthcare and Artificial Intelligence, pp. 261–267. Springer, Cham (2020). https://doi.org/10.1007/978-3-030-32161-1_32

5. Floridi, L., Cowls, J.: A unified framework of five principles for AI in society. Harvard Data Sci. Rev. 1(1) (2019). https://doi.org/10.1162/99608f92.8cd550d1

6. Blandfort, P., Karayil, T., Borth, D., Dengel, A.: Captioning in the wild: how people caption images on Flickr. In: ACM Workshop on Multimodal Understanding of Social, Affective and Subjective Attributes (2017)

7. Gomez, L., Mafla, A., Rusiñol, M., Karatzas, D.: Single shot scene text retrieval. In: The European Conference on Computer Vision (ECCV), pp. 728–744 (2018)

8. Gómez, L., Rusiñol, M., Karatzas, D.: Cutting Sayre's Knot: reading scene text without segmentation. application to utility meters. In: 2018 13th IAPR International Workshop on Document Analysis Systems (DAS), pp. 97–102. IEEE (2018)

9. Nayef, N., et al.: ICDAR2019 robust reading challenge on multi-lingual scene text detection and recognition—RRC-MLT-2019. In: Proceedings 15th International Congress on Document Analysis and Recognition, IEEE CPS, pp. 1582–1587 (2019)

10. Reddy, S., Mathew, M., Gomez, L., Rusiñol, M., Karatzas, D., Jawahar, C.V.: RoadText-1K: text detection recognition dataset for driving videos. In: IEEE International Conference on Robotics and Automation (ICRA) (2020)

11. Toyama, T., Dengel, A., Suzuki, W., Kise, K.: Wearable reading assist system: augmented reality document combining document retrieval and eye tracking. In: Proceedings ICDAR 2013, 12th International Conference on Document Analysis and Recognition, Washington D.C., USA, pp. 30–34, August 2013

12. Patel, Y., Gomez, L., Rusiñol, M., Karatzas, D.: Dynamic lexicon generation for natural scene images. In: Hua, G., Jégou, H. (eds.) ECCV 2016. LNCS, vol. 9913, pp. 395–410. Springer, Cham (2016). https://doi.org/10.1007/978-3-319-46604-0_29

13. Gomez, L., Patel, Y., Rusiñol, M., Jawahar, C.V., Karatzas, D.: Self-supervised learning of visual features through embedding images into text topic spaces. In: 2017 IEEE Conference on Computer Vision and Pattern Recognition (CVPR) (2017)

14. Gomez, R., Gomez, L., Gibert, J., Karatzas, D.: Self-supervised learning from web data for multimodal retrieval. In: Yang, M., Rosenhahn, B., Murino, V. (eds.) Multimodal Scene Understanding: Algorithms, Applications and Deep Learning, pp. 279–306. Elsevier (2019). ISBN 978-0-12-817358-9. https://doi.org/10.1016/B978-0-12-817358-9.00015-9

15. Mafla, A., Dey, S., Furkan Biten, A., Gomez, L., Karatzas, D.: Fine-grained image classification and retrieval by combining visual and locally pooled textual features. In: IEEE Winter Conference on Applications of Computer Vision (WACV) (2020)

16. Gomez, R., Gibert, J., Gomez, L., Karatzas, D.: Exploring hate speech detection in multimodal publications. In: IEEE Winter Conference on Applications of Computer Vision (WACV) (2020)

17. Lake, B.M., Ullman, T.D., Tenenbaum, J.B., Gershman, S.J.: Building machines that learn and think like people. Behav. Brain Sci. **40** (2017)

18. Terman, L.M.: The Measurement of Intelligence: An Explanation of and a Complete Guide for the Use of the Stanford Revision and Extension of the Binet-Simon Intelligence Scale. Houghton Mifflin, Boston (1916)

19. Karayil, T., Irfan, A., Raua, F., Hees, J., Dengel, A.: Conditional GANs for image captioning with sentiment. In: Tetko, I., Kůrková, V., Karpov, P., Theis, F. (eds.) Artificial Neural Networks and Machine Learning. Proceedings ICANN19, 28th International Conference on Artificial Neural Networks, Munich, Germany, September 2019. LNCS, vol. 11730, pp. 300–312. Springer, Cham (2019). https://doi.org/https://doi.org/10.1007/978-3-030-30490-4_25

20. Narasimhan, M., Schwing, A.G.: Straight to the facts: learning knowledge base retrieval for factual visual question answering. In: Ferrari, V., Hebert, M., Sminchisescu, C., Weiss, Y. (eds.) ECCV 2018. LNCS, vol. 11212, pp. 460–477. Springer, Cham (2018). https://doi.org/10.1007/978-3-030-01237-3_28

21. Narasimhan, M., Lazebnik, S., Schwing, A.: Out of the box: reasoning with graph convolution nets for factual visual question answering. In: Advances in Neural Information Processing Systems (NeurIPS), vol. 31, pp. 2654–2665 (2018)

22. Hendricks, L.A., Burns, K., Saenko, K., Darrell, T., Rohrbach, A.: Women also snowboard: Overcoming bias in captioning models. In: Ferrari, V., Hebert, M., Sminchisescu, C., Weiss, Y. (eds.) ECCV 2018. LNCS, vol. 11207, pp. 793–811. Springer, Cham (2018). https://doi.org/10.1007/978-3-030-01219-9_47

23. Rohrbach, A., Hendricks, L.A., Burns, K., Darrell, T., Saenko, K.: Object hallucination in image captioning. In: Empirical Methods in NaturalLanguage Processing (EMNLP) (2018)

24. Bhargava, S., Forsyth, D.: Exposing and correcting the gender bias in image captioning datasets and models. arXiv preprint arXiv:1912.00578 (2019)

25. Biten, A.F., Gomez, L., Rusinol, M., Karatzas, D.: Good news, everyone! Context driven entity-aware captioning for news images. In: Proceedings of the IEEE Conference on Computer Vision and Pattern Recognition, pp. 12466–12475 (2019)

26. Cheng, G., Ramirez-Amaro, G., Beetz, M., Kuniyoshi, Y.: Purposive learning: robot reasoning about the meanings of human activities. Sci. Robot. **4**, eaav1530 (2019)

27. Kuniyoshi, Y., Inaba, M., Inoue, H.: Learning by watching: extracting reusable task knowledge from visual observation of human performance. IEEE Trans. Robot. Autom. **10**, 799–822 (1994)

28. Ijspeert, A.J., Nakanishi, J., Hoffmann, H., Pastor, P., Schaal, S.: Dynamical movement primitives: learning attractor models for motor behaviors. Neural Comput. **25**, 328–373 (2013)

29. Bentivegna, D.C., Atkeson, C.G., Cheng, G.: Learning tasks from observation and practice. IEEE Robot. Auton. Syst. J. **47**, 163–169 (2004)
30. Ramirez-Amaro, K., Beetz, M., Cheng, G.: Transferring skills to humanoid robots by extracting semantic representations from observations of human activities. Artif. Intell. **247**, 95–118 (2017)
31. Tenorth, M., Beetz, M.: Representations for robot knowledge in the KnowRob framework. Artif. Intell. **247**, 151–169 (2017)
32. Heimerl, A., Baur, T., Lingenfelser, F., Wagner, J., André, E.: NOVA - a tool for eXplainable cooperative machine learning. In: ACII 2019, pp. 109–115 (2019)
33. Baur, T., Clausen, S., Heimerl, A., Lingenfelser, F., Lutz, W., André, E.: NOVA: a tool for explanatory multimodal behavior analysis and its application to psychotherapy. In: Ro, Y. M., Cheng, W.-H., Kim, J., Chu, W.-T., Cui, P., Choi, J.-W., Hu, M.-C., De Neve, W. (eds.) MMM 2020. LNCS, vol. 11962, pp. 577–588. Springer, Cham (2020). https://doi.org/10. 1007/978-3-030-37734-2_47
34. Zhao, R., Sinha, T., Black, A., Cassell, J.: Automatic recognition of conversational strategies in the service of a socially-aware dialog system. In: Proceedings of the 17th Annual SIGdial Meeting on Discourse and Dialogue, Los Angeles, CA, 13–15 September 2016 (2016)
35. Cassell: The Ties that Bind: Social Interaction in Conversational Agents. Reseaux Issue number 220-221, pp. 21-45 (2020)
36. Tartaro, A., Cassell, J., Ratz, C., Lira, J., Nanclares-Nogues, V.: Accessing peer social interaction: using authorable virtual peer technology as a component of a group social skills intervention program. ACM Trans. Accessible Comput. (TACCESS) **6**(1), 1–29 (2015). Article 2
37. Pecune, F., Chen, J., Matsuyama, Y., Cassell, J.: Field trial analysis of Socially Aware Robot Assistant. In: Proceedings of the 17th International Conference on Autonomous Agents and MultiAgent Systems (AAMAS) (2018)
38. Finkelstein, S., Yarzebinski, E., Vaughn, C., Ogan, A., Cassell, J.: The effects of culturally-congruent educational technologies on student achievement. In: Proceedings of Artificial Intelligence in Education (AIED), Memphis, TN, 09–13 July 2013 (2013)
39. Holstein, K., McLaren, B.M., Aleven, V.: Co-designing a real-time classroom orchestration tool to support teacher–AI complementarity. J. Learn. Anal. **6**(2), 27–52 (2019). https://doi. org/10.18608/jla.2019.62.3
40. Holstein, K., McLaren, B.M., Aleven, V.: Designing for complementarity: teacher and student needs for orchestration support in ai-enhanced classrooms. In: Isotani, S., Millán, E., Ogan, A., Hastings, P., McLaren, B., Luckin, R. (eds.) AIED 2019. LNCS (LNAI), vol. 11625, pp. 157–171. Springer, Cham (2019). https://doi.org/10.1007/978-3-030-23204-7_14
41. Holstein, K., McLaren, B.M., Aleven, V.: Student learning benefits of a mixed-reality teacher awareness tool in AI-enhanced classrooms. In: Penstein Rosé, C., Martínez-Maldonado, R., Hoppe, H.U., Luckin, R., Mavrikis, M., Porayska-Pomsta, K., McLaren, B., du Boulay, B. (eds.) AIED 2018. LNCS (LNAI), vol. 10947, pp. 154–168. Springer, Cham (2018). https://doi.org/10.1007/978-3-319-93843-1_12
42. Ishimaru, S., Kunze, K., Kise, K., Dengel, A.: The wordometer 2.0: estimating the number of words you read in real life using commercial EOG glasses. In: Proceedings UbiComp '16, 2016 ACM International Joint Conference on Pervasive and Ubiquitous Computing, Heidelberg, Germany, pp. 293–296. September 2016 https://dx.doi.org/10.1145/2968219. 2971398
43. Tonomoto, S., Iwata, M., Kise, K.: Preliminary experiments toward personalized nudging strategies extensive reading of English. In: Proceedings of CHI2020 Workshop on Detection and Design for Cognitive Biases in People and Computing Systems, 8 p., April 2020

44. Ishimaru, T.M., Kise, K., Dengel, A.: Gaze-based self-confidence estimation on multiple-choice questions and its Feedback. Submitted to Asian CHI Symposium 2020, Honolulu, Hawaii, USA, April 2020. https://doi.org/https://doi.org/10.1145/3391203.3391227
45. Yamada, K., Augereau, O., Kise, K.: Estimation of confidence based on eye gaze: an application to multiple-choice questions. In: Proceedings of the 2017 ACM International Joint Conference on Pervasive and Ubiquitous Computing and Proceedings of the 2017 ACM International Symposium on Wearable Computers (UbiComp 2017), pp. 217–220, 4 p. ACM, October 2017.
46. Grinbaum, A., Chatila, R., Devillers, L., Ganascia, J.G., Tessier, C., Dauchet, M.: Ethics in robotics research: CERNA mission and context. IEEE Robot. Autom. Mag. **24**(3), 139–145 (2017)
47. Devillers, L., et al.: Research ethics in Machine Learning, CERNA (2017). https://www.al-listene.fr/files/2019/05/54730_cerna_2017_machine_learning.pdf

# Democratizing AI for Humanity:
# A Common Goal

Amir Banifatemi[3], Nicolas Miailhe[1,2,3(✉)], R. Buse Çetin[1,2,3],
Alexandre Cadain[3], Yolanda Lannquist[1,2,3], and Cyrus Hodes[1,2,3]

[1] The Future Society, Boston, USA
nicolas.miailhe@thefuturesociety.org
[2] The Future Society, Paris, France
[3] AI Commons, Paris, France
http://thefuturesociety.org
http://ai-commons.org

**Abstract.** The AI Commons was born in 2017 from the collective efforts of a group of individuals and organizations towards sharing AI resources in order to harness it for social and economic improvement. Foundational workshops, reflections, and gatherings resulted in the identification and formulation of an open knowledge and collaborative framework. This idea has led to the formation of an international nonprofit organization – the AI Commons.

The organization has gathered experts in academia, industry, startups, international organizations, nonprofits and beyond to support the creation of a knowledge hub in problem solving with AI that can be accessible by anyone. The hub is based on the concept of a collaboration framework and access to AI resources. It is intended to help accelerate identifying problems that can benefit from AI capabilities on a global level. It also aims to be a catalyst for supporting diversity and inclusivity in AI applications and to inform governance, policy making, and investments around the deployment of beneficial AI solutions.

The AI Commons held a workshop on Oct 28th, 2019, in Paris during the Global Forum on AI for Humanity (GFAIH). The workshop followed previous sessions held at the Global Governance of AI Forum in Dubai (World Government Summit; February 2019), in Montreal (March 2019), and at the AI for Good Global Summit in Geneva (ITU, XPRIZE and UN agencies; May 2019).

**Keyword:** AI Commons

## 1 Background

We are entering a new phase of the digital economy that is increasingly characterized by AI-driven automation and decision-making. This stage of digital transformation is well underway, and it is already impacting business models, global value chains and social practices. In the last few years, AI has received strong interest from a range of players and has become a center of attention at all levels of industry and governments. As a general-purpose technology, the widespread potential of AI is gradually being

B. Braunschweig and M. Ghallab (Eds.): Reflections on Artificial Intelligence for Humanity, LNAI 12600, pp. 228–236, 2021.
https://doi.org/10.1007/978-3-030-69128-8_14

understood. Currently, we are at an expansion phase where the scope of AI technologies is exploratory, adoption in markets is at an early-stage, and much of its capability is yet to be tapped.

AI is nested in a digital ecosystem where data, algorithms, software, hardware and talent can converge. AI resources converge around online platforms whose business models have dominated the digital and data economy for over a decade. Through large returns to scale and network effects, platforms are capable of aggregating around them large and complete digital ecosystems. Hyper-returns to scale give platforms a definitive advantage in accessing and controlling data, which is essential for training machine learning models (Fig. 1).

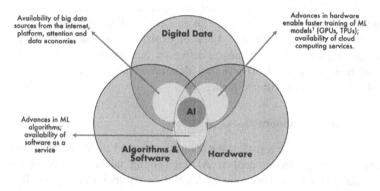

**Fig. 1.** The convergence of software, data and hardware lead the AI revolution. Source: The Future Society

As the AI economy emerges, platforms' value proposition is increasingly built around hosting software suites, and attracting talent and expertise to build, deploy and improve machine learning algorithms. For instance, Google TensorFlow, an open platform for machine learning development, relies on a large developer ecosystem which offers resources for learning (e.g. open courses), technical support, and community building. Finally, platforms have the critical mass to continuously invest in the development and mobilization of scalable computing power, essential to process data and enable learning algorithms. This convergence empowers platforms to anchor AI into their businesses to improve their services and reinforces oligopolistic market dynamics and a 'winner-takes-all' strategic landscape. This leads to a geographically and demographically skewed AI landscape; widening the 'AI Divide' between those who design, develop and deploy AI, and those who do not.

As AI research, development, deployment, and governance continue to improve, global challenges for an inclusive, sustainable future such as inequality, hunger, access to water and energy, and climate change intensify. With one decade remaining to achieve the UN Sustainable Development Goals (SDGs), the global community needs to accelerate the progress towards a sustainable future for all. As a general-purpose technology, AI holds great potential to address pressing global challenges including SDGs. For instance, to holistically combat climate change (SDG13: Climate Action),

mitigation (reducing emissions) and adaptation (preparing for unavoidable consequences) are important dimensions of the solution. Mitigation of greenhouse gas
emissions requires changes to electricity systems, transportation, buildings, industry,
and land use; while adaptation requires climate modeling, risk prediction, and planning
for resilience and disaster management. AI, and specifically machine learning, can
serve as a powerful tool for both mitigation and adaptation efforts for tackling climate
change.[1]

Amid the large potential positive impacts, AI technologies come with new societal,
economic and political risks and can exacerbate already existing challenges. For
instance, given the data-intensive nature of machine learning centric AI systems, risks
of surveillance, cybersecurity, and loss of privacy increase. Ratios of job losses versus
creation raises alarm as AI expands the scope of tasks that can be automated. Furthermore, AI raises a whole new range of challenges affecting human agency, safety,
security, inequality and inclusion[2]. Lack of explainability and accountability of AI
systems, more particularly deep neural networks, hinders our capacity to understand,
trust, and hold to account AI-powered decision-making in critical areas such as
healthcare, banking and criminal justice.

## 1.1    The Need to Democratize AI

For AI technologies to be a part of the solution, we need to democratize access to AI
resources (data, algorithms, applied AI engineering talent, computing power and
storage, and domain specific knowledge) and foster inclusion in AI. It is largely
observed that an intentional effort must be made to ensure that AI resources are more
accessible, and their benefits are equitably distributed.[3] Today, many international
organizations and countries have published both general AI strategies and principles
showing their support for a fair and inclusive AI. For instance, the OECD AI Principles
adopted by more than 50 countries emphasize the need for "stakeholders to proactively
engage in pursuit of beneficial outcomes for people and the planet, such as augmenting
human capabilities and enhancing creativity, advancing inclusion of underrepresented
populations, reducing economic, social, gender and other inequalities, and protecting
natural environments, thus invigorating inclusive growth, sustainable development and
well-being".[4]

Broader access to, and diversity of actors engaging with AI technologies can help
mitigate risks posed by AI (e.g. concentration and lack of fairness). There is a

---

[1] For discussion of use cases and risks see Miailhe, N. et al. 2020. "AI for Sustainable Development
Goals," Delphi - Interdisciplinary Review of Emerging Technologies, Volume 2, Issue 4 (2020).

[2] For additional information on the risks AI poses to societies, including risks particular to the global
South; see The Future Society and The World Bank, 2020. Harnessing Artificial Intelligence for
Development: A new policy and regulatory framework. (forthcoming).

[3] XPRIZE AI competition survey in 2016, and reports from AI For Good Global Summit, 2017,
2018.

[4] "The OECD Artificial Intelligence (AI) Principles - OECD.AI". 2019. https://oecd.ai/ai-principles.

correlation between lack of diversity of the AI field and the risks of acute inequality and discrimination due to algorithmic bias.[5] Interests, needs and socialization of those who design AI systems will necessarily be reflected in the AI they create. Expanding access in local communities including in the global South also helps to ensure AI applications are trained on local data and fit for local contexts. Furthermore, the deep knowledge gap separating most people affected by AI systems and their designers creates an information asymmetry that complicates and often threatens progress toward a more fair, beneficial and inclusive future. Understanding, accessing, and developing solutions with AI can help establish a sense of agency in the face of rapid advancements in technology and help address the knowledge gap in the development and deployment of AI technologies.

Enabling a more diverse range of actors to engage with AI can spark innovation and broaden the positive applications of AI technologies including AI for SDGs. Currently, AI research and applications are increasingly shaped by private interest and funding. There is a need for incentives and capabilities to develop AI applications that benefit society when these applications are not particularly economically attractive for private investors. Therefore, it is crucial to lay the foundations of frameworks and protocols that incentivize the emergence of AI applications which are less economically viable, at least in the short term.

## 1.2  Problem Space

The decentralization of problem solving can have a meaningful impact in how the AI promise can be achieved. The long term economic and societal value of solving many local yet urgent applications may not yet be visible to a large ecosystem of players driving the advancement in AI. It is, however, critical for this ecosystem to support the creation and distribution of AI applications by those who are in close proximity to urgent problems. Yet, there are persisting challenges for local problem solving: many problems are localized or not noticeable, and therefore with limited visibility to the world of entrepreneurs or stakeholders that would otherwise be championing their resolution. This is further compounded when problem size or scope have difficulties justifying large investments beyond grants or donations. These local problems, therefore, are left to the willingness of fragmented and non-sustainable support; leaving them outside of the purview of the best problem solvers.

Additionally, actionable knowledge on problem solving with AI is not accessible to non-experts and a broader public. The knowledge of solved problems with AI is mostly published in academic journals and conference proceedings as well as publications related to commercially available products and services. As of 2020, there is no commonly available structured source of usable information for non-experts to learn about and evaluate the use of AI for various problems. There is also a gap in formulating needs from a non-commercial perspective. As such, enabling local problem

---

[5] Crawford, Kate et al. AI Now 2019 Report. New York: AI Now Institute, 2019, https://ainowinstitute.org/AI_Now_2019_Report.html.

solving with AI requires democratizing access to digital ecosystems where broader AI resources including data, compute, and AI expertise cluster.

## 2    The AI Commons

Progress towards a more inclusive and prosperous society in which AI is expected to play a prominent role requires dialogue and collaboration that bring together a variety of stakeholders in a concerted effort. Such effort should seek to include individuals who may be the most affected by AI technologies and yet the least empowered to engage in AI development and applications. As such, the AI Commons has emerged from the need to enable more people to access and use AI resources with the ultimate objective of empowering communities beyond large industrial players or governments to harness the potential of AI. To truly democratize, decentralize and distribute its benefits; AI systems deployed across a range of communities should be designed with people whose perspectives reflect that diversity, and to build AI solutions that address actual needs. The AI Commons aims to support this by creating a collaborative ecosystem where AI resources (data, compute, AI talent and domain knowledge) are shared and used for AI-powered local problem solving.

### 2.1    History of the AI Commons

The AI Commons was founded by Yoshua Bengio and Amir Banifatemi in 2017 as a result of collaborations on the AI XPRIZE competition[6] (2016) and workshops organized under the inaugural AI for Good Global Summit[7] (2017). Further discussions with Konstantinos Karachalios underlined the opportunities and challenges in addressing global problems including UN SDGs with the help of AI and machine learning. AI Commons that was created as a non-profit association in 2017 in the United States and in 2018 in France to collectively respond to these challenges.

The need for academic and scientific support, governance for ethical and safe deployment, access to data and technical infrastructure emerged as common needs for AI-driven solutions to be sustainable and beneficial in addressing global problems thanks to the contributions of Stuart Russell and Francesca Rossi.

Additionally, in February of 2019 with help from the Future Society, a series of workshops organized during the Global Governance of AI Forum at the world government summit helped gather more validation on the proposed AI Commons collaboration framework, and brought more attention to the needed governance on promoting AI for good implementations. Further workshops were held in 2019 at

---

[6] https://ai.xprize.org/.

[7] Organized by XPRIZE and ITU: https://www.itu.int/en/ITU-T/AI/Pages/201706-default.aspx.

Mila[8], at AI for Good Summit, and during UNGA week in New York to further develop the focus of the organization.

Today, the AI Commons operates with a collective of volunteers and works towards publishing a public repository of beneficial AI applications in Spring of 2021. The repository aims to support problem-solving with AI by creating benchmarks for success and models of collaboration. In addition to above collaborations, the association also works with a diverse set of stakeholders to propose and facilitate initiatives that advance AI for the public good such as, IEEE, ITU, Partnership on AI, IBM Research, The Pontifical Academy at the Vatican, HEC, and University of California.

## 2.2    The AI Commons Model

The AI Commons proposes also a framework to incentivize broader identification of real-life problems that can be collaboratively solved with the help of the AI community. The framework will support the creation of a compendium and usable repository of actionable reference solutions that can be accessible by both experts and non-experts (Fig. 2).

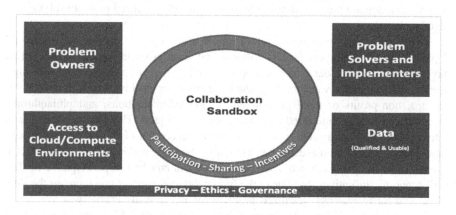

**Fig. 2.** The AI Commons Framework. Source: The AI Commons

The framework is based on curated communication and collaboration between two main groups: "problem owners", and the communities of AI practitioners, solvers and implementers. "Problem owners" encompass the group of individuals and organizations that have local and deep knowledge of a problem and its context, and either are championing or directly concerned with finding adapted solutions. Connecting problem owners and the communities of AI practitioners to solve acute and relevant problems collectively is the first and important part of the framework. Sharing mutual knowledge in a trusted and safe way is essential for creating communities that work together

---

[8] Quebec AI Insitute: https://mila.quebec/.

towards sustainable solutions. This collaboration would then rely on access to needed support such as cloud/compute platforms, qualified and usable data, and funding.

For instance, the AI Commons currently works with community hubs in three countries (Nigeria, Ghana, and Tanzania) to identify local problems and match these with AI researchers to create solution approaches and document them. The goal is to coordinate efforts locally and with other countries' solution developers in an open collaboration environment, so that future problem stakeholders and problem solvers can work jointly towards solving real problems and challenges. The work would be captured in an open access repository of reference solutions to be published in early 2021.

This simple collaboration model defined above as a "Collaboration Sandbox" allows AI solutions to be tested and iterated upon towards higher adoption, performance and robustness. It should also help reconcile performance with other critical indicators including privacy, safety, fairness, control, ethical value share, governance, risk management, and IP ownership. The framework will help activate the whole ecosystem working on the advancement of AI, as well as organizations and industry groups dedicated to capacity building and impact investing. It also intends to enable new participative models with economic incentives. Similarly, the framework can support and increase the flow of funding for increasingly localized problem solving in a sustainable way.

There are many groups interested in contributing to commonly needed AI deployments. For instance, NGOs, national and local governments/authorities might have problems and or data; researchers who have expertise in the science and engineering of data might want to share their expertise for positive applications for AI; startups, non-profits or local governments might offer solutions, and philanthropic organizations may be interested in funding specific projects. The framework will help activate the whole ecosystem working on the advancement of AI, as well as organizations and industry groups dedicated to capacity building and impact investing. It also intends to enable the wider ecosystem to identify and enable new participative models with economic incentives. Similarly, the framework can support and increase the flow of funding for increasingly localized problem solving in a sustainable way.

This collaborative ecosystem approach based on sharing AI resources intends to work towards making the knowledge and approaches to problem solving with AI benefit anyone and especially those who need it the most. This work needs to be conducted with partners that can support communities in being self-reliant in identifying solutions and supporting them with making their solutions robust and sustainable. As such, the AI Commons can also act as a platform to ensure cooperation between different AI for SDGs initiatives, following the 'SDG 17: strengthening the means of implementation and revitalizing the global partnership for sustainable development' (Fig. 3).

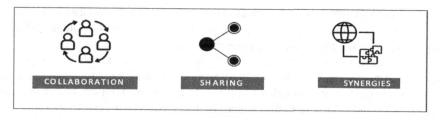

**Fig. 3.** The AI Commons' working model. Source: The AI Commons

The AI Commons' work is based on collaboration, sharing and building synergies among different initiatives with the same goal of democratizing AI resources to empower local problem solving with AI. Collaboration, sharing and building synergies are cross-cutting elements of the AI Commons initiatives.

A common becomes a reality when shared resources are made available in a sustainable way, with rules of access defined, along with governance to manage those rules. The availability of trusted data repositories (e.g. data trusts, data commons, data collaboratives) and low cost or subsidized access to cloud and compute collaborative environments as well as AI engineering talent are key enablers to help level the playing field for global problem solving. One of the biggest bottlenecks to harness AI is data availability and quality. Most AI capabilities such as neural networks require access to high-quality, massive, and reliable open data. Such big data can facilitate stakeholders to rapidly identify problem areas and customize solutions. However, at present a lack of access to large, quality data sets are a top barrier to AI innovation.

The basis of data democratization is ensuring data is available to everyone, which requires significant commitment from all stakeholders to share information and move against a competitive data-market environment. In this sense, the AI Commons furthers the idea of data commons[9], which seeks to aggregate government, private sector, and individual users' data into accessible and trusted data marketplaces. As such, a data commons is a curated data repository, organized by topic, community or interest, that is usable for AI models and is accessible to anyone[10].

Despite the huge impact potential and increased appetite to collaborate, data collaborative efforts are still constrained. The AI Common's Global Data Access Framework aims to tackle lack of access to data and help reconcile frameworks and protocols for data sharing and governance in order to help enable such AI systems to flourish. This initiative aspires to set in motion a global movement to significantly scale-up responsible access to data, empowering an unprecedented number of public, private and social sector actors to use data for public good. The promotion of data commons and data collaboratives being an essential part of AI development and usage,

---

[9] At the May 2018 AI for Good conference organized by XPRIZE, ITU and UN agencies, a 'Data Commons' concept was proposed as a key enabler for supporting projects that use AI to predict, monitor, measure and make progress towards the UN Sustainable Development Goals (SDGs). Supported by multi-stakeholder actors, the proposal was spearheaded by XPRIZE, along with Ocean Protocol, and reported by The Berkman Klein Center at Harvard University, among others.

[10] See also chapter 3 of this book.

the ITU and XPRIZE proposed to create working groups on AI and data commons to encourage data sharing, and call for participation by cloud and compute providers to help make compute capabilities available more widely.

Having access to tools and expertise as well as computing and data resources in an open environment creates a democratized opportunity allowing participation. The AI Commons achieves this through its collaborative sandbox bringing knowledge and resources together. This is further supported by i) creating a survey/repository and benchmark of beneficial solutions and checklists), ii) a framework to recommend availability and accessibility of data commons (Data Commons Program), and iii) partnership to provide cloud and compute resources to enable joint collaboration between problem owners and solvers.

The AI Commons is by design a collective effort of individuals and organizations to help scale AI for impact and for all. Its focus is to collaborate and leverage existing research, standards, frameworks, and other efforts made by various institutions globally, to help its mission. By working together and collaborating with other organizations on aspects of AI solutions' feasibility and deployment (including ethics, privacy, safety, diversity, transparency, protection of IP rights), the knowledge hub can be made available as a centrally accessible reference framework usable for the community on aspects of standardization, governance and policy making.

To help scale AI solutions, a template framework for precise solution scoping and their readiness for scaling will help facilitate funding and support for projects that have scaling potential.

AI Commons also collaborates with ITU and IEEE to evaluate usage of existing standards for responsible solution building. i.e. the upcoming P7000 standard. It also working with ISO/IEC SC42 to identify all current standards that can be useful in scaling AI solutions and helping with more data sharing, ethical and safe solution design, transparent and traceable outcomes of algorithms, and supporting efforts for better governance and support scaling the knowledge hub for impact.

Finally, the AI Commons sides with the mission of Global Partnership on AI (GPAI) grounded on collaboration and realizing the full potential of AI for the benefit of all. Launched with the participation of Canada, France, Australia, Germany, India, Italy, Japan, Mexico, New Zealand, the Republic of Korea, Singapore, Slovenia, the United States of America, and the European Union (EU); the initiative aims to "bridge the gap between theory and practice on AI by supporting cutting-edge research and applied activities on AI-related priorities." The AI Commons collaborative problem-solving framework and organically growing repository of actionable AI knowledge are valuable vessels for implementation of AI solutions in a way that respects human rights, inclusion, diversity, innovation and economic growth.[11]

---

[11] "Launch of The Global Partnership on Artificial Intelligence By 15 Founding Members (15 Jun. 20)". 2020. France Diplomacy - Ministry for Europe And Foreign Affairs. https://www.diplomatie. gouv.fr/en/french-foreign-policy/digital-diplomacy/news/article/launch-of-the-global-partnership-on-artificial-intelligence-by-15-founding.

# A Framework for Global Cooperation on Artificial Intelligence and Its Governance

Pekka Ala-Pietilä[1] and Nathalie A. Smuha[2(✉)]

[1] Chair of the EC High-Level Expert Group on AI & AI Finland, Helsinki, Finland
[2] Faculty of Law (FWO Fellow), KU Leuven, Leuven, Belgium
nathalie.smuha@kuleuven.be

**Abstract.** In this chapter we put forward a framework for global cooperation on Artificial Intelligence (AI) and its governance, with the aim to ensure that humanity can enjoy its benefits while preventing and minimizing its risks. The chapter is structured along three sections, focusing respectively on the *why, what* and *how* of global cooperation. First, we set out *why* AI requires governance and why its governance necessitates global cooperation. Particular focus is given to the need for a level playing field that secures citizen protection across the globe, enables socially beneficial innovation, and stimulates healthy competition to disseminate AI's benefits. Second, we list *what* the substantive areas are on which global cooperation on AI should be prioritized, and argue for a holistic approach along two dimensions. The first dimension is horizontal, and aims to identify minimum requirements that cover the entire socio-technical environment of AI in a transversal manner. In addition to AI-systems, we urge to consider the socio-technical environments of data and digital infrastructure, which are inextricably interwoven therewith. The second dimension is vertical, and aims at cooperation around domain-specific areas that require a more tailored approach to maximize AI's benefits for humanity, to prevent and minimize its risks and to address ad-hoc issues. Third, we assess *how* global cooperation should be organized. We stress the need to balance speed, holism and contextualism, and provide a number of guiding principles that can inform the process of global cooperation initiatives on AI and its governance.

**Keywords:** Artificial Intelligence · Global cooperation · Competition · Regulation · Governance · Data · Digital infrastructure

## 1 Introduction

Artificial Intelligence (AI), an umbrella term for a range of 'intelligent' technological applications, is not a new phenomenon [45]. Yet the combination of an increased availability of high computing power and large amounts of data, as well as advances in AI's research domain, significantly boosted the technology's possibilities [15, 34]. As a result, it is being used in an ever-wider range of applications and in ever-more domains – both in the public and private sphere. Given that these opportunities are accompanied by significant challenges and risks, attention to AI's governance peaked throughout the world. Today, it is widely agreed that – if we are to ensure that humanity can enjoy

© Springer Nature Switzerland AG 2021
B. Braunschweig and M. Ghallab (Eds.): Reflections on Artificial Intelligence
for Humanity, LNAI 12600, pp. 237–265, 2021.
https://doi.org/10.1007/978-3-030-69128-8_15

AI's benefits while preventing and minimizing its risks – global cooperation is a necessity [18]. Yet the motives behind the need for cooperation, the concrete areas of cooperation and the manner in which cooperation should take place often still remain debated. With the aim of diving into this debate, this chapter puts forward a framework for global cooperation on AI and its governance.

A large number of actors are already engaged in global cooperation in one way or another. Accordingly, global cooperation on AI does not take place in a vacuum. In addition, new cooperation initiatives around AI are regularly emerging – the Global Partnership on AI being an example [48]. Recognizing this multitude of efforts, we take a step back to consider the bigger picture that these initiatives are part of by shedding light on the overarching orientation they may consider, each from their own angle. Our framework is guided by three fundamental questions: *Why* is there a need for global cooperation on AI and its governance? (Sect. 2); *What* are the substantive areas on which global cooperation should take place? (Sect. 3); and *How* should the process of such cooperation be organized? (Sect. 4). Together, these elements provide the contours of a comprehensive framework that can guide cooperation across the globe.

The need for global cooperation on AI can be argued from various angles. Bearing in mind the dual aim of maximizing AI's benefits for humanity while preventing and minimizing its risks, in Sect. 2 we set out the importance of steering the relevant actors from a finite to an infinite mindset. The current 'race to AI' risks spurring short-term and protectionist approaches that result in a zero-sum game whereby, in the long run, everyone's gains are severely compromised. Considering the different motives that drive private and public actors towards competition, cooperation and coopetition, we argue for a level playing field around commonly agreed values for the development and deployment of AI. Such level playing field can not only provide a cross-border layer of protection against AI's risks, but also opens up the conditions for beneficial competition to foster innovation and materialize AI's benefits for all.

In Sect. 3 we list the areas of cooperation that should be prioritized to achieve this goal, bearing in mind the resource-intensiveness of cooperation initiatives. We argue for a holistic approach with a dual dimension. The first dimension is *horizontal*, and focuses on laying down minimum requirements to enable a trustworthy socio-technical environment around AI in a transversal manner. Cautioning against a myopic view, we believe this comprises not only the environment around AI-systems, but also the interwoven socio-technical environments of data and digital infrastructure. The second dimension is *vertical*. In parallel to establishing trustworthy environments, cooperation should also focus on domain-specific areas that require a tailored approach to maximizing AI's benefits, preventing and minimizing its risks, and addressing AI-related issues that arise ad hoc.

Having established *why* and in *which* areas global cooperation on AI should take place, Sect. 4 addresses *how* such cooperation should be organized. Preliminary, we raise the importance of striking the right balance between the need for speed given AI's fast-paced roll-out and impact, the need for a holistic approach and the need to consider the context-specificity of AI's concerns. Against that background, we urge cooperation partners to clarify the rules of engagement in advance and in an open manner. Moreover, we propose favoring existing cooperation mechanisms rather than the creation of new ones – all the while creating a network of networks across initiatives to allow for collective know-how to be built up and disseminated. While the need for speed imposes openness to differentiated cooperation, it remains essential for cooperation to be organized in an inclusive way, with a transparent way of working and mindful of power imbalances. Finally, we emphasize the need to establish accurate information streams to inform discussions, to set up feedback loops that improve cooperation outcomes and to secure AI-education for future generations who will need to continue today's cooperation efforts.

There is no silver bullet to ensure the success of global cooperation initiatives on AI. Nevertheless, by reflecting on an overarching framework in which such cooperation can take shape, we hope this chapter provides some useful indications.

## 2 The Need for Global Cooperation on AI

In this section, we provide a number of reasons to stimulate and accelerate global cooperation on AI and its governance. Notably, the underlying motivations for setting up cooperation initiatives typically also inform their scope and process. We first consider what distinguishes AI as a technology so as to warrant new governance mechanisms (Sect. 2.1). Second, we assess why these mechanisms require cooperation at the global rather than merely local level (Sect. 2.2). Finally, we list some of the challenges that may need to be overcome by aspiring global cooperation partners (Sect. 2.3).

### 2.1 Why AI Necessitates Governance

Melvin Kranzberg stated in 1986 that technology is neither good nor bad, nor neutral [32]. Technology is a tool created by human beings. It is shaped by the values of its makers and of the society they live in. Once technology becomes embedded in society, it can also start shaping society in turn. To ensure that this mutual shaping process respects and fosters appropriate values, governance mechanisms have been established to steer human behavior when developing and using technology. These governance mechanisms consist of many different tools – from non-binding organizational guidelines to sectoral standards to (inter)nationally applicable regulations. They can be applied ex ante (prior to being circulated on the market) or ex post, and are typically tailored to the technology and/or risks at stake. This also holds true for technologies based on AI, which are already covered by many existing (binding and non-binding) governance regimes, most of which predate AI's wide-scale incorporation in our lives. As a consequence, some of these regimes do not adequately capture the opportunities and risks that AI-systems generate in light of their specific properties.

There seem to exist many definitions of AI, with each definition laying emphasis on different aspects. Moreover, definitions are typically guided by the context in which they are established [6]. Nevertheless, regardless of the definition one upholds, AI-systems share a number of distinct properties that are generally accepted to constitute both its strengths and weaknesses. It is, for instance, precisely AI's ability to reason and learn autonomously, and to subsequently act thereon in an autonomous manner in the physical or digital world, that renders it so useful for human beings – as well as hazardous. The same can be said for AI's evolving nature, its remarkable speed in processing information, and the immense scale on which it can be deployed. Consequently, when we get it right, AI's properties can generate significant benefits that positively impact not only a happy few, but humanity at large. However, when we get it wrong, the very same properties are capable of causing significant individual and societal harm. AI-systems do not operate in a void, but are always part of the environment in which they are developed and used [25]. Therefore, the risks they entail are not limited to the technical realm, but also encompass ethical, legal, social and economic challenges that must be dealt with [9]. Most of these challenges are not new, yet due to the properties specific to AI they can manifest themselves in novel ways [50, 63]. In particular, AI-systems can pose new threats to human rights, to the democratic process and to the rule of law [4, 43, 44] (see also Chap. 9). Just as the decision to design, develop and use AI is intrinsically human, so is the decision to set the conditions under which this should occur, and the responsibility for those decisions [49, 50].

As a consequence, an increasing number of actors (often as part of existing regional or global cooperation initiatives) have called upon the establishment of governance mechanisms to secure the prevention and minimization of these risks, while at the same time fostering the maximization of its benefits. The European Commission's High-Level Expert Group on AI [25] as well as the OECD [46] for instance urged for measures to ensure "Trustworthy AI". This trustworthiness should emanate from the (demonstrable) fulfillment of requirements around the development, deployment and use of AI-systems by human beings. Hence, whether the term used is "Trustworthy AI", "Responsible AI" or any other denomination is of less importance than the actual requirements this term embodies.

As defined by the European Commission's expert group, the term "trustworthy" denotes the need to be (1) lawful, complying with all applicable laws and regulations; (2) ethical, ensuring adherence to ethical principles and values; and (3) robust, both from a technical and social perspective [25]. Throughout this chapter, the term *trustworthy* will be used as encompassing these three components. All three are necessary but not sufficient in themselves; they should work in harmony, overlap in their operation and be updated to ensure this harmony. To this end, existing governance mechanisms should be carefully scrutinized and, where needed, reshaped or complemented with new ones [52]. Fostering the trustworthiness of AI is not only essential to secure legitimate trust in the fact that, when AI-systems are used, this happens in a legal, ethical and robust manner. It is also required to enable AI's benefits, as a lack of trustworthiness will stand in the way of AI innovation and uptake by citizens and consumers, companies and institutions - and hence of the materialization of its opportunities.

## 2.2 Why AI's Governance Requires a Global Approach

Over the last few years, numerous countries and regions established their own AI-strategies. These strategies typically focus on incentivizing local stakeholders to join forces and maximize AI's benefits, and – to more or lesser degrees – to minimize the risks raised thereby. While local initiatives are necessary, they are not sufficient to duly tackle the challenges and opportunities at stake and to secure AI's trustworthiness [18].

In a globalized world, countries are increasingly interdependent. The policy choices pursued by one country can thus have a significant impact on others – directly and indirectly. This impact is particularly pronounced in the context of AI, a technology transforming entire economies and societies, with clear cross-border effects [28, 40, 64]. Consequently, the need for global cooperation on AI and its governance arises in a growing number of areas.

Global cooperation is an elusive concept and can be interpreted in multiple ways. Given that instances of truly 'global' cooperation are limited, one could even question the concept of 'global cooperation' as such. When referring to global cooperation throughout this paper, we intend to denote cooperation that takes place internationally or across-borders, with an as large as possible number of international actors that share certain interests, objectives or values, driving them to cooperate. It is, moreover, important to note that cooperation initiatives take place not only at the level of states, but also at stakeholder level, including for instance private companies, public institutions, research and academia, civil society organizations and individuals. In fact, cooperation increasingly takes place through mixed models, whereby governments and other stakeholders are represented around the same table.

The relationship amongst these actors can take various shapes and typically depends on the specific context. Drawing on insights from industrial organization, roughly three types of relationship can be identified: a relationship of competition, a relationship of cooperation and relationship of coopetition (or cooperative competition) [3]. Each of these relationships has a role to play in enabling AI's trustworthiness, depending on the issue at stake. Cooperation is not a goal in and of itself, and is not necessary for each and every AI-related aspect. However, even in areas where competition is preferred over cooperation – for instance in light of the stimulation it can provide to socially beneficial innovation – a certain level of pre-emptory cooperation may be needed to secure that such competition can take place under fair conditions and to the ultimate benefit of all.

As asserted by various authors, when it comes to AI, the current global landscape is marked primarily by a relationship of competition, particularly in light of the so-called 'race to AI' [3, 22, 35]. Virtually all national AI-strategies emphasize the desire to develop, maintain or strengthen a position of 'leadership' in developing and using AI, often with explicit references to the comparative position of rival states. And while this race to AI must not necessarily lead to a race to the bottom that sacrifices aspects like quality, safety and ethical values [51], such a scenario may nevertheless materialize if driven by the belief that AI's opportunities are part of a zero-sum or finite game, with set winners and losers [7]. This belief may lead to a unilateral focus on the state's own interest, triggering short-sighted – and often protectionist – measures, as well as a disregard for the negative externalities of its policies. A zero-sum game not only limits the scope of potential cooperation areas, but also hampers fair competition and undermines the incentives it can provide for beneficial innovation. As a result, the finite mindset may well become a self-fulfilling prophecy in which, in the longer term, everyone loses. Conversely, if a shift in perspective can be secured towards an infinite mindset, the protectionist approach can be cast aside and a reorientation can take place towards long-term growth and sustainable well-being.

Achieving this shift, however, requires a collective effort to establish a level playing field based on a common set of values to be respected when developing and using AI, and safeguarded by appropriate governance mechanisms. Once established, such a level playing field can protect citizens, as well as creating the conditions for healthy competition that allow AI's benefits to be augmented, scaled and widely disseminated. Through common rules and standards, a space of mutual trust can be fostered, ensuring that AI-products and services can travel across the globe without crossing red lines that may cause individual or societal harm. In addition, global cooperation can leverage know-how and capabilities from multiple actors and orient these toward beneficial applications that are not captured by market incentives. In this way, cooperation initiatives can help secure that AI's opportunities are enjoyed by humanity at large – and by those who would benefit from it most – rather than solely by the traditionally privileged.

Global cooperation on AI should not be equated with harmonizing regulation. Cooperation on AI can also meaningfully take place around non-regulatory areas, such as for instance the incentivization of cross-border research collaborations in AI for social good. Moreover, it should be stressed that not all aspects of the development and use of AI must be governed by regulation, nor must this necessarily occur at the global level. AI raises different challenges for different countries, some of which are better dealt with in a manner tailored to the local situation [51]. A balance must thus be found, whereby meaningful cooperation for the benefit of humanity is fostered, without overlooking the particular circumstances of individual states.

### 2.3 Challenges to Overcome

Global cooperation is both desirable and necessary to reach the aims set out above; some actors even explicitly included the intention to engage therein in their AI strategies [15, 68]. However, enabling such cooperation is not devoid of challenges. The urge to compete rather than to cooperate – and to prioritize one's own interests to the detriment of longer term and increased benefits for all – is pervasive at all levels that require cooperation. This encompasses not just the geopolitical level, but also the level of stakeholders (companies, public institutions, researchers), the level of international organizations that bring these stakeholders together, as well as within single organizations. Accordingly, several obstacles will need to be overcome.

First, as was already raised above, there is currently no universally agreed definition of AI. Moreover, there is no such thing as a single AI, as various techniques and application domains of the technology exist, each with their own benefits and risks. Furthermore, these techniques and applications continuously evolve. Given that different actors can interpret the scope of AI in different ways – and are sometimes incentivized to do so [51] – there is a risk of misalignment when cooperation initiatives are established. At the same time, rather than focusing on a strict delineation of AI, we propose to consider a holistic approach to the technology, as outlined in more details under Sect. 3.1, thereby largely overcoming this definitional obstacle.

Second, the stability of cooperation initiatives typically hinges on the underlying motives that drive actors to cooperate rather than compete. Generally speaking, competition can occur at two levels: at the level of values and at the level of markets. With the former, we refer to the political and ideological values underpinning the organization of national or regional societies. With the latter, we refer to the space of trade in which economic (public or private) actors are engaged. Many national and regional AI-strategies have focused on positioning their jurisdiction – including their citizens, companies and organizations – in the best possible position to compete in and benefit from the global AI market. Such competition is typically not limited to the trading of goods and services, but also extends to establishing the best regulations and standards for AI, with the aim to turn national standards into the global norm. Competition also focuses on attracting AI resources, such as AI researchers and developers, AI-developing companies, AI-enabling infrastructure and financial investments – all of which influence one's position on the global AI market.

As long as the competing actors have a similar underlying value-system, these values will also be reflected in their way of competing. This opens up a basis for cooperation regarding the conditions that AI's socio-technical environment should meet to ensure that competition ultimately benefits all. However, when actors have differing value-systems, overcoming competition in favor of cooperation is significantly more complex. Substantive areas for cooperation can still be identified in those instances where economic interests, or the desire to attain a specifically delineated objective, may diminish the importance of the value discrepancy. Yet the agreement that can be reached in such scenario risks not only being less far-reaching but also less stable, as any change in those interests – whether through internal or external factors – can terminate the underlying motive for cooperation altogether.

Third, even where value-systems are more closely aligned, global cooperation on AI can be complicated by differing priorities.[1] While Artificial Intelligence is a subject appearing on the agenda of most (geopolitical) actors, it is far from the only one. The fact that AI-based technologies are already transforming our lives on numerous fronts does not render other transformative (human-made or natural) phenomena less important to focus on. As the establishment of cooperation initiatives requires both time and resources, engaging in cooperation on AI means less resources are available for (cooperation on) other goals. Moreover, even when sufficient partners are ready to spend their resources on AI-related cooperation, the partners' priorities may not necessarily align when it comes to the substantive domain or concern that should be addressed first. It can in this regard also be noted that, while individual and societal interests impacted by AI often coincide, under some circumstances, these interests can instead collide. Depending on the underlying societal values and their hierarchy, cooperation actors may be driven towards different approaches when faced with colliding interests.

Finally, and closely linked thereto, is the differing social and economic conditions of the cooperation partners. Not all actors – whether countries or stakeholders – have an equal starting position when engaging in cooperation. Those with less financial means or in more vulnerable circumstances not only encounter more difficulties in finding a

---

[1] In this regard, we also refer to the recommendations we propose in the final section of this chapter, focusing in particular on clarifying the rules of engagement between cooperation actors and ensuring a transparent cooperation process.

seat around the cooperation table, but might also struggle to find cooperation initiatives that are sufficiently tailored to their particular needs. It is evident that the challenges and opportunities faced by countries who still lack basic connectivity infrastructure will be different from the challenges and opportunities of highly advanced nations that dominate the global AI landscape. This uneven position will have an unavoidable impact on their respective priorities. Global cooperation on AI can help bridge the digital divide and is necessary to secure that AI is not used in a manner that further deepens it [28]. At the same time, efforts will be needed to ensure that potential differences in value-systems, political priorities and socio-economic conditions can be overcome to bring as many as possible global actors together.

## 3  Areas for Global Cooperation on AI and Its Governance

Having established *why* global cooperation on AI and its governance is needed, we can now focus on *what* areas should be cooperated on. AI is a multifaceted technology and can be used in a myriad of manners and domains, for better and for worse. As the establishment of global cooperation initiatives is resource-intensive, prioritization of cooperation goals is needed. Not all aspects surrounding AI's development and use need to be addressed through global cooperation. As a general rule, we believe that areas of increased risk require increased cooperation, and should be addressed as a matter of priority. Setting commonly agreed rules in this regard is essential to prevent and minimize AI's risks not only at local but also at global level. In addition, we also consider cooperation essential to establish a level playing field that is based on a shared set of values. This will not only secure citizen protection across the globe, but also enable socially beneficial innovation and stimulate healthy competition to disseminate AI's benefits.

To achieve this, we argue for a holistic governance approach, along a dual dimension. The first dimension is **horizontal** (Sect. 3.1), and aims at identifying minimum requirements for a level playing field to secure trustworthy AI in a transversal manner. Not only AI-systems, but the entire socio-technical environment around such systems should be considered (a). Moreover, in addition to the environment of AI-systems, it is essential that the interwoven socio-technical environments around data (b) and digital infrastructure (c) are also taken into account. While many cooperation initiatives around AI are still myopically focusing on AI-systems alone, it is only by considering these three environments collectively - the *'system-data-infrastructure trinity'* - that AI's trustworthiness can truly be advanced. The second dimension is **vertical** (Sect. 3.2), and focuses on domain-specific areas where cooperation efforts should be tailored to the context or sector. This encompasses areas in which specific benefits for humanity can be realized and maximized (a), where AI's risks must be prevented and minimized with more immediate urgency (b), and areas where the need for cooperation can arise in a more ad hoc fashion (c). We believe that the horizontal and vertical dimension of AI governance should be addressed in parallel.

## 3.1 The Horizontal Dimension of AI Governance

What is it that makes us trust financial institutions sufficiently to hand over our savings to them? What is it that inspires our trust in the aviation system, so that we dare step on a plane flying over 10.000 meters above the ground? It is not the trustworthiness of the bank's staff, nor the trustworthy reputation of the airline. Rather, we trust the broader socio-technical environment around these systems. We know that financial institutions are subjected to regulatory requirements, that standardized procedures are in place to ensure the quality of their services, and that – in case something goes wrong – there is a possibility for redress to ensure we get compensation. Similarly, we know that airplanes are built in accordance with certain standards, that they undergo multiple verifications prior to and during their deployment, and that the pilots flying them have the certified competences to man them. Moreover, we know this not only for the banks and airlines that are established in our home country, but we trust these environments across the globe, due to the global cooperation on and harmonization of the relevant standards, processes and regulations.

By analogy, securing the trustworthiness of AI cannot be limited to considering individual AI-systems, but must extend to their broader socio-technical environment. We consider the socio-technical environment of AI to be an overarching concept, encompassing three distinct environments that each need to be rendered trustworthy: the socio-technical environment around AI-systems (a), the socio-technical environment around data (b) and the socio-technical environment around digital infrastructure (c) – or the 'system-data-infrastructure trinity'. Each of these three environments form a distinct yet interlinked web, which means they ought to be considered holistically. For each, it must be assessed which minimum requirements the systems, processes and actors involved should meet to be rendered trustworthy, as well as the human skills that are necessary to meaningfully engage with these environments.

For some aspects, binding regulation will be the most appropriate governance mechanism to secure the aims sought. In this regard, we argue for a risk-based approach, whereby elements that carry a higher extent of risk for individuals and society should be addressed more stringently. For other aspects, however, different tools should be explored, such as voluntary standards or certification mechanisms. In each case, it must also be established to which extent the mechanism should be imposed ex ante or ex post, and which entity should be responsible for its enforcement. By arguing in favor of a holistic approach that covers the trustworthiness of the entire socio-technical environment around AI rather than just the system, and by considering the interwoven environments of AI-systems, data and digital infrastructure comprehensively rather than in isolation, we wish to counter the myopia that existing initiatives at times suffer from.

### (a) Building a trustworthy environment for AI-systems

As explained above, regardless of their shape, AI-systems do not exist independently but are part of their broader socio-technical environment. They influence this environment and are influenced by it. To secure their trustworthiness, a systemic approach is thus required, focusing on the trustworthiness of all actors and processes that are part of this environment [25]. This includes inter alia the social, legal and economic context in which the systems are used, the design and technical specifications of the systems' software, the purpose for which they are deployed and the business model in which they fit.

Concretely, as a first step, the various actors and processes that are part of the systems' environment should be mapped. Specific attention is needed for people who may be negatively affected by AI-systems even if not directly engaging therewith. As a second step, minimum requirements that ascertain and enhance the legality, ethicality and robustness of the socio-technical environment of AI-systems should be identified. These requirements should reflect – by priority – those aspects posing the largest individual and societal risks, and those aspects needed to establish a global level playing field. Finally, the identified requirements should be globally agreed on and, where needed, complemented with new ones.

As many risks are context-specific, a large number of standards or procedures will need to be established at sector- or application-level, so as to tackle the risks specifically arising within that context. This, however, does not take away the need for standards and procedures that are context-agnostic and apply horizontally – especially since the same AI-system can be repurposed for different contexts. Regardless of the sector in which AI-systems are used, those interacting therewith or subjected thereto must be able to trust in the fact that basic safeguards are in place. For instance, they need know that certain guarantees are foreseen to protect their human rights, that the accuracy and robustness of the systems are duly verified or certified by competent experts where necessary to safeguard those rights, that the necessary documentation and tools are available to render the systems auditable by independent authorities, that measures have been taken to counter the impact that these use of these systems may have at work or on the labor market, and that – in case something goes wrong – accountability and redress mechanisms are available.

We believe that finding agreement on these requirements is significantly more important than the quest for an agreement on AI's definition. They should be met regardless of whether it concerns a basic algorithm, a sophisticated deep-learning system or any other automated decision-making process that may or may not fall under the ever-changing AI definition. Safeguarding these minimum requirements can take numerous (complementary) shapes, from principle-based regulatory provisions to certifiable standards. In our view, both are necessary, with the former ideally informing the latter. As noted above, the risk-based approach that increases the stringency in case of increased risk can be of help. Several initiatives have started preparatory work in this field [11, 15, 27, 46, 48, 56, 74], increasingly also across borders. As AI-systems often consist of components developed or used in different countries, these requirements must be agreed on globally to ensure that they are met regardless of their place of development. Encouragingly, while each of the existing cooperation initiatives on AI highlighted slightly different aspects in light of their mandate, so far, most established similar outcomes. Nevertheless, many of the current requirements are non-binding and not yet sufficiently concretized to secure accountability by those involved. Moreover, few of them have sufficient attention to the necessary skills and competences that may need to be certified.

In addition, besides identifying the minimum content of these requirements, cooperation efforts must also focus on the processes that are necessary to demonstrate and verify the fulfillment of these requirements, for instance through standardized reporting or audit procedures.[2] We believe that agreement on these procedural matters is equally if not more important than agreement on the requirements' substance. To illustrate: two countries may, for instance, demand a different level of demonstrable accuracy of an AI-system. However, without a commonly accepted procedure on how the system's accuracy should be measured, demonstrated or verified, neither country will be able to assess compliance with its standards. Consequently, to avoid that trust in the socio-technical environment of AI-systems will remain local and volatile, agreement on the demonstrability and verifiability of the requirements' fulfillment is essential.

### (b) Building a trustworthy environment for data

Whether it's referred to as the new oil or the new electricity, the role of data in our economies and societies is growing in importance, and this trend will undoubtedly persist. Not all AI-systems necessitate big data. Yet many AI-systems nevertheless heavily rely thereon. For those systems, the availability of quality-controlled, thorough, comprehensive and representative data is necessary to materialize the benefits they can achieve [14]. Data plays an essential role throughout those system's entire lifecycle. At the same time, storing and processing data comes with significant responsibility [23, 24], even more so when it concerns personal data (see Chap. 3). In that case, such data can be considered as a constitutive part of a person's identity [20] and is therefore typically accompanied by a protective right of control thereof [38]. Given data's relationship to AI, securing a trustworthy socio-technical environment for data that enables its availability and protection across borders and secures the trustworthiness of all actors and processes involved, should be part of any global cooperation framework on AI.

This means that the parameters of data's socio-technical environment must be mapped, and that global cooperation on defining their substantive and procedural dimensions should be stimulated. While this mapping exercise is well underway - and actors on regional level (such as the EU) have started setting out some of the constitutive elements of a trustworthy data environment - political convergence on these issues at global level is still limited. Certain countries implemented particularly protectionist stances in this field, under the not always justified guise of national interest and security – thereby fostering a zero-sum game approach and creating obstacles for mutual trust and growth opportunities. Matters are further complicated by the large diversity of issues at stake. As data is contextual, certain requirements will need to be specified at domain-level. Yet the fact that it can be reused and repurposed for numerous applications – including applications that were not foreseen or foreseeable at the time the data collection took place – render horizontally applicable policies an indispensable base layer for a trustworthy data environment. To this end, and without the ambition of being exhaustive, we list below a number of data-related issues that should be addressed in global cooperation fora.

First, a convergence of approaches should be sought on data's legal status, particularly including ownership and intellectual property rights thereon. Such

---

[2] It can be noted that a number of initiatives have started work in this regard, including ISO [70], CEN-CENELEC [65], ETSI [67] and NIST [72].

convergence is not only useful as regards first-hand data, but also for secondary and tertiary data, including 'new' data that originates through the combination of other data points. Data's applicable property regime – which also governs its accessibility – typically differs depending on the category of data (personal, non-personal or mixed; pseudonymized or anonymized; public or confidential) and context (such as business-to-business (B2B), business-to-consumer (B2C), business-to-government (B2G), government-to-citizens (G2C) and other variations). Whereas in certain contexts – such as the B2B domain – ownership questions are often settled through contractual clauses, these matters are typically less straightforward when consumers or governmental actors are involved. Since different models are conceivable, fostering a mutual understanding around these issues at global level is fundamental, and can subsequently form a basis for further convergence where needed.

Second, and closely linked thereto, is the governance of personal data – a data category for which the term 'ownership' is, in fact, often deemed controversial for various reasons [26]. In recent years, awareness around the (mis)use of personal data, especially when emanating from consumers or citizens and used to influence their behavior, has steadily grown. The *MyData* movement and other initiatives greatly stimulated the empowerment of individuals through increased data autonomy [36, 71]. While codified in multiple human rights instruments, the right to personal data protection is not absolute; it must be considered in relation to its function in society and be balanced against other fundamental rights (see Chap. 9). Tensions can arise between individual and societal perspectives, for which concepts like data trusts and data commons have aimed to provide (partial) solutions (Chap. 3). In addition, (extra-EU) countries formulated the right to personal data protection in different ways and with different safeguards, and some still lack any specific data protection law. Even in countries where personal data is protected, mechanisms for protection are not always efficient. The emphasis on self-determination through consent is, for instance, increasingly deemed problematic [8, 59], given the substantial asymmetries of information and power that are often at play and that may render meaningful consent an illusion. For AI-systems and their data to travel within a trustworthy environment, common definitions for data categories, common regimes for (shared) data ownership and protection, and common procedures to determine which regime is applicable, should be established across borders.

Third, individuals, objects and organizations produce millions of data points every day, that could be harnessed for a myriad of beneficial uses. These data points are, however, not always collected and - if they are - this collection sometimes only occurs by a small number of large players who currently dominate the data space. Data can not only provide significant value, but can also be used as a means of amassing power – whether in the private or public sphere [41]. Legal clarity on the property and use of data will not necessarily reduce the power asymmetry between consumers, citizens and smaller companies on the one hand, and incumbent entities on the other. Depending on the regional regulatory and market structure, governments can be one of these dominant entities or they can be entirely dependent thereon. Whichever the case, a concentration of power in the form of data hoarding rarely results in anything other than a zero-sum game with suboptimal outcomes. A lack of access to the necessary datasets to provide a service plays a major role in this regard. Consequently, cooperation to incentivize data sharing under fair conditions – including through federated learning models – as well as measures to ensure that market concentration does not lead to (private or public) abuses, should be encouraged. Moreover, the creation of open (annotated) data sets, common data pools and data commons can help balance existing power asymmetries. Just as is the case for open source repositories of AI codes and the sharing of (already trained) neural networks, much work is still needed to foster cooperation on access to open data sets. Such access is particularly useful for researchers and not-for-profit organizations who rely thereon to conduct fundamental research or work on socially beneficial projects. In addition, a comprehensive regime for data philanthropy within a trustworthy data environment can also stimulate the development of AI-applications that benefit humanity as a whole, rather than data incumbents [53].

Fourth, cooperation is needed on technical standards for the digitization, storage, processing and encryption of data. Data's interoperability and portability hinges not only on its legal and market environment, but also on the manner and format in which data it is collected and kept. Moreover, the value of datasets is highly dependent on their quality and integrity, for which common measurement procedures should likewise be developed. Besides agreement on the (legal) definition of anonymous and pseudonymous data, harmonized procedures on a given anonymization or pseudonymization method - including the potential demonstrability of compliance therewith - can likewise enhance trust. This also holds true as regards requirements for data encryption and security. Similar to the context of AI-systems, we believe the focus should lay not only on the substantive dimension of these requirements, but also on commonly agreed standards to measure, demonstrate and verify the steps and processes followed for their fulfilment.

Last, attention must be paid to the appropriate collection and use of data. The datafication of society is an increasingly common phenomenon, spurred particularly by the aim to realize the benefits that sound data analysis can provide [39]. At the same time, this has also led some to mistakenly believe that everything is quantifiable and measurable, and that the collection of sufficient data can unambiguously inform policy-making [47]. Data should, however, not be equated with objective facts. It concerns a (partial) representation of the world, which is always shaped by a specific interpretation and needs to be interpreted in turn to be of use [23]. Hence, to secure a trustworthy socio-technical environment for data, it is important to foster the necessary competences and literacy for the appropriate handling of data, including the awareness of its inherent limitations when used to draw conclusions. Especially when data-driven applications are used to inform policy-making, common guidelines on providing basic information – such as how much data a given dataset contains, how it was collected, whether and what kind of sampling was used, what data is missing, and in which manner data points are being used as proxies – would not be a luxury.

### (c) Building a trustworthy environment for digital infrastructure

The importance of digital infrastructure as an enabler of various digital technologies has rendered it one of the most desired assets for both private and public actors. AI-systems cannot function without an underlying infrastructure that supports their development and use, and through which their accessibility towards users is enabled.

Moreover, the data that AI-systems rely on depend on digital infrastructure for their storage, processing and transfer. As the deployment of remote tracing applications to fight the COVID-19 pandemic has shown, entities controlling the digital infrastructure do not even require AI-applications or access to (personal) data in order to nevertheless extract value therefrom and have an influence on societies [60, 61]. Consequently, securing a trustworthy socio-technical environment for AI must necessarily go hand in hand with securing a trustworthy environment for digital infrastructure.

The term digital infrastructure refers to a range of elements enabling digital services, including the internet backbone; the connectivity of systems through broadband, mobile telecommunications, Wi-Fi networks and communication satellites; cloud computing; data centers; platforms to develop and operate AI and other software systems as well as API's. Global cooperation in this field is rendered particularly difficult in view of its connection to discussions on sovereignty and national security. Geopolitical competition over infrastructure has proven to cause negative spillover effects on state relationships in other domains too, thereby affecting the potential success of cooperation in this field. It is, however, precisely because of digital infrastructure's importance that global cooperation on its environment must be sought. Besides the need to avoid a zero-sum game approach and a loss of benefits in the longer term, cooperation can also help counter the risk that negative consequences will be suffered primarily and most severely by those who are already more vulnerable. Convergence on the substantive outcomes that cooperation in this field should lead to is still difficult to define. Here below, we nevertheless list four aspects that we believe global cooperation fora should address.

First, discussion is needed on the evolution of the global digital infrastructure and its critical points of control. As a function of market and technological developments, a limited number of actors emerged – often referred to as 'gatekeepers' – that have a strong influence on these control points, as well as the conditions for access to the underlying infrastructure. The capability to influence the development of, and access to, digital infrastructure comes with significant responsibility, as the shape of digital infrastructure is capable of shaping society – a capability that can be used in ways that enhance the infrastructure's utility for the benefit of individuals, companies and other stakeholders, but also in ways that can harm them. Global cooperation initiatives on AI should therefore duly reflect on the governance mechanisms needed for the evolution of the digital infrastructures on which AI is run. Such governance mechanisms should extend not only to the infrastructure's technical requirements, but should also focus on ensuring the responsibility of the actors involved, as they form an inherent part of the infrastructure's broader socio-technical environment. In particular, a dialogue is needed on (and with) the gatekeepers for internet access, for storage and processing capacity, for the accessibility of applications, for the digital marketplace and for news curation. Special attention should also be given to the gatekeepers of the infrastructures that shape digital identity (such as social media platforms).

Second, cooperation efforts should focus on bridging the digital infrastructure divide. While some countries are rolling out 5G, others still lack basic connectivity infrastructure [1]. This has a profound impact on the ability of the citizens in those countries to meaningfully participate in society, and on the economic progress that they can achieve. It is futile to speak of the many benefits that AI can generate as long as basic digital capacity is not secured. Global cooperation is hence needed to support countries across the globe with the build-out of digital infrastructure where this is lacking or underdeveloped. Only once such capacity is in place – as part of a trustworthy environment that governs it – can we truly start materializing the benefits of AI for humanity. Global cooperation initiatives such as the Digital Public Good Alliance [66] and the Global Data Access Framework [69] can help foster this [58].

Third, attention is needed for the environmental footprint of AI's digital infrastructure. Data centers, cloud services and connectivity equipment consume a large amount of energy and thereby significantly contribute to emissions, with the ICT sector as a whole being estimated to use around 5 to 9% of the world's total electricity and generating over 2% of all emissions [14]. It is projected that, in the next few years, ICT operations will start representing up to 20% of global electricity demand, with one third stemming from data centers alone [58]. To reduce our negative impact on the environment and tackle climate change so as to preserve our planet for future generations, states must take their collective responsibility – and enforce such responsibility also upon the private actors active or incorporated within their jurisdictions. In its Communication on "Building Trust for Human-Centric AI" [16], the European Commission already raised the need for AI developers and deployers to foster environmental well-being, which constitutes one of the seven requirements for Trustworthy AI put forward by its High-Level Expert Group. This need goes beyond AI-systems and also includes the broader digital infrastructure – and entire value chain – on which AI-systems rely. A trustworthy environment for digital infrastructure must secure attention to its sustainability and ensure that the benefits realized with AI today will not jeopardize the future of next generations. Given the cross-border nature of environmental harm, the environmental requirements that AI's digital infrastructure should meet must be agreed at the global level.

Last, we highlight the need for global cooperation on digital infrastructure's security, especially when such infrastructure is critical. The importance of digital infrastructure for states' daily operation – from the functioning of hospitals or transport services to services affecting national security – was already raised above. Evidently, the more we rely on digital infrastructure to operationalize our essential services, the more vulnerable we are when this infrastructure proves to be defective or comes under attack. Since an increasing number of private and public actors procure (part of) such infrastructure abroad, it is essential that the trustworthiness of this infrastructure can be ensured across borders. Beyond technical robustness and safety requirements for AI-systems, similar requirements should therefore be discussed for their underlying digital infrastructure.

## 3.2   The Vertical Dimension to AI Governance

Building a trustworthy socio-technical environment around AI – covering the *system-data-infrastructure trinity* – can help ensure that it embeds appropriate values and that it is used in a manner that fosters rather than hampers human capabilities. A trustworthy AI environment can also help minimize the possibility that the technology is underused out of mistaken fear, a lack of clear rules or other obstacles that may result in opportunity costs [19]. At the same time, the risk remains for AI to be intentionally misused or to inadvertently cause harm. As the concrete materialization of AI's opportunities and risks is often linked to the domain and application in which it is used, the horizontal framework that was set out above needs to be complemented by domain-specific cooperation initiatives, allowing for a more tailored approach where needed. Some of these domains can even start constituting (socio-technical) environments in and of themselves, for instance when linked to a specific sector such as healthcare, transport or education. Rendering these environments – and particularly the development and use of AI within such environment – trustworthy, will necessitate domain-specific expertise. Moreover, in some instances, a specific focus on one particular issue or problem – considered against a holistic background and from multiple angles – might be more conducive to finding solutions. Here also, we believe that an increased level of risk typically calls for an increased level of cooperation to assure a coordinated approach.

Domain-specific areas of cooperation can broadly be captured along three axes: areas aimed at maximizing AI's benefits for humanity (a), areas aimed at preventing and minimizing AI's risks for humanity (b) and areas dealt with on an ad-hoc basis, typically in light of new or unexpected challenges (c). Rather than listing the numerous vertical cooperation domains for AI, in what follows we briefly address these three overarching axes. It should be born in mind that the type of relationship that different actors are engaged in (competitive, cooperative or coopetitive) as well as the cooperation initiative's organizational set-up (which is further described under Sect. 4) will to a large extent shape – and be shaped by – the substantive domain in question.

## (a) Cooperation on maximizing AI's benefits for humanity
AI can enable a multitude of beneficial applications. The fact that the technology is being oversold (often for commercial reasons) can at time lead to unfeasible expectations. Nevertheless, a realistic perspective of its capabilities acknowledges AI's potential to contribute to individual and societal well-being in numerous ways. To maximize AI's benefits for humanity, we see the need for cooperation on two main fronts.

First, cooperation is needed to secure the minimum requirements for a level playing field that provides a base layer of protection, and that enables market competition to take place under fair conditions. By eliminating distortions to competition and ensuring that all actors can contribute, such a level playing field can stimulate and incentivize beneficial AI research and innovation and ensure that the fruits thereof can be accessed by all. Achieving this result requires not only transversally applicable rules, but also attention to the developments taking place in specific sectors and domains.

Second, cooperation is needed to materialize socially beneficial AI-applications that are not fostered by market competition. While claims are being made about AI's benefits, it is not always specified who the beneficiary of those benefits are. This question is rightfully receiving renewed attention, and efforts are increasingly focusing on the benefits' wider dissemination. Moreover, as already noted above, situations can arise whereby one group of individuals benefits from an application while another group is harmed, and where individual benefits are traded off against societal harm – or vice versa. These situations are not always straightforward, and the perspective with which one looks at them is often colored by the underlying value-system of the onlooker. Nevertheless, global cooperation can help ensure that the beneficiaries of AI's benefits also encompass those people who are most in need.

Initiatives aimed at developing so-called 'AI for social good' applications have been mushrooming [2, 12, 62], and are often aimed at advancing one or more of the UN Sustainable Development Goals and its 169 targets [57]. Examples are AI-applications that help reduce humans' negative impact on the environment, render the provision of healthcare more accessible, optimize the allocation of scarce resources in developing countries or foster educational opportunities. Cooperation initiatives can bring together the necessary systems, data and infrastructure to build and scale such applications in various domains. In this context, it is however important to be attentive to local and cultural specificities, for instance by having due regard to the preservation of local languages and customs. Moreover, it is not because AI applications are not built for profit, that their careless use cannot cause harm. Accordingly, it is essential that these applications – however beneficial their intended aim may be – meet all relevant requirements and are built with the help of domain experts that can steer them towards their most relevant uses. As AI is but a tool towards an end, cooperation efforts to maximize AI's benefits for humanity in specific domains should first clarify the goals to be achieved, and only then identify to which extent AI can help therewith.

### (b) Cooperation on preventing and minimizing AI's risks for humanity

The use of AI can lead to several types of harm. As with any technology, this harm can stem from a malicious use of AI and be caused intentionally, but it can also arise out of negligence. It can affect individuals and groups, private and public organizations, as well as entire economies, societies and humanity at large. Moreover, in certain situations, the only way to detect and counter AI-driven harm is by using AI-applications as a shield and countermeasure. Given AI's digital nature, the adverse effects of its negligent use and misuse are typically not limited to the country in which it is developed, but can easily wreak havoc in other countries too – or can even be built to do precisely that. No country can control these risks by itself. Therefore, the prevention and minimization of AI's risks for humanity is par excellence an area for which global cooperation is not a choice, but an absolute necessity. For these reasons, competition between global actors may more easily be overcome in this field, as competitors are naturally forced to seek mutual aid and protection from those risks, which opens the door to cooperative and coopetitive relationships.

The various manners in which the use of AI can harm humanity can be linked to a specific domain or application, and hence often require tailored approaches. These include, for instance, the use of AI in cybersecurity attacks that target states' critical infrastructure [54, 55], the use of AI for disinformation purposes which threatens democracies [4] and, more broadly, AI's dual-use risks [5]. The use of AI in the military, especially when having the potential to cause lethal effects, requires heightened attention [42]. Across the globe, calls are also increasing made by civil society organizations and private actors alike to regulate the conditions under which AI-enabled (remote) biometric identification should be deployed. In addition, consideration should be given to critical risks for humanity in the long term.[3] Several international fora have ongoing discussions on some of the above risks. However, we believe that the speed and efficiency with which (state) actors are currently engaged in these discussions is not proportionate to the risks involved.

### (c) Cooperation on ad hoc matters

Besides domains that can be anticipated, periodically the need will arise to organize global cooperation on AI-related issues in a more ad hoc manner. These can concern AI's positive or negative consequences – or both. The developments surrounding the COVID-19 pandemic for instance made it clear that, in times of crisis, AI-systems can be used for numerous socially beneficial applications [37], that the exchange of qualitative data can contribute to saving lives [31] and that the control points of the infrastructures on which AI-systems run (including AI-driven tracing applications) are more crucial than ever [61]. At the same time, AI-systems have been used to fuel the spread of mis- and disinformation about the virus, the harm of which goes far beyond the medical realm. It is the collective task of all actors involved to remain attentive for new matters that may require the setting aside of competition in favor of ad hoc cooperation at the global level. While the development and use of AI still brings with it many unknown unknowns, the establishment of sustainable networks of global cooperation can help foster their anticipation.

## 4    Organizing Global Cooperation on AI and Its Governance

The annals of global cooperation precede the second world war, yet it is in the aftermath thereof that such cooperation truly started taking off [17]. This leaves us with a long and rich experience of how global cooperation has been organized – on issues as diverse as nuclear weapons, aviation safety, space or the law of the sea – which can be drawn from in the context of AI. Many existing cooperation initiatives already touch upon matters that are (directly or indirectly) related to AI's concerns, from their own perspective. These initiatives have beaten tracks, distinct ways of working, ingrained procedures and established actors. As global cooperation on AI is thus embedded in a pre-existing setting, a close link exists between *how* such cooperation is organized (the process and shape) and *who* is involved (the cooperation organizer and partners). Inexorably, the cooperation process will be influenced by the actors around the table as well as by the type of table. Bearing this interwovenness in mind and acknowledging the numerous actions that are already taking place the field of AI, in this section we put forward seven elements that can help guide the organization of both existing and new global cooperation initiatives.

In particular, we address the need to: balance speed, holism and context-specificity (Sect. 4.1), clarify the rules of engagement of cooperation partners (Sect. 4.2), favor

---

[3] A number of research centers scattered around the world have the specific aim (and funding) to develop applications of Artificial General Intelligence and Artificial Consciousness. Regardless of the likelihood that this aim proves realistic or successful, the magnitude of risk that would be raised thereby calls for a common global stance and vigilance.

cooperation through existing fora rather than creating new ones (Sect. 4.3), develop a network of networks to build up collective wisdom (Sect. 4.4), being open to a model of differentiated cooperation (Sect. 4.5), secure an inclusive and transparent way of working, mindful of power imbalances (Sect. 4.6) and establish feedback loops while preparing for cooperation by future generations (Sect. 4.7).

## 4.1 Balancing the Need for Swift Action, a Holistic Approach and Attention to Context-Specificity

As the scale and pace with which AI is being developed and used is growing, so is the need for swift cooperation. Consequently, a red thread that should shape the organization of global cooperation on AI is the need for speed and efficiency. It has become increasingly clear that the transformative influence of AI goes well beyond the simple sum of the influence of individual AI-systems. While we are still in a steep learning curve as regards the technology itself and its impact on individuals and society, AI-systems are already being rolled-out in virtually all domains of our lives. Speed is therefore of the essence to secure that this roll-out occurs in a manner that fosters AI's benefits in the long term and in a manner aligned with our values, rather than in a manner hampering them. The importance of speed, however, needs to be balanced off against two other elements, namely the necessity of a holistic approach on the one hand, and sufficient attention for domain-specific concerns on the other.

The holistic approach we argued for above requires attention not only to the socio-technical environment of AI-systems, data and infrastructure, but also to the large variety of angles through which AI's challenges and opportunities can be considered, necessitating the diversity and inclusivity of cooperation partners. At the same time, AI's challenges and opportunities are often context-dependent, requiring appropriate attention for domain-specific concerns that require more tailored measures. These three elements – speed, holism and context-specificity – are, evidently, not always harmonious. The more parties at the table and the more pieces of the puzzle to consider, the less likely it is that the desired speed of action can be attained. The shape of the cooperation initiative, as well as the type and number of actors taking part, will have an inevitable influence on the speed of the process. A careful balancing exercise is hence needed, requiring often difficult trade-off decisions from the global cooperation partners. For areas where the risks are particularly extensive and irreversible, speed may temporarily need to be prioritized over holism so as to secure a fast base layer of protection.

## 4.2 Clarifying the Rules of Engagement

Setting up a global cooperation initiative – whether through a multi-stakeholder partnership or intergovernmental process – is typically a time- and resource-intensive process. To avoid a waste of these resources and enhance efficiency, the rules of engagement between cooperation partners need to be clarified and rendered explicit prior to the cooperation's initiation. If the initiative is to be fruitful, all of its participants need to be seriously committed to the defined mandate and goals, and must communicate their expectations in advance – both internally and externally – to allow for common engagement rules to be agreed on. The rules of engagement will likely depend on the substantive area of cooperation, and on whether the actors start the process from a stage of competition, coopetition or cooperation.

As noted under Sect. 2, for global cooperation initiatives to succeed, competition need not always be entirely eliminated. When competition takes place on top of a level playing field based on common values, it can foster beneficial AI-applications and stimulate a race to the top – in terms of both regulation and innovation. However, when competition is taking place at the level of value-systems, it typically affects the partners' relationship far beyond the field of AI, thereby rendering cooperation more difficult. Potential cooperation partners should therefore reflect – and come clean – on the type of competition at stake and the envisaged relationship within a cooperation initiative. The underlying value-systems governing the political, social and economic views of the respective partners will necessarily contribute to the manner in which the cooperation rules of engagement will be shaped, thereby determining not only the initiative's outcomes but also its durability.

### 4.3   Building on Existing Cooperation Structures

Over the last century, numerous international organizations were set up with the specific aim of fostering cooperation amongst states and other stakeholders, each with distinct compositions, mandates and collaboration processes. Many of these organizations are in the position – or already took decisive steps – to include the issues raised by AI on their agenda. Some of these organizations have a working scope that also encompasses issues around data and digital infrastructure, while others are solely focused on the immediate environment of AI-systems (or even narrower, on maximizing its benefits through 'AI for social good' projects). Therefore, prior to establishing a new cooperation structure, it is advisable to map existing cooperation initiatives on AI, so as to assess the new structure's added value. Given the need for speed, we believe that – as a default – the use of existing cooperation initiatives should be favored over the creation of new ones. This is particularly the case when those organizations have a broad mandate and can thereby foster a more holistic approach. Of course, in order to enable fruitful cooperation on AI and its governance, these existing initiatives may need to include new and more diverse cooperation partners, and will need to ensure the involvement of domain experts – yet many of them have set procedures in place to do so.

Only where, after a thorough mapping exercise, existing cooperation initiatives appear to fall short, can the establishment of new cooperation fora be justified. This is for instance the case when no existing organization has a mandate to address the relevant issue, and where obtaining such mandate would be an unduly lengthy process. A new initiative could also be justified when no existing organization can engage in swift and fruitful cooperation on a specific matter due to burdensome, inefficient or non-inclusive processes. Each time a new forum is created – or a new mandate is defined within an existing cooperation forum – the delicate balance between speed, holism and context-specificity as outlined above must be considered.

### 4.4   Developing a Network of Networks

In some instances, the working scope and mandate of existing cooperation initiatives can (partially) overlap. Overlapping mandates have not only led to organizational competition, but also to geopolitical competition within these organizations. Indeed, in light of the first-mover advantage for (state) actors in terms of regulatory impact, it has been argued elsewhere that the race to AI also brought forth a race to AI regulation [51]. This regulatory race at organization-level is at least in part fueled by the differing composition of the organizations in question, though competition can also take place between organizations with similar memberships.

While these overlaps carry a risk of duplication of work, inconsistency and waste of scarce resources, they also secure that the same subject matter is looked at from different perspectives, which may limit the risk of gaps. Thus, the Council of Europe will for instance have a particular focus on the human rights risks raised by AI, while the OECD's perspective will be colored by the lens of economic progress and world trade. Both organizations may converge on the need for legal, ethical and robustness requirements for AI, yet they will consider this need from their specific angle. A multiplicity of initiatives can also avoid the risks of a herd mentality or of a concentration of regulatory power at the global level, which could start from the best of intentions but evolve into an undesirable regulatory monopoly. In this sense, the various organizations in the global cooperation field can maintain a balance of power amongst them and – in the ideal case – work towards the most optimal outcomes by competing with each other in a race to the top.

Where cooperation mandates overlap, it is however important to secure the dissemination and cross-pollination of information between the relevant initiatives. This will enable a mutual learning process and thereby maximize the chances of a regulatory race to the top – effectively establishing a relationship of coopetition between these organizations rather than competition. The dissemination of information can take many shapes, but should ideally be as speedy and as efficient as possible. In practice, existing initiatives within international organizations have for instance allowed other organizations to partake as an observer. Thus, the Council of Europe's Ad Hoc Committee on AI (CAHAI) counts the OECD, the European Commission, UNESCO and the UN Panel on Digital Cooperation – each having partially overlapping mandates – as observers in its meetings. The status of observer has also been granted to states that do not have a Council of Europe membership, yet have an interest in its work, and to other types of stakeholders. In turn, the European Commission's High-Level Expert Group on AI likewise comprised observers representing (non-member) states, stakeholders and international organizations - including the Council of Europe and the OECD.

The practice of inviting observers from regulatory competitors generates a network effect that allows for collective knowledge building – both on the subject matter and on cooperation processes – thereby benefiting all actors involved. In addition, some organizations have set up more concrete mechanisms for information sharing. For instance, in 2019, the OECD launched an AI Policy Observatory [73] in cooperation with the European Commission, containing a repository of state- and stakeholder policy initiatives around AI. Such information gathering and dissemination helps compensate the unavoidable overhead costs that a multiplication of work generates, and contributes to the mutual advancement of cooperation efforts. By maintaining a dialogue across cooperation initiatives, a network of networks can be created and informal coordination can be secured.

## 4.5  Maintaining Openness to Differentiated Cooperation

Given the borderless nature of AI's positive and negative impact, cooperation initiatives should ideally gather the widest group of (geopolitical) actors, aiming towards truly 'global' participation. However, and particularly in light of the potential value-based discrepancies highlighted above, this may not always be possible or desirable – nor is it always strictly necessary to achieve relevant outcomes. The European Union is a primary example of a cooperative framework in which differentiated integration has proven to be essential to advance multinational agreement on certain matters. Essentially, the EU has inbuilt mechanisms that allow for countries to opt-in and opt-out of a cooperation regime for certain substantive matters, and for a smaller group of countries to pursue closer cooperation in some domains when other countries are hesitant to join [13, 33]. In this manner, enhanced cooperation need not be delayed but can be initiated by like-minded countries – with an open invitation for other countries to join the cooperative regime at a later stage.[4] When modelling this feature to the global stage, openness to differentiated cooperation in the context of AI can prove an asset for countries willing to invest time and resources in finding agreement on certain issues amongst themselves.

At the same time, it should be born in mind that the enhanced cooperation by some countries is liable to create externalities upon those remaining outside the cooperation framework. Those externalities can be both positive or negative. When positive, external countries are only likely to join the initiative at a later stage if the benefits they can gain from joining minus the costs thereof outweigh the positive externalities. When negative, external countries are only likely to join if the costs of joining are lower than the negative externalities they face by remaining outside. Alternatively, to the extent the costs of doing so are lower than the costs of joining, they may also choose to boycott the enhanced cooperation initiative through political, economic or other means. In this regard, it is also important to consider the unequal geopolitical and economic circumstances in which countries at the global stage find themselves. Sensitivity is needed for asymmetries of bargaining power – including when it comes to accessing the cooperation table.[5]

Being mindful of the above, we believe two approaches ought to be combined. On the one hand, cooperation should be sought with an as large as possible group of partners, especially to seek agreement on the requirements for trustworthy socio-technical environments around AI's *system-data-infrastructure* trinity. As a general rule, cooperation initiatives should be open and collaborative, and welcome new partners that share the initiative's vision, values and goals. The size of such a group and

---

[4] It should be noted, however, that the EU Treaties only allow for the use of this mechanism when no agreement can be found with all EU member states. At the same time, EU countries have also pursued 'differentiated cooperation' outside the scope of the EU Treaties.

[5] Such power asymmetries are often accompanied by an asymmetry of the (negative) consequences endured by the development and use of AI at global level. Attention should therefore be paid not only to the opportunities and risks generated by AI, but also to the potential shifts in power that AI may induce – whether between and amongst countries, or between and amongst public actors, private actors and individuals [24, 30].

the diversity of actors may make it difficult to achieve consensus that is far-reaching in the short term, yet the immediate focus should lay on identifying minimum require-ments allowing a basic level-playing field that can be further built upon. Once started, the trust-building through this cooperation process can grow, which – ideally – grad-ually increases the convergence of views and extends the cooperation scope. On the other hand, and simultaneously so, like-minded partners willing to seek closer coop-eration and reach further consensus should advance through a differentiated coopera-tion approach. When doing so, they should however secure consistency with the outcomes of wider cooperation initiatives. Even when starting off at smaller scale rather than at the global level, such cooperation can have a positive impact and act as a catalyst for broader agreement in the longer term.

## 4.6  Securing an Inclusive and Transparent Way of Working, Mindful of Power Imbalances

For cooperation to be both swift and efficient, the teams representing the cooperation partners and partaking in the negotiations should have a clear mandate to conduct negotiations, as well as the required knowledge of the area of cooperation. Given AI's multifaceted impact, a multidisciplinary approach is required, allowing for the relevant issues to be considered from all relevant angles. This necessitates inclusive, diverse and gender-balanced negotiation teams, and specific efforts to ensure participation from multiple stakeholders, ideally comprising a balanced representation from the public sector, the private sector, research and academia, and civil society organizations. In addition, cooperation initiatives need to be equipped with sufficient resources, and secure clarity and transparency on monetary contributions in advance. Mechanisms must also be foreseen to ensure that those actors willing to participate but lacking the necessary financial means – particularly when it concerns developing countries or civil society organizations – are not hindered thereby. Not only those with the ability to accelerate or contribute AI-capabilities, but also those meant to benefit therefrom – and that may be adversely affected thereby – should have a seat around the table.

In this regard, specific consideration should be given to the manner in which past injustices might shape today's power asymmetries. Often still, the discourse within global cooperation initiatives on AI and its associated values is driven by more eco-nomically developed countries [29], reflecting a power imbalance to which past geopolitical developments directly or indirectly contributed. There is a risk that these power structures are maintained within cooperation initiatives, even when aimed at outcomes that are meant to benefit humanity at large [41]. Structural inequities can not only be perpetuated through opaque algorithmic decision-making that may render asymmetrical power relations more obscure [1], but also through cooperation frame-works that insufficiently acknowledge the disparate manner in which the use of AI-systems affects global populations. This can concern the extraction of data from more vulnerable populations [10], the economic exploitation of ghost workers in weak labor markets [21] or the beta-testing of AI-applications in countries with less safeguards [41]. Countering these practices necessitates the participation of those countries and populations that have historically been underrepresented at the discussion table and are still exposed to the consequences thereof.

Finally, it was already mentioned that transparency on the parties' goals, intentions and expectations is a necessary precondition for durable cooperation. However, transparency is equally important during the cooperation process. Thus, the way of working, procedures for agreement, budgetary implications and conditions for welcoming new cooperation partners should be clearly set out. Procedural transparency is not just important within the initiative, but also externally. The legitimacy – and hence the success – of cooperation outcomes also hinges on their acceptance by those whom cooperation partners represent, be it citizens or other stakeholders. Legitimacy stems not only from a valid political mandate or board decision, but also from transparency about the cooperation process and accountability for the decisions taken in its context.

## 4.7   Establishing a Feedback Loop and Preparing for the Future

To achieve meaningful output, cooperation initiatives must secure adequate sources of input. Given AI's rapid scientific advances, a bridge must be created between cooperation partners and the research community, allowing for a constant information stream that ensures accurate, updated and scientifically sound input to form the basis of cooperation discussions. This research should not just focus on providing information that advances the cooperation initiative, but should also map the concrete impact of the initiative's outcomes. Ideally, a feedback loop is created, whereby the effects of the cooperation outcomes – for instance, a set of requirements for AI-systems – are monitored, and the extent to which they achieve their aim – for instance, a global level-playing field in terms of AI safety – assessed. Subsequently, these findings can serve as new input for the cooperation process and facilitate the evidence-based improvement of cooperation outcomes. This is particularly important in light of the uncertainty surrounding the most optimal governance models for AI at this stage of the technology's uptake.

In addition, the need for cooperation on AI must also be considered in the longer term. Although the urgency to cooperate forms a red thread throughout this chapter, this does not exclude the importance of looking ahead. Global cooperation on AI is unlikely to be a short-term undertaking, and is set to have continued importance for years to come. It is therefore necessary that – both at state and stakeholder level – investments are made in future cooperation resources and capabilities, particularly in the form of educating the cooperation teams of tomorrow. Citizens – whom the cooperation partners not only represent but of which they are also composed – need to be educated about AI's capabilities, limitations and impacts. An increased level of awareness and education on AI not only empowers individuals at home, at work and in the public sphere, but can also help ensure that, in the long run, they are sufficiently equipped to continue an informed and collaborative cooperation process on AI over the next decades. We are convinced that the establishment of a durable global cooperation framework on AI and its governance is a marathon, not a sprint.

# 5  Conclusions

Global cooperation knows many shapes. In the sections above, we did not seek to describe the numerous variations of cooperation initiatives that one can find in the context of AI today. Instead, we took a bird's eye perspective and aimed to set out an overarching framework in which such cooperation can take place, by setting out its core dimensions. Our framework was guided by three fundamental questions: *why* is there a need for global cooperation on AI and its governance; *what* areas should cooperation initiatives focus on; and *how* should cooperation be organized.

Many consider the global landscape of AI to be characterized by competition, despite the fact that – to attain the dual aim of maximizing AI's benefits while preventing and minimizing its risks – global cooperation on AI and its governance is indispensable. We, however, believe that this aim is globally shared, and see hopeful indications that the need for cooperation thereon is increasingly acknowledged and addressed. To secure its realization, a balancing exercise between three elements must be mastered: speed, holism and contextualism.

First, the need for quick action cannot be overstressed. The technology's fast development and deployment require an equally fast response, especially in areas where the likelihood and extent of risk may be significant. This implies that cooperation through existing cooperation initiatives should be favored over creating new ones, given the significant time and resources the latter typically requires; that differentiated cooperation structures should be considered so as to incentivize countries with aligned values and objectives to progress even if agreement cannot yet be reached 'globally'; and that our learning curve about AI's potential and limitations must become at least as steep as the curve of its rollout.

Second, a holistic approach is essential. This entails that requirements should be adopted to counter risks and enable a global level playing field at horizontal level, aiming to secure not only the trustworthiness of the environment of AI-systems, but also of data and digital infrastructure. These three socio-technical environments are interwoven, and it is only by considering them collectively that the ideal of Trustworthy AI can be approached. In addition, establishing a level playing field can foster healthy competition, thereby stimulating beneficial AI innovation and the wide dissemination thereof. At the same time, a holistic approach also requires a diversity of perspectives around the cooperation table, to secure that AI's challenges and opportunities are considered from multiple angles and that humanity at large – with particular attention to those who are most vulnerable – is represented.

Third, the importance of context-specificity needs to be acknowledged. Not all aspects pertaining to AI require binding regulation or harmonization, nor do all aspects require global cooperation. Some countries may require a tailored approach to deal with AI's impact based on their specific situation. In addition, a tailored approach is needed for certain domains in which AI can particularly help materialize benefits for humanity, areas where AI's risks are particularly pronounced, or domains where the need for cooperation arises on an ad hoc basis. The manner in which cooperation can take shape in those domains will largely depend on the underlying relationship of the willing cooperation partners and – in case of a competitive relationship – whether such competition takes place at the level of markets or at the level of value-systems.

AI is not a force of nature, but a tool designed by human beings. Consequently, whether, when, how and for what purposes AI is used, is an entirely human responsibility. All stakeholders across the globe – regardless of their nationality, ideology or value-system – carry this responsibility, and they carry it collectively. This raises citizens' legitimate expectation that, for all those areas where cooperation is needed to maximize AI's benefits for humanity and prevent and minimize its risks, actors across the world will roll up their sleeves. With this in mind, in this chapter we aimed to offer some guidance for the actors involved. Undoubtedly, we only managed to scratch the surface of the many complexities at stake. Nevertheless, we hope to have provided a framework that invites further reflection on how global cooperation on AI and its governance can be approached.

**Acknowledgement.** The authors are grateful for the helpful remarks received from Leo Kärkkäinen and Barry O'Sullivan on an earlier draft of this paper. They also acknowledge the useful comments suggested by Bertrand Braunschweig.

# References

1. Benjamin, R.: Race After Technology: Abolitionist Tools for the New Jim Code. Polity, Medford (2019)
2. Berendt, B.: AI for the Common Good?! pitfalls, challenges, and ethics pen-testing. Paladyn J. Behav. Robot. **10**(1), 44–65 (2019). https://doi.org/10.1515/pjbr-2019-0004
3. Brandenburger, A.M., Nalebuff, B.J.: Co-Opetition. Currency Doubleday, New York (1996)
4. Brkan, M.: Artificial intelligence and democracy: delphi - interdiscip. Rev. Emerg. Technol. **2**(2), 66–71 (2019). https://doi.org/10.21552/delphi/2019/2/4
5. Brundage, M., et al.: The Malicious Use of Artificial Intelligence: Forecasting, Prevention, and Mitigation (2018)
6. Buiten, M.C.: Towards intelligent regulation of artificial intelligence. Eur. J. Risk Regul. **10**(1), 41–59 (2019). https://doi.org/10.1017/err.2019.8
7. Carse, J.P.: Finite and Infinite Games. Ballantine Books, New York (1986)
8. Cate, F.H., Mayer-Schonberger, V.: Notice and consent in a world of Big Data. Int. Data Priv. Law. **3**(2), 67–73 (2013). https://doi.org/10.1093/idpl/ipt005
9. Cath, C., Wachter, S., Mittelstadt, B., Taddeo, M., Floridi, L.: Artificial intelligence and the 'Good Society': the US, EU, and UK approach. Sci. Eng. Ethics **24**(2), 505–528 (2017). https://doi.org/10.1007/s11948-017-9901-7
10. Couldry, N., Mejias, U.A.: The Costs of Connection: How Data Is Colonizing Human Life and Appropriating It for Capitalism. Stanford University Press, Stanford (2019)
11. Council of Europe: Terms of reference for the Ad hoc Committee on Artificial Intelligence (CAHAI) (2019)
12. Cowls, J., et al.: Designing AI for social good: seven essential factors. SSRN Electron. J. (2019). https://doi.org/10.2139/ssrn.3388669
13. Dyson, K., Sepos, A.: Which Europe?: The Politics of Differentiated Integration. Palgrave Macmillan, Basingstoke (2010)
14. European Commission: A European strategy for data. European Commission, Brussels (2020)

15. European Commission: Artificial Intelligence for Europe (2018)
16. European Commission: Building Trust in Human-Centric Artificial Intelligence (2019)
17. Farer, T., Sisk, T.D.: Enhancing international cooperation: between history and necessity. Glob. Gov. **16**(1), 1–12 (2010)
18. Feijóo, C., et al.: Harnessing artificial intelligence (AI) to increase wellbeing for all: the case for a new technology diplomacy. Telecommun. Policy 101988 (2020). https://doi.org/10.1016/j.telpol.2020.101988
19. Floridi, L., et al.: AI4People—an ethical framework for a good AI society: opportunities, risks, principles, and recommendations. Minds Mach. **28**(4), 689–707 (2018). https://doi.org/10.1007/s11023-018-9482-5
20. Floridi, L.: On human dignity as a foundation for the right to privacy. Philos. Technol. **29**(4), 307–312 (2016). https://doi.org/10.1007/s13347-016-0220-8
21. Gray, M.L., Suri, S.: Ghost Work: How to Stop Silicon Valley from Building a New Global Underclass. Houghton Mifflin Harcourt, Boston (2019)
22. Harari, Y.N.: Who Will Win the Race for AI?. https://foreignpolicy.com/gt-essay/who-will-win-the-race-for-ai-united-states-china-data/. Accessed 15 July 2020
23. Hasselbalch, G.: A Framework for a Data Interest Analysis of Artificial Intelligence. Mediamocracy (2020)
24. Hasselbalch, G.: Making sense of data ethics. The powers behind the data ethics debate in European policymaking. Internet Policy Rev. **8**(2) (2019). https://doi.org/10.14763/2019.2.1401
25. High-Level Expert Group on AI: Ethics Guidelines for Trustworthy AI (2019)
26. Hummel, P., et al.: Own data? Ethical reflections on data ownership. Philos. Technol. (2020). https://doi.org/10.1007/s13347-020-00404-9
27. IEEE: IEEE Ethics In Action in Autonomous and Intelligent Systems. http://ethicsinaction.ieee.org/. Accessed 16 July 2020
28. ITU: Assessing the Economic Impact of Artificial Intelligence. ITU, Geneva (2018)
29. Jobin, A., et al.: The global landscape of AI ethics guidelines. Nat. Mach. Intell. **1**, 389–399 (2019)
30. Kalluri, P.: Don't ask if artificial intelligence is good or fair, ask how it shifts power. Nature **583**(7815), 169 (2020). https://doi.org/10.1038/d41586-020-02003-2
31. Kleijssen, J.: Technologies numériques, intelligence artificielle et lutte contre la COVID-19 : la contribution du Conseil de l'Europe. Obs. Brux. 121 (2020)
32. Kranzberg, M.: Technology and History: "Kranzberg's Laws". Bull. Sci. Technol. Soc. **15**(1), 5–13 (1995). https://doi.org/10.1177/027046769501500104
33. Kroll, D.A., Leuffen, D.: Enhanced cooperation in practice. An analysis of differentiated integration in EU secondary law. J. Eur. Public Policy **22**(3), 353–373 (2015). https://doi.org/10.1080/13501763.2014.956781
34. LeCun, Y., et al.: Deep learning. Nature **521**(7553), 436–444 (2015). https://doi.org/10.1038/nature14539
35. Lee, K.-F.: AI Superpowers: China, Silicon Valley, and the New World Order. Houghton Mifflin Harcourt, Boston (2018)
36. Lehtiniemi, T., Haapoja, J.: Data agency at stake: MyData activism and alternative frames of equal participation. New Media Soc. **22**(1), 87–104 (2020). https://doi.org/10.1177/1461444819861955
37. Luengo-Oroz, M., et al.: Artificial intelligence cooperation to support the global response to COVID-19. Nat. Mach. Intell. **2**(6), 295–297 (2020). https://doi.org/10.1038/s42256-020-0184-3
38. Lynskey, O.: The Foundations of EU Data Protection Law. Oxford University Press, Oxford (2015)

39. Mayer-Schönberger, V., Cukier, K.: Big Data: A Revolution that Will Transform how We Live, Work, and Think. Houghton Mifflin Harcourt (2013)

40. McKinsey: Notes from the AI Frontier: Modeling the Impact of AI on the World Economy. McKinsey (2018)

41. Mohamed, S., Png, M.-T., Isaac, W.: Decolonial AI: decolonial theory as sociotechnical foresight in artificial intelligence. Philos. Technol. **33**(4), 659–684 (2020). https://doi.org/10. 1007/s13347-020-00405-8

42. Morgan, F.E., et al.: Military Applications of Artificial Intelligence: Ethical Concerns in an Uncertain World, 224 p. (2020). https://doi.org/10.7249/RR3139-1

43. Muller, C.: The Impact of Artificial Intelligence on Human Rights, Democracy and the Rule of Law. Council of Europe, Strasbourg (2020)

44. Nemitz, P.: Constitutional democracy and technology in the age of artificial intelligence. Philos. Trans. R. Soc. Math. Phys. Eng. Sci. **376**(2133), 20180089 (2018). https://doi.org/10. 1098/rsta.2018.0089

45. Nilsson, N.J.: The Quest for Artificial Intelligence: A History of Ideas and Achievements. Cambridge University Press, Cambridge (2009). https://doi.org/10.1017/CBO978051181 9346

46. OECD: Recommendation of the Council on Artificial Intelligence (2019)

47. O'Neil, C.: Weapons of Math Destruction. Penguin Books Ltd. (2017)

48. Partnership on AI: Joint Statement from founding members of the Global Partnership on Artificial Intelligence. https://www.gov.uk/government/publications/joint-statement-from-founding-members-of-the-global-partnership-on-artificial-intelligence. Accessed 16 July 2020

49. Russell, S.: Human Compatible: Artificial Intelligence and the Problem of Control. Viking (2019)

50. Smuha, N.A.: Beyond a human rights-based approach to AI governance: promise, pitfalls, plea. Philos. Technol. (2020). https://doi.org/10.1007/s13347-020-00403-w

51. Smuha, N.A.: From a "Race to AI" to a "Race to AI Regulation" - regulatory competition for artificial intelligence. SSRN Electron. J. (2019). https://doi.org/10.2139/ssrn.3501410

52. Smuha, N.A.: The EU approach to ethics guidelines for trustworthy artificial intelligence. Comput. Law Rev. Int. **20**(4), 97–106 (2019)

53. Taddeo, M.: Data philanthropy and the design of the infraethics for information societies. Philos. Trans. R. Soc. Math. Phys. Eng. Sci. **374**(2083), 20160113 (2016). https://doi.org/10. 1098/rsta.2016.0113

54. Taddeo, M.: Just information warfare. Topoi **35**(1), 213–224 (2014). https://doi.org/10.1007/ s11245-014-9245-8

55. Taddeo, M.: Three ethical challenges of applications of artificial intelligence in cybersecurity. Minds Mach. **29**(2), 187–191 (2019). https://doi.org/10.1007/s11023-019-09504-8

56. UNESCO Ad Hoc Expert Group (AHEG) for the Preparation of a Draft text of a Recommendation the Ethics of Artificial Intelligence: First version of a draft text of a recommendation on the Ethics of Artificial Intelligence (2020)

57. United Nations ed: The 2030 Agenda for Sustainable Development. Presented at the (2015)

58. United Nations Secretary-General: Road map for digital cooperation: implementation of the recommendations of the High-level Panel on Digital Cooperation (2020). https://undocs.org/ A/74/821

59. Van Alsenoy, B., et al.: Privacy notices versus informational self-determination: minding the gap. Int. Rev. Law Comput. Technol. **28**(2), 185–203 (2014). https://doi.org/10.1080/ 13600869.2013.812594

60. Veale, M.: A critical take on the policy recommendations of the EU high-level expert group on artificial intelligence. Eur. J. Risk Regul. 1–10 (2020). https://doi.org/10.1017/err.2019. 65

61. Veale, M.: Privacy is not the problem with the Apple-Google contact-tracing app. http:// www.theguardian.com/commentisfree/2020/jul/01/apple-google-contact-tracing-app-tech-giant-digital-rights. Accessed 01 July 2020

62. Vinuesa, R., et al.: The role of artificial intelligence in achieving the Sustainable Development Goals. Nat. Commun. **11**(1), 233 (2020). https://doi.org/10.1038/s41467-019-14108-y

63. Yeung, K., et al.: AI governance by human rights-centred design, deliberation and oversight: an end to ethics washing. SSRN Electron. J. (2019). https://doi.org/10.2139/ssrn.3435011

64. Yeung, K.: Responsibility and AI - a study of the implications of advanced digital technologies (including AI systems) for the concept of responsibility within a human rights framework (2019)

65. CEN-CENELEC Focus Group on Artificial Intelligence. https://www.cencenelec.eu/news/articles/Pages/AR-2019-001.aspx. Accessed 13 Sept 2020

66. Digital Public Goods Alliance. https://digitalpublicgoods.net/. Accessed 15 July 2020

67. ETSI Specification group on Securing Artificial Intelligence. https://www.etsi.org/committee/1640-sai. Accessed 13 Sept 2020

68. Executive Order on Maintaining American Leadership in Artificial Intelligence. https://www.whitehouse.gov/presidential-actions/executive-order-maintaining-american-leadership-artificial-intelligence/. Accessed 16 July 2020

69. Global Data Access Framework. https://www.unglobalpulse.org/policy/global-data-access-framework/. Accessed 15 July 2020

70. ISO/IEC JTC 1/SC 42 - Artificial intelligence. https://www.iso.org/committee/6794475.html . Accessed 13 Sept 2020

71. MyData. https://mydata.org/. Accessed 16 July 2020

72. NIST. https://www.nist.gov/topics/artificial-intelligence. Accessed 13 Sept 2020

73. The OECD Artificial Intelligence Policy Observatory - OECD.AI. https://oecd.ai/. Accessed 16 July 2020

74. The Partnership on AI. https://www.partnershiponai.org/. Accessed 16 July 2020

# Author Index

Printed in the United States
By Bookmasters